SELF-SIGNATURE

MOTIFS OF LIFE ALTERING EXPERIENCES

UNWITTING ENTRAINMENT OF SELF-ORGANIZING MOTIFS: TRAGEDY AND TRIUMPH!

By

Dr. DON J. FEENEY, Ph.D.

SELF-SIGNATURE MOTIFS OF LIFE

ALTERING EXPERIENCES

Published by: Consulting Psychological Services, P.C.

CONTENTS

CHAPTER 5

CHAPTER 6

CHAPTER 7

CHAPTER 8

CHAPTER 9

CHAPTER 10

CHAPTER 11

CHAPTER 12

DEDICATION

To Kelly, my lovely, one-of-a-kind daughter, confidently expressing her Beaming Signature Motifs through her brave engagement, challenges, and the planting of new horizons, all while manifesting her emerging talents and strengths, with resilience and shared, creative growth in her joie de vivre.

EINSTEIN, in his general theory of relativity regarding gravity, stated that matter tells space time how to curve, shape, design itself Spacetime tells matter how to move, behave!

Feeney, in his theory of Self-Signature Motifs states Self configuration tells our life space-timelines how to curve, shape, and design pathways of Motifs, and these pathways of life space-timeline Motifs Formatively moves the Self throughout its journey

PRÉFACE

The purpose of this manuscript involves the dynamic demonstration and delineation of life-altering experiences ascollaborative products of one's unwitting participation. Such unwitting collaboration involves interaction and interfacing with self-organizing schemas embedded in catastrophic motifs. The synchronization of embedded design schemas inherent in one or more aspects of a person's lifestyle, resonating with people, places, things, and unfolding events (geopolitical, psycho-social-cultural domains), is described as a dynamic principle of this unwitting collaboration.

The manuscript aims to illustrate the ironic timing of synchronized entrainment occurring in perfect harmony. For example, someone taking two extra minutes to drink a Starbucks coffee saved his or her life by creating just enough delay to miss the horrific 9/11 tragedy. It also explores unexpected consequences in everyday events.

There is an adage: "... when you're up to your neck in alligators, it's hard to remember your original objective was to drain the swamp." The unexpected consequences of becoming unwittingly distracted in either dangerous or excessively escapist diversions of pleasure can lead to entrainment of disastrous proportions. Addictions, divorce, financial ruin, damaged careers, etc., can all result from unwitting distractions in entraining motifs that lead to one's demise. Even with good intentions, caring contributions can inadvertently foster co-dependency patterns, compromising the fundamental essence of an individual's life experience and character.

The manuscript aims to illustrate these dynamics and other aspects of unwitting entrainment in life-changing events by examining a-causal events that develop into a collection of schemas forming through self-organizing motifs. These motifs display standard schemas with resonant attributes. The manuscript investigates the physics and metaphysics of human experience, seeking to understand the synchronization of a-causal events that lead to sudden, dramatic tipping points in life.

The manuscript also focuses upon fortuitous and disastrous coincidences of synchronizing events, such that the order of chaos and the chaos of order are viewed as equally possible outcomes of life-altering experiences. Emphasis is also placed on multiple dimensions of interconnectedness at the implicit and explicit levels of human consciousness and behavioral experience.

The manuscript emphasizes that the foundational role of various organizing motifs is integral to transformative life experiences. It examines how good and evil manifest through formative self-organizing patterns that drive changes in life.

The twelve chapters of the manuscript move from random and non-causal events to key motifs, trauma, asymmetry, illusions versus reality, shifting boundaries of motifs, depth perception, evil and the right stuff, glimpses into mystery, the arrows of time, multidimensional consciousness, and mastery of synchronization in multi-dimensional life experiences.

Case examples are shown at the personal, psycho-social, and cultural-political levels of hierarchical experience. One example can be seen in the current Bush administration's response to the horrific events of 9/11. The Bush administration's invasion of Iraq to promote democracy now risks becoming a breeding ground for terrorists and a cause of civil war. The U.S. aid in the 1980s to the Afghanistan War against the USSR only strengthened fighters like Osama Bin Laden, who later became the terrorist leader of Al Qaeda, which sponsored the 9/11 attack on America. The U.S. supporting elections in Palestine was an act of democracy that coincidentally led to the terrorist group Hamas being elected, further destabilizing the Middle East.

In each of these scenarios, the original goal of democracy was overshadowed by the distraction of creating political adversaries, causing the U.S. to go "off course" from the mission of draining the political "swamp" of terrorist regimes. These ironies of coincidental twists of significant events show only a small part of how unwittingly, subversive organizing patterns can merge into unforeseen outcomes. These outcomes can lead to life-changing experiences, shocking in their scope and effect on one's lifestyle. How can a lover's quarrel escalate to one partner trying to jump from a moving car, police intervention, or the vengeful killing of children to punish a spouse or parent for leaving?

Pathological distractions are the self-created alligators pulling us into dangerous waters. These unwitting entrainments are the focus of this manuscript. How efforts to clear dark waters of problematic concerns may unknowingly align with deadly distractions stirring turbulence instead of calm is illustrated. When couples try to resolve communication issues, rhythmic, mutual interruptions can escalate into tipping points of explosive, disintegrating proportions, nearly guaranteeing chaotic confusion that hinders even the simplest exchanges.

The manuscript examines these and other dynamic concerns as functions of interconnected motifs resonating with subconscious entrainment. The matching and mirroring of intensity and configuration motifs in partners' communication can trap them in a deadlock. The manuscript expands the concept of subconscious entrainment to include fortunate, coincidental events that are unforeseen and unpredicted but develop at multiple levels of harmonious resonance. Examples may include natural physical events and psycho-physical phenomena in a person's life. Multiple simultaneous occurrences like tornadoes in a community, political upheavals, and turbulent interactions among friends can all unify in non-causal yet coincidental resonance. These synchronizations can happen at various levels of organization, from immediate psychosocial events to broader, more complex ones. They involve interconnected, entraining themes that influence one's lifestyle with far-reaching, long-term implications, affecting conditions from birth, early childhood, family dynamics, community, to cultural contexts. These ideas are the core assumptions of the manuscript. They represent the principle of interconnectedness of reality, which is emphasized throughout the writing.

The manuscript emphasizes that formativeness is essential to creating one's reality. As such, the design structures of how we entrain and interface with ourselves, one another, and the world at large alter the formativeness of our reality. It is the motif of interacting design structures that selectively entrain, construct, and reconstruct, which life-altering experiences have the highest probabilities of manifesting themselves in our life experience.

Motifs develop within a framework of fluidity, lacking a fixed, absolute form. They are asymmetrical design elements with related themes, patterns, and structures, each displaying distinct yet coherent organizational features. Each family has unique traits compared to others, varying in their proportional distribution and intensity. Additionally, each family member exhibits specific ratios of inherited traits proportionally balanced relative to one another. For example, consider the Payton Manning football family, which reflects its own set of dynamics, embodying a microcosm of the "whole within the individual." While each son is highly talented and skilled as a professional NFL quarterback, each still has a unique and distinctive personality, with proportions of outgoing and gregarious or subtle and nuanced traits. Each member embodies a distinct, holistic motif—a collage of family process traits—without any single member or theme mirroring the entire family exactly. However, they are similar or "familiar" to each other. Although no single family member can represent the group, each exhibits characteristics that indicate their affiliation with the larger family unit. Motifs are comparable to fractal patterns seen in chaos theory.

These attributes allow them to represent unfolding, unique, formative themes that self-organize in similar but slightly different ways, modeling organic life forms at various levels of manifestation. In other words, human beings are unique and similar, both within themselves and between each other. They are ideally suited to serve as templates for unique, unfolding formative themes capable of multi-faceted and multi-dimensional entrainment. These are the foundational ideas that the manuscript explores and identifies as active in the a-causal manifestations of life-changing events, which can cause sudden shocks to one's reality and lifestyle. This manuscript aims to show that life-changing experiences often arise through one's unconscious synchronization and entrainment with self-organizing patterns.

The manuscript promotes dynamic perspectives, understanding our deep-rooted interconnectedness and the powerful non-causal effects of expanded altered consciousness as tools for choice, selectivity, and creating empowered pathways for future living.

It explores life-changing encounters throughout a person's development—from birth trauma, the first day of school, and adolescence to the loss of loved ones, threats to careers, financial hardship, acts of terrorism, legal issues, natural disasters, and cultural upheavals. These experiences shape an individual's lifestyle. This manuscript offers meaningful perspectives and frameworks that promote self-mastery and transformation through such encounters, suggesting they may be crucial factors in personal growth and life transformation.

This manuscript elaborates on proactive perspectives essential in constructively and creatively encountering life-altering experiences. It argues that nothing happens by chance, that good things happen to bad people and vice versa, and that random spiraling can lead to an out-of-control runaway system (e.g., the Martha Stewart case, where defending herself led to her crime). These facets and nuances will be explored throughout the manuscript.

An unintended chance encounter can set off a chain of events leading to an unexpected yet meaningful outcome. The discussion includes learning to boost intuitive awareness, assessing future implications from current events, and broadening one's consciousness as interconnected within global networks. Blind dates, chance meetings, and fortunate discoveries will be examined through interconnectedness, using ideas like Synchronization (Jung, 1964) and Chaos Theory (Glick, 1985). Perspectives on the arrows of time and future memories will also be examined, along with how entrainment and six degrees of connectedness help foster synchronization.

The ability to predict, influence, and improve one's quality of life at individual, psycho-social, cultural, and global levels has traditionally been based on the idea that scientific knowledge equals power. However, science (Glick, 1985) has increasingly shown that greater knowledge reveals chaotic complexities of staggering scale. The realization that multi-system events—such as weather, population growth, and global ecological changes—are so overdetermined that precise predictions are nearly impossible. Lorenz (1962) demonstrated this with weather forecasting, showing that weather deviations produce mathematical graphs representing geometric forms known as fractals. Fractals are self-replicating natural mathematical patterns—from river formations to galaxies.

The metaphor of fractals helps explain self-similarity and recurring motifs in family systems, although it is not an exact symbolic method. Motifs go beyond fractals in their organic and creative nature. Not only are they self-replicating, but they also self-design their unique formats. Motifs are alive, organic, and self-generating. Fractals follow an algorithm or recipe; motifs are beyond that formulation, although they can be roughly approached in a manageable and straightforward way. For example, the value of π is commonly approximated as 3.14. The actual value of π is infinite! It was calculated by a computer storage company, which broke the world record by computing π to 105 trillion digits.

These fractal structures may also exist within the synchronizing schemas embedded in self-organizing motifs. Life-changing experiences involve an impairment of the skewed asymmetry that, if not counterbalanced, can lead to a runaway system reaching a critical point. This sudden shock is the core of a life-changing event. Disrupting dynamic, asymmetrical motifs alters the motif's ability to generate life processes. The motif evolves from its innate creative and organic properties, shaped by distinctive proportional relationships among its traits and characteristics. Subsequently, it changes and shifts course in response to compromised complexity. Shock and trauma disrupt, impale the motif on its complexity, interfering with, paralyzing, and freezing its synchronized flow of asymmetry. It is now being tripped up by its disrupted complexity, which self-interrupts its movements, once harmonized and synchronized in its asymmetrical flowing motif. A story once recounted the encounter between a millipede and a frog on the garden floor. As the story goes, the frog grabbed the millipede with its thousands of rhythmic, smoothly moving legs flowing rhythmically across the garden's ground. The frog asked the millipede, "How do you do that?" The millipede stopped, seized, and, shocked, froze! The millipede is surprised to find itself paralyzed, fixated, and unable to actualize its organic motif. Its motif has been altered into distorted fixation, entangled by its complexity. What results are life-changing, life-altering motifs disrupted in their ability to reactivate their unique complexity of organic, flowing formativeness!

The degree of disruption in shocked motifs influences their impact on one's life. All motifs have an inherent asymmetry, which contributes to their uniqueness.

Severe disruptions in this asymmetry occur when proportions are badly misaligned. For example, Islamic fundamentalism (Not Islam per se) lacks the balancing and flowing complexity of its natural beauty.

Complex, interconnected forces with significantly interweaving themes and schemas can be challenging to manage. Such imbalanced or distorted themes may also appear in people's lives, whether in a seven-year marriage cycle that needs realignment or in perceived experiences of luck, fate, and destiny. These themes can surface at any level, from personal experiences to global politics and terrorism. The manuscript explores how synchronicity (Jung, 1964) increases the likelihood of experiencing life-changing events.

Synchronization, or the timing alignment of internal and external events in a person's life, may or may not enhance one's unique asymmetrical motif. As complexity increases, there is a greater need for interweaving and aligning the intricacies of events. Without such re-sequencing and timing with new events, they can lead to significant life changes rather than improvements. The phrase "all change is stressful" is a truism, as even positive change requires recalibration of one's unique traits, qualities, and their harmony with ever-evolving new and changing events and scenarios. Numerous accounts exist in which individuals experience significant good fortune—such as winning the lottery, receiving substantial inheritances, or achieving best-seller status on the New York Times list. These events often bring about considerable upheaval, complex challenges, and require rapid adaptation to new circumstances.

Too much of a good thing, as well as adversity, can lead to overwhelming outcomes.

In these cases, we are likely to end up like the millipede in a frozen state of paralysis of various forms.

Since the Big Bang, asymmetric formative influences have shaped human history and development. New research on mind-body studies, electromagnetic resonance, and brainwave patterns (Briggs, 1992) shows how dynamic multi-system effects influence physical and human existence. The manuscript suggests that individuals can increase the chances of fortunate events aligning with their motifs by recognizing and embracing the hidden order within chaos. Synchronization creates a deeper sense of meaning and purpose in life. Prior works (Feeney, 2001) have examined how individuals experience formative motifs inherent in their existence, converging with external events that shape their reality.

The manuscript suggests that meaning and purpose can be found even in life-threatening events by uncovering hidden order within chaos. However, managing complexities properly is essential; otherwise, progress can be significantly hindered. Once again, complexity is a gift and, if ignored, a potential curse! There is no such thing as a simple person "just being themselves," as even merely being alive and sitting in a chair can be challenging. Just ask an 80-year-old nursing home resident. The propositions and methodologies will demonstrate how key motifs function as synchronized entrainment. These inherently asymmetrical motifs relate to an individual's psycho-social-cultural environment in potentially transformative ways. Working through the complexities of motif phase transition convergences fosters personal growth, pushing individuals toward higher levels of functional organization, reinforcing that "what does not kill you makes you stronger." These convergences happen at least six times, as mentioned throughout the manuscript, referring to stages in our development.

At the same time, phase transitions can unleash dark, destructive forces, as seen in terrorism, 9/11, and other catastrophic events. Marriages, careers, and communities evolve through the ebb and flow of chaotic dynamics. The manuscript explores how seemingly random meetings and events are space-time configurations of unique motifs. Einstein's General Theory of Relativity (Discovery Channel, 2006) explains how physical matter curves space-time, creating distinctive formations that influence life paths. This curvature in space-time reflects the hidden order within chaos in human experiences.

As Einstein suggested, matter density influences space-time structures. A person's strong, tangible thoughts, beliefs, and actions matter and significantly shape their space-time path in many subconscious ways. Aspirations, expectations, and hopes formed during childhood often manifest in unexpected and noticeable ways. It is true: if you build it (your dream house or nightmare), it will come to pass!

The manuscript demonstrates how human biology inherently values and expresses meaning and purpose, which manifest through formative design structures. These structures promote synchronization between the mind and body, shaping behavior and life choices.

People unconsciously follow paths shaped by hidden motives. Shared structures and self-organizing patterns create entrainment, aligning individuals with events, places, and people in fractal formations. This phenomenon explains why people repeat relationship cycles, face similar life challenges, or experience periodic relapses of addiction. Recent studies (Discovery Channel, 2004) indicate that brainwave patterns change before a person becomes aware of an upcoming experience, reinforcing the idea of entrainment. As an organizing, goal-oriented process, formative influences may intuitively impact future events.

The manuscript presents intuitive recognition and transformation tools, illustrating how to harness chaotic life sequences for growth. It explains how individuals can use these insights to embrace lucky moments and navigate life's unpredictable patterns. By recognizing and applying these tools, the manuscript encourages dynamic perspectives, understanding our deep interconnectedness and the powerful, non-causal influences of expanded altered consciousness as tools for choice, selectivity, and empowered synchronization of future experiences.

It explores life-changing encounters throughout an individual's development—ranging from birth trauma, the first day of school, and adolescence to the loss of loved ones, threats to careers, financial ruin, acts of terrorism, legal troubles, natural disasters, and cultural upheavals. These experiences shape and challenge the complexities of a person's motif in a non-causal way, prompting subtle, asymmetrical patterns inherent within the individual. A person's pattern is altered, and self-organizing properties may be emphasized unevenly, leading to exaggerations, omissions, and skewed extremes. However, just as energy and information are neither created nor destroyed, the potential for recovering fully functioning, self-organizing patterns is not lost but conserved in collapsed states, awaiting reconsolidation at some later, healing point. This manuscript offers meaningful perspectives and frameworks that promote self-mastery and transformation through such encounters, suggesting they may be crucial factors in personal growth and life change.

This manuscript aims to explore proactive perspectives essential for constructively and creatively facing life-changing experiences. It asserts that nothing happens by chance, that good things can occur to bad people and vice versa, and that random spiraling can lead to an out-of-control runaway system (e.g., the Martha Stewart case, where defending herself led to her crime). These aspects and nuances will be thoroughly examined throughout the manuscript. Our unwitting, intertwined motifs align with the gravitational shaping and dovetailing curves of traumatic experiences flowing into and merging with our lives as contributors to our challenges.

An unintentional chance encounter can trigger events that lead to an unexpected yet meaningful outcome. Cultivating intuitive awareness, recognizing potential future implications from current events, and expanding one's consciousness as interconnected within global networks provides access to possible entrainments. Blind dates, chance meetings, and fortunate discoveries will be explored through the lens of interconnectedness, using concepts like Synchronization (Jung, 1964) and Chaos Theory (Glick, 1985). Perspectives on the arrows of time and future memories will also be reviewed, along with how ideas like entrainment and six degrees of separation contribute to synchronization.

Significant transitions happen at different developmental stages, marked by important life events that support overall growth. Transition periods—such as ages 0-3, 4-6, 8-12, 13-17, 19-24, 25-29, 30-34, 35-39, 40-44, 45-49, 50-55, and beyond—can bring varying levels of disruption. Just as the universe goes through inflationary expansion phases, acting like a cosmological and biological organism, individuals experience rapid growth spurts at different points in their development. Each of these growth moments is a phase change where motif complexities must be processed, so the individual's unique motif flow becomes stronger for refinement, expressiveness, and woven into their new fabric of daily life.

These formations may also exist within the synchronizing schemas embedded in self-organizing motifs. Life-changing experiences involve skewed asymmetries and complexities that can develop into runaway systems reaching a tipping point if they are not balanced and synchronized. This sudden shock embodies the core of a life-changing experience. The asymmetry of life-changing motifs unevenly aligns and offsets growth cycles in a complementary way, where opposing features balance each other (e.g., pros and cons of a debate). This primarily results from neglecting the complex ratios of characteristics and qualities unique to the person's motif. However, the level of imbalance in these motifs determines their influence on a person's life. All motifs inherently possess asymmetrical complexity, each with a distinct ratio of proportional qualities and characteristics that define their uniqueness. Due to their organic, living nature, these ratios of proportionally distributed traits can grow and evolve. Motifs are formative and constantly evolving, and as Pi expands, motifs become limitless in their formative capacities.

The manuscript provides tools for intuitive recognition and transformation, demonstrating how to harness chaotic life sequences for growth. It explores how individuals can use these insights to embrace fortuitous moments and navigate life's unpredictable patterns. By recognizing and leveraging the hidden order in life's chaos, individuals can unlock the potential for profound personal transformation.

Individuals can unlock the potential for profound personal transformation within the hidden order in life's chaos.

INTRODUCTION

These are the times that test the human spirit, which extend far beyond simple frustrations and obstacles interfering with our goal attainment.

Renewed determination and/or strategy adjustment are the usual requisite resources. However, overwhelming events' unpredictable, incomprehensible emergence threatens an inner sense of control, resourcefulness, and future optimism. An employee losing his job due to poor performance is a predictable, comprehensible outcome within the range of personal control (presuming the presence of required resources, level of function, and motivation). Due to management reorganization, job loss may occur shortly after an employee is hired, including after a selection process lasting two years. Such a sudden turn of unpredictable, incredulous events challenges one's predisposition toward inner control, resourcefulness, and future optimism.

Seligman (1975) describes these traits as shaping an individual's optimism about future endeavors. Harmful and destructive interpretations can develop when these traits are threatened or undermined. The employee might begin to repeat thought patterns of distorted beliefs (subjectively logical), such as "Just my luck," "I am destined never to find the right job," "God must be punishing me," and so forth. These are emotional reactions and theories about the nature of reality and the universe. They raise questions about free will versus predeterminism and why some people's lives seem cursed while others feel blessed. Although common sense suggests that everyone has free will and choice, many positive-thinking, energetic individuals still encounter unpredictable chaos and badly timed events that obstruct their best efforts.

These types of negative thoughts, unfortunately, reflect a lack of awareness and ignorance of the complexity of the individual's unique characteristic motifs. Many frustrating, negative beliefs that come from unproductive efforts are more a result of not recognizing what the actual complexities and requirements are. It takes time, attention, and effort to understand them! What are called successes or failures are simply signs that these complexities haven't been worked through and addressed. Proper attention must be given to that connected part of the new developmental stage, as well as how thoroughly that interweaving has occurred, and its impact on outcomes. Someone who lands a sales position and works more independently might feel stifled and blocked in an office job, unable to reach their full potential. Their sense of failure isn't due to a lack of talent or ability, but rather because they haven't recognized their circumstances and the unique environments where their complexity can flourish and harmonize with their new challenges. The only true failure is not recognizing the individual's unique abilities, talents, and effective ways of functioning that require a new environment for their capacities and potential to develop. When they do, we call it success!

It has been said that if you want to make the universe laugh, make plans. Relationships are known for this. Intelligent, beautiful women searching for the "right partner" spend months, even years, sorting and selecting their dates, only to find that their one right person (Mr. Big) happens to be married, gay, dying of an incurable disease, or leaving town to tour the world.

Signature motifs are inherent resource states that shape the fundamental capacity for performative organizational schemas, designs, and action plans. In this way, their formative influence is powerful! When life-changing events disrupt our plans and schemas—especially when our dreams do not unfold as expected—it can be devastating and disheartening, altering one's trajectory, goals, and objectives. I once had a friend who planned to attend law school, get married, have children, enjoy a beautiful home in a wealthy suburb, and make much money. He expected great abundance. He dedicated himself to his legal studies and achieved excellent results. After marrying his partner and finding the perfect home to buy, he realized these milestones depended on passing the bar exam. Successfully passing the exam would enable him to start his career at a law firm and benefit from the professional and personal advancements he had diligently pursued. However, there was a problem: each time he took the bar exam, his scores improved, though the margin by which he failed decreased, but he still did not pass. Even after many years of studying law, connecting with different attorneys he admired and wanted to model himself after, despite being well-versed, he still failed the exam! Despite extensive study, guidance from mentors, and extra effort, he could not pass the bar exam. It was frustrating that he was always just one or two points shy of passing. He grew discouraged and disheartened, wanting to sue everyone and everything that hindered his licensure as an attorney, even though he had earned his Juris Doctor degree. He could work as a legal consultant or conduct legal research for law firms, but he couldn't pass the bar exam for years. Eventually, he switched to real estate and became extremely bitter and depressed, to the point of withdrawal and isolation. Despite multiple attempts, he experienced significant personal and financial challenges due to not passing the bar examination. These difficulties included strain on his marriage, living in accommodations below his aspirations, and postponing starting a family, all of which he attributed to limited finances and resources. His patience with his plan was tested by that life-altering obstacle to his dream of becoming a lawyer. Although he had other options, he realized his intense dream of being a legal eagle was utterly shattered. It was an all-or-nothing situation for him, and when it didn't work out, that experience fundamentally changed his life.

One day, he went to a racetrack hoping to win back the money he believed he would have earned as an attorney. He wagered all his money on a favored racehorse, aiming to recover his losses from not practicing law. Despite good odds, his horse lost by a nose, and he lost all his money. Reminiscent of failing his bar exams "by a nose," this event crushed him. He was upset, complaining and shouting at the ticket taker that his tickets were no longer valid because the horse he bet on should have won, and how unfair it was! While complaining and panicking to those around him about how close he came, a child approached and said, "There are many other races and many different bets. Why are you putting all your money on this one race when you have so many more to run?" The man realized he had focused on the prize without considering the uncertainty or the process. He acknowledged his abilities and ambition to serve his community with lawful and fair actions. He recognized that his commitment to fairness, ability to administer justice, and skill in organizing effective Community Action Groups were well within his capabilities if he leveraged his network and engaged in legal initiatives within community movements—tasks he had previously thought were exclusive to lawyers. The concepts of justice, proportion, and deservingness—the principle that all individuals should receive an equitable share of community resources—and his awareness of disparities were qualities he could cultivate rather than depend on luck. By understanding his focus on balance, schematic justice, and the specific needs of different funds and resources, he could avoid spending his life in despair over not reaching his dream of becoming the ideal attorney, especially since he already possessed the talents to advocate in his community. Ironically, the French word for attorney is advocate! Signature motifs can lead to healing, life-changing moments when we remember we have the formative resources and knowledge to rise above fixations and preoccupations with the prize. Recognizing the vast complexities of our formative motif capacities allows us to identify and develop inherent talents, capabilities, and life themes that may not have been fully utilized. Formative growth and learning are crucial for overcoming major life trauma.

It is not just the frustration of failing to achieve a significant goal or objective (e.g., becoming a millionaire or being married with children by age 30) that threatens to unravel us. Instead, it is the perception and interpretation that, try as one might, unforeseen, overwhelming events that thwart our personal best are inevitable. As the old Saturday Night Live character Emily Litella used to say, "It is always something." Ironically, the actress who played this character died shortly thereafter of cancer.

Instead of always tackling challenges head-on or withdrawing when faced with difficulties, it can be beneficial to develop self-awareness. Recognizing our unique traits, complexities, and how we express them helps reduce many problems that might seem impossible to overcome. The old saying about trying to clean the kitchen floor while wearing muddy shoes comes to mind! This doesn't mean we are doing something wrong, but rather that some aspects of our approach may not be helping us effectively.

Some schools of thought propose that human behavior is partly shaped by genetics and biochemistry, with roughly 60% of personality being temperamentally inherited at birth. Other perspectives emphasize the strong influence of environmental, social, and cultural factors in shaping behavior. Existentialists, however, argue that meaningful perceptions and interpretations are choices made through an individual's free will. Each viewpoint highlights a particular aspect of human experience. Nonetheless, all resemble the story of the three blind men and the elephant—each perceives only a part and mistakes it for the entire picture. The interplay between free will, determinism, and locus of control is a key theme in this work, representing a range of control areas that individuals may experience as they grow and develop.

One example of such a range includes:

1. Direct control (e.g., "I can start my car whenever I want, presuming it is in good condition").

2. Indirect control (e.g., "I can drive at my desired speed, traffic conditions permitting").
3. Little or no control (e.g., "I am stuck in rush hour traffic").

Although primarily a personal decision, perceptions and interpretations of such experiences can be shaped by predispositions, the environment, and free will. Furthermore, biochemistry and how a person's car functions may be factors within an entrainment system that introduce stress-related elements affecting the experience. The range of options broadens when we consciously recognize different levels of complexity and our freedom to choose various paths. Our motives help us develop unique ways of deciding what may or may not be permissible, in harmony with the new complex motives we encounter. We must pay attention to how our motives interact with their surroundings.

Mastering influences in life requires a deep and thorough understanding of complexity. Grasping complexity makes our lives easier by offering a clearer road map that matches our experiences. Whether learning to drive a car or use a computer, understanding "how it works" is crucial for mastery. Misconceptions and illusions about how human experience functions (or is meant to function) can create chaos, impacting how we interpret and respond to overwhelming, life-changing events. What makes "chaos" chaotic is the feeling that there is no rhyme or reason. The problem worsens when such events destroy plans, efforts, and preconceptions about how our lives are supposed to unfold. It's our blind spot in how we contribute to organizing our ingrained motifs, which are often a hidden and confusing set of variables.

While chaos theory (Glick, 1985) has shown that a hidden, implicit order exists within seemingly random events (e.g., weather patterns, wave motion, and fractal patterns in geography), how does this apply to human experience? This question is central to this work. Each person's movement through life involves nonlinear patterns of belief and behavior (Feeney, 2001). These patterns are complex, intentionally designed frameworks (templates) of uniquely non-symmetrical patterns of thinking, feeling, sensing, and acting when facing tasks, challenges, and more. These patterns are interconnected and reflect reality proportionally. They manifest in symbolic and literal forms of expression across multiple representation systems, including visual, auditory, kinesthetic, tactile, and olfactory systems, as well as interoceptive and exteroceptive senses. Some individuals intricately weave highly complex visual and auditory systems into how they visualize and verbalize their understanding of reality.

At the neurological level, our nervous system contains complex, interconnected cell assemblies that reflect these patterns. These neural assemblies are widespread across the human brain's cortex. Beliefs and behavior patterns operate within a web-like network. Motifs resemble neural cell assemblies of interconnected, patterned complexities, both physically in the brain and symbolically in actions. The entire system vibrates when one part, or chord, is stimulated. For example, a belief about aging can activate multiple ideas of optimism or pessimism, thoughts about life after retirement, companionship, and more. Emotions, feelings, attitudes, and behaviors also resonate with these beliefs. These patterns probably resemble fractals or chaotic structures. The influence of such beliefs on a person's self-view and growth can be either empowering or destructive. These belief and emotion motifs can trigger intense despair or confidence-boosting affirmations. Unconscious thought motifs can spread these deviations, serving as key points of change in life and possibly throughout the lifespan.

This manuscript shows that human beings move within dynamic patterns organized in hierarchies of motifs (Feeney, 2001). Understanding these hierarchical levels and their interconnected, weaving patterns—psycho-social-cultural—with the larger world will be examined as a crucial part of mastering life. Recognizing one's participation in multiple pathways as a foundation for various outcomes is essential for this understanding. Participation is seen as an unconscious choice that contributes to and results in life-changing experiences. The deep impacts of chaotic, traumatic early childhood events will also be explored as factors that influence this participation.

The manuscript aims to provide a meaningful, comprehensive framework that recognizes interconnected and interlocking motifs and their empowering, transformational roles. Unhealthy solutions in relationships, career decisions, psychosocial living arrangements, and geopolitical relations all involve intensified integrations of entrenched motifs. Helping the reader expand their unique artistic motif through synergistic entrainment enhances their formative nuances, leading to higher levels of functioning in life and the world. The focus will be on how core motifs can trigger significant life changes and ways to support transformational healing.

It will be shown that formative motifs serve as vital, creative elements of existence, shaping both crisis and renewal in human life. Motifs function asymmetrically, often seeming illogical, with connections that appear unrelated. Their complex, multidimensional self-organization will be demonstrated. Recognizing uncommon patterns in our unconscious entrainments empowers transformational awareness, helping to resynchronize our motifs. Ultimately, this work aims to reveal how individuals can skillfully engage with interconnected motifs, turning unpredictable, life-changing experiences into meaningful purpose and clarity.

CHAPTER1

PLAYING DICE WITH THE UNIVERSE

Chance, A-causal Events, and Interconnection can be both thrilling and overwhelming. The devastating impacts of war, terrorism, and other profoundly life-altering events can have significant and lasting effects.

Loss of a loved one, financial ruin, winning the lottery, or being chosen as this year's Heisman Trophy winner in football are just a few examples of life-changing events that leave us in disbelief, wondering how such things could ever happen to us. This work explores the dynamics of these events and promotes mastering these previously unknown challenges. In this chapter, the ideas of chance, a-causal events, and holistic interconnection serve as a starting point into the complex realm of life-changing experiences.

This manuscript assumes, as Einstein once said, "God does not play dice with the universe." Einstein observed that events which appear unrelated and lack an apparent causal link may nonetheless exhibit resonance and connection, even when occurring at vast distances from one another. He illustrated this idea in one of his famous thought experiments, using the humorous phrase "spooky action at a distance."

Fascinating cosmological dynamics occur within the same universe where human experiences unfold. People don't need to travel millions of miles to feel a deep connection among seemingly unrelated events. Fateful events unexpectedly come together and influence important parts of life—such as work, love, and friendship—often seeming like unsolvable mysteries. In many ways, motifs are complex forms of entanglement that can happen across space and time. This indicates that the past and future are entangled, as well as events that seem geographically distant.

Therefore, this work suggests that nothing in life happens purely by chance or just plain luck, though at times

It may sometimes seem like a game of luck, but we are part of the equation shaping the outcome. This is not about fatalism or a grand design but about understanding the influential forces of the universe, such as attraction and repulsion (gravity and anti-gravity), as well as electromagnetic fields. These forces created stars, planets, and even life itself. Motifs act as entangled properties that attract and can repel, reflecting effects of varying degrees of synchronization. Both success and failure, along with everything in between, can be seen as the synchronization of what we attract through affirmations and what we repel through differentiation, which has become part of our own self-organizing, representational systems.

Whether a specific person, situation, meeting, or coincidence of events was intentionally meant to happen is a significant question that will be thoroughly examined in this work.

Currently, scientific theories indicate that the formation of the universe and life involves various principles and properties, such as species evolution, the Big Bang Theory, quantum mechanics, and the theory of relativity. Ironically, the more advanced the governing principles become, the more uncertainty and relativity are recognized in the universe. Probability and statistical analysis are essential tools for predicting outcomes based on the likelihood of different events.

Einstein did not believe in pure chance, dismissing the idea that the universe and everything in it were accidental. He wanted to believe in a stable, static, infinite universe. One of his scientific contributions, the cosmological constant—which measures the rate of expansion in the universe—was initially included to balance his equations but was later removed. Ironically, this very concept predicted the expansion of the universe. Such an "accident" should not be considered random or preordained. Instead, it reflects an a-causal inevitability arising from the underlying structure of the universe at the subatomic level—specifically within energy loops, strings, and spin networks (Smolin, 2001, on quantum gravity). These quantum formation events are themselves based on principles of uncertainty and probability. At these fundamental levels of existence, linear cause-and-effect predictions no longer apply. The key impact of Einstein's idea was that he intuitively conceived the cosmological constant from a self-organizing instinct while consciously rejecting it because he believed the universe should be fixed and unchanging. Could it be that Einstein was more insightful than he was "smart" enough to realize? Our unconscious mind is quite remarkable.

Specific a-causal events, by definition, cannot be individually predicted in terms of time, place, and configuration. Statistical probabilities are referenced when deciding whether a specific

Professional gamblers, for example, understand odds and use them to bring meaning and order to what might otherwise seem chaotic. Winning or losing becomes more about skill, intuition, and strategic finesse than just randomness or luck.

Similarly, securing a job through timely networking involves both luck and certain skills, much like gambling. If "God does not play dice with the universe" and "spooky action at a distance" exist, then many unknown forces operate behind the scenes, influencing outcomes. This includes mysterious "dark" matter and energy in the universe and unexplored "dark" DNA regions involved in genetic switching. The influence of these unseen interconnections on significant life events will be discussed in later chapters. As we sharpen our skills and intuition, life becomes less about chance and more about expertise. It becomes more of an exercise in skill and strategic decision-making. Playing with integrity and taking calculated risks are essential in navigating life-altering experiences.

When highly improbable events occur, several questions arise:

1. Are they merely coincidences?
2. Do they show any underlying cause that has yet to be identified?
3. Were they somehow meant to happen, predetermined by fate or an omnipotent entity?

These questions are exemplified in the life of Dr. Elisabeth Targ, a research psychiatrist who, in July 1998, published a remarkable double-blind study (Western Journal of Medicine) regarding prayer and healing. She studied forty healers across America who prayed for the health of advanced AIDS patients. Her findings revealed significantly fewer AIDS-related illnesses among the patients who were prayed for. In 2002, she received $1.5 million for further research, including the study of glioblastoma multiforme—a deadly form of brain cancer. Later that year, she was diagnosed with and soon died from the same disease. She had been prayed for by healers, creating a striking resonance with the very study she was conducting. She passed away on July 18, 2002, at 11:11 P.M., precisely 111 days after her diagnosis.

The coincidences persisted even after her death. One of Dr. Targ's prayer healers had a dream in which Dr. Targ appeared to be speaking to her husband from a distant European location, repeatedly saying, "Ya vas liu bleu." Later, Dr. Targ's father translated this phrase from Russian as "I love you." Dr. Targ was fluent in Russian and had traveled widely. It is uncertain whether this was a message intended for her husband from an unknown source or merely a coincidence.

Mathematicians like John Allen Paulos argue that the most unlikely event is the absence of coincidence. Probability theory indicates that surprising anomalies are bound to happen in an information-rich world. Irving Good, a statistics professor at Virginia Polytechnic Institute, pointed out that over a ten-year period, a person experiences more than five million minutes, providing plenty of opportunities for extraordinary events to occur.

However, others, like cognitive scientist Josh Tenenbaum, argue that the human brain is wired to recognize patterns and assign meaning to unlikely events. Some researchers believe that intuition about coincidences is linked to the ability to predict probability accurately. Still, even though humans may be good at identifying a-causal events, the question remains: why do they happen in the first place?

Research suggests that global consciousness might influence real-world events. The Global Consciousness Project, led by Princeton University psychologist Roger Nelson and Dean Radin, examined whether worldwide events—such as the 9/11 attacks—affected random number generators. Their results showed a significant rise in variance (statistical noise) just hours before the attacks and a return to normal by the end of the day. Similar patterns appeared during other major global events, like the March 11, 2004, Madrid terrorist attacks. These results challenge the idea that coincidences are purely statistical probabilities.

Physicists have also discovered that observation impacts reality, as shown by quantum mechanics experiments on light's behavior. This indicates that we cannot separate ourselves from what we observe—we are fundamentally part of the system.

This study argues that transformative events are not just the result of chance but are connected occurrences shaped by individual perceptions, choices, and the core frameworks that govern the universe. Future chapters will delve deeper into these complex dynamics, showing how understanding these principles can lead to a more proactive and insightful approach to life.

Einstein understood that changing one part of the universe could impact the whole. He saw this interconnectedness to matter, energy, and time. His famous equation, $E = mc^2$, shows that matter and energy are never lost but are transformed from one into the other through the constant of the speed of light. He also understood the proportional and structural relationship of the relative space-time continuum.

He explained the implications of space-time and motion, noting that increasing an object's speed converts energy into matter, expands space—changing its structure and, consequently, its purpose—and slows down its time clock. This happens because the time interval stretches as space expands with the object's increasing velocity. It suggests a connection between matter (human beings), speed (the pace of life), space (the area traveled), and time (the duration of life). Altering one aspect of a person's experience can change their entire existence, creating a new balance in their overall lifestyle. This principle applies to individuals and includes all people, places, things, events, encounters, career paths, romantic relationships, family dynamics, health, and other facets of life.

Recognizing our fundamental nature and our capacity to evolve and reshape ourselves is crucial. You don't need to travel near the speed of light to undergo transformative changes. Core patterns of life-changing transformations are embedded in the heart of the "stuff"—atoms, molecules, quarks, and so on—that constitute our existence. Scientists like Brian Greene (1996) suggest that all matter and energy are made up of complex, vibrating energy strings at the subatomic, quantum gravity level (Smolin, 2001). Particles seem "solid" only because these strings—which operate across at least eleven-dimensional, folded subatomic structures—vibrate at such high speeds, close to the speed of light, that they exceed a critical frequency, creating the illusion of solidity.

The complex nature of these multidimensional strings, their capacity for self-alteration, and their influence on everything they compose, including human beings and consciousness, remains a mystery. However, if we are made of pure formativeness, can we not physically, mentally, psycho-biologically, and consciously experience change through our actions and interconnected experiences with people, places, and things? If pure form exists at every level, can conscious experiences transform themselves through self-awareness and synchronization?

Because of our interconnectedness, we face the challenge of affirming and reinforcing, through creative repetition, the "formulations" of network assemblies—such as images, visualizations, identity traits, roles, nationality, religion, and global worldviews—within our psychobiological and socio-cultural boundary structures. These formulations propagate our unique motif. It can be compared to solving an identity "Rubik's cube" in no fewer than eleven dimensions while simultaneously influencing millions of others seeking their own interconnected solutions. How life-altering would that be—or perhaps, how life-altering is it already? Could successful resolutions be more easily achieved if we viewed personal and political challenges as manifestations of pure formativeness?

If, as Einstein stated, "God does not play dice with the universe," then what appears as "spooky action at a distance" may reflect an inherent interconnectedness in the cosmological universe and within each human being. Each person's unique "universe" of formative motifs—comprising the distinctive structures that define them (Feeney, 2001)—resonates with the wholeness of their inner and outer lives. The interconnectedness of these motifs (distinct organizing patterns) functions like a spider's web—pull one strand, and the entire network vibrates. This "web" of motifs is interconnected not only within a person (mind, body, emotions, etc.) but also across their psychosocial world (relationships, career, social activities, and family constellations). Perhaps it is a matter of learning to pull our strings instead of allowing others in the outside world to pull them for us.

The experience of seemingly random yet life-altering events is dynamically orchestrated through our participation in various levels of formative motifs. While these events may not be precisely predictable due to the multiplicity of overdetermination, high probabilities can be discerned through a greater understanding of one's unique formative motif. However, such discernment requires comprehension of interconnectedness as a fundamental property of motifs.

Each human being's interconnectedness within themselves reflects an unavoidable interconnectedness with all the events of their life—from birth to death. While some may attribute this to the "Hand of God" or an "Omnipresent Being," such interconnectedness is—it is our shared reality. All humans are made from the elements of stars—the remnants of burnt-out stars that created complex elements from which life formed. Similarly, when we "burn out," we leave behind complex components, such as organ donation, where hearts, kidneys, and pancreases become life-sustaining elements for others.

Each human being's unique arrangement of complex elements represents a single motif tile within the grand mosaic of humanity. The illusion of separateness and detachment in space, time, and relationships results in events and coherences that seem improbably real—what Einstein called "spooky action at a distance," yet Entanglement of Motifs is very real.

Interconnectedness is the fundamental nature of the universe (Bohm, 1985), functioning as a seamless whole (Bell, 1982) at both cosmic and human levels. Events in one area of life (such as career decisions or financial choices) ripple into many others, affecting self-esteem, living standards, and even the risks related to poverty and wealth. These connections resonate across various aspects of life, including work, love, and friendship, often leading to significant consequences. Are we cultivating a field of dreams, or are we growing weeds? Understanding how interconnected life events produce formative effects helps us become "professional gamblers" in our own lives, making decisions we hope will "pay off." How we participate in the "games" of our lives determines the outcomes that shape our experiences, whether they bring blessings or curses.

Choice through "organismic" participation means that our unique pattern of motifs resonates with others that share similar yet asymmetrical configurations. Due to this asymmetry, certainty is impossible (as per the uncertainty principle), and we can never predict exactly what will be attracted or resonate into our lives. Additionally, motifs can interface with multiple other formative patterns, creating layers of complexity. Understanding these patterns necessitates an appreciation of the interconnected mosaic of motifs, a defining property of the universe.

Interconnectedness is a vital part of both human and cosmic existence. However, what is truly interconnected is the mosaic of formative motifs that constantly "flip" in and out of perceived reality, much like an Escher painting. In one of his works, birds fly across one side of the painting, gradually becoming diffuse until they re-emerge as fish on the other side. Similarly, human experiences and motifs undergo figure-ground reversals, transforming within a vibrant kaleidoscope of change.

Common idioms—such as "the cup being half empty or half full," "one man's meat is another man's poison," and "one person's loss is another's gain"—illustrate a simple version of this complex interplay of interconnected formative "flips." Human beings share multiple boundaries. One person's property boundary may mark another's beginning, much like how our relationships constantly shape and redefine our lives. The concept of six degrees of separation suggests that every individual is connected to others through a chain of no more than six intermediaries.

The multidimensional nature of our psychosocial and cultural interconnectedness aligns with the ancient saying: "If you move a grain of sand on the beach, the order of the entire universe is altered." The convergence of one person's formative motif with countless others creates mind-boggling permutations, with far-reaching consequences. Martha Stewart was imprisoned for lying to authorities, not for insider trading. Could she have predicted that her attempt to protect herself would lead to such a life-altering event? The repercussions on her family, company stock, employees, and the broader cultural perception of her brand illustrate the complexity of interconnectedness.

These initial patterns influence and echo throughout our psychosocial-cultural fabric, leading to surprising, life-changing events. This work contends that events that lack explicit causality may arise from converging underlying motifs that interact and intersect in complex ways that are not yet comprehensively understood. Interestingly, Martha Stewart's experience might lead to an unexpected transformation, as discussions arise about her launching a new talk show after her release from prison.

Guiding Tracks

The integration of formative motifs, such as those identified by Stewart, is evident throughout an individual's personal development. This work aims to help understand how each person contributes to creating their multifaceted entrainment. Discovering multiple boundaries of interfacing formativeness is a crucial step in that process. The following chapters will explore how this is achieved and where it leads. The next chapter on motifs lays the foundation for understanding how boundaries function as levels of interconnection.

CHAPTER 2

THE NATURE OF FORMATIVE MOTIFS ARTISTIC FORMULATIONS

This chapter discusses the nature of motifs and how they can be

Involved in healthy, fortunate experiences and relationships or dangerous, lethal entanglements. For example, motifs can represent fantasy ideals within hypnotic, addictive relationships. Delusional motifs of synchronized entrainments suggest the influence with which formative motifs create powerful hypnotic dynamics between such couples. Partners may appear as sailboats navigating the unpredictable forces of nature. However, this is not the case. Their unwitting entrainment of motifs has triggered a whirlwind of chaotic drama. It is important to understand that motifs possess a self-organizing guidance quality that continues in synchronized entrainments of an unwitting consciousness.

Imagine the motion of a spinning gyroscope. After winding the string around the center rod and pulling, the inner spinning wheel keeps it upright. Whether held in the palm or on the tip of a pencil, it maintains its position and orientation for as long as it spins. Humans may also have their unique spin and gyroscopic movement that helps them stay on a particular life course and be resilient against outside influences.

This unique inner gyroscopic movement, having its unique signature, is what I have termed the sensory motif.

Artists use motifs when moving their paintbrush or sculpting a statue. This unique artistic movement and design distinguishes Picasso from Michelangelo. Each has his motif. Motifs are not static; they evolve and shift, as exemplified by the evolving states of Picasso's or Chagall's work.

Each person is a unique artistic motif expressed through their movement, manner of being, and personal signature. The internal movement of this motif provides gyroscopic stability and structural design, anchoring individuals on their life paths. This internal dynamic creates a distinctive framework that helps develop a person's core identity.

A signature of the self is demonstrated through unique character themes and patterned behaviors that persist throughout the self's developmental stages. Previous research has shown the emergence and ongoing presence of an organizing motif—often called the individual's signature—throughout a person's life. Pearce (1985) references Piaget and Innholder's (1964) work on early childhood development (from concrete to abstract formal operations), suggesting the emergence of a post-biological ego identity (Erikson, 1950). Pearce states this identity develops through sensory-motor connections and emotions toward a fluid mental world of creative power and expression. He notes that this organizing identity exists from the beginning of life but remains in a latent form, serving as a growth blueprint that requires stage-specific attention and development. He emphasizes the critical importance of models (motifs) for developing this identity blueprint or organizing principle.

Pearce suggests that early developmental language learning occurs in the womb, where small micro-muscular movements parallel verbal sounds of the mother. Condon and Sander (1974) found, through sophisticated analysis of high-speed sound movies of scores of newborn infants, that so-called random movements immediately coordinated with speech when speech was used around the infants. Computer studies verified a complete and individualized repertoire of body movements for each infant synchronized with speech (moving a left elbow slightly on hearing a 'k' sound as in "cough" or "cat"). Their studies of older children and adults revealed patterns of synchronization to be permanent and universal. They found that movements in adulthood had become microkinetic, detectable only by instrumentation, and still unique to each person.

These findings align with other studies (Bernard & Sontag, 1947; Bordy & Axelrod, 1970; Klaus, 1972). The only exception is autistic children, who showed no body-speech patterning. This exception may indicate suppressed synchronization performance rather than its absence. What is important about these findings is that the newborn has a distinct, unique repertoire of movements (motif), with this synchronization occurring within twelve minutes after birth. Pearce accepts that twelve minutes is too short for full synchronization to develop. He suggests that the infant structured this patterned response at some level of design while in the womb. He proposes that the drive for this patterning is innate. That internal purpose only needs stimulation from the external environment to interact with, allowing it to take shape and manifest. This is a fundamental example of intent or purpose existing before the ability to "do." Along with many other types of in-utero learning, this is documented by Verny and Kelly (1981). This inherently unique self-structuring character emerges in varying degrees of refinement, depending on environmental factors, early childhood experiences, physiological conditions, etc. (Dabrowski, 1967, 1970). Chomsky (1967) suggested that language is innate, encoded in the genes.

Briggs (1988) explores research on the subtle feeling-tone "themes" in the lives of creative people. Beneath language and thought lie complex shades of emotion between love and hate that influence events related to these themes. Briggs demonstrates how metaphorical and imagery-rich language can reveal the complex, organized feelings of lifestyle themes, often oversimplified in traditional thinking and expression. There appears to be a nonverbal structure or lattice framework beneath language and thought, guided by its organizing principles. Hung (1964) mentioned archetypes that operate within the self.

This nonverbal structure can be communicated through sensory motifs. A motif is a repeated pattern in design. The sensory qualities within motifs (visual, auditory, and kinesthetic) mainly convey thematic or symbolic ideas embedded in the motif. The design of the motif might initially be understood at the sensory level, such as a child's attraction to handling and shaping clay into bold, colorful forms. As the motif develops, it can express emotions, reflecting a child's personality, and become more vibrant and charismatic through molding and actively engaging with life's tasks. The motif can then evolve into cognitive and spiritual expressions. These stages of development align with the concept of the triune brain (MacLean, 1972), which describes brain structures that are sensory (reptilian), emotional (limbic), and cognitive (new neomammalian).

The earlier material suggests that people are naturally equipped with a motif and purpose to organize their lives toward health and harmony. According to Dabrowski (1967, 1970) and Dabrowski and Piechowski (1977), personality development occurs through five sequential levels. They describe dynamic aspects that support this upward self-organization, guided by a personality ideal that encourages harmonious unity and integration. The innate guiding unity of this personality ideal reflects inherent motifs and the aim of achieving unifying wholeness. Sensory motifs help define an individual's ideal personality.

Sensory motifs are an inherent structural schematic that determines the shape or design of what makes each of us unique. It is ever unfolding. The motif appears to function as a uniquely individualized domain of energy, distinguished not by a solitary pattern or defined sets of personality or behavioral patterns, but rather by the emergence of an interconnected family of interacting patterns. Humans are complex, and no single pattern fully captures individual uniqueness. That is why most individuals resist being categorized. I advocate using the model of a family of interactive patterns to grasp this complexity.

This model suggests that humans operate in inherently patterned ways that can be modified at the behavioral level but remain essentially unchangeable at the core of the self. Like a tree, the core pattern is innate, but its growth and branching can vary. Various innate behavioral patterns—such as speaking, walking, working, loving, and relating—share similarities while exhibiting distinct differences. These interconnected patterns are called a family of interactions. Our work behavior influences and interacts with our patterns of relating at home, but behavior at work is not identical; it is only similar (for example, people might be high achievers both at home and at work, but more active at work and more passive at home). Early childhood behaviors and belief patterns influence how we function as adults. Patterns established in one aspect of life can be present in others; for instance, patterns regarding love and intimacy developed during childhood may impact adult experiences. This reflects the presence of sensory motifs across different aspects of life.

The entire meaning of motifs lies in the numerous patterns and events that shape a person's life. It is like puzzles that ask how many faces you see hidden in a collage of objects and figures. Letting go of old habits and trying new perspectives can help reveal these patterns. That is why understanding the family of interactive patterns is important to grasp how the motif is perceived. This clarifies the configuration of the motif.

These configurations are like ripples caused by dropping a pebble into a pond. As waves expand, some hit the shore and bounce back, creating new wave patterns. The interactions and interference of these colliding waves form shapes and arrangements that repeat in similar but slightly different ways. These similar yet unique configurations are called a family of interactive patterns. Since motifs are not learned but are inherent structures to develop, these interactive patterns are the pure, distilled expressions of what is already innate.

A simple example of this is your signature. Every time you sign your name, there are usually small or noticeable differences in how you sign. Still, you can always tell your signature from others because certain traits and shapes appear from the various patterns in all your signatures.

The sensory motif appears in a family of interactive patterns. These motifs suggest unique configurations based on movement. We are constantly in motion, whether staying still or being very active. Without movement, there is no life. However, the kind of movement I refer to is a special one called flow. Csikszentmihalyi (1990) explains how flow occurs through focused sensory and mental interaction, creating qualities of various forms and designs, like a tennis player flowing back-and-forth, which creates form, skill, and art. Individuals may experience a sense of self during flow experiences involving elements of form and art, which they describe as moments when they feel truly themselves. The sensory motif within the self is essential for each person's unique sense of a meaningful life. It is the core of the self.

Motifs showcase their unique patterns and traits in these flow states. Interactive motifs usually, but not always, involve exchanges during various activities—either alone, like reading a book, or with someone else, like playing ping-pong or making love. Flow is a process that encourages the development of a family of interactive patterns. That is why such a process is so naturally rewarding. Consequently, a strong sense of purpose arises in these states.

The resonance between an individual's unique sense of self and how their lifestyle manifests has been measured as the meaning of life. Ebersole and Quiring (1991) discuss meaning in life depth (MILD) as a cognitive content process using a five-point scale to measure the depth of meaning. They indicate that the more precisely interactions of self and environment resonate with that person (design qualities or motifs), the greater the sense of meaning. It is postulated that the self has unique form and design qualities that necessitate resonant interaction (art, music, etc.) specific to that self's motif. Experience takes on meaning in terms of what one discovers as identifiable external forms symmetrical with internal organizing principles. As the individual experiences a matching of external and internal organizing experiences, he or she feels a sense of meaning and purpose in life.

Frankl (1963), in Logotherapy, emphasizes the importance of finding meaning and purpose in life. Each person's organizing traits seem to have a unique signature that causes some experiences to resonate more strongly with certain individuals than with others. When resonance occurs, the person feels a sense of purpose in their self-experience. This can be called a purposeful self that resonates or connects when symmetry is found in experiences that reflect their organizing principle. Although unique to each person, this ordering process is essential for the joy of flow experiences to emerge in such unselfconscious moments (Csikszentmihalyi, 1990). During these times, the individual feels joy, absorption, or fascination.

Motifs can be expressed in flowing, artistic forms arranged in unique, sensory sequences. A person's motif, a specific shape or configuration, will have distinct expressions. For example, some individuals might say, "See how they feel about ideas" or "Get feelings off their chest." They then start sharing them verbally, which could represent their syntax of experience.

However, motifs are more than just sequences of senses. They are complex and structured designs that begin to appear in people's life characters. Motifs extend beyond simple interests and hobbies; they are the unique signatures of the self. They act as templates that create an inherent sense of order and beauty within us. Functioning like organizing gyroscopes, they shape the syntax of experience. They are fluid rather than fixed, involving a subtle, flowing order and creative design. As a result, they foster a sense of purpose, which emerges as these flow states are experienced and transformed into their distinctive artistry, form, and style of expression. Motifs can be seen in how people navigate through interactions. However, motifs are more than just a style of interaction; they embody a unique signature and blueprint for how individuals move through life.

For example, some people may become very absorbed and intrigued by abstract symbols of ideas. Albert Einstein was one of those. In developing his theory of relativity, he would become absorbed and intrigued by what he called "thought experiments." He would imagine the effect of time and space if he were riding a beam of light to the ends of the universe and back. His motif was one of manipulating abstract symbols in relative frames of reference where time and space are fluid. Such a motif involved contrast and juxtaposition of different levels of abstraction. Notice the interplay of an absolute, universal oneness contrasted against his emphasis on how relative the universe can be. Indeed, he sought oneness throughout his life, as evidenced by his search for a unified field theory of universal forces. His penchant for relative frames contrasted beautifully with his search for pure truth and a universal constant ($E=mc^2$). His motif utilized a paradoxical structure as he pursued unification through relativity.

Interestingly, his motif of enjoying the relative nature of a holistic universe never got him to dinner on time with his wife. He was late, but then it was all "relative". Einstein often incorporated the concept of juxtaposing parts and wholes in different designs. His beautiful thought of gravity as acceleration, contrasting standing on a moving elevator, standing on the earth's surface, or falling weightlessly in a unified field without contrasting upward force or acceleration, utilized juxtaposition as a motif of gravity.

Other people, such as engineers or tool and die makers, might have a more concrete way of expressing themselves. They often focus on motifs in settings involving physical forms and tangible impressions, like Ford Motor stamping plants using new tool and die template designs. The subtle details in these motifs tend to highlight engineering and the adjustments they make to create physical, visible forms. Musicians enjoy the tactile sensation when playing chords, harmonizing with syncopated rhythms, and switching between patterns and arrangements. While these structural patterns are most obvious in music, they appear in many other fields as well. These design elements have an architecture—or Arche-texture of feeling—that act as self-organizing templates. They help spark and guide the development and precise expression of these unique patterns in the moment. Each person has an intrinsic motif or a set of interconnected qualities. The more we are aligned with our sensory motif as a guiding principle of self, the more empowered, harmonious, and resilient our relationships with ourselves and others will be.

Developmental stages through which motifs self-organize and emerge are not necessarily free of hazards and challenges. Many cases of deprivation occur in early childhood or later years, such as trauma, oxygen deprivation, or marasmus in children. These hardships can limit crucial developmental interactions. However, as Frankl (1963) demonstrated, meaning and purpose can develop even under difficult conditions. It seems that, because life conditions can become so traumatic and deprived, it is even more important to access one's unique motif in life. As both Frankl (1963) and Csikszentmihalyi (1990) suggest, individuals might need to perform at their best during times of extreme adversity. A sense of meaning and purpose is often cultivated through flow experiences, as people are driven to engage their sensory motif. This could be an alcoholic hitting rock bottom, a child abuse victim confronting their abuser, or an earthquake survivor discovering resilience to survive. In each case, it is the consistent sensory theme that empowers individuals to take risks and face their fears. Their motif enables them to find flow and purpose despite adversity.

The organizing and empowering motif experience causes fears, terrors, and anxieties to peak and become part of a larger, holistic, self-organizing identity. One's sensory motif is the experience of an unchangeable, unwavering sense of self at the core. It empowers and energizes remarkable abilities such as belief, positive expectation, and creative imagination for problem-solving. It provides a sense of permanence in an otherwise chaotic world of trauma and turmoil. The degree to which the self can access and resonate with its character or motif through external interaction (Csikszentmihalyi, 1990) determines how well meaning and purpose are fulfilled.

Impairment of developmental growth caused by trauma can result in dysfunctional, state-dependent learning. State-dependent learning (Rossi, 1986) suggests that what is learned, remembered, and performed is connected to the state in which it was acquired. When re-evaluating one's psycho-physiological state during an experience, memories, learnings, and behaviors are organized within that state's context. Cheek (1981) found that intense stress leads to altered states, which can be viewed as a form of spontaneous hypnosis that encodes state-bound problems and symptoms. Lienhart (1983) proposed a theory of multiple personality based on state-dependent learning, suggesting this process creates conflicting cues and fragmented memory systems across different times and contexts. In treating traumatized clients (Erickson & Rossi, 1980; Rossi, 1980), it was observed that bypassing "learned limitations" and accessing response potentials could facilitate integration. This approach requires a specialized method to enable creative reorganization. Erickson (1980) used age regression to bypass resistant, present, state-dependent learning. When state-bound, a client's dysfunctional behavior gains its own "functional autonomy," persisting despite the client's will or ego (Rossi, 1986). Therefore, employing a specific method or motif to promote integration is essential. When Erickson accessed the client's resources, he likely used a therapeutic motif, originating at pre-verbal stages and strengthened through cross-context, state-dependent learning. Motifs can serve as the unifying element in re-integrating dysfunctional, state-dependent learning. Smith and Jones (1993) suggest that traumatized clients can re-integrate with experiences that reverse the fear of the "new," offer opportunities for personal choice, and restore a sense of security in their ongoing identity.

The developmental nature of motifs allows for the reorganization of chaos and confusion into coherent experiences. Motifs assist in restructuring and reintegrating dissociated, state-dependent experiences. Csikszentmihalyi (1990) describes higher-order effects that occur during absorption in pleasurable flow experiences (such as making love, watching a child sleep, sculpting clay, etc.). The flow experience is essential to each person's unique sensory motif.

The motif is an open system that responds to nuances, sensations, feelings, perceptions, memories, and fluctuations in cognition. It seems to emerge from an interaction between the individual's inherent organizing nature and the learning environment.

The therapeutic value of sensory motifs becomes clear when working with clients who feel "stuck" or fixated in limiting life situations. By engaging with the encoding and organizing aspects of sensory motifs, thoughts, emotions, and behaviors can be released and used creatively. Developing these sensory motifs helps promote the emergence of deeply rooted life themes that are essential to the client's sense of meaning and purpose. When clients connect with these motifs, they activate creative, organizing, and thematic processes, such as creating music, growing flowers, building houses, or coaching teams.

The intricate organizing principles of sensory motifs become apparent when people do their life's work. Regardless of their field—whether it's music, art, business, machinery, or others—their choices reflect their unique internal organizing principles and show their movement in a flow state of purpose. The experience of this organizing movement within the client when accessing such uniquely personal experiences is a feeling of "I cannot not do this." When there is a love of repairing old cars or painting sunsets, there is the sense that one could not avoid doing these activities even if one tried. There seems to be a match or congruence between what the person loves to do and an internal organizing structure or principle of self. A sense of alignment exists when this match between activity and internal organizing forms or structures exists. As the artist paints a version of a sunset, there can be an experience that all is well with the world (Csikszentmihalyi, 1975).

The principle of self-organization, as expressed through sensory motifs, aligns the client's internal resources. This concept parallels Pearce's (1985) discussion on the necessity of models in identity development. Alignment and resonance within this broader organizing field facilitate an individual's empowered mental and sensory integration. Addressing only problem areas can obscure the core organizing principle. Focusing only on solving a problem can hide the underlying pattern.

Resilient Motifs

The interactive effects of motifs within family and social environments have been extensively researched in studies of resilient children. Resilience is the ability to restore one's unique psychological identity after being distorted by adversity. Emma Werner (1992), in Overcoming the Odds, presented findings from a 40-year longitudinal study of 210 resilient children on the Hawaiian island of Kauai. The research revealed a complex interplay between the child and their environment. Resilient children utilize internal resources—such as vitality, confidence, and self-righting abilities—and external support systems, including extended family and social connections.

Many resilient children, often required to take on responsibilities in dysfunctional family situations, develop self-reliance and a deep understanding of their core abilities and talents. Stripped of conventional family support, they are forced to refine their inner strengths and skills—whether in writing, art, dancing, or carpentry—to survive. This process leaves only their inherent core motif intact. By emphasizing their unique talents, these children cultivate vitality and charisma, becoming more self-directed and more attractive and likable to adults.

This likability increased the chances of securing mentorship from supportive adults, who could guide them along positive life paths. Werner's research confirmed that resilient children were especially skilled at attracting the right mentors—people who helped them succeed. Importantly, this mentoring support could happen at any stage of life, whether at four or forty years old—it was never too late for positive guidance.

External support from mentors, teachers, coaches, and community leaders was key in helping resilient children overcome obstacles. These children seemed to have "good luck" in selecting mentors. For example, one resilient teenager with strong interpersonal skills charmed his girlfriend's mother and was invited to move in, securing a stable and protective home. Because of their self-reliance, resilient children naturally create opportunities by choosing the right mentors.

Honoring and refining their innate qualities helps shape and define a resilient child's core. Just as engineers strengthen thin steel plates in automobile hoods by stamping unique angles and textures to boost durability, adversity fortifies these children, refining their core through life's challenges. However, for these qualities to fully emerge, supportive mentoring is essential.

Resilient children maintain a strong sense of coherence and trust in overcoming challenges. They have a clear, private understanding of who they are and attract the support needed to develop their unique abilities. While resilience is often described as the ability to "snap back into shape" after adversity, this metaphor holds a more profound truth: the shape they return to is the structure of their sensory motif. Essentially, resilient children recover from adversity and regain alignment with their inherent strengths and capacities. The strong, magnetic quality of someone actively working within their motif often attracts the right mentor at the right time. For example, African American athletes rising from complex backgrounds often find support from a coach or mentor who recognizes and nurtures their potential. This process functions like a self-correcting gyroscope, maintaining balance by aligning the individual's inner core motif with external opportunities.

The interactive nature of resilience—balancing internal strengths like vitality and competence with external mentorship and support—mirrors the family of interactive patterns model of the motif. An individual's inner motif and external environment dynamically interact, reinforcing and affecting each other. Building and trusting your motif enhances balance and encourages a positive life path.

The inner motifs are honing and refining with interactive support and encouragement from significant others. This interaction assists in shaping and sculpting the individual's unique design and core motif.

The idea of maintaining one's shape and being able to bounce back from adversity suggests that a coherent, core consistency is operating to bring one back into form. That core consistency is the sensory motif, functioning as an inner and outer gyroscope, allowing resilience and a return to a unique form.

Motifs' interactive, perpetuating nature attracts and generates ongoing development, support, and enhanced refinement. Thus, motifs can adapt and recover when faced with challenges due to their resilience.

Self-Organizing and Developmental Motifs

Motifs must be nurtured and developed from early childhood throughout life by focusing on their unique organizing qualities. Their developmental nature means that they can organize and guide a person's growth over time. Motifs enable the reorganization of chaotic and confusing states into more meaningful experiences. They help to reorganize and reintegrate what are called dissociated, state-dependent experiences.

Individuals who have experienced physical, sexual, or emotional harm in childhood often dissociate different parts of themselves and suppress specific memories. These disavowed aspects, psychological wounds, and traumatic memories are often linked to state-dependent experiences, which, when triggered, can reactivate the trauma. For example, sexual intimacy may elicit physiological or emotional states associated with memories of past abuse.

Motifs can help people discover their artistic talents and intrinsic interests while organizing aspects of their fascinations and joys. Accessing these powerful organizing structures supports individuals in making personal sense and meaning out of life experiences that may be in conflict intellectually. For example, traumatized clients can begin to work through and reintegrate painful and detached parts of their life experiences and repressed feelings by first accessing empowering, core motifs. This can reconnect them with the joy of their organizing and their artistic talents, whether they involve music, art, poetry, or even the artistry of engineering, mathematics, and similar fields.

Motifs offer an inherent framework for organizing life experiences. While these experiences may not always seem logical, the motif has a unique, creative "logic" that is nonlinear (not a straightforward cause-and-effect pattern). The core self's self-organizing nature acts as a filter, allowing conflicting or nonsensical personal experiences to be integrated into a coherent sense of continuity or meaning.

When filtered through one's motif, many personal losses and rejections can help in the meaningful reorganization of events, such as times when one lost touch with and strayed from one's true self. When relationships struggle, it can often be linked to becoming rigid and narrow in demands and not adhering to principles of mutual growth and expansion. Partners find that many of their intimate relationship issues leading to fixation are connected to being distracted from their unique life motif. When aligned with one's motif, partners feel complete and whole and enjoy the personal freedom they can share.

Motifs clearly have an internal gyroscopic structure that assists in organizing and developing personal growth. They are the formative, nonverbal structures or templates that affect the shape and form of our beliefs and how we make sense of our world.

Computers provide a helpful model for understanding how this template process functions. The computer employs a special template design to rearrange and reorganize written material from its original form into a specific format. The text remains unchanged; only the format is adjusted according to the template. No matter their chosen field, individuals can experience a sense of unity and healing from traumatic issues by discovering their own organizing themes.

Many traumatized individuals struggle with intrusive memories and denial simultaneously. That is, repetitive thoughts and images of painful losses and fears of helplessness in personal relationships may involuntarily enter the person's awareness. There is often an attempt to deny and suppress these inner mental experiences. Entrancement is usually involved at this stage.

Motifs help individuals emerge from entrancing, recurring mental experiences. They enable self-directed management of a person's inner mental states. Motifs foster the creation of organized, self-experienced feelings of intrinsic wholeness. As a result, they provide a powerful, organizing, and motivating ("motif-ating") model that offers a safe, stable structure for resolving both conscious and unconscious traumatic struggles.

Ironically, the aspects of trance occur more easily with uniqueness and individuality, as novelty seems to promote absorption. A heightened emotional state arises from engaging deeply in enjoyable flow experiences. These are unique to each person's motif. Whether making love, watching a child sleep, or sculpting clay, these activities offer a flow experience that reflects an individual's unique character.

Facilitating access to an individual's distinct character structure may help redirect attention from traumatic fixation, thereby enabling greater focus on and engagement with the individual's inherent strengths and empowering qualities. With awareness of the trauma event in mind, accessing and engaging one's signature motif juxtaposes these fixations and facilitates the reconsolidation of cognitive processes so that there is a positive, confident reframing of the person's resources to mitigate whatever the traumatic event may have been. Signature motifs represent empowered states of consciousness that, when associated simultaneously with the reexperienced trauma event, support reintegrating and reconstruing the event's shock fixation into a flowing, release of a corrective emotional experience. What seemed to be a shocking dead end, like a deer frozen in place, immobilized in the headlights of an oncoming Mack truck, now becomes a revelation of new, creative frames of perceiving and options of creative, alternative available courses of action for intervention. One's signature motif is an open system of the way one's Selfhood is designed and therefore serves as an architectural schematic of an asymmetrical blueprint that organizes its sense of the individual's self-experience responding to changes and fluctuations in feelings, sensations, perceptions, memories, cognitions, and external conditions. When juxtaposed with unhealthy experiences and events, it serves as a righting "gyroscopic" re-orientation, reestablishing balanced Selfhood within the individual concerning perceptions, cognitions, affect, and behaviors required for this righting orientation to occur. Treating trauma requires careful establishment of resource states and when accessing simultaneously dual awarenesses of trauma and resources, powerful reprocessing and reintegration may occur. Though alternating attention in cross-shifting patterns while focusing on aspects of trauma could be helpful, incorporating highly empowered states of one's signature motif while simultaneously or sequentially alternating accessing these trauma dimensions may provide intensive reconsolidations and reconfigurations at a significant level of change. Treating trauma necessitates the careful establishment of resource states. By simultaneously accessing dual awarenesses of trauma and resources of signature motifs, powerful reprocessing and reintegration can occur.

The manifestation of motifs appears to result from the interplay between the intrinsic organized nature of the individual and the environment in which learning takes place. Differentiating unique signature qualities of one's motif from such interactions assists in identification and access. When Madame Marie Curie was pursuing the discovery of a radioactive substance now known as radium, she had to sort through tons of ore and dirt. She processed hundreds of pounds of material to obtain a small quantity of radium. She had interacted with tons of material mixed with hidden traces of radium. She processed hundreds of pounds of material, ultimately producing a small, refined amount of radium. The pursuit of one's multifaceted motif involves distilling through a myriad of manifestations in which it is embedded.

Pattern manifestations of motifs are all-pervasive in every area of one's lifestyle (work, love, friendship, etc.) and need to be recognized and differentiated as they overlap from one area to another. Motifs emerge at the overlapping interface of where lifestyle patterns interact. They are like a multifaceted, crystalline structure where multicolored light can shine through, yet the purity of the crystal structure is preserved.

Therapeutic values of motifs emerge when their unique design is accessed by individuals stuck or fixated on limiting life conditions. By accessing the coding and organizing features of sensory motifs, thoughts, emotions, and behaviors can then be reorganized and utilized. The development of sensory motifs serves to nurture the emergence of embedded life themes critical to the partner's sense of meaning and purpose. When partners access these motifs, creative, organizing, thematic processes are set in motion.

For example, creating music, growing flowers, or building skyscrapers can access unique, inherent abilities and talents, helping partners get in touch with a core sense of self. In entranced relationships, the core concept of the self can become obscured by the idealized fantasies associated with entrancement. While it is still present, the motif is now hidden and camouflaged by the luster and fusion of entrancement.

Regaining that musical motif within creates harmony. This harmony enables individuals to authentically express their true selves, which, in turn, allows resonance and harmony in their relationships. Just as there is a psycho-bio-physical connection to relationships, there also exists a structural hierarchy of motifs in each of us. Accessing the sensory motif taps into these organizing structures at the mind-body level.

For example, while men generally may have a hard-wired perceptual biological-physical response to female proportions, it is also clear that each of us individually has our own inner concept and aesthetic of beauty. These idiosyncratic perceptual-biological-physical wired-in responses to beauty are as much inherent as they are learned. Our sensory motif is the inherent, structural design of what we find individually beautiful.

Accessing sensory motifs of one's talent, art, ability, aesthetic interests, and so on opens doorways to unique character-designing empowerment. These unique, organizing structures suggest what we love to do, play, or even become. Sensory motifs provide foundations for identity and self.

Knowing that you may have an innate organizing structure of spatial positions with your hands and fingers, for example, can help you pursue relevant activities like playing the piano, typing, or writing. Motifs can suggest broad areas of effort from which refined expressions of these inherent structures and forms can develop (from brain surgeon to computer technician). The challenge is discovering these inherent motifs and their specific applications and manifestations.

Growing and developing dexterity, for example, can be discovered and manifested in how a person lives their life and relates to others. Individuals may develop greater finesse and become adept at "handling" complex relationships. Recovery from entrancing relationships requires access to self-organizing structures already inherent within us.

Indeed, we can become victims of hypnotic entrancement by failing to develop our unique, character-shaping motifs. It is at this point that the entranced partner's fear of losing their identity turns into a pursuit of discovering their core self, their defining motif. However, the distinctive qualities of entranced partners' artistic motifs may only be expressed through selective hypnotic experiences. These often involve strange and sometimes frighteningly distorted manifestations of their true form.

In their own way, partners express their unique motifs through distorted caricatures and cartoon-like versions of their true artistry. Their wild roller-coaster ride risks losing their sense of identity as they know it. However, this process can also lead to the discovery of their true self or characteristic motif. Partners choreograph their relationship like dramas or scenes from a Shakespearean play.

From their most survival-driven and need-based functions (control, power, fear, etc.), partners see symbols of their core motives in each other's physical and personality traits. They are often unaware of the practical, everyday realities. Instead, they favor a private, illusionary, fantasy world, even if it means tapping into their darker, mystical inner selves.

This fusion of fantasized reality in a hypnotic, dreamlike relationship can cause problems when trying to navigate relationships with friends, family, children, and important events. In hypnotically induced relationships, these kinds of real-life issues are often lost to partners who are fused in hypnotic mindsets, with logic and fantasy of their own. Their problem-solving skills regarding real-life issues are as compromised as their perception of reality.

Discovering one's life work (purpose in life) through motifs can heal entranced relationships. Regardless of the field, the choice and application reflect unique internal organizing principles. Using these internal principles supports the healing process by promoting balance and stability for partners who have become disengaged or overwhelmed. When an individual's passions align with their internal organizational principles, it can foster a restorative sense of integration, which is especially valuable for partners who need this cohesion. The expressive motif of unique style and structure helps partners reestablish their distinct sense of identity.

This principle of self-organization, expressed through sensory motifs, aligns individual resources. The harmony and resonance within this larger organizing field of structure, design, and inherent "architecture" support the client's empowered mental and sensory integration. It's all too easy to focus on the problem of the addictive relationship that needs resolution and overlook the inherent organizing motif already at work within each partner.

As previously noted, motifs are deeply expressed, especially in flow experiences, which occur through focused sensory and mental engagement and result in various forms and patterns. These flow experiences activate the motif's unique, transformative design and structure, awakening participants' sense of self. The sensory motif is essential to a person's sense of meaning and parallels the core of the self. Engaging partners in unique flow states helps them experience greater meaning and self-worth.

Using the concept of sensory motif, it is postulated that the self has unique form and design qualities. These require aligned interactions (with the inner and outer world) such as art, poetry, music, or machinery that is idiosyncratic to the self's motif. This term extends beyond a particular state of consciousness or emotional condition; instead, it signifies an intrinsically organized collection of traits and attributes that fundamentally represent the core aspects of the self. Just as Picasso maintained a distinct artistic motif, every individual possesses their own unique style or guiding principle. That means finding a medium that matches and reflects our unique qualities, talents, and artistry is important. The danger in addictive relationships is that, instead of reflecting our uniqueness, they tend to reflect a hardened, stereotyped image of what we think we should, ought to, or must be. Rarely is this what we truly are.

As a unique expression of a motif, the flow state creates a meaningful experience. Partners in flow recognize external forms that align with their individual, asymmetrical motifs, which overlap or integrate enough to form a synchronized whole. Such complementary formation of asymmetrical motifs bonding and supporting each other fosters a relationship of flowing together, like puzzle pieces fitting almost perfectly and reflecting the internal principles that define their sense of self. Interestingly, individual differences can create unity within asymmetrical patterns. This is where two unique people connect and become one by sharing their distinctiveness, forming a special, mutual bond. When partners demonstrate alignment and strong rapport, they achieve a shared sense of harmony. They can move and communicate as separate sensory selves through talking, acting, and even dancing together. Their unique bond is truly one-of-a-kind to them. When this bond weakens or dissolves, their connection may also fade. Partners in flow exhibit a distinctive timing and movement in their give-and-take interactions, mirroring how each partner's internal sensory motif comes together to synchronize.

When a person is doing his or her life's "artistic" work, it could be said that they feel a sense of meaning and purpose in life. One does not have to be a painter to be an artist. Indeed, a mechanic can be very artistic in his work, rebuilding rusty old engines. There is a sense of resonance where meaning and purpose in life emerge. The internal motif is aligned with the external world of manifested interaction. We express our unique inner motif in whatever medium, field, profession, or life endeavor allows a meaningful, flowing expression of this motif. Even the interests or hobbies we choose—for instance, steelworkers who enjoy hunting, fishing, and woodworking—are expressions of their inner motifs through hands-on experiences. Couples have more chances to share, integrate, and build synchronization when each partner develops their motif.

Recognize that each person's organizing properties seem to have a unique signature or pattern. In other words, some experiences will resonate more with certain partners than others. This is because some experiences more closely mirror the unique inner motif of partners who use their hands and tactile touch. For example, the steelworker responds positively to hands-on activities, such as hunting, but not to activities involving sitting and listening, like opera. The system he relies on is touch, not hearing or sight. It's not only about representational systems, but also the distinctive movements a steelworker makes, much like a pianist's precise timing and sequences. The steelworker's literal hand movements are a physical metaphor for how he handles daily experiences—perceiving the world as something to physically handle, build, create, touch, and validate. When attending an opera, he is more likely to enjoy the experience by engaging with the rhythm through tactile movements, such as tapping his hand, rather than relying on visual or auditory input. The literal movements of motifs are unique because they can express themselves both literally and metaphorically at the same time, in the present moment. Partners can resonate more deeply by tapping into the individual motif of a person's sub-modalities to build rapport and connection.

Self-signature motifs involve both literal and figurative patterns and configurations. The continual recurrence and progression of these motifs result in the formation of cycles, asymmetric patterns of repetition, and iterative structures. For instance, a piano player improvising may use specific finger movements and patterns based on those movements to create new patterns. This process includes repeated perception and intuitive motion with variations, which helps to drive the music's momentum and energy. Motifs have a repetitive, iterative nature that affects writing, orientation, behaviors, and interactions with others. These factors can lead to different outcomes, such as creating musical and artistic nuances in a jazz composition or managing substance use, resulting in recurring patterns in both cases.

The cyclic gyrations of self-signature motifs are repetitive iterations of asymmetrical variations on literal and figurative themes of expression and representation. They produce gyroscopic effects that help with guidance and alignment. The steel worker's hand movements and gyrations symbolize physical and constructive actions, influencing his behavior and those around him. They also show physical and constructive patterns, affecting his actions and interactions with others.

The dynamic, asymmetrical variations of thematic hand movements, gestures, fingering, and so on, create a gyroscopic-like effect that orients and guides the steel worker, giving him a sense of stability in who he is and what he is doing during these gyrations. Just as a spinning top produces a gyroscopic effect used in guidance systems like jet airliners and rockets to space, gyrating, iterative cycling motifs of asymmetrical theme variants act as righting, orienting, and aligning forces, providing the individual with a sense of meaning, purpose, and direction. The motif iterations and gyrations serve as the individual's compass, helping determine whether their direction is correct. Even when a gyroscope is placed on its side, it stays oriented as long as it spins. No matter the event's severity, the gyroscopic movement corrects the instrument, keeping it aligned with its course and restoring its purpose.

An important note about gyroscopes, rotational movement, and related topics is that at the subatomic level, Fermions have a property called 1/2 spin, which is not an integer.

This means that spin at this microscopic level refers to asymmetry in how a particle can be rotated to return to its original pattern or shape. In other words, there is a geometric patterning at the subatomic level; it does not spin in terms of motion but reorients, returning to the same configuration after a set number of turns. If you turn the configuration of a fermion by partial, fractional degrees, you will get the original pattern or motif. Conversely, Bosons have whole integer spins, meaning that full turns of one or two times bring the system back to its original state. For example, no matter how many times you turn it, a map of an hourglass stays in the same configuration, which is called a spin of 1. When rotating an irregular object, such as the Statue of Liberty, each rotation results in a distinct configuration or perspective due to the object's asymmetrical structure. This asymmetry requires fractional partial turns, resulting in varied configurations and positions. The point is, even at the microscopic quantum level, asymmetry plays a critical role as it forms the basis of what we call matter in our everyday reality.

When there is resonance, it can be said that each partner feels as if their experience together has purpose. At that point, one can refer to what might be called a "purposeful self," which resonates and responds positively when symmetry or balance is found. Resonance can happen not only between partners but also with tasks at work and play. This occurs in experiences that display features like the qualities and attributes of a partner's inner motif.

Partners feel more comfortable and connected when their motifs share similarities that foster internal, organizing experiences. In other words, some partners might appreciate the structure of an engineer's blueprint because they relate to and find a certain similarity and harmony with their internal networking design. Compatible partners can enjoy and accept each other's differences because they share a similar, though asymmetrical, template or motif, which becomes more complete when interacting.

Asymmetrical motifs in an overlapping, integrative arrangement between partners interact smoothly, shaping the purpose and structure of each person's unique inner experience. There is a comfortable imbalance in their asymmetrical systems, which is essential for the joy of flow states. These two individuals share similar yet distinct aspects of their connection. Although motifs tend to be asymmetrical because of their personal and individual nature, there is a natural ease when we express our true selves in healthy, meaningful ways with one another. The asymmetrical parts of our motifs are often admired with hope by each other, while the symmetrical parts act as a bridge to promote understanding in the relationship. Partners need creative variation and flow in these interactions. Maintaining the asymmetrical aspects of our motifs in empathic relationships provides stimulation and challenge, encouraging play and purpose. The flow state is crucial for connecting with these motifs of design and order. In fact, aligning the unique designs of inner motifs with the external flow of movement and energy creates a sense of power and transformation, leading to growth and abundance in the future.

In the previous chapter, we explored the life cycle's birth, life, death, and rebirth stages. Partners who are deeply engaged in a relationship typically progress through various stages: initial introduction and envisioning a future together, navigating the development of their relationship, undergoing periods of separation, and reestablishing their connection in more meaningful and enriched ways. Working through the hypnotically "fixated" phases allows them to give rebirth to their artistic motif from within.

The birth of a unique motif experience is not without pain or a sense of loss, as seen in a mother's labor of love during childbirth. The motif may develop through three stages, such as when artists create their work. First, there is gathering ideas, visions, and data and collecting information to start and explore the "project" of discovering one's motif. Second, there is saturation, where the artist is overwhelmed by the vision and deepens their work, making important discoveries. These discoveries are journeys of artistic effort, allowing the entity to build and shape itself within the artist's character. (Think of Mozart's efforts in writing classical music; he became obsessed with its composition after being inspired at age five.) As the self-signature motif develops, it becomes more complex and reflective, possibly reaching a comprehensive stage. At this stage, the motif is entirely realized elegantly and comprehensively. Finally, the self-signature motif appears in artistic vision and design and becomes tangible. This shows in their work, whether painting, writing, music, or accounting.

As partners explore their vision, obsession, and fulfillment of entrancement, they can emerge as unique "works of art" in their own lives. The partners can incorporate the discoveries and obsessions from their relationship experience. They can emerge and embrace their own realities. The end of an entranced relationship can signify the reawakening, rebirth, and expression of their motif. Each partner can then create their own artistic motif, allowing its design and character to develop through various aspects of their lives.

The following two cases illustrate the healing and therapeutic value of motifs. By identifying, accessing, and utilizing the unique design architectures of each client's motif, resolution and recovery become creative outcomes.

Appendix: Case Presentation

The following two cases demonstrate the empowering effects of accessing client sensory motifs. The therapeutic benefits of aligning with this organizing field showed how resonance with it creates the joy of flow experiences. The clients were seen in an outpatient setting for eight to twelve weekly sessions in short-term outpatient therapy. Notably, when the concept of organizing life purposes was introduced, all clients involved appeared to progress faster in their treatment. Clients dealing with various issues reported increased optimism and energy when accessing experiences of life purpose. They seemed to handle their problems with greater self-acceptance and self-esteem, and in each case, they resolved their presenting issues. The follow-up to these cases was limited to the duration of the therapy itself.

Case 1

A married subcontractor was referred to probation for stress and causing a public disturbance. He had become quite irate and angry at a contractor, so he stole some of the contractor's tools and equipment in retaliation.

In the sessions that followed, many issues were explored:

1. His tendency to attract conflict and chaos into his life.
2. The codependent nature of his relationship with his mother.
3. His desire for power.

In one session, the client became livid, almost explosive, expressing his frustration over being deprived of his financial compensation. He also felt limited and constricted in his relationship with his mother. He seemed to take perverse pleasure in losing his earnings, as it gave him an excuse for one of his expressive tirades.

When asked about his interests and sources of motivation, he said that he finds great satisfaction in applying his expertise to ensure compliance with building codes. He also seemed to enjoy being deprived of his earnings, often leading him to deliver expressive tirades. His main activities centered on construction, deconstruction, and reconstruction, working on building, arranging, and reorganizing parts related to those processes. As a child, he enjoyed taking his building blocks apart and rebuilding them into new forms. For him, this represented freedom, power, and self-expression. He loved this process and said he could "do it all day." He was constantly building and rebuilding but never truly finishing, as he would undo what he had done and rebuild it again. This mirrored his mood swings.

He carried a visual diagram resembling a Lego set, illustrating a building's internal structure—wires, plumbing, skylights, sprinklers, and more. He could draw this layout using horizontal and vertical lines, triangles, and right angles, like the skeletal framework of electronic circuitry. He used this map as a reference for his idea of the perfect building safety feature. His schematic was creative, and he could revise this image as needed. He believed everything had to fit, and he loved exploring new arrangements. As a child, he played with these toys for hours in the attic. He enjoyed working with tiny chips because they allowed him to build and dismantle his creations freely.

After reviewing the situation, he noted that the central organizing principle, sensory motif centered on building and construction, was not followed, resulting in a mismatch with the intended structured approach. It was suggested that his explosive rage and uproar reflected his energy for "building up" to a peak experience and then tearing down whatever was created in his path.

He found comfort in the idea that he was strongly shaping his understanding of design by criticizing how his contractors strayed from the "correct blueprint" of their agreements. This realization made him feel less helpless and outraged. He even took a twisted pleasure in intensely focusing on creating a precise design or schematic of an alignment—whether for a building, a sprinkler system, or wiring—and then stripping away all the "fat" and excess material.

As he identified with this organized patterned motif in its sensory form, he began integrating issues related to power, personal integrity, and a differentiated self. Accessing his organizational motif in a sensory format enabled him to move away from intertwined relationships, promoting a more balanced separation. He started responding with humor instead of intense rage. He gradually became more centered and focused, and he continued to make suggestions on how this motif operated in his life.

The outcome showed relief from stress, better coping skills, and a newfound appreciation for his freedom and power for self-nurturing and validation. He appeared impressed with his internal structuring process, as if he truly had "something to offer." He was able to release his hidden dependence on mother-like oppressors, whom he had previously directed his anger toward because of his alienation from his purpose. His stress and conflicts decreased as he became more in tune with his life's purpose.

Case 2

The client was a forty-year-old nurse seeking therapy to address her divorce, feelings of fatigue, and thoughts of suicide. She had a fifteen-year-old daughter going through adolescence and seeking independence. The client expressed dissatisfaction regarding several aspects of her life. She reported difficulty when comparing herself to affluent peers, conveyed a lack of fulfillment in her nursing profession, and indicated frustration concerning the absence of a romantic relationship. She put in only minimal effort in her work and personal relationships.

She felt her life was going nowhere and had no point. She seemed down and listless, believing she had little to offer despite being an attractive, healthy woman with a stable job. She had been raised in a highly educated and intellectual environment. Her father was a country club member, yet she felt she didn't belong there. She never truly felt that she fit into that lifestyle.

It was noted that she did not fully adhere to the intellectual, upper-middle-class value system in which she was raised. She feared standing up for her desires, her father's disapproval, and her mother's rejection.

When asked what she truly enjoyed, she initially struggled to answer. However, she remembered a stage comedy skit where she played one of the Saturday Night Live comedians. She loved performing, embracing spontaneity, and transforming life events into memorable experiences. She even dramatized her struggles in therapy in a very theatrical way. She saw herself as Scarlett O'Hara from *Gone with the Wind* and seemed to embody that character in her real-life actions. She also loved mysteries and challenges. Her dramatic approach to life involved expressing her emotions openly, whether it was dealing with depression, portraying a role, or creating a character. This seemed to help her find solutions in her life. She longed to be an actress, a profession that would let her showcase and express the many sides of her creativity. Her personality reflected a pattern of a multifaceted diamond, needing to highlight each unique facet to its dramatic extreme, culminating in a synchronized brilliance! Acting allowed her to explore and develop these aspects of herself.

Rather than being pathological, this orientation could be a path-finding tool for her life's purpose. She demonstrates creativity and artistry, enlivening her work through performance and infusing her art with vitality. Her mother, a former artist, had tragically taken her own life at the age of forty-three. The client believed her mother had been full of self-doubt and had stopped living up to her artistic potential.

It seemed likely that the client feared repeating her mother's fate. She needed to reaffirm her artistic purpose, especially in creative acting. It was suggested that she had grown up with a negative view of an artistic life. However, if she allowed herself to embrace and go with her artistic process, she could fully explore her talents. This realization excited her—she understood that she could access and experience the joy of acting in a way that resonated with her deeper self. She needed encouragement to follow her truth and purpose.

She was also interested in psychology, as it allowed her to work with people who were "acting out" their pathology—something she was deeply familiar with in her own family. She found that psychiatric patients, when acting out their wild dreams, bizarre delusions, and distortions, often exhibited vitality and expansiveness. This resonated deeply with her motif, which required a varied and dramatic enhancement of her multifaceted nature. She felt a profound connection to this experience.

She needed to act and perform creatively in real life, creating exaggerated dramas that gave her existence meaning and purpose. She withdrew and appeared sad instead of sharing her true feelings.

It was suggested that what she truly wanted was to be an actress. At that moment, she sat up straight, smiled, and acknowledged her desire to study acting as an artistic experience. This realization changed her outlook, allowing her to pursue ambitions and ideas that she had finally kept to herself. She began to appreciate her multifaceted personality's harmony, symmetry, and organizing motifs, recognizing how rich and colorful it could be.

Another benefit of discovering her acting motif, playing different dramatic roles in her life, was that she realized that when she was happy, sad, up, or down, she might be "acting a part" rather than genuinely being herself. This helped her align with her feelings and address them directly instead of dramatizing the situation. She could also enjoy acting out the drama of her joys and sorrows as a way of coping and expressing herself, while developing a mindful sense of who she is as a unique individual experiencing human moods and changes.

CHAPTER 3

TRAUMA AND FORMATIVE MOTIFS

Human beings can emerge from traumatic upheavals through formative properties known as motifs.

The importance of understanding trauma becomes clearer when describing its nature. Trauma can take many different forms. Losing a job, going through a divorce, family estrangement, serious car accidents, terrorism, and similar events all threaten a person's sense of stability and routine. However, it's crucial to recognize that shock, trauma, chaos, or crisis is any experience that disrupts how a person organizes and structures their life. Job loss can disrupt sources of income, personal stability, and self-esteem. But if the individual is self-employed, upholds their values, and stays productive, they can maintain their sense of order and organization in life. What makes the unknown frightening is its ability to change the unique way a person's life is arranged and designed.

Events that appear chaotic and overwhelming can be seen as changes to the current order of an individual's life, bringing a new set of circumstances. If life is about unique formative patterns in a person's lifestyle, events that strengthen these organizing themes are considered beneficial. Events that threaten the very foundation of an organization are seen as trauma. For example, a woman who was widowed after 48 years of marriage and whose husband died six years ago recently passed away herself. She described her life as unbearable without the organizing support of her spouse.

However, loss is not only about disturbing a person's current life pattern. It also creates a new pattern, which might seem chaotic compared to what came before. What appears chaotic and unexpected can also serve as a shift to a different way of shaping one's life. The first experience of loss and death can feel like an empty void as the physical world seems to fall apart right before your eyes. Such losses involving physical death break apart and disrupt a long-standing routine that has lasted for decades. The event gains new meaning if the spouse recognizes that her "loss" might have been her partner's "gain" if his quality of life had become severely impaired.

The main idea is that the same event can have different aspects, each showing changes. What appears chaotic or uncertain may contain underlying shifts in themes. Far from being just disorganized chaos, the unique organizing power of mobilizing themes creates radical design structures that transform the existing order into renewal. The chaos caused by losing a loved one is also part of a natural biological reordering process.

Emotional pain and grief are both consequences of loss and serve as fundamental elements in restructuring motifs. Events can either break down or incorporate new structures, depending on how they impact the existing design of the status quo. If the widow can access an alternative, embedded design structure compatible with the one suggested by the loss (such as a model of temporary versus permanence, a background in life sciences, acceptance of loss as part of life, or holding on to things before releasing them; a model where her life continues with meaning and purpose, or, perhaps, if he did not die, she was planning to leave him anyway), then redesigning the status quo can help turn chaos into a renewed organization of the familiar. Chaos challenges the current order with its patterns of reordering, which may include subtle, embedded asymmetries that are unique, unexpected, and ultimately shocking. At first, this might be experienced as trauma and upheaval, with no apparent rhyme or reason. The common question "Why me?" often emerges during such times. The degree to which these initially developed ordering patterns exist before trauma greatly influences the potential to reduce its harmful effects. This resource is often found in survivors and explains how the ability to adapt increases resilience and strength during difficult times.

The capacity for formativeness, which arises from each person's unique motif as a vital resource, enables innovative transformational configurations in contrast to apparent devastation. Formativeness drives energized motifs that produce indirect, non-causal, and asymmetrical innovations in creative design structures, sometimes called fractals. Developing and refining the ability for formativeness is a key marker of various higher intelligence levels. Navigating the complex array of competing design structures requires considerable resourcefulness. Transformative experiences demand the use of advanced cognitive resources. This is precisely what makes formative motifs powerful.

Developing the capacity for formativeness in each person's motif enhances the connection between different design orders. Asymmetrical patterns (skewed irregularities) are highlighted in this process and serve as bridges linking one configuration to another. It's similar to discovering irregularly designed puzzle pieces that fit together to reveal a picture not previously visible. Unlike traditional puzzles, many different configurations can be created based on higher-ordered arrangements. Examples of such interchangeable frames can be seen in complex, didactic exchanges (such as in the controversy of the Iraq War, the Israeli-Hamas conflict, etc.). This reflects how asymmetry embeds all formative motifs. Acquiring and utilizing diverse mosaic techniques enhances our capacity to manage an extensive array of intricate patterns. In short, we become skilled at solving our life "puzzles." Traumatic effects may motivate change but can hinder creative, out-of-the-box thinking. Trauma often impairs higher brain functions.

A guiding principle is self-selective perception, where part of our inner self resonates with specific formative influences in our external, psycho-social-cultural environment. Recognizing which aspect of our inner motif or formative self is active helps us understand how an entrainment has aligned with our life. These can be life-changing events of such complexity that they seem disturbingly impactful. Carefully examining which elements of our formative identity influence, direct, and interact with the external environment—particularly in response to trauma—raises important questions about the extent of our alignment. Alignment refers to the consistency between our core self and our core behaviors. It differs from mere unhealthy adaptation or reactive tendencies rooted in genetic or biochemical survival mechanisms (though not entirely separate from them). The level of misalignment increases the risk of trauma convergence.

Alignment is where our significant behavior in work, love, and friendship reflects the relative or proportional presence of our formative motifs' redesigning capabilities and qualities. For example, an employee at a restaurant may work in a fluid, colorful, charismatic, expansive fashion that highly aligns with aspects of his core motif. However, he hides the subtle, complex nuances that are a deeper part of his mosaic motif. Therefore, only a partial or proportional presence of core aspects of his motif is aligned in his work behavior.

The qualities of formative aspects built into one's self-selective, organizing criteria reflect the degree of alignment with one's core motif of formativeness for transformative redesign. The quality of the self-selective criteria one uses indicates how beliefs, values, needs, and emotions are allowed to reshape the habitual patterns perceived, interpreted, and acted upon in dealing with everyday reality. Entire schemes are formed through self-selective criteria. Someone who was adopted, regardless of how loving the foster parents are, may still wonder what was so unlovable or unworthy about him/her that his biological parents did not want him. Such traumatic early childhood experiences, no matter how irrational the interpretive schema may be, can become a self-selective criterion through which future life experiences are filtered, perceived, interpreted, and acted out. The outcomes are tragic, skewed, and lead to missed alignments with core motif qualities of uniqueness that could have served as intrinsic resources of love, worth, and a sense of belonging. Maximum alignment between core motifs and behavioral expression reflects a self-selective criterion that optimizes high proportions of core motif qualities throughout one's internal and external experiences. The presence of such high-quality self-selective criteria creates a schema that fosters reality entrainment of high-performance states. These are known by many names (flow states, being in the zone, finding the groove, etc.). Professional athletes, artists, actors, politicians, parents, and children all excel with this type of alignment.

These states of alignment access one's greatest potential to reorganize, integrate, and "solve" the puzzling disruptive effects of life-altering experiences. Motifs have a complex ability to organize and help integrate unexpected, life-changing experiences. However, the self-selecting criteria utilized by the individual may constrain the empowering, formative motif of the individual as renewed creative formative designs may not be considered, believed or sustained. It would be like describing flying in a modern jet airliner to someone raised in the dark ages! One wonders if the French sage Nostradamus may have felt that way in considering sharing his prophecies with those of his time!

These chaotic, unpredictable experiences are woven into our lives in some vague, resonant way, often at an a-causal level. They represent some of the most puzzling phenomena we encounter. Their presence may be linked to a certain degree of missed or misaligned parts of our lives. The way we 'solve' or assimilate them is usually transformational—we change because of them, yet paradoxically become more of who we already are, which will become clear later. Transformation involves a complex realignment with our unique sensory self. If we don't realize we have this property within our humanity, how can we align with what is unknown? It's like the "Dark Matter" drawing us in. It's similar to solving a Rubik's cube puzzle. Multiple facets (three-dimensional in the case of the cube) must be considered simultaneously with each move to find the solution. This idea applies to other complex issues like international politics, family dynamics, lifestyle management, and more. There is a crucial difference between these complex systems and a Rubik's cube. In a Rubik's cube, the patterns all balance out in the final solution and are symmetrical. Real-world complex systems, however, are uneven and irregular—mood swings, varying closeness in family bonds, allies and adversaries in international politics, etc.

Asymmetry in patterns means that real-world complexities are not resolvable in black-and-white absolutes (who the good and bad guys are depends on who wants what from whom and when). For example, international politics, by definition, involves numerous countries that are asymmetrically aligned. Russia cooperates with the U.S. on terrorism, economic trade, and disarmament agreements. While Russia functions as an ally in this way, in other ways, it can be quite adversarial. Russia allied with Germany and France against the U.S. in the Iraq War. Russia also supports skewed elections in Ukraine, which the U.S. opposes.

Asymmetrical imbalances in complex systems like these demand artful, nuanced innovations. There is no ultimate solution. Could the Middle East conundrum be one of these asymmetries? Final solutions resemble fascism. Instead, innovative actions are designed to address the continuously emerging, moment-to-moment challenges in such systems. A well-known adage describes these situations: "The more things change, the more they remain the same." However, it is important to stress that this does not mean complete uniformity. The French phrase is "C'est la vie," meaning "such is life." Similar conditions exist in everyone's complex lifestyle. It is a microcosm of asymmetrical patterns. One person's best friend might be friends with one of our enemies. Alliances and alienation occur within families and between them. It is common for a successful business executive to spend long periods away from their spouse and children to provide a comfortable life for their family. These asymmetrical systems possess all the traits of formative motifs. The interconnected parts are constantly in flux. These changing patterns of core elements form the motifs. These complex movements shape the effects that motifs have on our life patterns and direction.

Significant experiences often occur when fluctuations reach a critical point of imbalance. This so-called tipping point is a crucial, evolutionary growth stage that challenges our development. There are at least six stages of growth in human development, and reaching such a point in our lives may be one of them. This is where the property of skewness can no longer be managed with adjustments alone but instead requires more transformational measures. Realigning core motifs with innovative actions becomes necessary. Understanding the empowering characteristics of motifs is essential in navigating systemic transformations. It's important to remember that complete, perfect alignment can never be fully achieved or maintained in evolving, asymmetrical systems (except, perhaps, the artist within).

The self-selective criteria of each person's (or country's) way of perceiving and interpreting the world contribute to this skewedness. It can create a resonance (polarization of attitudes, behaviors, and chain reactions) so extreme that usual counter-balancing measures no longer function (as when one skids on ice, where slamming on the brakes increases speed). It is at such critical moments that genuine re-alignment with the core properties of one's re-organizing motif can be so empowering. Both individuals and nations must understand how to align their self-selective criteria with the fundamental characteristics of their inherent values and principles. However, their values, in and of themselves, may embody asymmetrical properties that emerge in convoluted, interweaving bewilderments of manifestations. For example, the commandments say not to kill, but human carnage has persisted for eons. One day, a scholar stated that the commandments were misinterpreted! It was supposed to read: "Thou shalt not Murder!" One may need a good lawyer to grasp the fine points of values and ethical behaviors that indeed could be considered asymmetrical. My intention is not to delve into controversies but rather to underscore the inherent complexities in our well-meaning efforts to treat each other with kindness and respect.

The term organic is utilized in the sense that actual motifs have an asymmetry that is asymmetrical to itself (Wittgenstein). At this level of abstraction (skewedness turned on itself), congruent alignment can never be perfect for more than the moment. Resistance to such organic evolution of motifs is the breeding ground for life-altering experiences. It will later be presented how this expansive feature re-establishes innovative, moment-to-moment problem-solving in life-altering experiences.

Meaning and purpose can be recognized through formative alignment with core motifs even in extreme, life-threatening situations. This manuscript's propositions and technologies will reveal startling conclusions: that formative motifs (Feeney, 2001) within the individual act like strange attractors (Glick, 1985) from chaos theory. Additionally, the individual's formative motifs are fractal-like, as they interact asymmetrically and interconnect with one's psycho-social-cultural environment in chaotic yet meaningful convergences. It is suggested that these convergences are transformational phase transitions that elevate an individual's functioning toward higher levels of organization. Life-altering crises can become empowering with proper motif alignment. At the same time, it is argued that these phase transitions—such as life events like divorce, illness, IRS audits, a teenage son getting a DUI, or a clinical depression diagnosis—all occur within a short period and also represent stages where dark, destructive forces may operate. Examples like terrorism, 9-11, exploding trains in Madrid, and Tokyo demonstrate how being at the wrong place at the wrong time can cause sudden traumatic shocks to a person's life.

We can become caught up in a contextualized reality that may result in severe consequences if not recognized and restructured. Entrainment is the synchronization of similar motifs (not necessarily core ones) moving together—like laser beams, a troupe of choreographed dancers, traffic flow, or fans of a sports team. Individuals can be entrained with each other and/or a series of connected events (such as a mosaic or kaleidoscope). Consider how herds of buffalo run together, entrained, racing off a cliff. Entrained lifestyles driven by social trends—like seeking a better job, spouse, or family—can lead to destructive outcomes in one's life.

Partners we marry, communities we live in, and more arise from the ebb and flow of motif dynamics in our psycho-social and physical worlds. The manuscript shows that seemingly random encounters are patterns appearing in unique space-time configurations. For example, one day, a young married couple ate lunch at a Ponderosa Steakhouse in the summer of 1972. The young husband, eating lunch with his wife, saw the psychiatrist who had supervised him almost two years earlier walking down the aisle of the restaurant. The young man pleasantly greeted the psychiatrist and said in a playful but profound manner, "Hello there, Dr. G! How have you been? Got any jobs out there in the state hospital?"

A new alcohol rehabilitation unit was recently established. Since the psychiatrist knew the hospital's assistant superintendent, he said he would recommend the young man because he believed the dynamic, change-focused treatment program would suit his style. Six months later, the young man started his first year of a career that would span fifty years, eventually becoming a clinical psychologist specializing in alcohol, drug treatment, and other disorders. It was an ideal fit, something the young man had never initially considered as a career.

The young man was curious and open-minded, like a visitor at an art show. He was receptive and open to new experiential possibilities. He moved through a moment-to-moment, non-self-conscious state of awareness. As will become clear, such states play a crucial role in life-changing experiences. A convergence of synchronization dynamics was connected to this event, which seems unpredictable and random. The perfect fit nature of the event reflected an a-causal convergence of motifs.

When Jung (1964) studied with Sigmund Freud and the concept of synchronization, he referred to a collective unconscious from which all humans draw their archetypes and personal life synchronizations. Although research has not confirmed Jung's idea, researchers report having experienced these phenomena in their lives. Precisely defining these constructs to capture their complexity poses significant challenges. Nonetheless, formative patterns exist within individuals, societies, cultures, and more—whether we are aware of them or not. They may seem mysterious, but convergences are common in everyday life. Such convergences involve space-time configurations that maintain coherence of unique motifs within and across our inner and outer worlds. This flow of interconnected motifs within and between an individual and their environment is the essence of these convergences. It represents formative patterns that vary in their levels of attraction and resonance. Motifs are organizing, energizing templates that orchestrate collections of events, much like a magnetic field rippling through iron filings to form unique patterns. Unlike magnets, however, people move through multiple energized fields, which mutually shape, contour (including individuals, locations, objects, and events on various scales), and create creative and sometimes unexpected experiences.

In his General Theory of Relativity, Einstein (Greene, 1996) provides examples of space-time convergences. He explains that the degree of physical matter present exerts a curvature in space and time. What we perceive as "gravity" is the configured curvature that bends and contours space and time in unique ways. Similar curvatures and contours have been observed in computer models of chaos patterns (e.g., weather systems, water flow). These patterns create unique, formative motifs.

Einstein demonstrated how such curvatures work in daily life. He pointed out that two people standing far apart on the Earth's equator and walking north toward the North Pole at the same time would eventually meet at the same point. This occurs because the Earth's surface curves, causing what starts as parallel movement to intersect. In high school math, students learn that parallel lines never cross, but this is only true in flat space-time. Einstein's insights show that space-time is curved, so paths that seem parallel locally can eventually meet.

As matter becomes denser, curvature becomes more pronounced, and clocks run slower. Therefore, the density of matter uniquely shapes the paths in space and time. However, matter density is not just about mass—it also involves shape changes in how matter motifs interconnect and modify each other's properties. Traveling at speeds close to light can further alter space-time contours.

Acceleration, similar to that of a rising elevator, can generate "artificial" gravity by altering space-time patterns. Additionally, the "spin" of an object—referring to its angular velocity and orientation—can influence gravitational curvatures through a phenomenon called "frame dragging," which modifies space-time's characteristics. This indicates that formation configurations are constantly interconnected and influence each other, as demonstrated by the fact that all objects, regardless of size, fall at the same rate in a vacuum. At speeds close to light, contraction of space, time dilation, and an intriguing convergence—often overlooked—appear to occur. The photon, traveling at the speed of light, never ages and never truly goes anywhere because it is already there before it leaves, as it is one with the universe. From the photon's relativistic perspective, it reaches its destination instantly before departing. For humans, we experience time and space as we move from point to point in a continuous flow. Motifs spend time nourishing the ongoing process of shaping our experience. These motifs exist before the event occurs and become part of the individual's new experience and location. Often, trauma, shock, and sudden change happen suddenly, catching people off guard, seeming to appear out of nowhere. This reflects the experience of trauma as an immediate event, often without understanding how it happened. There may be objective knowledge about the events, but the subjective experience of shock and impact feels instantaneous or caused without clear reason, simply happening as impact. While some call this shock and awe, trauma creates a moment that feels like it has no beginning or end, a timeless unity with the experience. This might explain why it's so hard to detach from that trauma unity, as the merging of trauma energy and the altered self-concept appears to have no clear origin or destination. When the core of that motif is freed and reprocessed, it gains self-recognition in its own "Light," its inherent, empowered Being. This process brings renewal and strengthens its original, timeless, formative qualities. Of course, this perspective is from the photon's point of view earlier. From a human perspective, the development and differentiation of individual identity related to trauma require both time and space. Motifs serve as structural frameworks and organizational patterns that shape and influence associated elements, fostering specific relationships and connections. Both trauma and triumph can happen internally within a felt moment. Objectively, however, time and space are essential for healing and growth after trauma. Interestingly, quantum physics describes the objective role of the observer and the subjective role of light waves, suggesting that there are times when the subjective and objective overlap in ways that are both traumatic and triumphant. The phenomenon where observation influences experience—often linked to mindfulness—also involves entanglement, a quantum property where two particles can influence each other instantly, even across large distances. Although no definitive mechanism has been proven, research confirms entanglement exists. In Einstein's relativity, the idea of the photon existing in a state of oneness is rarely emphasized. I believe that oneness unites relativity and quantum physics. It's possible that entanglement—what Einstein called "spooky action at a distance"—illustrates this unity. Oneness also extends to entanglement itself. It suggests that two particles can, although seeming distant and independent, maintain a meaningful connection once entangled or sharing similar motifs, spanning space and time. This interconnectedness resonates across both realms, highlighting a fundamental unity within the quantum universe. Some suggest that entangled particles, once synchronized into a shared motif or spin, could merge into a single entity, eliminating separation—merely two reflections of the same particle. For example, in a fish tank, you see one goldfish, but refraction at different angles makes it look like there are two, even though there is only one. This exemplifies the universe's oneness. Remember that old New York City vendor joke, where a customer asks for a hot dog, and when asked what they want on it, replies, "Give me 'one' with everything." That is the only joke you will find here. Enjoy your "one with everything."

A core idea of this work is that there is a parallelism between a person's real-world experience of time, their mind-body connection, and their daily psychosocial-physical life events. This parallelism is more about correlation than causation. One chapter will explore how space-time patterns influence life-changing events. You do not need to move at light speed or near a black hole to feel the connection between life events that echo in parallel themes. People's life paths often cross in remarkable, synergistic ways. For example, the 1911 sinking of the Lusitania was turned into a movie, which was then shown on the maiden voyage of the Titanic. A Titanic survivor who watched the Lusitania film later wrote a story about the Titanic disaster. These kinds of overlapping life experiences happen more often than one might expect. Probability alone doesn't fully explain the strange timing of these events, especially on a large scale.

The study of human psychobiology naturally supports the creation and reinterpretation of meanings and values. The "density" of an experience—its gravitational effect on formative design—is influenced by the strength of personal emotional involvement. This influence is physically reflected in the brain through thought patterns, beliefs, neural activity, and even neuromuscular responses. Neurologists have discovered that mental rehearsal and visualization reinforce neural connections and cell assemblies in the cerebral cortex. Repeating mental activities shapes pathways between neurons, reorganizing the brain. Changes in mental motifs lead to corresponding shifts in neurological patterns, aiding learning, memory, and automatic habit formation.

Yamamoto (2004) found a strong connection between martial arts masters and students, as well as a link between brain wave patterns and computer interactions. The U.S. Air Force is also exploring mind-machine technology for fighter pilots. These studies highlight the profound power of entrainment.

Both "mental mind" and "physical mind" connect through parallel pathways, with their shapes and curves forming key motifs (Feeney, 2001). These motifs unknowingly bring people together, sharing space-time contours within a "curved" psychosocial matrix. This leads to events and encounters aligning, often described as "six degrees of separation" or "small world" phenomena. Individuals may think they are on their paths, but they move within interconnected contours, unknowingly sharing trajectories with strangers through patterns of "strange attraction."

Strange attractions manifest repeatedly—cars maintaining the same speed beside us, familiar strangers commuting on the same train, people attending the same sports bar, university course, or even sharing the same jail cell. The fractal patterns of strange attractors, often hidden within chaos, can lead to fortuitous events and tragic collisions. This manuscript explores methods for identifying, understanding, and harnessing these convergent motif points. By recognizing how motifs entrain one another along parallel "tracks," individuals can transform chaotic potentials into transcendent pathways. Why do people keep meeting the same unhealthy partner, repeating similar types of mistakes or mishaps, periodically reliving tragic/comic events every 5-7 years, relapsing asymmetrically in alcoholism and drug abuse, or being crisis-prone? This has more to do with repeating cycles of fractured patterns misaligned to their unique core motif. If one is not resonating with parallel themes in one's formative motif, then one could risk resonating in an unhealthy, interconnected physical world (people, places, scenarios of life events, etc.), which can have tragic, life-altering consequences. Recent studies (Discovery Channel, 2004) have revealed that an individual's brainwave patterns will alter BEFORE becoming conscious that an anxiety-provoking experience is going to occur. Such is the entrainment of convergence. Learning to attend to such precursors and trigger points can have life-altering consequences. Ignoring them could create events that alter our lives.

An important feature of converging motifs is a common property they share with what's known in chaos theory as the self-similarity patterns of fractals. These will be more fully presented in the section on motifs. For now, it can be said that it is the property of these patterns that contribute to the chaotic unpredictability in one's lifestyle. What can appear as good or bad ("luck"), fortune, coincidence, accidental, or being in the "right (or wrong) place at a certain time with or without certain people, places, or needed resources all reflect a convergence of "chaotic" patterning in resonating motifs. The context of how motifs embed amongst themselves designates their web of interconnection. Because of the complexity of such a matrix, the interconnections may be enfolded many degrees from one another. In other words, it can be like a game of "Mouse Trap," where one action sets off a chain reaction, ultimately causing the lab to explode. That life events are separated from one another in time or space does not mean they are not connected by contouring flows of formative designs that could, if left unchecked, "blow up" in the face of one's life-altering experience.

While the "Mouse Trap" game implies indirect cause and effect at a distance, this is misleading. In the human experience, it is not at all clear what is interconnected to what at any given juncture of our space-time configuration. Just what we are resonating with and what matrix of design structures is being interfaced can change from moment to moment. This is the property of fractal patterns of chaos that operate in the motifs of human experience. It is part of the asymmetry referred to previously. The structure of multi-tiered, folded DNA molecules helps explain how a matrix of formative patterns functions. There is much debate about the epigenetic (dynamics that influence on/off gene switches in multi-tiered enfolding) function of DNA and ecological influences of selective activation. The enfolding of the DNA molecule (the spiral helix, as it is sometimes described) reflects a motif (design structure) that exists at the quantum scale (sub-atomic, with its eleven dimensions referred to as membrane theory) and at the cosmic level (solar systems, galaxies, local groups, etc.).

Interconnection between levels may not become apparent unless a "critical mass" or overload at one level floods over into or impedes their flow. For example, water flowing down mountain ranges into rivers, fed into by numerous streams, may go unnoticed. Yet, melting spring water from a previous winter's massive snowfall may suddenly burst into a deadly flash flood. This work focuses on why one person is caught in a flash flood on a highway, while another, passing earlier, avoids it. Some would say that life cannot be controlled, that the Earth is a complex organism with an unpredictable life of its own. I believe that critical mass permits quantum leaps between levels of hierarchical organization (between lifestyle path and transformational levels). Such "leaps" may permit contours and convergence between physical and psycho-social realities. While it is generally accepted that no one can control overwhelming forces of nature, how is it that birds and elephants (creatures inferior to the intellect of human beings) know when to run and get out of harm's way (they can sense vibration changes in electromagnetic fields)? No animal died in the tragic tsunami in Southeast Asia. If the Earth (and some scientists say this of the universe itself) is a "living, complex organism," then humans need to resonate with it at the organic level rather than skewed, selective intellectualism.

How humans alter the Earth (climate, terrain, resource extraction, deforestation, etc.) may clash, to some extent, with an "organic motif of the awesome forces of nature." The devastating tsunami in Southeast Asia highlights how man-made resorts in island paradises create a false sense of security regarding Earth's natural power. Selective perception filtering leads to ignoring the interconnectedness of life's complex systems, which can result in being at the "wrong place at the wrong time." This is not to say anyone can have an "omnipotent" view. However, if creatures can still "get out of the rain," perhaps we have lessons to learn from them. This work will examine these and other profound implications in later chapters. Developing a more holistic, organic perspective will be discussed as a powerful resource to help us "beat the odds" of losing our lives in life-altering events.

This principle of parallelism influences how we perceive time in our daily lives. The way individuals prepare themselves mentally, physically, and emotionally each day can significantly affect long-term results, leading to either positive or negative outcomes. Holistic perception matters every day, not just during major crises. Without recognizing our connections across multiple, layered levels through each action, we risk unintentional life-changing experiences. Achieving this requires a shift in perspective and a broader understanding that fosters deeper insight. Years ago, intriguing images were displayed on poster boards, featuring a maze of colorful, blurry, chaotic markings and other elements. They made little sense with our usual daily view—walking, eating, talking, working, etc. However, when viewing these confusing images with "soft eyes," remarkable three-dimensional figures and scenarios appeared. Sometimes, we focus so intently on something that we overlook the full range of levels and patterns emerging within that event. Exploring this way of focusing deserves more attention later in this work. Humans don't need to control the universe but do need to stay open to its natural creative forces, which can enhance their chances of success. Learning the fundamental rules of this game would certainly help.

Anyone can find themselves in unexpected and unlikely situations at any time. Whether you're a Martha Stewart caught in a courtroom, a Jessica Lynch in the Iraq war, a tragic victim of the horrific 9/11 World Trade Center attack, or have been lucky (or unlucky, for some) enough to win the lottery, these moments are increasing the chances that life-changing events can happen to anyone. Carl Jung (1964) called this synchronicity, where seemingly unrelated events, people, places, or experiences align to create a sense of resonance or unexpected meaning or purpose. For example, a chance meeting on an airplane where two strangers— the heads of IBM and American Airlines— sit side by side, start a conversation, and as a result, IBM computers are installed in American Airlines reservation centers in 1954. This event marked the beginning of computerization in society and helped develop the Internet.

Periods of transition and change can lead to chaos, confusion, and feelings of being overwhelmed. From birth trauma and the first day of school to adolescence, loss of loved ones, threats to careers, financial decline, acts of terrorism, the presence of attorneys in one's life (by the way, there is an old Chinese curse: "May there always be lawyers in your life"), natural disasters (such as the tsunami that killed over 160,000 people in South Asia), cultural upheaval, comets, and the "End of Days" scenario—these are just a few examples of major, life-altering experiences. This work aims to develop a meaningful set of frameworks and perspectives that offer an enlightened view of the realities that are so impactful. To move beyond the waves of chaotic upheaval, understanding that nothing happens by chance requires a significant expansion of our worldview and cosmological perspective. It can be argued that an all-powerful being is the ultimate cause of all events. Alternatively, some suggest that negative events happen to virtuous people and that life's fairness is inherently uneven.

While the nature of such life-altering events may always be a mystery, exploring the apparent validity of the idea that formativeness is an essential property of our universe is a meaningful and innovative use of what we know through human experience.

One final point is how "irrational" and oddly disjointed, even nonsensical, motifs can appear. As noted earlier, this results from their asymmetrical and skewed traits, which, if not addressed and balanced properly, can lead to deviations and potentially uncontrolled outcomes. This is evident in the "mad" genius of the artist, the clever cunning of a criminal mind, or executives obsessed with success who end up divorced, alone, and imprisoned. However, lucky and beneficial outcomes can also come from skewed motifs. For example, when someone tries bowling for the first time and scores impressive results (known as "beginner's luck"), they might say they weren't "trying" to bowl but just "threw the ball" without much thought. Researchers (Csikszentmihalyi, 1990) have shown that being unselfconscious during activities enhances performance in flow states.

The natural "organic" flow of motifs in "Beginners" demonstrates this unselfconsciousness. People often form meaningful connections when they are relaxed and not trying hard to make a good impression. As a colleague of mine once said, "Watched water never boils." Beneficial uncertainty is a key aspect of resonating motifs strengthened by the "organic" alignment of simply being oneself in the present moment. Unfolding motifs, initially resonating with the immediate experience, become quite fortunate and empowering. Without changing the complexity of configurations in matrices (such as lifestyle scenarios involving people, places, and things), which gradually connect, initial experiences of motifs can lead to challenging synchronization.

The consequence can be "mismatching" or faulty construct design schemes, leading to irrational beliefs, emotional conflicts, and less-than-optimal behaviors. I recently reconnected with a friend I hadn't seen in eight years. She recalled with familiarity how unchanged I looked physically. During our talk about current events and travel, she mentioned a friend overseas who shares my first name. Although they hadn't been in contact for a while, she hoped he was safe. She said that seeing me reminded her to call her friend. She reconnected with two old acquaintances—one from her earlier years and one from another area, both sharing the same first name—which led to changes in her life. She whimsically remarked on this deeply and left with a warmth she hadn't felt before.

However, because she had not matured in the configuration of her motifs (she wore the same hairstyle and clothing fashion of ten years prior), she missed important ways of connecting herself to the experience. She again felt isolated, struggling to connect and find worth in these friendships. In misaligned understandings of innovations in interconnecting with these past relationships, her advancement of appreciation and meaning was lost. Without forming meaningful connections to beneficial attributes that were once accessible, she chose to disregard them. She left with lingering feelings of loneliness that have persisted from the past to the present. She did not realize she could have such connectedness here and now if only she could embrace what was emerging.

Motifs have unfinished business property and challenges in matching advancements of embedded, multi-faceted interconnections. This is a consequence of their asymmetrical, skewed nature. The resonance with this person I had not seen for eight years occurred both at the literal level (my first name was identical to her friend's) and at the figurative level (images and symbols of travel, worldviews, separation in time and space, and reassuring reunion either in person or on the phone). Such multifaceted, embedded levels create a resonance of formativeness that is similar but never perfectly identical. This illustrates the inherent asymmetry of a motif. A saying about history states that it tends to repeat itself. However, a more accurate statement would be that it rhymes with itself with recurrent variations on its themes and schemas. Is our life and history like a poem that rhymes and recurs? What are the schemes and rhythmic cadences of this poem? Isn't this definition simply akin to our own recurring themes? Do we not repeat our history but with variant themes and schemas?

The next chapter will elaborate on the dynamics of asymmetrical motifs and their role in fostering a-causal, life-altering experiences.

CHAPTER 4

MOTIFS GONE WILD

Asymmetry And Life-Altering Deviations Of Bounded Motifs there is a need in all growing life forms for fertile ground into which roots can sink—tapping into growing resources—and open space, time, and energy are essential for people to spread their wings. Human beings also need resourceful places to establish themselves and expand during times of growth. These resources nourish the roots and wings of our motives, expressed as a lifestyle, to develop and thrive. Consider planting an apple seed. If the ground is too hard or too soft, roots cannot reach deep for nutrients or anchor themselves securely. If upward, expansive growth is restricted or distorted, its long-term potential may be limited. You can see in urban sidewalks how plants push through cracks in the cement and the corners of buildings. However, the consequence of continued persistence frequently results in distortion and misrepresentation. As a result, growth may never fully reach the broad range of its original complexity. However, the hardships of its journey may contribute to its unique character. When a grain of sand embeds itself in an oyster, the foreign particle irritates the shell. The oyster responds by producing a substance that can become crystalline to protect itself. Over time, that grain of sand has "provoked" the oyster to grow this substance around it, which turns into a beautiful pearl. The next time you face an irritation caused by a person, place, or thing, consider meditating on the oyster. Envision the beautiful pearl that grows around the irritation, transforming it into something valuable. In this way, you foster your personal growth and turn challenges into opportunities for improvement.

In the film *Field of Dreams*, several characters reflect on unfulfilled ambitions from their earlier lives, such as aspirations to become professional baseball players, even though they have achieved success in professions like medicine or writing. In everyone's life, to some degree, there are areas where opening one door of a career choice or life decision means closing another. It might have been marrying someone at a young age for reasons like love, youth, romantic illusion, lust, or other factors, only to regret not marrying the "other" one that was lost. When our early choices are restricted, limited, or made prematurely—such as teenage pregnancy, declining college to care for financially strained parents, suffering severe abuse and trauma, or damaging trust and intimacy—our formative motives can become skewed. If left unadjusted and misaligned with our unique opportunities, this can limit growth and self-expression. Fortunately, for the doctor who wanted to be a professional baseball player, he realized that if he hadn't become a doctor, he wouldn't have been able to save a dear friend at risk in his immediate future. At that moment, he recognized that he made a core choice aligned with his motif of healing. Although it may not have been the most pleasurable pursuit, it was the most satisfying expression of his true identity.

The more severe the trauma and restrictions of roots and wings in a person's life, the more skewed the distortions of self-identity, self-esteem, and reality testing become. Self-limiting beliefs and self-defeating behaviors can lead to abusive relationships, job instability, and chronic health issues. The tendency for self-perpetuating and self-fulfilling prophecies becomes prevalently skewed in negative, destructive forms—possibly throughout life—if left to their own devices.

Such a skewed design should be distinguished from each person's natural tendency to develop a wide variety of derived expressions. Just like a flowering garden with diverse but similar plants, multiple variations—like roses or orchids—have roots and wings to convey a healthy, skewed design of their beautiful asymmetries. Few, if any, distortions or twisted, knotted structures are present in plants whose growth and survival are threatened by disease, which requires a significant deviation from their core motifs. While how one faces adversity is characteristic of an individual's unique style and temperament, the extreme measures taken for survival may push them beyond a range where their full potential can be realized.

A person in such skewed conditions of disrupted growth would encounter intense struggles to return to their core uniqueness origins. Recovering personal realignment is essential in such cases. Here, exposure to life-altering experiences can be traumatic and triumphant. The adage "If it does not kill you, it will make you

stronger" may apply. Constricted motifs in a person's life may make them prone to life-altering experiences. A middle-aged man who faced sexual and physical abuse in his early years unsurprisingly had trouble with long-term relationships. He tended to select abusive women, detached from emotional intimacy, who themselves suffered personal guilt and shame for having been abused. What became life-altering for him was not the repeated abusive experiences of abandonment as an adult but rather the startling revelation that such a way of living was "oddly comfortable."

The predictability of expecting abuse offered him an odd sense of control and "normality" (based on what had become familiar). Chaos hits when he encounters someone who loves him. Such a change in his attempt to make changes (pursuing healthy connections instead of seeking to correct unhealthy relationships co-dependently) served as a crisis. How was he to behave and express himself with someone who only had positive, constructive things to say and do with him? There was nothing to "change" in his partner.

The need to work through the complexity of his motif was very clear, and without refining and reworking how he progresses with his growth and meaningful development on new levels of understanding and experience, he would remain stuck at that level of functioning. It would be an endless Groundhog Day cycle until he learned and moved forward.

The apparent change was within himself and his expectations. He tended to self-destruct in potentially healthy relationships in the past. When he met this healthy lady, she wouldn't go away, no matter how much he provoked, baited, or critiqued her behavior. He was 35 years old, divorced, with two children aged six and eight. He was quite intelligent, physically strong, and mechanically inclined, with a love for music and the guitar.

Yet, he was often embarrassed about his past abuse and constantly criticized many of his talents, abilities, and quirks (he liked to play music until 3:00 A.M. when no one was around).

While he needed to work through the traumatizing history of his abuse, it was the shock of meeting someone to whom he was deeply attracted— and who was attracted to him—that catalyzed his motivation initially. Part of his healing and recovery was to discover many of his hidden talents and abilities through the non-judgmental enjoyment of his behavior intrinsically. Whether it was music, intelligent dialogue, or emotional sensitivity, he discovered that refraining from self-evaluation of his performance allowed him to simply be himself in the activities in which he was engaged.

The entrainment of his previous abusive lifestyle had attracted numerous unhealthy women into his life. Ironically, he had "met" the new, healthy partner by accident. He had been hit by this woman driving her car just after he had entered his car, parked in front of his home. He was going out on a date with another one of his "typical" unhealthy partners when this person slammed into his car. The accident pinned him in the car, and he had to be pried out by the local fire department. It prevented him from keeping his date. He ultimately broke up with his unhealthy partner and started dating the woman who hit him with her car.

Like the proverbial two-by-four piece of wood needed to get the horse's attention, it finally "hit" him—what had been missing in his life.

Having experienced physical abuse, this immediately caught his attention. However, the person who hit him was very kind and gentle—completely different from what he had known. He later said that he had been at his wit's end with many failed, unhappy relationships when this person entered his life (by crashing into the driver's side of his car). This is not to suggest that his readiness for change "caused" the accident. Instead, it showed his willingness to embrace new, life-changing opportunities whenever they appeared.

It was somewhat ironic and dramatic; however, the way she had entered his life—literally "stopping him in his tracks" through the collision that disabled his car. Had it not been for such a physical encounter—altering his pathway that day—he might still be entrained on a lonely road of life. Another curious feature of the accident is that it was the first snowfall of the year on a road upon which she had driven many times without incident. The timing of the weather, road conditions, and both he and she being at the same geographical point in time all suggest a contouring effect, correlating multiple factors simultaneously.

She was also divorced, not currently in a relationship, and open to new opportunities. Of course, no one can definitively determine cause and effect. Meeting someone whose needs and lifestyle goals align with one's own at a particular time can result from various factors beyond mere coincidence. Later, other ironic and unique encounters will be shared, highlighting themes for further exploration.

Synchronizing experiences such as the previous one are not necessarily one-to-one correlations of perfect timing. Rather, because lifestyles have motifs that are asymmetrical (skewed unbalances of design and order), it is highly improbable that there would be a perfect fit. Instead, a series of indirect, intermediate steps would be involved in how scenarios may move as an entrainment of contouring motifs. This can be exemplified in the concept of six degrees of familiarity, where it has been calculated that we know somebody who knows somebody, and so on, to the sixth degree of personal encounter, who knows someone that knows us. Approximately ten years ago, it was commonly stated that many individuals knew someone associated with actor Kevin Bacon. We are never more than six degrees of separation from every other person in the world. Such multifaceted, nonlinear interrelationships among people, places, things, and natural events (such as the weather—consider what global warming involves) are what is more likely in asymmetrical entrainment.

An example of such asymmetrical correlations with varying degrees of synchronized connections occurred during the horrific event of 9/11. For the first time in my friend's life, he had been vacationing overseas in the south of France. On that fateful day, his serene vacation was shocked by the surreal news that two American commercial airliners had crashed into the New York World Trade Center's twin towers. Events unfolded in incredulous ways. He had been enjoying a piano recital at the Hotel Negresco in Nice when it was interrupted by this devastating news. He was too far from his hotel, so he walked frantically, trying to find a hotel with a television to gain more information, as the one at his hotel was not working then. After almost an hour of frantically searching for a television, he located a small hotel north of Côte d'Azur (the Riviera's coastline).

Entering the hotel and finding the reception area, he sat down to watch an ongoing broadcast of the horrors that would change America and him forever. As he watched, two more people entered the room. They were a married couple from Chicago who were also on vacation and staying at a different hotel. When he met this couple, he realized they were also Americans searching for news and that they lived less than forty-five minutes from his home, a southern suburb of Chicago. As events unfolded, the wife, who worked for the Chicago Sun-Times, and my friend, an author, connected when they returned to Chicago, collaborating on articles about terrorism.

When my friend returned to Paris for his flight home to Chicago, he found that all flights into and out of the U.S. had been indefinitely canceled. After contacting the U.S. Embassy in Paris, he received the name and phone number of a Parisian home where he might wait out the delay. Fourteen years before 9/11, he had been told about a stockbroker who had lived in Los Angeles, California, and moved to Paris. Interestingly, the name and number of the Parisian home he was given belonged to that stockbroker. This person was the son of the De Sousa family in Paris, a reputable and well-established family. He additionally assisted my friend in arranging alternative travel with another airline after the original carrier ceased operations.

To add to the series of contouring events, my friend met a Moroccan woman at the start of his flight from St. Louis to Paris. Surprisingly, she worked as a passenger customs relations officer at Charles de Gaulle Airport in Paris. She got to know him, and when he returned to Paris, she helped him at the airport by guiding him to the right time and place for his return flight home, which included a layover at Heathrow Airport in England. Interestingly, the Moroccan woman was Muslim and had a lot of empathy for Americans like my friend. It turns out that my friend's grandfather came from Lebanon eighty years ago with a French bride.

As fate would have it, my friend and the Moroccan woman fell deeply involved and started planning to live together in

America. My friend told me that before he left, he had come across books in a brochure about terrorism. He reflected on how distant that entire topic seemed from his life. It later happened that after his return, he would write his book on terrorism and contribute significantly to a large series of volumes on the same subject. He was asked to examine terrorism from a unique angle, and his prior (though unrelated) research made him especially suited for it. My friend also mentioned that he hadn't traveled much and that it was just his luck to choose the time around 9/11 to take his first trip overseas.

9/11 was truly a life-altering event, and the impact on my friend, America, and the world continues to be felt to this day—and will continue so into the future. The contouring entrainment of timing, multiple encounters with resourceful people along the journey, and his relevant contributions toward this life-altering event (his writings and consultations) can be viewed from many perspectives. The first possibility is that all his encounters were purely coincidental. Another perspective suggests that Americans meeting one another overseas is not much of a surprise. However, the unique details of these contouring events seem to defy probability and chance. Meeting people at such a uniquely tragic point in time, encountering the couple from Chicago whose wife worked for a newspaper, my friend being a writer, the good fortune to reconnect with a stockbroker he had only heard about 14 years ago, and then being given his name from among the many kind French people taking in Americans at the time—all of these events seem remarkable. Lastly, meeting an Arab woman who worked at the airport and provided essential guidance to be at the right place at the right time, reminiscent of his grandfather's marriage and journey to America with his French bride, adds depth to the experience.

When I interviewed my friend, I asked him about his experiences and what he made of it all. He said that when he first decided to make plans for the journey, he had been playing the piano and had written a song about themes of "saying goodbye or endings and beginnings." Interestingly, he played the piano both at the start and the end of his voyage. He was following his music or sense of harmony. When asked how he met the Moroccan woman in St. Louis, he shared that she had been on vacation in Los Angeles (where the stockbroker he learned about 14 years ago had lived before moving to Paris). He was attracted to her because he recognized, though he was unaware of this at the time, similar physical features to members of his own family.

He said he remembered saying, "Bless you," to her when they finished talking while waiting in an airport ticket line. Though she was Muslim, she was drawn to him by that message, and the rest, as they say, was history. Throughout his journey, he developed a curious, observant consciousness, sensing that the trip was taking on a unique "life of its own." This awareness seemed to act as a strange attractor, aligning his actions, movements, and interactions in a uniquely entraining way. Whether this was intentional, and to what extent, will be explored throughout this work.

For now, the contouring entrainment of human consciousness may be examined as a possible expression of asymmetrical motifs. Interacting in indirect, complex, and nonlinear ways—rather than through straightforward cause and effect—characterized my friend's experience during his first trip to Paris.

Reflecting on the events of 9/11 worldwide, one can always "Monday morning quarterback" (hindsight) what should have been done to prevent it. However, there were warning signs: the 1993 bombing of the Twin Towers, the Clinton administration's identification of Osama Bin Laden as a dangerous figure in global terrorism, intelligence reports from Indonesia months before 9/11 warning of general threats, and warnings given to the Bush administration upon taking office in January 2001 regarding the dangers of terrorism. However, the 9/11 Commission agreed that there was no specific information detailing the exact strategies and tactics the terrorists would use.

Having considered these factors, it seems fair to suggest that the Bush administration lacked a sense of urgency or priority in responding to terrorism. The depiction of President Bush with a blank stare and speechless while talking to a grade-school class reflects his shock and unpreparedness for such an event.

The administration's lack of awareness is common in those confronted with life-altering experiences. The fact that such events are total shocks and traumas—whether to an individual or an entire country—reveals how unwitting participation in entraining contours can create motifs that spiral out of control. This unwitting participation refers to the broader failure of the U.S. government to fully grasp America's role and vulnerabilities on the global stage. When the USS Cole was attacked overseas by suicide terrorists, there was no significant effort to analyze such events from a global perspective, explicitly considering the possibility that world terrorism would eventually reach American soil.

America's long-held illusion of safety, reinforced by the two vast oceans separating it from distant lands, led to a prevailing belief in isolation as security. This misguided perception made it easy to ignore the increasing number of warning signs. It is akin to the people of Indonesia watching the ocean recede, unaware of the impending tsunami about to overwhelm them.

The illusion of separateness, isolation, and disconnection blinds us to our unwitting participation in danger. For example, the 9/11 hijackers were able to rent cars, take flying lessons (focusing on takeoffs but not landings), appear on security camera footage, and board commercial airliners carrying metal box cutters without any scrutiny. Even more astonishingly, two weeks after 9/11—while European airports were patrolled by armed military personnel with automatic weapons— Chicago's O'Hare Airport had a single, somewhat overweight patrolman sitting on a stool in a terminal corner, eating a double-scoop vanilla ice cream cone. Unless he planned to fight terrorism by raising potential attackers' cholesterol levels, not much had changed.

An important caveat is the equally problematic overreaction of targeting anything that resembles "the enemy." This pattern of extreme responses continues, as seen in the looming potential for war with Iran over its supposedly peaceful nuclear program, which was estimated to be three to eight years away from weapons capability. However, politically persistent war motifs—exemplified by the Iraq invasion—threaten to escalate tensions. In a recent statement about Iran, President Bush even referenced the possibility of "World War III," illustrating how entrenched perspectives may shape future global conflicts. The entrapment of such synchronizations could culminate in the ultimate asymmetrical motif—a Pyrrhic victory.

Motifs inherently possess asymmetry. This means that while they may follow a familiar theme, they are never identical in detail. When these variations occur naturally, they allow for growth and development. Curiously, minor genetic variations in species enable evolutionary adaptation (or, in some cases, harmful mutations). However, when rigid motifs—such as isolationism—and imposing "sameness" constructs upon others are blindly upheld as perceptual filters, even the world's strongest nation can be led unwittingly into a false sense of security, like a lamb to the slaughter. If motifs of strength and geographic distance remain unchallenged, they will fail to evolve into healthier, more adaptive perspectives of global integration. Search for integration would require recognizing how asymmetrical and uncategorizable events may appear. Both within our country and beyond its borders, we need to see the functional and differential effects of not only what people do and say but also the consequences of what they evolve into. Observing asymmetrical ripple effects, interactions, and emerging patterns would seem to be more intelligent than focusing only on simple behaviors. It's not just about what a person says but what they do. Instead, it's about what a person achieves in the long term through their involvement in the complexities of this country and others. These complexities relate to the asymmetrical matching patterns rippling through our psychosocial and political culture. Otherwise, these blind spots will continue to serve as breeding grounds for catastrophic events, like 9/11.

Despite experiencing Pearl Harbor on December 7, 1941, fighting valiantly in World War II, and emerging from the Cold War, the U.S. government continues to fall into the same old pattern of isolationism. Even in the era of the Internet and multinational corporations transcending borders, America often operates under the illusion of global safety, repeatedly letting its guard down. Now, more than twenty-five years after 9/11, millions of undocumented individuals have crossed the U.S.-Mexico border—any of whom could be potential terrorists. The curious phenomenon of isolationism does not just mean physical distance from European and Asian allies. It could also mean that, through joint ventures and integrated cooperation, the United States might engage in and possibly finance and direct many global changes unilaterally. This is shown in the imbalance of contributions to NATO, where America provides funding that European countries do not. In the South Pacific, we are largely in charge even while working with countries like Australia and the Philippines. An individualistic mindset can sometimes be linked to isolationism. It's important to understand the real effects and wide-ranging implications of these themes in their true form, rather than stereotyping them in ways that cloud our perception. This helps us recognize emerging patterns more clearly.

A crucial theme regarding motifs, life-altering experiences, and chaos is that they seem to correlate in proportional ways. When motifs fail to expand and evolve into more creative forms, life-altering experiences can act as catalytic converters, inducing chaotic upheavals that break entire systems apart. Motifs, like individuals and nations, are formative design systems that require interaction with other systems for growth and sustainability. An imbalance—either through rigidity or dilution—can threaten their viability.

While plants and flowers grow naturally, they still require the right conditions and careful watering—not too much, not too little. Similarly, motifs, whether personal or national, must maintain healthy interactive boundaries to thrive. A consciousness of unfolding motifs is necessary for this to happen. This sense of consciousness—often referred to as purpose, mission, or patriotism—serves to advance thematic motifs by addressing potential blind spots, while also upholding and reinforcing cultural integrity and the nuanced complexities that arise in international interactions involving such motifs.

This can be quite challenging. No single leader represents all factions. There is a fluid process of turbulence and fluctuation, inundating various emerging ideas that surface at any time, each reflecting the complexity of multiple motifs simultaneously. The extent to which these complexities are synchronously integrated influences each other in asymmetrical ways, thereby affecting which motifs take precedence. One might assume that power and influence are the main factors, but ironically, power and influence are simply expressions of the synchronization of complexities that have come together.

There is an old phrase that captures this: "Nothing is more powerful than an idea whose time has come." That idea is the integration of the complexity of motifs. Synchronizing formative motifs can be seen throughout history. Examples of ideas whose time has come include the American Revolution, the French Revolution, the Russian Revolution, and even the Chinese Revolution, as well as in our modern times. A somewhat less volatile kind of revolution is the "revolution" of the Make America Great Again movement, which has challenged our political, social, and cultural norms. Regardless of political viewpoint, it's clear that the influence of an idea becomes most significant when the complexity of its underlying motifs aligns with the prevailing context. It will evolve, expressing its unique motifs, patterns, ratios, and proportions. The intensification of synchronized motif complexity is both formative and impactful. However, their formativeness continues to evolve and is not fixed.

Events like 9/11, monthly international trade deficits in the billions, and outsourcing jobs overseas (not to mention the impact of the internet and the World Wide Web) remind us of America's ties in a global community. Ignoring these effects or following corporations like Wal-Mart in prioritizing overseas expansion reflects an unhealthy approach to international involvement. It is not wrong for Walmart to seek global growth; it aligns with progress and prosperity. The issue is that it often overshadows and, in many cases, dominates other cultures and countries. America seems more like a target than a partner to work and share with. An American motif appears to swing with a global mood shift: on one hand, aggressively fighting the war on terror (invading Afghanistan, Iraq, and promoting democracy in the Arab world, Eastern Europe, and Asia), and on the other, engaging in corporate globalization that weakens the middle class through deficit spending, tax cuts, and unfair trade deals. For example, the U.S. trade deficit with China grows by billions each month. Ironically, while the U.S. government fights a war on terror to defend the American way of life, its economic policies might be weakening it at the same time. Such is a world with limited harmony in motif complexities. The need for nuanced, balanced, proportionate approaches in our motifs could help synchronize our complex ideas of living, where the delicate balance of connection and genuine empowerment could thrive internationally and make America safe again for future generations.

The American ideals of capitalism and rugged independence struggle to thrive in such a contradictory environment.

Mistaking corporate America's prosperity for the well-being of all Americans is a flawed and risky assumption. American individualism must go beyond the illusion that isolation equals safety—whether that means ignoring global threats or confronting them alone, as in Iraq. It took President Bush a second term to start engaging with other major world powers (besides England, which was already aligned). Yet, the administration's strict belief that corporate success automatically benefits the public has created a fragile economy. At this point, deficits have grown so large that people debate which is a greater threat to America—terrorism or the national debt. The deficit in 2025 is projected to be over $35 trillion and still rising!

One of the most striking aspects of motif entrainment is how ideas coalesce with supporting elements to create interconnected effects. For example, America's single-minded approach to global influence—often likened to a bull in a "China shop"—was evident in its leadership during the elections in Iraq, Ukraine, and Afghanistan. This raises an important question: Do elections alone signify the existence of a true democracy rooted in that culture? As we in America have a constitution congruent with and supporting democracy at its deepest roots, what are the constitutional roots in other countries that hold elections, and how grounded and ingrained are they in the fabric and motif of those cultures? The issue remains highly controversial. The fact that much of the world holds a negative opinion of America should be concerning, regardless of whether those people vote in U.S. elections. Countries and governments are composed of people, and true safety for America lies in fostering genuine respect and mutual understanding between cultures. Being feared or intimidating may temporarily suppress opposition in the Arab world, but it will ultimately breed more insurgents and future threats akin to Osama Bin

Laden. What new wars will America have to fight tomorrow because of the seeds it plants today?

Entraining Contours

The skewed nature of rigid, truncated motifs—as well as motifs that have lost their boundaries—tends to attract synchronizations of multiple events.

Actions and policies do not exist in a vacuum. Our expanding universe has been described as a gigantic loaf of raisin bread, where all the "raisins" (symbolizing galaxies) move outward proportionally. It is not the galaxies themselves that expand but the space-time continuum that stretches, keeping everything in harmony. This is an analogy for a universe entraining itself in a self-organizing motif.

However, when motifs expand in skewed but restrictive ways, it resembles warped baked bread expanding in its warped baking pan, distorting the proportional spread of raisins. Cultures and civilizations become jammed together, losing the space and time necessary for organic evolution. This warped distribution of cultural collisions mirrors what happens when the U.S. government seeks to reshape the world in its image, disrupting the natural proportions of global interactions. Motif complexities oversimplify and lose their artistry, synchronization and resonance uniqueness. In this context, motifs become limited.

Organizing Principles

At various points, we all become interconnected through organizing principles. Whether a minister dealing with spiritual matters or an FBI agent addressing homeland security, each operates within a set of organizing principles that selectively shape their reality. A country's behavior similarly influences global dynamics, shaping how thoughts, emotions, and actions interact with the world.

A minister, for example, may attract and engage with people, places, and events aligned with his spiritual focus. Like iron filings arranging themselves around a magnet, his presence organizes reality along these "magnetic" lines of influence. Similarly, consciousness itself serves as a contouring field, aligning events in a seemingly coincidental but deeply interconnected manner.

Consider Ashley Smith, who was held hostage by alleged murderer Brian Nichols. She used spiritual teachings from The Purpose Driven Life to encourage him to surrender. Was it mere coincidence that he kidnapped her, a recovering drug addict grappling with her struggles? Or was it an example of the synchronizing effects of contouring motifs, where the trajectories of their lives intersected at a crucial moment?

Physical matter, ranging from planets to subatomic particles, influences and is influenced by gravitational and electromagnetic forces. As Einstein showed, gravity is the warping of space-time by massive objects. Similarly, human consciousness creates waves of influence that shape social and spiritual interactions in ways that go beyond direct cause-and-effect relationships. Expanding contours of interacting motifs in outer space or social environments generate waves with multiple facets and nuances, much like multifaceted prisms, diamonds, and crystals. The combined effect of these complex interactions surpasses linear cause and effect, leading to a form of over-determinism where entanglement and measurement can occur because the system's complexity acts like an organic whole, resisting reduction to simple cause-and-effect. At this point, entanglement between events and individuals, across space and time—past, present, and future—can interact in ways that produce intricacies beyond basic cause-and-effect models. Addressing this requires reconfiguring system interactions to form a cohesive and interconnected unity of expressive diversity. Imagine a mobile hanging from a roof, swaying in the wind, with asymmetric parts so that if one part moves or is pulled, all the others reverberate similarly.

Both gravity and electromagnetism arise from the movement of particles within a field. In the same way, the movement of human consciousness generates entraining waves that shape lived experiences. Numerous studies (Grof, 1992; Calhoun, 2005; Yamamoto, 2005; Bateson, 1962) suggest that consciousness operates as a kind of physics governing human experience. NASA researcher Loelisk has even proposed that Earth functions as a holistic, self-regulating entity similar to a living organism. The synchronicities observed in Earth's biophysics and human events align with Albert Einstein's suggestion that modern physics is compatible with the experience of synchronized human interactions.

Proportionality and Motifs of Trauma

When bad things happen to good people, it does not necessarily mean they deserve it. There has never been a clear explanation for why tragedies befall some individuals and not others, even when circumstances seem equal. However, this is not a study of deservedness or causation but rather an exploration of factors that may contribute to or correlate with life-altering experiences.

Professional gamblers have learned how to play games of chance in ways that increase their odds of winning. If we could understand the "games" in which we are unknowingly participating—through the types of consciousness we project and absorb—would our chances of "winning" in life also improve? Consider the Indonesian tsunami, where no animals lost their lives. What level of consciousness were they operating on that increased their odds of survival? How could so-called "dumb" animals like cats, dogs, and chickens survive while intelligent and loving human beings perished? It is this deeper level of awareness that this study seeks to examine.

Studies have revealed that almost all living organisms possess guidance systems (such as magnetite) that allow them to navigate their environments. The waves of "consciousness"—not necessarily in the human sense—resonate proportionally to their surroundings. Nonhuman creatures trust their senses, intuitions, and visceral bodily awareness to guide their every move. In contrast, humans rely more on logic, reason, and ego-driven models to navigate life. While this approach enhances predictive power in controlled settings (such as laboratory experiments and legal contracts), experience tells us that life has no guarantees.

Therefore, the degree to which an individual's motif is misaligned with their core self and persistently reinforced sets the stage for life-altering experiences. What hidden distortions in our perspectives might contribute to seemingly random events—like being the one out of ten thousand taxpayers selected for an audit? It may seem strange, but how do external events correlate with internal experiences? What are the "mechanics" of coincidences and accidents that seem destined to happen?

Fate is a matter of choice, yet choice creates cause-and-effect outcomes. Free will and destiny often function as reciprocal forces. Understanding this circularity helps us recognize the internal and external conditions that influence one another. Destiny frequently presents us with choices—such as whom we decide to marry. Choosing one partner shapes our path, limiting other options. Once a decision has been made, it is irrevocable, and one must accept the resulting consequences. However, we can always make new choices moving forward. We could re-decide on new courses of action, understanding the ramifications of our rippling effects of interfacing motifs with one another.

Life-altering experiences bring forth the unintended consequences of our past decisions, affecting both the immediate and distant future. For instance, marrying at nineteen may provide stability but later lead to divorce, financial burdens, and emotional distress. Poor choices, made impulsively, can challenge our sense of control and purpose.

Mistakes are crucial for learning. But what exactly constitutes a "mistake"? Given the complexity of life, even ultra-sophisticated computers would struggle to predict the long-term consequences of our decisions. Recognizing misalignments with our core selves is crucial. Human intuition, when effectively accessed, surpasses even the survival instincts of animals.

A distorted or skewed personal motif can resonate with a series of events that contribute to devastating life experiences. Consider the case of a man who consistently expected hidden "catches" in every job he took. His motif was shaped by passive-aggressive hostility, a fear of commitment, and deep-seated resentment from past traumas. Each job he accepted collapsed after one to three years. Despite valid reasons for job issues— such as sudden changes, sales, or bankruptcies—he showed entitlement and passivity.

It was as if he approached each position with rigid expectations that would never change. His mindset, "set in stone," led to growing resentment and a reinforced sense of victimization. Every job reinforced his belief that he was destined for failure, and he became increasingly convinced that his life was cursed with bad luck. While many people experience job frustrations, his resistance to life's uncertainties distorted his perception, making him feel personally targeted.

To this day, he moves from one "cursed" job to the next, trapped in a cycle of trauma and victimhood. His inability to accept the fluid nature of life continues to contour his experiences, reinforcing his belief that he is fated for disappointment. This case highlights the powerful impact of personal motifs on life trajectories and the importance of aligning with one's core self to break destructive patterns. These patterns extend beyond mere beliefs and imprints, shaping a person's lifestyle through complex configurations that include neurological, somatic, behavioral, and cognitive elements. These structured complexities form the foundational basis of unhealthy, irrational, and distorted beliefs. These skewed structural configurations of asymmetrical motifs are what needs to change for the beliefs, the imprints, and the behaviors to develop a lasting stabilization.

More than our Psychology

It could be argued that self-fulfilling prophecies influence much of our life experience, as our expectations and how we genuinely measure our self-esteem strongly shape the quality of our lives. While it seems that a person's psychological state can indeed affect their quality of life, this does not account for sudden, unpredictable traumas that can happen to anyone. Dying in earthquakes, plane crashes, or being at work in one of the towers of the World Trade Center on Monday morning, 9-11-2001, for example, have nothing to do with self-esteem, early childhood experiences, or expectations set. Instead, self-determinism and choice are replaced by feelings of chaos, loss of control, and anxiety about the unknown. In other words, randomness! Scientists and researchers face challenges in creating purely random sets of events for their studies. True randomness is the complete absence of bias or prejudice, where events happen spontaneously and without causal influence. For instance, obtaining a purely random sample of adolescents for a drug study requires a method or schema for selecting participants in an entirely unbiased and uninfluenced way. Motifs and unfolding asymmetries in each person's life are intentional and systematic, with unique configurations that influence and are influenced by predisposing factors rather than individual agency. There is a tendency to see cause and effect as if one action directly causes another or one person does something to another. However, this is more of an illusion and an oversimplification of the true complexity. When internal organizing factors are mobilized, there is a non-local, holistic effect operating, which only appears to have a singular cause-and-effect relationship. In reality, it is the collective effect of multiple motifs interacting and resonating. Because we have difficulty perceiving this resonance within and between our motifs, it does not mean it isn't there—it just means it's hard to detect. The tsunami that struck Southeast Asia years ago was devastating. The tragic loss of hundreds of thousands of lives resulted from a series of interconnected factors: fissures beneath the ocean, the shape of the ocean floor, depth variations, seismic activity, and more. These interwoven, asymmetrical factors and resonances synchronized holistically, culminating in the phenomenon we call a tsunami—an enormous wave of water. Although it manifested as a powerful wave, it was the result of countless resonances and dynamics. Tragically, many people unwittingly synchronized their presence with these factors, making them victims of this massive natural event.

Seligman (1992) has illustrated how to cope with negative experiences (keep the mind focused on aspects such as it being temporary, situational, and not personal). But coping style does not address chaotic disasters with life-and-death consequences as far as meaning and purpose. The reasons why some individuals survived while others did not encompass a range of possibilities, such as divine tests or punishment, efforts by malign forces, the inherent randomness of life, the occurrence of unfortunate events, and the belief that challenges can lead to greater resilience. The shuttle disaster in January 2004, involving a complete loss of life upon re-entry, was found to be caused by damage to its heat shield (loss of tiles). Despite enhancements to the subsequent shuttle, it remains unclear why this specific flight with these astronauts suffered critical damage to its heat shield at launch, sealing its fate from the beginning. Yet, as in 9/11, some experts raised questions about safety issues resulting from cost-cutting budgets. This is not what the politics of such rational thinking wanted to hear. If reality does not fit into budget designated frameworks, then reality is pressured to conform to the budget. This is contrary to the reality of NASA's mission statements and, therefore, confirmative to disastrous, life-altering outcomes.

As with any such tragedy, the pain and grief become augmented when no real meaning and purpose seem to be served. The psychological state of the astronauts is not responsible for the occurrence of this disaster. However, is their way of thinking, their psychological state of mind, synchronized with that of NASA's budgetary constraints? Are they unwittingly cooperating and entraining with disaster through sheer, unwitting participation with such bottom-line consciousness? One could simply say that being motivated to be an astronaut would place one in a high-risk position (sitting on top of a rocket loaded with millions of gallons of liquid explosives certainly seems riskier than a walk in the park, unless it's Central Park, New York at midnight). A more meaningful perspective is to view the organizing principle of what motif was operating at NASA that would have entrained the entire mission on a contouring track of disaster.

NASA had been undergoing a period of cost-cutting before this mission, as reported by CNN. Any enterprise, no matter how noble and grand its mission, involves financing and accountability. Consequential to this background setting was the issue of time efficiency and meeting predetermined and perhaps even unrealistic and unsafe timelines. It appears that even chaos and random outcomes may have telltale signature motifs spelling future perturbations. Indeed, this aligns with the predictions of chaos theory, despite the seemingly contradictory nature of "predictive chaos." Glick (1985) describes how flowing water wheels can spin both forward and backward when their varying patterns of motion (known as fractals) encounter "tipping points" (or a turning point not unlike the last straw that broke the camel's back), which operates with its signature motif known as the "butterfly effect." The metaphor comes from the graphed-out patterns of random movements within a defined space and time (contours of entrainment). Examples may be two cars interweaving their driving between parking lots, weather patterns over a geographic area, spinning water wheel motion, or the classic example that the beating of a butterfly's wings in Africa can cause it to rain in South America.

Curiously enough, while I am not a mathematician, I have observed patients suffering from alcohol, drug abuse, and gambling addiction cycle through "trigger behaviors" (activities that lead to addictive behavior) in a style and frequency similar to fractal patterns of predictive chaos. What many psychotherapists would call disturbances in lifestyle (and indeed they are) could also be considered as perturbations of predictive chaos in the life of an individual. Here again, we find signature motifs of perturbations that are indeed random and chaotic yet continue to present unique, hidden ordering patterns within. These unique signatures reflect hidden motifs within both human and natural events. When they interact, the contouring interfaces of man and nature may well design (not destine) individuals being at the wrong place, wrong time, and wrong vehicle.

Attributions of faith, God, destiny, etc., are not precluded from such a perspective. Rather, such a perspective of entraining, contouring motifs offers a mechanism by which such experiences and encounters become manifest. Research into such dimensions would be strongly recommended at such a juncture.

Being cognizant of hidden order both in the lifestyle of individuals and in nature may further raise the question of influence. Far from behavior being determined in one's head alone, the patterns of triggers (and tipping points) that could operate in troubling conditions such as addictive behaviors may also operate in affective disorders such as mood swings, depressive spirals, and frequency and intensity of anxiety and panic. Mood swings among the population often follow a "butterfly" pattern, peaking around holidays, late summer, and early spring—periods when suicide rates are higher. While psychodynamic factors are certainly a contributing cause in these conditions, behavior never occurs in a vacuum but rather in a context. Skewed patterns can be influenced by social, cultural, financial, and governmental contexts (like NASA), or natural events (such as weather and earthquakes). are all possibilities. Alignment along these multi-level and multi-dimensional systems would imply that some individuals skewed in some perturbed motif entraining with some financial/governmental operating in some mechanical/physical device all similarly (but never equally) perturbed possibly suggests linkages or tracks to disaster. Admittedly, without research and rigor, this is quite speculative. However, the discovery of hidden orders within chaotic patterns known as fractals has been well researched over the past twenty years. That these fractals are unique motifs that serve in synchronous alignments among human and nonhuman systems and dimensions is not such a far stretch. Look at the advances in robotics both in Japan and America. The U.S. government is currently utilizing mind and machine interfacing with its F-14 fighter pilots. Because the number of cockpit operations is becoming so demanding, these pilots are being trained on biofeedback-like computers on how the alteration of their brainwave frequencies can influence electronic hardware. We are not too far from a future where a pilot's thought (or wish) can become the plane's command. Perhaps Walt Disney's theme song of "When You Wish Upon a Star" has more basis in reality—especially future reality—than ever before.

According to neuroscientist Paul Whelan of the University of Wisconsin (Szegedy, Maszak, 2005), ninety-five percent of our daily activity is done unconsciously. The intuitive, snap judgment that occurs in deciding to drink Coke over Pepsi, children's expressions causing you to feel euphoric or aggravated, that song on the radio taking you back decades in time, are all examples of the conditional, unconscious associations of our hidden inner states. Whelan suggests that, without such conditioned learning automated at the unconscious level, daily living would be chaotic. It allows us to drive cars, carry on conversations, tie our shoes, walk, talk, and chew bubble gum without having to attend to every step or detail. It is what cognitive neuroscientists call the adaptive unconscious. It helps us understand the appropriate meaning of such statements as "prostitutes appeal to pope" and "children make nourishing snacks," weeding out the perversity of illicitness and/or devouring of humans.

This inner organization of the unconscious involves neural codes that engage complex brain structures and neurotransmitters. The hidden order of the unconscious includes a "thinking without thinking" (non-awareness) core of deep metaphors and imagery. Gerald Zaltman (Szegedy-Maszak, 2005) created a patented method to access the core structures of motivation in consumers to determine what they are driven to purchase. He developed the Zaltman Metaphor Elicitation Technique, which involves ways of eliciting networked concepts and constructs (cognitive images) that influence behavior and thinking. He designed a children's hospital in Pittsburgh using this method. By accessing metaphors (constructed images) associated with people, places, events, purchases, emotions, and so on, he was able to tap into the ninety-five percent of the brain that motivates us at the unconscious level.

There have been other studies regarding the hidden, unconscious ordering of meaning and imagery by Gladwell in his bestseller Blink (2005). He demonstrated that the Coke can's red and white colors activated a variety of brain structures out of people's awareness, motivating them to action, memory recollection, and self-imaging. There appear to be multi-channel crossovers in brain structure interconnections that permit multi-modality crossover from images and language to memories, feelings, and action that are highly synchronized.

Although more will be explained later about their synchronized crossover, it is presented here to show how a human mind-brain system resonates and entrains with core organizing motifs. The metaphors embedded in a context involving people, places, emotions, and products are expressions of core motifs aligning and shaping with external events, unknowingly drawing people into life-changing experiences. Neuroscientific studies support the idea that the mind/brain system can synchronize in unconscious, subtle ways during complex events. This capacity for multi-faceted synchronization with people, places, and things appears to be a fundamental aspect of how the brain's neural structure is organized. Furthermore, such multi-layered synchronization can occur simultaneously across various events. For example, when a person experiences multiple traumatic events in a short period—such as losing a job, a spouse, a home, and perhaps even their mental stability during a nervous breakdown—it may indicate several cascading events that synchronize to produce a critical tipping point.

Life-altering events are usually a compilation of chain-reacting breakdowns that cascade like dominoes, forcing a quantum-level change. It's not one domino event but the synchronization of resonating assemblies of "domino" events clustering together where the whole is greater than the sum of its parts. This is the "tornado's" tipping point of concentrated force entrained into a synchronization of life-altering proportions. It is not the loss of a job but a career. It's not the loss of a wife but of the one and only soul mate with whom you have shared years of experience. It is not a single event (though 9/11-type disasters can be powerful singularities that are a "perfect storm" building and converging, but this is not what destroys the will to live!). The cumulative effects reach a critical point, which can become life-threatening.

Life-altering events involve the potential loss of hope and future. Being alert to the entraining contours of one's synchronizing constructs, images, and core themes can assist us in reconditioning our adaptive, unconscious participation. Life-altering events are the belated culmination that we have been consciously out of control of our behavior for quite a while. Translate "out of control" into "out of contact" as far as self-awareness is concerned. The life-altering event may be that wake-up call to that exquisite realization. Aligning our conscious and unconscious behavior requires intricate sorting out and working through the skewed nature of our misaligned motifs (realigning adaptive unconsciousness with our genuine core of self-motif). Acting out misaligned skewed in one's "adaptive" but malfunctioning motifs only exacerbates imbalances in the delicate synergy of an individual's or even a country's genuine core identity and constitutional construction.

Zaltman speaks of core metaphors involving interconnecting constructs. These metaphors are integrated into external situations, products, emotions, or events (relevant associations to the colors of a Coke can). What's at issue here is if such associative metaphors are misaligned with core constructs of a person's self-motif (concepts of self, value, purpose in life, unique ways of sensing and perceiving one's own reality experience, etc.). Over or under non-adaptive unconsciousness can powerfully contribute to misaligned motifs. This is especially valid if human motivation is driven by this ninety-five percent factor of unwitting unconscious conditioning. Skewed motifs can occur at all levels of reality, including the individual and national levels.

Skewed in National Policies

When motifs are skewed in such distorted ways that misalignments with core motifs become extreme, therein lies the breeding ground for life altering experiences. These experiences come in the form of chaos in that the self-designing system of the individual or country no longer can function. Alcoholics Anonymous has a phrase for this: It's called "hitting one's bottom." Chaos is a natural part of life, no matter what one does. However, our lives become lightning rods when we unwittingly participate in the game of life in self-reflexive ways deviant from our core nature and self.

Volcanoes are necessary for the earth to rejuvenate itself. Yet, building a house near such an entity and then feeling doomed when it blows (Mt. St. Helens) would be a curious way of saying one's life is cursed to be blown away! Yet, when we go through our lives with mistaken beliefs and distorted expectations or live within a culture or civilization that does not practice what it preaches, we are unwittingly participating in skewed contours like an "accident waiting to happen."

It has been stated that democracies are the best insurance against terrorism. Life in the post-9-11 world has found the U.S. government advocating democracy throughout the Middle East. While there are hopeful signs like the Iraq elections (as mentioned earlier), this is no guarantee that cultures in other parts of the world will resonate to democracy the way the West has over the centuries. While the vote on this policy motif is probably years out into the future, learning from our past to protect our future is essential.

Power as a Skewed Motif

Asymmetry in cultural motifs is not necessarily a flaw but can create unique deviations, like tectonic plates subducting beneath one another under extreme pressure. Without the necessary space and time for full expression, this layering effect forces motifs into contorted and evolving shapes, reshaping design structures. As continents are reshaped through such encounters, cultural motifs can collide, generating shockwaves that ripple throughout civilizations. The 9/11 attacks were the final, catastrophic eruption that triggered an all out war on terrorism. Natural and man-made disasters seem inevitable, especially when world leaders behave like rigid, unyielding "plates" refusing to shift even an inch.

During the 2004 U.S. presidential election, President Bush stated that the war on terrorism would be ongoing for years, implying that it could never be won permanently. However, he later reversed his stance, claiming victory in the war was already being achieved. Terrorism, structured as a decentralized, multi-centered, and multi-celled network, remains resistant to eradication—eliminating one center leaves others intact, much like trying to remove a spider's web. What, then, is a realistic outcome, and what strategies are required under these conditions? What is the role of power and might in a war driven by ideology and faith as well as military action?

It has often been said that the pen is mightier than the sword. Regarding terrorism—especially Al-Qaeda's vision of jihad—the perversion of religious texts to justify violence is perhaps more dangerous than their physical attacks. The battle for civilization's hearts, minds, and souls is crucial because where ideology leads, culture and society will follow. The chaos and asymmetry of terrorist organizations stem from distorted religious motifs. How does America protect itself from such zealotry? Authority should be effective, not an end in itself. If a culture claims divine righteousness, it must have the honor and courage to stand firm in its beliefs. However, how can America elevate the argument so that power remains a means to an end rather than becoming an end itself? Compassion and intervention—saving people whether they want to be saved or not—can lead to further conflict. Misalignment of motifs breeds disastrous, life-altering consequences.

Osama Bin Laden was one of the world's most wanted criminals, yet he perversely enjoyed admiration and protection from segments of the Muslim world. Despite a $300 billion war budget, terrorism persisted, as did Bin Laden's freedom for years. Can democracy truly be installed in regions where cultural motifs and values are undermined by Western influence? Meanwhile, fear and terror were repeatedly emphasized by the U.S. Secretary of Defense, particularly before congressional budget appropriations—coincidence or calculated strategy?

While America must protect itself, manipulating public fear reduces intelligent adults to frightened children, seeing threats in every shadow. The flawed intelligence leading up to the Iraq War, falsely justifying military action with claims of weapons of mass destruction, raises critical questions: How can the American public make informed choices when fear distorts reality?

The problem with terrorism is further complicated by the constant fear it instills, much like a modern-day "cry wolf" scenario. The emphasis on military power overshadows cultural diplomacy and international cooperation. America was not attacked by invading armies but by terrorists who weaponized its achievements. The U.S. military can dominate physical landscapes, yet history shows that no force is stronger than an idea whose time has come. When cultural motifs are distorted by oppressive Islamic regimes and exploitative Western policies, paradoxical alignments of terrorism accelerate. Is it coincidental that political figures once supported by the U.S., such as Bin Laden during the Soviet Afghan War and Saddam Hussein during the Iran-Iraq War, later turned into adversaries? The notion that "the enemy of my enemy is my friend" is flawed; a wolf in sheep's clothing remains a wolf.

Distorted Contours of International Motifs

Survival and self-interest dictate international policies, both at governmental and corporate levels. This echoes the story of "The Emperor's New Clothes," where illusions remain unchallenged. When 9/11 occurred, all commercial flights were grounded—except for those carrying Bin Laden's family out of the U.S. The priority of maintaining alliances with wealthy aristocracies has contributed to radicalization. America promotes democracy yet aligns with autocratic regimes when convenient. During the 1980s, the U.S. supported Saddam Hussein during the Iran-Iraq War, leaving him in power after the Gulf War. These contradictory policies perpetuate the very threats they aim to eliminate, fueling fundamentalist extremism.

Ironically, what has impressed the Arab world most about American military actions is their rare consistency. President Bush's unwavering stance on Iraq—whether one agreed with it or not—was a departure from the usual diplomatic double-talk. Yet, compromising international policies creates dangerous precedents. While the United States did not originate terrorism, certain policies have contributed to its increased prevalence. Today, similar contradictions persist. For example, the U.S. rewarded Pakistan for its assistance in the war on terrorism with F-14 fighter jets, exacerbating India's security concerns. To maintain balance, America then sold military equipment to India. With both nations possessing nuclear capabilities, the U.S. inadvertently perpetuates future conflicts rather than resolving them.

These asymmetrical policies create a perpetual sense of insecurity, ensuring that war never truly ends. Defense contractors benefit from these conflicts, as government contracts—often awarded without competitive bidding—fuel a military-industrial complex reminiscent of the 1960s. Is democracy truly good for business, free trade, and international relations? The divisions in America have rarely been more intense. Meanwhile, Pope John Paul II, widely regarded as a unifying spiritual leader, has passed away, raising questions about where new leadership will emerge in this post-9/11 era. When

Pope Benedict later quoted a 12th-century critique of Islam, it only deepened religious divides. In a century increasingly defined by religious and ideological conflict, such statements can only inflame tensions.

Abraham Lincoln once said, "A house divided cannot stand." While America is not in a civil war, political and ideological divisions threaten its unity. The nation only comes together when attacked—by then, the damage has already been done. In the 1980s, America ignored the rise of Islamic fundamentalism and Saddam Hussein. In the late 1990s, internal political conflicts distracted from growing global threats. If the only time America unites is in response to crisis, then perpetual war will remain its destiny, and future tragedies like 9/11 will continue to be written into history.

Ego and Eco Certainty

American interests, particularly those driven by multinational corporations and NGOs, can become so self-centered that congressional lobbyists, in their pursuit of money, often forget what America truly stands for as a nation. Distorted corporate priorities—covering oil, agriculture, cheap labor, border policies, and the military-industrial complex—shape America's future and impact the lives of its citizens in crucial ways. This hardly encourages harmony with others.

Without genuine leadership that prioritizes unity over division and emphasizes our shared values rather than our differences—much like the late Pope—these unchecked and conflicting interests will only intensify. Achieving unity is difficult when the parts do not fit together smoothly, are uneven, and have different priorities. However, given the asymmetries present in an organization, it is the leader's responsibility to understand the broader complexity and interconnected trends involved in asymmetric unification. Leadership through motifs often involves irregularities and challenges, aiming creatively toward a unified whole. This approach is not always democratic, but it is undoubtedly not terroristic. The foundation of meaningful progress lies in recognizing the interconnectedness of individuals, nations, and global structures. Understanding these interconnected dynamics and their influence on future shaping is essential for navigating the challenges ahead. This exploration of interconnected motifs and their role in shaping transformative experiences will be the focus of the next chapter.

CHAPTER 5

FUNDAMENTAL MOTIFS

Contours of Connection: Losing Illusions and Winning Realities Why do some young adults in their early twenties have a need or even compulsion to be married for fear their lives will end? Why are others equally driven by some fictional myth or dream to be a doctor, a lawyer, a CEO, an entrepreneur, etc.? How do we, as individuals and countries, come to places in our life cycle where, if we are not such-and-such an identified achiever, billionaire, captain of industry, or whatever, our lives are (to us) depressingly useless? Which God do you worship? The gods of money, success, fame, fortune, immortality, and supremacy are all up there on many of our lists. Having dreams and visions of ourselves in the future can serve as healthy guides. It is all too easy to confuse the dream of what we want to do in life with who we are in life. It's easy to over-identify with our fictional role-playing on many of our lists. Alfred Adler (1954), one of the original students of Sigmund Freud (but you can forgive him for that), once stated that all human movement is compensatory in striving to overcome some sense of inferiority. Social interest was his "cure" for the neurotic striving for superiority over others (as well as one's self-perceived deficits). His measure of mental health was the degree to which an individual (or a nation) moved in their compensatory efforts with an attitude of making contributions to the common good of all (interest in social connectedness).

He believed we integrate thoughts, feelings, and actions to pursue a meaningful goal or ideal. Note: Adler's design resembles a motif. However, the motif construct is more comprehensive, incorporating fully how one's uniqueness is an implicit and explicit signature of formativeness manifested throughout one's mind-body continuum. It is embedded in the inherent nature of one's unique, psycho-biological consciousness of being, from the biometrics of eye scans and fingerprints to the exquisite physiques, mental, emotional, and unselfconscious flow nuances of ballerinas and baseball players. Such individual design, therefore, is not only a product of a person's subjective interpretation. Each person's unique motif shapes the nature of their subjectivity. Indeed, it constitutes the idiosyncratic construction of what it means to be subjective, forming the "quantum gravity" foundation of one's space-time life continuum. It empowers free will in a uniquely innovative way.

Understanding the complexity and importance of our uniqueness and how it influences our lives and those around us is a challenging task that often requires deep insight and reflection. Without clear guidelines, structured mentoring, and age-appropriate educational opportunities, individuals may face challenges through trial and error. This is often seen in situations where curiosity leads to unexpected actions. Such instances are more likely when individuals become deeply invested in idealized fictional concepts, which can cause significant changes in their behavior or thinking. Purposeful efforts to shape one's lifestyle might involve power, attention, revenge, or disillusionment, leading to life stories of "...if only things had been different, I could have been a..." (Fill in the blank here refers to being some grand success). Adler's Individual Psychology views each person as a unified, indivisible whole. This is a key point, as all conflicting parts of a person (emotions, beliefs, behavior problems, etc.) are methods or strategies (one's modus operandi) employed to pursue conceptual ideals through concealed or private reasoning. This semi-unconscious aspect of an individual allows for complex synchronization of unwitting influence. It is a potential risk that an individual may not realize (unwittingly) that they "know" something at another level, which they are unknowingly seeking!

The problem Adler was addressing involves a compulsive, insistent form of compensation, which goes like this: "If I don't become President of the United States like my father, my life will mean nothing." Idealization and self-devaluation become major motivations that distort and skew perception rules (or perceptions one has created, often unconsciously, about how to see or interpret one's reality) involving oneself and others. It can take the form of believing that one and only person is "my soul mate partner." It may be "getting into the Ivy League College" or "Making that million-dollar (or now billion-dollar) annual salary." A significant number of individuals from Generation X faced major challenges after the market downturn of the 1990s. They can't believe how their lives have turned out! Many have moved back in with their parents, entered unhealthy relationships or marriages, or are constantly chasing that "golden ring" of a career move or breakthrough.

Nations, too, can dream of being number one (as do most colleges, companies, individuals, and communities). Having the "Bomb" (Atomic) means a nation has "arrived" and joined the elite club. It reminds me of people striving for membership in elite country clubs, societies, or discos (remember Studio 54 or Faces). What we won't do to worship our god. Speaking of which, notice the rivalry between East and West in trying to be the number one world religion. What kind of idealization is unknowingly at play here? What could such private logic involve in a life-changing, global nuclear world?

What connects mythmaking, major life events, chaos, and recurring themes? The answer relates to human nature. Human beings have a pattern-seeking instinct to create order and meaning from chaos. When horrific tragedies like 9/11 burst into our reality, the shock and chaos challenge us and compel us to figure out why it happened (what caused it, what it means, how to understand it, prevent it from happening again, and what to do about it).

As with all shocking events, it is only human to impose our interpretation, our patterning on how to make sense of it all. A creative admixture of fact and fiction is usually infused throughout our analysis and interpretation. Such an admixture emerges in our government's response to 9/11.

The myth or fictional messages sent to the American people and the world in general were that Iraq's dictator had weapons of mass destruction, that it was a training ground for the 9/11 hijackers, and was developing nuclear capabilities which could be directed to America. The Bush administration hammered away at America and the world regarding life-threatening "realities"! It was an all-or-nothing issue. If it walked like a duck, talked like a duck (and just happened to wear a garb), then it must be a terrorist, so "Duck!" The ability we teach our children to differentiate right from wrong, good formativeness from poorly formulated (lacking valid criteria from which to measure degrees of genuine risk), seemed to be strangely absent at such high levels of expected maturity in decision-making.

After the war was launched in 2002, no weapons of mass destruction or verification of their other threatening warnings proved to be true. The strategy involved initiating the war regardless of the circumstances, including instances where the initial justification may not have been accurate. At that point, even if no genuine threats were identified, the operation would have to continue until it concluded, as withdrawing prematurely could pose serious risks. Focus was placed on the gradual promotion of a democratic culture. The belief was that the American people could not understand the issue's complexity, so it was necessary to simplify it into good and evil to motivate their limited understanding.

After identifying clear enemies, like the "bad guys," and acting on this understanding—such as invading Iraq—it's understandable that many of these efforts, strategies, and beliefs become self-perpetuating and self-justifying. The more we act on or believe in something, the more it seems real and justified. If humans are creatures of habit, then their choices and decisions today can easily lead to imprisonment and deadly fates later on. The roots of our life-changing events can be planted years in advance. Like in wars, the difference between our goals and the stories we tell ourselves triggers a chain of events that tend to reinforce itself. We continue "fighting our wars" because it has now become our way of life—or death.

Couples who marry in their late teens or early twenties may face significant challenges around their fourteenth or fifteenth year of marriage, especially after having two or three children, as they start to feel that life is moving quickly and opportunities might be slipping away. This period can often be marked by considerable upheaval. The husband or wife might look back and see personal adventures, careers, and encounters they never experienced, now as gaps and regrets in their lives. Old insecurities about dating, fitting in, belonging, rebelling against authority, and acting "wild and crazy" (like adolescence) tend to surface as they try to recover from poorly made decisions, which are now being re-evaluated.

If partners continue to do what they've always done (as governments sometimes do), never re-evaluating and dealing with the reality of the here-and-now needs, then self-perpetuation of archaic roles and expectations will inevitably evolve into some life-altering experience. Lack of course correction and synchronization of marital vows with evolving partner needs can lead to a "tipping point" crisis. When chaotic patterns reach such a point, paradoxical uncertainties and life-altering consequences emerge. What once worked now not only fails but often makes things worse in unpredictable ways. It has been a rule of thumb in marriages that the "contract" of implied quid pro quo (what has given and received) needs to be revised every seven years, plus or minus two. While this is only a generalization, it points to the critical need to remember that partners may continue to grow, but the relationship may remain the same. This points to a critical dynamic of living.

What force would cause us to change our usual habits of doing the "same old-same old" when those habits keep evolving on their own? That force is a life-changing experience. It is the chaotic clash with a person, place, or event that in some way breaks down a shield or the self-maintenance of limited, blocked creative impulses. What nearly guarantees the occurrence of such transformative experiences is strict adherence to the status quo, which widens the gaps between current realities and past, idealized notions of how "it should always be."

The decision to marry, pursue higher education, or choose a career marks the start of a definitive path. This involves embracing one opportunity while permanently passing up another. As an old proverb suggests, it is impossible to step into the same river twice—unless, of course, time travel becomes possible. Each moment is unique in its multidimensional complexity. Like each snowflake, it has a one-of-a-kind, distinct quality that has never existed before and will never exist again (even our memories lack its full complexity, which is why and how we can continue to learn from our past to enrich our future now). We can never go home, as Thomas Wolfe said, and that means we can never undo a past decision. Still, we can revisit and make similar decisions again, which is a natural outcome of life-changing experiences. The twists, turns, curves, and spirals of our chosen lifestyles can lead us into surprising, shocking, and awakening realizations about the illusions and myths we've been living with. Repetition of trauma in similar yet different ways may perpetuate itself through the very contexts and frameworks that sustain their resurgence over time. The good news is that, since each moment (even trauma) is unique, there is always a nuance that differs with each recurrence. That's where intervention can begin to unravel and reformulate corrective, emotional evaluations, enabling empowering changes. Yet, as the light bulb joke goes: "How many therapists does it take to change a light bulb? ... An answer could be 'one is too many and a hundred are too few.' It's the light bulb that does the changing." It can hurt to emerge from the darkness, and one might dislike facing the truth of their life in the light of day. Sometimes, unwittingly following familiar patterns seems easier than using one's wit in new, self-healing, and self-affirming ways.

Unconscious patterns of deletion, distortion, and overgeneralization in our lifestyle choices can inadvertently align us with similar distorted themes present in our external environment. Awakening to our false gods and challenging our myth-making beliefs is an essential consequence of life-altering experiences. While recovering alcoholics, drug addicts, and others dealing with excessive fixations may comprehend what it means to "hit the bottom" of one's illusory way of life, we do not need to be off on lost weekends to encounter trauma.

Unjustifiable Trauma

Child abuse in any culture within the civilized world is completely unacceptable and unjustifiable. Children born into such homes, environments, or societies where terrible acts of abuse occur may also try to survive by creating false lifestyles or worshiping false gods. They have learned to view themselves as tragic, unfortunate victims. Experiencing trauma can be deeply distressing and confusing, making it understandable that individuals might adopt a victim identity after such events. However, a major concern arises when people internalize this victim role, as it can reinforce negative experiences and block personal growth. This is a corruption of their original motivating force, intended to be a source of empowerment. Such formative contamination leads to an autoimmune-like response, where individuals become allergic to themselves and turn against their well-being.

This perpetuates faulty lifestyles and false gods (self-gratification and lost boundaries of self). The scandal of child abuse by priests in the Catholic Church surfaced after decades of trauma. Some would say that the real God of the universe has a reason for everything. Whether that is true or not, it only substantiates that "God only knows" why such traumas occur. I, not being God, do not know such things. However, I have learned that the universal realities in which human beings live have built-in mechanisms that erupt like fuses with faulty wiring. Children born into families (or churches) where the adults have serious faults in their mental "wiring" may be the "fuses" that "blow the whistle" on such transgressions. They are unwittingly entrained by birth and/or placement in faulty settings to be at risk for abuse.

Life-altering experiences involving child abuse are an unfortunate example of how irrelevant one's inherent character or personal value is toward having "caused" such conditions to occur. The casual nature of life-altering events refers to the intertwining of skewed motifs interlocking with dangerous contours of disaster. It is not about God's judgment that one person (or child) deserves to be tortured and another (because it did not happen to him/her) was more deserving and therefore spared. While most intelligent adults accept that bad things happen to good people, when bad things continue to happen to the same people throughout their lives, that same intelligence could easily come to the opposite conclusion (that maybe they are not so good!).

To prevent such irrational thinking, it's important to understand that the patterns of living motifs are continuously active. Because much of our motivation is unconscious, childhood experiences can easily carry over into adulthood. Since ingrained habits of distorted life patterns reinforce themselves, adults with a history of abuse often unknowingly continue to resonate with skewed motifs. This isn't just a psychological issue; it also involves real-time physical events. For example, helping the "wrong" homeless person on the subway and getting mugged, or your house being the only one hit by a tornado in the area. It could be a woman who recently left a life as a nun and, during her first intimate relationship, contracts AIDS. Although these events can happen to anyone, repeated "coincidental" accidents in someone often surrounded by chaos and trauma usually indicate underlying patterns affecting their psychological, social, and physical experiences. These may involve subtle energies and subconscious patterns at play.

Mind-Body-Real Time

Some find the concept of the mind-body connection fairly easy to understand. However, when linking one's consciousness (including unconscious motivation) with real-time physical events in daily life, such connection is often overlooked. Nevertheless, many studies connect human consciousness with physical phenomena. Studies (Kosslyn, 2005; Carpenter, 2005) have shown how conscious imagining affects brain neurons, causing micro-muscular movements. These findings have been applied to improve performance in sports, business, and personal goal achievement. The human brain is essentially a highly complex electrical circuit. This electrical activity produces electromagnetic fields linked to changes in a person's mind and brain activity. Brain scans using functional magnetic resonance imaging (fMRI) have revealed different electromagnetic patterns during various altered states of consciousness. States like relaxation, tension, and aggression each have unique electromagnetic signatures. Researchers have also hypothesized electromagnetic profiles for certain psychiatric disorders, such as psychopathy, schizophrenia, and obsessive-compulsive disorder, based on fMRI data. Split-brain studies show that the left hemisphere of the brain does not communicate with the right hemisphere, which can lead to conflicting signals. As a result, the verbal left hemisphere cannot relay perceptions to the right, while the right hemisphere experiences sensations that feel indistinguishable and lacks control.

As the human mind/brain can be influenced by external electromagnetic fields (since it is one itself), it has been demonstrated by Dr. Giacomo Pizzolatto (2005) at the University of Parma, Italy. His research demonstrated that mirror neurons located on either side of the frontal cortex would fire simply by observing others' actions as if they were doing it themselves. The ability to influence, be influenced, and entrained through empathic resonance of electromagnetic fields generated through observation, mirroring, and empathizing is a powerful reality. When teachers and students in martial arts training communicate over separate space by resonating mental fields that appear to be electromagnetic (much the same as tuning into a station on your radio), the influence of such entrainment is quite powerful.

Entrainment of resonant fields can be self-perpetuating with built-in resistances to change. This can be seen when rapport is established between two people. Once entrainment is engaged, it can require a great deal of energy to break free. Fictional beliefs and myths can establish strong patterns of influence that may result in significant adverse outcomes. Witness fundamentalists in various religious sects. Theirs is a literal truth grounded in invariant rigidity. The logic of Islamic fundamentalists is clear to them that terrorist acts are the way to Allah. Despite the horror, pain, and suffering, they are so entrained that they cannot reflect on their literal fixations.

When locked in a vacuum, entrainment leads to chaotic runaways. For example, when Muhammad Atta, the leader of the 9/11 terrorist groups, was radicalized in Europe (Germany), his feelings of alienation became entrenched in fundamentalist extremism. Before that point, he was a discouraged achiever who couldn't get into his local university. It was the isolated, intense focus of extremism entrained with Islamic fundamentalists that appears to have converted him to the dastardly personage from whence he came.

Small Distinction/Big Difference

Synchronization of chaotic events can occur in small changes that progressively accumulate exponentially into massive deviations. Terrorists like Muhammad Atta turn to Islamic fundamentalism, creating an almost schizophrenic literalism (mistaking the image for reality) of radical asymmetrical motifs. Such warped asymmetry is then synchronized with the 9/11 horror. When enough people cross a bridge, as seen with London's Millennium Bridge, they may walk in sync, causing spontaneous synchronization. At a certain threshold, a phase transition from randomness to coherence can emerge, leading to the rhythm of the crowd's walking resonating with the bridge's frequency, and it swings wildly, shattering itself into pieces.

A person's path in his/her lifestyle may cohere and resonate with other people, places, or events in unwitting and unexpected outcomes. Our life-altering experiences can inculcate multidimensional factors (states of one's consciousness, family constellations, cultural, spiritual background, etc.) in situations where we are either unaware or only minimally conscious of the underlying influences guiding our actions.

Fictional beliefs and rationales in our lives create resonant rhythms and space-time frameworks that can influence our life paths and those of others, often leading to unexpected, aperiodic outcomes. Recognizing the interconnections among cognitive processes, imagery, motor neuron mapping, empathic mirror neuron activity, resonant electromagnetic fields between individuals, and the links between states of consciousness and real-world phenomena emphasizes the potential for reciprocal influence and entrainment among people, environments, and events. Studies (Discovery

Channel, (2002).) Some theories propose that electromagnetic fields could play a role in brain-mind pathways that affect interactions with the physical environment, suggesting potential entrainment effects. Dr. Michael Persinger (Discovery Channel, 2003), a research psychologist, has used electromagnetic fields to alter emotional states in research subjects, activating brain centers to release hormones that promote relaxation. He claims that these electromagnetic waves can be directed into people's brains to induce emotional states such as fear and anger. Target populations can then be encouraged to blame certain groups or sources as the cause of these negative emotions (blaming some ethnic group as the basis of these fears).

When the capacity for mutual influence between cognitive processes and external environments is considered, it is evident that perceptions, such as fiction, myths, beliefs, and interpretations, can have an impact on shaping reality. As an adage goes, "If you believe it's real, then that's what's real for you, and

'You're right!" We connect with the world not just through words, but also through rhythm, sounds, images, and vibrations. Most communication between people (93%) is nonverbal (tempo, pace, volume, intensity, syntax, and nuance of spoken words).

You might have watched old westerns where cowboys and Native Americans clashed, and war drums rhythmically sent signals between tribes. Custer heard those signals beating as urgent warnings at the Little Bighorn. He knew it wasn't the Blue Man Group, either.

Profound life changes often come from seemingly minor or insignificant interactions. The tsunami in Indonesia devastated both residents and tourists. Understanding why some survived while others did not involve analyzing a complex array of variables that may require advanced computational methods. Still, it can be helpful to consider what specifically brought them together. This region features some of the world's most stunning and visually impressive landscapes. The beauty of its beaches, clear water, and exotic, luxurious atmosphere made it a top destination. The resort vibe, with its many pleasures, entertainments, and indulgences, created a paradise of relaxation and richness. It was a horrific shock when Hell arrived in the form of the tsunami.

Indonesia is an attraction with its exotic beauty, emphasizing the raw elements of nature. These raw elements of nature (beautiful palm trees, beaches, unique culture of the residents, panoramic ocean vistas, etc.) attracted people worldwide. As fate would have it, this raw, elemental environment, so connected and entrenched with tectonic plates, faults, and earthquakes, adds dangerous hazards to this heaven on earth. This area of the world, underdeveloped as part of its raw beauty, lacks a warning system that could have saved thousands of lives. Both people of wealth, as well as professionals (doctors, lawyers), and art connoisseurs are drawn to such scenic vistas.

Those who survived were the ones who made split-second decisions to turn the right way, climb to higher ground, follow the right person, etc. Survival of the fittest in this scenario was in timing, coordination, and knowing which person, guide, or "mentor" to follow to get out of harm's way as soon as possible. In this way, some small children survived while some adult, strong swimmers perished. As in all disasters, timing is everything when it comes to survival. Strength may be more about how to follow the right resource, network with the optimum subgroup, and/or zigzag in just the right way to negotiate a deadly obstacle or source of destruction. The ability to survive and prosper often depends on how effectively we adapt to environments that are either supportive or potentially detrimental.

The Tracks of Entrainment: Space-Time Zones

If timing is everything, then timing and rhythm of rapport and synchronization are all relative to speed and motion. Einstein illustrated that nothing can exceed the speed of light. The paradox of light is that physicists know that, from the spacetime framework of the photon, it has no mass and has arrived before it ever left! Only from our subjective frame of relativity do we perceive it moving! Einstein stated that speed is always constant (186,000 miles per second) no matter the context. Therefore, what changes is time and space (the faster one moves compared to light speed, the slower time will pass and the more space will expand). Intriguingly, if we moved at the speed of light, no time would pass, and space would completely expand. Going at the speed of light, that person would experience no time at all traveling to any point of the universe, no matter how long the distance. This is a kind of oneness or singularity. It has an eerie similarity to the singularity of a black hole's supermassive gravity, which collapses into no formative thing at all. That, too, is a kind of oneness at the other end of the continuum of expansion and contraction (kind of how the universe itself endlessly recycles).

Formativeness seems to take on a super-symmetry (illusions of perfect balance in design) at these extremes of perfect unification, where particles are matched by their opposites but lack unique revealing configurations of distinctive motifs. It is the small discrepancies that exist in the Standard Model that reveal an asymmetrical design inherent in the universe. These could be the tipping points, if you will, of perfect harmony when matching experiences occur at macroscopic and microscopic (cosmological and sub-atomic) levels of extreme limits of organization. If it were possible to exist ubiquitously at the extreme boundaries of reality, such as at light speed or within a black hole's center, one might observe a phenomenon where the infinitely large and small dimensions converge and intertwine. These differing aspects concerning speed limits and the expansion or condensation of matter and energy reflect the relationship among fundamental scientific principles. The physicist Stephen Hawking (Discovery Channel, 2006) believes that information is preserved at both extremes. Formativeness never really ends but is itself reformed, repackaged into higher levels of formativeness (or meta-formativeness). The Holographic nature of formative information, if you will.

Living on Earth, the space-time changes we experience are more metaphysical (subjective psychological phenomena). Time and space seem to change depending on our consciousness frames of mind (time flies when having fun, yet watched water "never" seems to boil). Yet, time and space phenomena, even on Earth, may not be strictly psychological. Deepak Chopra did studies of people listening, dressing, and reexperiencing cultural fashions from when they were twenty years younger. He observed that many of their aging vital signs returned to youthful levels.

The Consciousness Effects of Mental States on Physical Reality

Doctors have demonstrated the consciousness effects of mental states and their influence on physical reality. Persinger (2002), Radin (2002), and others previously cited. The issue here is: what is the "speed of light" in each lifestyle? How does each person live in that ageless, timeless, and spaceless phenomenon while being grounded on Earth?

The answer appears relatively straightforward: when each person lives in their "here and now," the experiences of present moment time and space become an everywhen and everywhere. Such a principle is found in the teachings of all the great religions of the world and will be explored later. For now, this construct will be described as the speed of light on Earth—a constant phenomenon that establishes a maximum speed for terrestrial processes.

Flow states of unselfconsciousness—streams of forgetting oneself while immersed in some mind-body activity (playing the piano, shooting free throws, runner's high, any non-self-conscious interactive flow of attending)—offer a glimpse into this mode of being.

Everyone is unique and has their own pace and style. As mentioned in previous sections, the degree of alignment (or misalignment) one has with their own unique motif determines optimum levels of performance. Learning how to maintain and enhance alignment with motifs during shocking and/or disastrous, life-altering experiences is a key to survival and thriving. Even more important is being able to discern one's contours, pacing, timing, and entrainment—as these can serve as early warning systems when dangerous or risky engagements begin to occur. Re-engagement into motifs of traumatic "flow states" may be experienced as anxiety and/or panic states.

The types of people to whom we are attracted, the careers we choose, and the ways we enjoy ourselves all express the unique contours and multiple entrainments of our motifs. We may have fictions or fantasies of meeting that fabulous, charismatic femme fatale or that dynamic hunk of a man. Before the tech bubble burst in the late '90s, many young adults in their twenties dreamed of millionaire bank accounts and Beamer cars parked in three-car garages.

What is important to grasp is that the entrainment of our unique contouring motifs usually means joining in a constellation of synchronizing events. Just as violins have their timing and placement in an orchestrated piece of music, we, too, uniquely synchronize facets of our motifs to some larger, orchestrated sources of life events. If we are not aware of what social arena some facet of our motif is entrained to, we may be playing a role in a larger system that puts us at risk.

Teenagers may think it is "cool" to smoke, party, and "hook up" in promiscuous ways with peers. While such activities may be part of "experimental periods," indulging in facets of their motives (self-expression, release of energy, or just being "out there") can lead to deadly, life-altering experiences—drug overdoses, addictions, loss of life, or long-term shame and self-esteem issues.

At a more subtle level, it has been said that our lives can be altered by a small change, whether we button our shirts from the top to the bottom or the bottom to the top. Being home for that call from a potentially significant other may determine who you ultimately marry, where you live, how many children you have, and whether you live longer and prosper.

It seems astonishing that such small details could have long-term, impactful effects on our lives. Nonetheless, consider those caught in the Indonesian tsunami—some had the rest of their lives shaped by a seemingly minor decision like whether they turned left or right in the last seconds.

Long-term effects from small, seemingly trivial events are less obvious in daily interactions. However, the patterns of future outcomes—entrainment—are very similar. To understand this, it's important to grasp linear and nonlinear cause-and-effect, which is a key concept in chaos theory.

Symphony of an Evening's Spring

Envision a tranquil spring evening, characterized by a subtly blue sky marked with distinct orange-hued clouds and a prominent moon positioned in the upper-left quadrant of the horizon. Three birds fly by in formation, followed by two or three slightly larger groupings. People walk almost in slow motion compared to cars zooming by. Two couples, walking to the right at nearly 45-degree angles, arrive at their parked cars nearly simultaneously. Cars continue to come and go.

The branches of a nearby tree wave back and forth in staggered rhythm while the moon remains motionless, growing brighter as the night sky deepens into richer shades of blue. People continue to crisscross one another's paths at varying speeds while three cars revolve counterclockwise in the parking lot—entering, leaving, or slowing to a halt.

Amid this remarkable (yet daily) occurrence, a dandelion feather seed floats by to piped-in Latin music, seeking to plant itself on a concrete patio.

Time continues to pass. The contrast of the bright moon against the darkening blue ocean of sky becomes more vivid. Who—or what—is orchestrating such a multifaceted New York Broadway-like production in this shopping mall suburb of Chicago?

There is a non-linear relationship (not a direct 1:1 ratio) between the timed, rhythmic movements of people, cars, lights, the moon, clouds, and sounds. Yet somehow, there is a multifaceted harmony of entrainment. Anyone or anything that enters this dynamic environment quickly finds a place and rhythm within its lively movement.

Rather than a linear, 1:1 lockstep ratio, there are 2:1, 3:1, etc., proportional series of rhythms into which people, places, and physical events (e.g., the asymmetrical waving of tree branches in the wind) harmonize in a mysterious symphonic way. Two people may pass a third; their speeds differ, yet proportionally they entrain in a non-linear flow.

Even my observations are drawn into some coherent, organizing principle—one determined by an inherent lowest common denominator encompassing a multitude of variable possibilities. The speed at which a car drives by entrains with—and is entrained by—the rate of conversation of a group of young people sitting by the road.

While I pause for thought and reflection, another dandelion seed, higher up, goes flying by. Six people walk by—the first person with the most distance, followed by the next two groupings of people with unequal distances between them—yet all three groupings seem to move as an orchestrated whole.

Illusions of Single Events

When the wind blows through the leaves of a tree, only one leaf cannot move. Each leaf is rooted to a twig of a small branch, which is rooted to that of a larger branch, which is rooted to even larger branches, and eventually to the trunk itself. As the branches and leaves all wave in response to the wind, each leaf moves in some variable ratio (not quite 1:1 linearly) because of the range of flexibility and variety of connections.

Whether we intend to or not, the very instant we enter some situation of time, place, person, and/or event (going to a shopping mall, out for a drive or walk, at the office, talking with our child and/or spouse), there is an instant entrainment pulling (like the moon on the ocean's tides) to entrain into some symphonic whole. Space, time, and our geometry are on a continuum of inseparable oneness. This entrainment typically exhibits nonlinearity, characterized by a variable ratio that operates within a defined range or continuum according to an underlying organizing principle.

By observing several lanes of traffic during rush hour, one can discern the dynamic movement of vehicles as they transition between lanes with calculated precision, adjusting their speed from slow progress to rapid acceleration when opportunities arise. Naturally, navigating peak traffic periods may occasionally result in encountering setbacks or challenges.

Shifting from one assembly of events, each with its organizing principle (or common denominator), to another marks the end of one moment in time and the beginning of the next. One cannot not be part of the scenario one is in. As the organizing timing principle of a scene of events changes, so will all its participants. When the wind blows through the trees, the attached leaves have to move with it. As the wind changes, so will the organizing range of principled movements of each leaf.

Such shifts involve changes in the space-time continuum (gradated zones) within our Earth-world experience. Human beings do not travel at the speed of light. However, they do move within a unique, entrained, orchestrated symphony of fleeting collages of simultaneously occurring events. As the wind shifts and the organizing principle of ranges of ratio motifs changes, we transition from one moment or snapshot time frame to the next.

What Is Time?

It can be said that time does not move. Instead, there are snapshots of sequenced event configurations organized by proportions or ratios of synchronizations, each with its motif. Imagine still frames on a movie film strip rhythmically streaming through a projector light, synchronized in their unique way (the old 8mm speed). Passing through or out of synchronization from one motif (speed cycle) to another invokes a new organizing principle. This usually occurs when the sequenced event configurations can no longer be accommodated in an alteration of motif re-synchronization. Therefore, there is an alteration in what we call "time," passing from one synchronization of the space-time frame to another. What is that classic movie line: it is not the spoon that bends, but rather it is our mind!

We call the illusion created by the synchronization of these "still frames" of event configurations—flashing in a certain way through the "LIGHT of the NOW of the PRESENT MOMENT of CONSCIOUSNESS" (positioned or sequenced one after another)—the arrow or direction of time.

In a motion picture, there is an illusion that the characters are moving. The projector displays frames so rapidly that they exceed the critical flicker fusion frequency, making individual images indistinguishable to the human eye. Instead, it sees blurred boundaries, creating the illusion of uniform, uninterrupted motion—and what we call "time."

It is our projections, synchronized through motifs of consciousness, that alter our sequenced, mosaic events—and thus, what we call reality.

The ratios and proportions are all relative to the speed with which the entire system is synchronized to move. As speed increases, movements become more refined, resulting in increasingly significant outcome variations. If a journey proceeds at 80 miles per hour and an incorrect route is taken, the deviation from the intended course will amount to 80 miles after one hour. At a speed of 8 miles per hour, the deviation would be 8 miles in one hour. The faster rate of change provides less room for margins of error. Rushing into traffic, or a marriage, or a job can have equally deleterious and dire consequences. Successful alignment means minimizing the number of time frames that lead us off the designed sequence of our desired motifs.

Our motifs are consistently integrated comprehensively and coordinated with the temporal, spatial, individual, and event-related contexts—collectively referred to as space-time on Earth—with which we engage. Thus, synchronizing specific assemblies or events can change space-time frames and influence our thoughts, emotions, actions, and engagement.

The psychosocial environment, encompassing established behavioral expectations, rules, norms, attitudes, and ritual activities, exerts an influence upon individuals, who likewise shape that environment in return; these dynamics may correspond with or diverge from one's fundamental motivations. Certain events trigger key elements of our core theme. For instance, going to church might reach a spiritual part of ourselves. It could also trigger latent resentment toward authority or feelings of guilt. Whatever is stirred, it will be a unique frequency within our broad range of core motifs.

I remember participating in a personal encounter group some years ago and marveling at how each person I met brought out a different facet of our personalities — interactions of humor, intensity, playfulness, irritation, etc. It was as if the one-on-one interpersonal universe could create pockets or packets of distinct phenomena, each with its own unique set of fleeting, ephemeral traits, pacing, and nuanced dialogue between each paired encounter.

Events in settings like malls, churches, family gatherings, or office coffee breaks are shaped by distinct organizational patterns. They are as varied and multi-phased as whirlpools in a river. One could try to give them names and labels. Yet, over time, one might simply run out of words when trying to describe these endless encounters. It's as if reality has its space-time fabric on an earthly level. We are never not on some point of their infinitely complex grid or fabric.

We are always connected with something, someone, or some series of synchronized, shaping events. Recognizing that our presence, no matter the time or place, inherently forms membership and participation—regardless of how objectively or subjectively we perceive ourselves at that moment. For example, sitting in a restaurant and overhearing a couple discuss their plans to start a family, or watching someone quickly walk to the restroom, can evoke personal memories or biological awareness. Hearing the conversation may remind you of when you began your own family, while seeing someone move swiftly to the restroom can stir an internal awareness of biological urges. Some people can sense or hear others feeling the emotional impact of the song "You'll Never Walk Alone.Sights, sounds, smells (notably), movements, and physical sensations—internal and external—act as channels for communication and influence among people, environments, and objects.

When individuals engage in behaviors such as snapping gum while chewing, playing music from their cell phone, or speaking in quick, lilting tones, their actions may influence others in the vicinity and serve as communication to those present. We may filter and screen out most of their background noise.

Nevertheless, 93 percent of all communication and influence is non-verbal, and 95 percent of our process is unconscious. Even if we don't smoke, being near groups exposed to secondhand smoke is still harmful. Inevitable as it may be, observation can subject us to some of the most significant influences of all time in the history of mankind. That is, what is "watching television"? Watching is observing and vicariously participating. Yet, researchers have indicated that it can entrain observers (watchers) into increases in violence, dangerous risk-taking behaviors, chemical and alcohol abuse, sexual acting out, and decreasing motivation in other constructive life endeavors (vis-à-vis homework).

Watch someone yawn. Listen to another laugh, cry, share a tragic story, or look at you and walk by in an exotic, provocative way. What images, feelings, or sensations come up? These empathic connections and internal resonances are your mirror neurons (described earlier) in action. They are examples of picking up energy in electromagnetic fields (Drs. Persinger and Radin, 2002), which activate and are activated by brain waves in our mind/brain/body systems. Changes in sensations and perceptions lead to shifts in conscious and unconscious awareness and functioning (Ross and Rossi, 1986, 1992). Hypnotic states and induction use these perceptual shifts of space, time, and fixed attention to reality. We experience—and influence—these alterations daily.

The irony is that such mutual social influence might be a necessary source of interaction that humans need to maintain a sense of energy, identity, and belonging. Leo Buscaglia said nearly twenty years ago that each person has strong social needs for interaction, such that we all require a minimum of twenty-five hugs each day to feel nurtured. He was not talking about being frisked by a policeman or attacked by a mugger. Still, it would be a nightmare if that were the only type of intimacy we ever learned to seek.

There are risks of influence and entrainment involved with such social hunger. Unwitting participation in entraining unhealthy interactions, negating self-esteem, and feelings of powerlessness can all result. Repetition and recycling of these interactions can ultimately lead to disastrous, shocking, life-altering experiences. When many people cross a bridge and unintentionally begin to synchronize their steps, they can generate vibrations that may compromise the bridge's structural integrity. Similarly, repeated patterns in addressing and overcoming everyday challenges can gradually weaken our foundations.

The interaction of different elements within our design, which can occur non-linearly and coordinately, may seem somewhat complex. After reviewing many life-altering events, people have repeatedly stated that they never saw them coming. This can range from such trauma as successive job loss in a long-term career, not realizing (or controlling for) the profession itself was altering in nature and foundation.

One story, shared by a salesman in a men's department store, described how he had been gradually laid off from various national financial trading firms. During that series of events, often called "when the bubble burst," he lost three consecutive positions in major trading firms severely impacted by falling markets. Seeking new jobs, he was always the most recently hired person. As conditions worsened, the rule for layoffs was that the most recently hired employees were the first to go. As a result, he has been phased out of his long-term career and is now learning to work with people in a more personal retail sales setting. While he's managed to land on his feet, he now earns less than he did in high school. He is returning to where he started—directly from high school into a specialized finance field—and is now picking up where he left off 25 years ago.

There is a strange reality that seems to stick to life-changing experiences. Because the patterns and shapes are so subtle, complex, and broad in their possible interactions, the end of an underdeveloped theme (misaligned, if you will, at times) becomes clear. The gap between where it has grown and where it has lacked growth is highlighted and exposed by how far we can progress through life stages—until unbuilt foundations eventually come to light during life-changing events. It is our limited personal growth that blinds us to risky patterns and lifelong pursuits that, without expanding our foundations, can lead us to a head-on crash with narrowing paths and even dead ends.

The fiction and myths of our lifestyles will be revealed and "snapped" into awareness as we experience the emperor's new clothes of our lifestyles. Chasing illusions, entrainment, and fictional myths in our lives without appropriate feedback loops and reality checks is akin to driving through a blinding blizzard. Unable to "see" where you are going nor with whom or what you're traveling, it is only a matter of time until you encounter the "twilight zone" of life-altering experiences.

CHAPTER 6

LOSING ONE'S MIND, FINDING OUR SENSES COLLAPSING AND EXPANDING BOUNDED MOTIFS.

Life-altering experiences can result from unwitting participation in

an entrainment of sequential events, skewed in their paradoxical, chaotic interactions creating a tangled path of disaster. They are embedded in the membranes of interconnected dimensions—such as weather conditions, the neighborhood we live in, sunspots and solar flares, stock market changes, a wife coming home nervous and upset at 3:00 A.M. on Saturday, butterflies fluttering in South America, forgetting to pay your electric bill so the alarm clock doesn't wake you up for work on time—causing you to run late in New York City on the morning of 9/11/2001, and so on.

How each person's life patterns overlap and intersect, and a collection of organizing events can shape, merge, and sometimes create strange attractors or asymmetrical motifs—unintended patterns in which individuals unwittingly participate. These motifs serve as organizing frameworks involving complexity and coordination of embedded quirks, tendencies, oddities, and uncertainties, often skewed in dispositional ways that no single variable can fully explain. This includes tendencies to engage in drama, face challenging situations related to failure and success, or have a propensity for life-and-death issues—whether in insurance sales or needing coverage—frequently losing items like keys, directions, or even loved ones, or being connected to others who have or will experience loss—directly or indirectly—in ways that influence communities, nations, and the world.

The list goes on. There is no one reason for this but rather a collage of similar factors (like a family whose members have a constellation of dramas, traumas, and triumphs in their unique fashion or motif— consider past president John F. Kennedy and his family with its unique asymmetry of proportional trials, tribulations, and triumphs). Individuals may become attuned to these distinctive and compelling motifs in a largely unconscious and unintentional manner.

Such a model of life-changing experiences suggests that, while anything can happen at any time, a person might be influenced by multiple layers of forces that go beyond just a conscious choice and free will. Motifs shape what we are aware of and can perceive. When Columbus first found America, he anchored his three ships in the Gulf waters where natives, who had never seen such things, lived. They could not see the ships for three months because this reality was so unfamiliar. It was the village medicine man who first learned to see the ships, then taught the villagers (not our pop music group) how to tune into such a motif.

We live in a universe that does not revolve around us as its center. One can mentally visualize a desired future, but what or whom did that person interact with to initiate such endeavors in the first place (if there is a "first place")? Entraining field forces include—but are not limited to—the singularity of the individual mind. Instead, they represent a formative assembly or constellation of multidimensional interconnections from which emerging motifs entrain. We may be shaped by inherent patterns from conception onward. Who and what our parents are, along with all the psycho-biological-social-cultural variables involved, act as entraining synchronizations from the very beginning of our lives.

This entrainment can involve the weather, butterflies, postage stamp prices, and even whether your mother named you after a famous president. The unexpected, the ironic, and paradoxically, seemingly superficial and extraneous details—appearing irrelevant at the time—can synchronize an entrainment's nuance with life-changing consequences. It's not about being in the wrong place at the right or wrong time. It's about the space-time of our synchronizations, which already entrain us into life-changing experiences.

The language we utilize has constructs (love, commitment, achievement, loyalty, happiness, success, value, etc.), each with multiple meanings, operational definitions, and derivations of nuance, which challenge effective communication within ourselves and with those with whom we interconnect. Puns, jokes, humor, and tragic comedies of unbelievable misunderstandings (what are plays like Romeo and Juliet, not these?) are examples of the multifaceted meanings language can assume.

We can be entrained with one derived meaning of a construct. At the same time, our partner operates from a very different version (e.g., "Love means leaving me alone for twenty minutes when I first get home from work" versus "Love means coming up to me when you first get home and embracing me for twenty minutes"). Entrainment with discrepant linguistic forms and meaningful expressions may lead to synchronizations of conflict and divorce, or agreements to disagree—if meta-levels of formative diversity can be appreciated and enjoyed.

When people are socialized and educated to grasp language, concepts, definitions, and nuances as part of everyday life—like the Kennedy family—these aspects naturally fit into their lifestyle. In that case, it is crucial to recognize the entrainment that such derived meanings, purposeful operating definitions, and values can establish in the synchronization of our lives. Sometimes, the most paradoxical and unexpected outcomes of life-changing experiences can emerge.

Both chance and predictable events can significantly influence future outcomes due to their paradoxical effects.

A key feature of unwitting entrainment is the repeated linking of unrelated entities—such as objects, people, locations, times, situations, and events—in surprising and unexpected ways. Note the late-night TV talk show with David Letterman, who had a fun segment called "Stupid Human Tricks," where one act showed how a mousetrap, a sucker, and a blowgun could synchronize so he could catch a marshmallow in his mouth. (You will have to watch the re-run to learn how.) Although this technique is simple, it allows different objects with different functions to sync up using unique forms of entrainment.

On a more significant level, the government put Capone in prison for tax evasion because of a synchronization of functionally unrelated operational constructs, such as Al Capone, bootlegging, criminal, Internal Revenue Service, difficulty of conviction, etc.! Whoever heard of a criminal paying taxes for illegal acts, much less going to jail for not doing so?!

Another example of seemingly unrelated and divergent constructs achieving synchronization can be seen in the recent case involving C.I.A. agent Valerie Plame Wilson. What was the synchronization that caused this highly regarded agent to be betrayed through the exposure of her identity by the very secret organization dedicated to secret functions? What synchronization is created by the following seemingly unrelated elements: the Iraq War, weapons of mass destruction, the justification for invasion, a book by the agent's husband, Ambassador Joe Wilson, exposing the absence of weapons of mass destruction, Karl Rove, the C.I.A., and a reporter named Novak? The entrainment caused by such a synchronization—the agent's spouse challenging the validity of the Iraq War in his book, revealing how these weapons were nonexistent and thus could not be used as a justification for the war—led to retaliation in the form of exposing his wife's covert identity as an agent by the very agency sworn to protect such secrecy and American interests.

Synchronization of the Small

Unexpected, paradoxical entrainment occurs because we live in a universe of highly complex interconnections far beyond what our common-sense logic would suggest. This applies to microscopic levels as well as the macroscopic psycho-social-political-cosmic realms. At the cellular level, the cell's main communication center is not in its nucleus but at its membrane, where it interacts through resonant signals with millions of other cells and the organs and systems they comprise. Synchronization happens here and can lead to health or illness. If the brain can synchronize bodily functions, then our consciousness can align with that synchronization, and so on.

The reverse of this is also valid: how mind-body synchronization (or loss of synchronization, which is a form of dysfunction) can interconnect. Surprisingly, the construct of the "membrane" itself (as the brain of the cell) is also applied at the quantum level, as that thin "sheet" of energy touches every point in our universe and is closer to us than the clothes we wear. Known as the eleventh dimension, it continually interacts with other membranes, recycling and recreating this and other universes (see The Endless Universe, 2006). (Talk about interconnection!)

At the quantum level of reality (which is closer to our surface reality than we realize), all possible outcomes of a "particle-wave" (life event) position and speed are possible. This means the event can take any form (wave and potential or particle occurrence), occur anywhere (position), and happen at any time (speed in terms of its rate of change). How it (the event) is measured determines its speed, known as collapsing the wave function into a specific particle or occurrence.

In human terms, this means we all have human potential flowing through us like energy waves in an ocean. Our level of consciousness determines when and where these waves collapse (in their interference patterns with the waves of others). This impacts real-life outcomes in careers, relationships, and personal identity. When a certain threshold or tipping point is reached (according to chaos theory), these waves will crash into each other, "beaching" themselves into a series of unfolding (and unpredictable) events, as has been illustrated.

Our participation in a gathering or series of events is a form of synchronization that interacts selectively based on specific thematic criteria, or the motif of interaction. We focus on particular, thematic aspects of our self-motif in different situations. Playful, energetic, charismatic, conflicted, and painful qualities may emerge in various social, personal, and work contexts. We might encounter a series of erotic-like interactions where only exchanging glances happen. The possibilities are endless.

Driven by the choices of our motifs of consciousness, the imagination can run wild as emotions and desires activate entrainment. Entrainment into uncontrolled assemblies of organizing events—such as a series of erotic encounters, conflicts, confrontations, or opportunities that seem to unfold systematically or sequentially—can reflect our conscious and unconscious states of mind. We attend to and attract what we resonate with and have synchronization with. We may or may not be aware of what emerges and the messages (frequencies and vibrations—both verbal and non-verbal) we are sending or unwittingly receiving. This is how we can be drawn into events, encounters, and evolving progressions that may or may not be beneficial to our lifestyle.

What seems like impulsiveness or emotional acting out can have its origins in unwitting entrainment that interacts and meshes with unacknowledged aspects of ourselves. We are not always aware of what motifs of consciousness are operating. Aspects of these motifs are projected onto our external world, where entrainment can now occur.

At the same time, we are capable of absorbing representations of the external environment (introjects), which subsequently exert an influence on our internal processes.

We need to learn about our recognition, awareness, and focused connection with sensory entrainment (vibrations, intensities of sight, sound, physical or emotional sensations), as well as our empathic internalizations (meanings, interpretations, symbolizations). All of these identify sources of mutual influence on our motifs of consciousness and the synchronization formed. Our interconnectedness, which may encompass aspects of consciousness, intuition, and spirituality, ensures that we consistently remain part of something greater than ourselves. We are also simultaneously (and somewhat paradoxically) a whole "universe" within the integrity of our unique lifestyle—our individual motif of core self.

Respecting the vast range of multidimensional interconnection, dynamic synchronization permits access to our possible futures. Opening our perceptual horizons to the almost infinite number of possible combinations and permutations with which one may join and synchronize (entrainment in various assembly organizations) is a first step toward creating our future. It is critical to recognize that we are already synchronized and participating in an unfolding assembly (or assemblies) of organized events. If such entrainment were sustained, it could be stated that a future has been established within current synchronizations.

To more fully grasp this concept, it is helpful to recall how physicists have described the expanding universe. They (David Greene, 1992) use the metaphor of baking raisin bread. As the "loaf" expands, the raisins rise and separate from one another in a synchronized, proportional fashion. One might refer to this as an expanding "motif of raisin bread" (tongue in-cheek, of course). Space (the bread) evolves as the universe expands between the galaxies (the raisins), pushing them outward and away from each other in one synchronized, simultaneous whole assembly of organization. This is perfect harmony.

The people, places, and situations with which we connect—consciously or not—harmonize in motifs of synchronized, unfolding oneness. Whatever motif is contemplated forms synchronizations with other motifs (no matter how seemingly unrelated) throughout one's spacetime. This includes derived, linguistic constructs that can be potentially shocking in nature. What are we asking for—unwittingly?

One can observe these synchronized assemblies moving as organized units of flow in groups of cars in traffic, packs of people walking down a city street, or constellations of negative emotions. Our participation (and mutual influence) can carry us into future times and places heretofore unknown and unseen.

While Einstein said that God does not play dice with the universe, scientists argue that the chance element could be eliminated if one could calculate all the multiple vector forces involved in a dice throw (speed, angle, gravity, friction, etc.). Interestingly, MIT and Stanford University students have approximated such variables in games of chance like blackjack and roulette. They were so successful in Las Vegas casinos that they were barred from entry. The future may not be as completely unpredictable as one might think.

Cosmologists (Brian Greene, 1998) have proposed that we might not live in just one universe but in many, known as the multiverse. Likewise, we can simultaneously participate in multiple assemblies of events (multiverses) without realizing it. Such participation can influence our future outcomes and life-changing encounters. Expanding our perceptual awareness across multiple dimensions becomes necessary if we are to identify which tracks we are on, what is influencing us, and where these synchronizations might lead us.

Predestination can be viewed as outcomes that are predetermined based on our chosen paths. Continued participation in gatherings of synchronized, life-changing events—whether consciously or unconsciously—forms the very foundations and sets the tracks of our entrainment, outlining non-linear pathways (multiple states of consciousness with their associated people, places, and things). At this point, shocking and unexpected synchronizations of seemingly unrelated elements often lead to life-changing events.

We never do one thing at a time. Dropping a pebble into a pond does not create just one ripple, but many. Who we meet, where we sit for a cup of coffee, where we go to school, and with whom we speak are all associated with multiple possibilities.

This indicates that our intentions, aspirations, and circumstances can influence the objectives we pursue, including career paths and personal goals.

Fatales, gorgeous hunks, etc., without fully realizing what we are getting ourselves into. That beautiful, vibrant femme fatale may awaken a dreamlike consciousness of vitality, lost love, passion, and the sense of completion of some missing part or ideal in one's life journey—be it a soulmate, a vision of perfection, a peak performance, or a sense of finally arriving at some idealized quality of life.

It may also entrain one into years of hellish conflict and loss. The complexity and ramifications of pursuing such illusions, images, and idealizations (idolatries, if you will) may have life-altering consequences.

Forming our illusions and ideals can sometimes lead us to pursue individuals with needy or narcissistic tendencies, marked by a constant need for external validation or approval. Marrying and starting a family with such a person can tie people together—directly or indirectly—for the rest of their lives. You can be divorced, but once you have lost it, you can never be single (or a virgin) again.

The consequences of divorce can indeed be life-altering. But so can the professions we merge with and identify ourselves through over the long term. Becoming a doctor, lawyer, politician, skilled tradesperson, or entrepreneur all come with tremendous benefits—and tremendous liabilities.

A doctor might win the Nobel Prize in physics. A musician may become the king of pop. However, the eccentricities that may have assisted their success might also link the first to incest (Einstein married his second cousin) and the latter to criminal accusations (Michael Jackson faced charges as a child predator).

The career or profession we choose can be inextricably tied to the risks, liabilities, and vagaries of our dark sides. It could be argued that elements of Darth Vader's character from Star Wars exist, to some extent, within us all. Does it play a role in the profession we choose? The old story of Dr. Jekyll and Mr. Hyde reflects the dual—or multi-sided—nature of ourselves, our careers, and our lifestyles.

Yet, it's not necessarily darkness, evil, or negativity that leads us into unintended complications culminating in life-altering experiences. Sometimes, it's simply the nature of adventure and the human need to explore and discover other worlds, other realities—and in the process, other parts of ourselves.

Parents must sometimes let children learn from their own mistakes to shape their unique impact on the world. The courage to suffer one's own death—psychological and/or psychosocial—and be reborn is not easy (Perls, 1972).

Spirals of Entrainment

The entrainment of our motifs in both daily and long-term endeavors almost always involves mutual interactions. These interactions, whether occurring internally or with other individuals, locations, events, or circumstances, can arise at any point within a cycle where elements influence each other. If left unchecked, unhampered, or otherwise uninterrupted, these cycles can spiral toward devastating, disastrous, life-altering experiences.

As mentioned earlier, one could simply go to a coffee shop and sit down to read—an appropriate public setting for such an activity. People may enter, mill around, talk, sit at various tables, and eventually get up and leave. Occasionally, someone may sit across from you and silently stare.

Initially, this matter may be disregarded. You continue your business. But as time progresses, you begin to feel the other's scrutiny in a not-so-subtle fashion. Looking up, you—or "I"—see the person stir restlessly in his seat, averting my glance. I return to my reading, only to feel once again the sensation of being examined, like under a microscope.

This time, I deliberately focus my attention, looking directly into the eyes of the person seated less than five feet away. I smile whimsically, pause my reading, and wait to see what unfolds. He looks away again, his face flushing from pale to red as he stirs even more uncomfortably.

As I continue to relax and hold his gaze with a gentle smile, his nonverbal restlessness intensifies—anxiety spiraling upward. I notice a walkie-talkie on his table and begin to wonder if he's some kind of security guard.

The longer this non-verbal interaction continues, the more the spiral escalates—until he begins to visibly squirm. I eventually break off the exchange and return to my work. Shortly after, he gets up, walks past my table, and disappears—without ever saying a word.

There was no clarity about why he was there or why he behaved in such an asocial way. But one thing is certain: I felt very uncomfortable. The unspoken "communication" between us carried a subtle anomaly in expected social behavior. At that moment, there was no casual awareness—no glances, silent nods, or respect for social space.

Both he and I entrained one another. And when I deliberately drew attention to this—through my non-verbal, direct focus—it intensified the entrainment already in motion. It spiraled faster until it paradoxically interrupted itself through reflection. The interaction formed a synchronization. Entrainment triggered a self-sustaining feedback loop. Focusing on the entrainment caused it to peak, then fade.

More complex spirals of interaction occur where events are entangled with higher levels of interface. These will be examined shortly. It is important to understand that spiraling systems, often nonlinear and involving multiple simultaneous connections, can seem stable before quickly shifting into increased activity and transformation.

In the previous example, the shift occurred through alternating attention and disengagement, resulting in a higher level of awareness—a nonlinear shift in perception toward the act of perceiving itself. This subtle change produced nonlinear effects—not just cause and effect, but multiple ripple effects folding inward, eventually disrupting the entrainment. Steady focus changed the synchronization of nonverbal behaviors.

While helpful, such a dynamic might not be so desirable in a marriage or a job.

The potential for identifying and teasing out motifs that resonate with complex, assembled life events is infinite. Miscommunications, distortions of intention, or flawed interpretations can create runaway divergences—spirals that cascade into chaos.

For example, language confusion can push a married couple to the brink of stress. The husband, feeling frustrated while parenting their 7-year-old son, might say to his wife:

"And you never support me—you are always spoiling him!"

She perceives the accusation as an ultimatum, feels hurt, guilty, and angry, and then responds defensively. They are caught up in the blame game, losing sight of effective parenting. If this dysfunctional communication continues, it could affect other parts of their relationship. Eventually, it could endanger the marriage.

The son might internalize the belief that he caused his parents' conflict or potential divorce. He could misinterpret these childhood events and unconsciously assign himself the blame for their unhappiness.

Feeling selfish, ashamed, and unworthy of having his own needs met— having been labeled a "spoiled child"—he grows increasingly resistant to experiences that challenge his sense of identity. Criticism from significant others may reinforce a distorted self-motif: that he is an outsider who disturbs and disrupts relationships.

This might include authority figures—spouses, bosses, teachers, or even his children's teachers—anyone with the power to label him "unacceptable" or "not enough." A group or assembly of such figures could manipulate him into compliant behavior that violates his self-integrity.

Alternatively, his resistance to this perceived pressure to comply might spark a devastating stubbornness, alienating him from his wife, family, and community. The result? Life-altering experiences of rejection and divorce.

Distorted motifs can surface in patterns of passive-aggression, borderline personality dynamics, and addictive behaviors.

The possibilities are endless for how we can be drawn, often unwittingly, into participation with numerous assemblies and groupings simultaneously.

For example, consider the person in the previously cited case. He may be caught in a constant pursuit of multiple advanced degrees, frequently changing jobs in search of something that both improves and destabilizes—transient in structure but consistent in its recurring pattern—across both family and work environments.

A person with such a constrained, skewed self-image might stay married but rarely be truly present at home. They may remain in the same general career field, but their time at specific jobs would likely be brief, perhaps two to three years. Ironically, this person tends to be drawn toward jobs or companies that are inherently unstable and prone to layoffs. Even their marriage might be with someone needy but unstable and chaotic. Life events echoing these themes are likely to be drawn into their orbit.

The multifaceted combinations of entraining with simultaneous assemblies of events, each aligning with and reflecting such a motif design, would be numerous and long-term. Chronic instability and external interventions would become likely necessities, which, paradoxically, would only intensify the motif's adaptive resistance. This resistance, often stubborn and reactive, would conceal a hidden dependency on compliance, all in pursuit of a narcissistic center of attention.

The interconnections of a motif within multiple forms of entrainment are vast. The motif's structural design both influences and is influenced by the organizing themes of various assemblies—life domains, social circles, work environments, family relationships, and more. Whether these assemblies match or resonate with the underlying motif scheme determines the level of engagement and intensity of participation.

Attention is often "fixated" on needs, strong emotions (like love or fear), physical or sensory stimulation (such as loud noises, rapid movement, or visual stimuli), or personal beliefs and expectations. How our attention and perception are directed shapes our cognitive map—our selective framework for seeing and organizing reality. This map, or template, entrains us selectively from all potential arrangements of life events, guiding us into synchronizations that conform to our inner design.

Returning to the earlier example, the individual's motif was centered around the contrast between transience and permanence. This internal structure led him to join and attract various groups, most of which laid the groundwork for destructive, life-changing experiences.

The template or model of motif design effectively maps out how an individual selectively entrains with the external world. It guides how various facets of one's internal structure draw in external experiences, determining which nuances become emphasized in life's interactions. This template defines which organizational patterns of reality resonate with a person's motif.

An individual's level of developed consciousness is a key factor influencing this motif design, thus the participation template. In this context, "consciousness" refers to maturity of values, personal integrity, and the depth of self-knowledge and awareness of reality beyond the self. Levels of consciousness are crucial and will be explored more deeply later. For now, it's important to understand that one's level of consciousness directly shapes how they perceive, interpret, and map their reality. It affects the interpretations individuals derive from experiences and the experiences with which they engage.

It is equally important to realize that how we perceive and interpret an experience reflects as much about who we are as it does about the experience itself. Our "rules" for interpreting reality—what could be called a perception—are not unlike how one approaches an inkblot in a Rorschach test. What we see is what we get.

Nevertheless, the difference is important in real life: who we are shapes the specific "inkblots" we are attracted to. From the perspective of quantum mechanics, it is similar to the "collapse of the wave function," where many probabilities merge into a single, definitive event. On a human level, any state of consciousness can collapse into a clear sequence of experiences, each with multiple connections and implications for our lifestyle.

"The good, the bad, and the ugly"—thank you, Clint Eastwood.

It is all an expression of the self, emerging in a specific time, place, and context. In summary, wherever you are, you attract experiences that align or resonate with your current state. If we function at higher, healthier levels of consciousness, these experiences can be enriching and transformative.

The awareness of motifs shapes how we organize and form our perception of reality. These motifs influence everything: our beliefs, values, attitudes, and relationship behaviors.

Still, terrible things can happen to highly functional people, and they often do. No one can say precisely why. Still, it might be because unwitting involvement in complex entrainment can merge realities where, as the saying goes, "no good deed goes unpunished."

Why? Because dysfunctional layers of context and lower levels of consciousness are realities we must contend with. Synchronization between people, places, and events tends to gravitate toward the most common denominator of energy, ego, survival, power, and instant gratification.

The involuntary synchronization at these lower frequencies, with apparently unrelated forces, can profoundly impact one's life.

Take Oprah Winfrey, a compassionate leader who founded a school for girls in Africa. For years, she has been a fierce advocate for protecting children from abuse. However, despite her good intentions, she discovered that at least one of her employees had been abusing the very children she sought to uplift.

Who would have imagined that Oprah—of all people—would become unknowingly entangled in perpetrating the very harm she has dedicated her life to preventing?

Life-altering experiences can, indeed, result from an unexpected synchronization of unrelated factors that reshape a person's lifestyle, identity, and direction.

Shields of Energy

Mismatches between healthy consciousness and unhealthy, lower-level functioning realities create significant risks.

For example, have you ever tried driving the speed limit on the Dan Ryan Expressway in Chicago? They do not call it the "poor man's Indy 500" for nothing. If you attempt to drive strictly by the speed limit, you may be putting yourself at risk for a real-life-altering experience. Traffic commonly moves 10–15 mph over the speed limit, so not keeping up may be unsafe.

Similarly, we can be perceived as unacceptable when we attempt to operate at a markedly different level than the majority norms of our environment, whether in our workplace, families, or communities. People tend to disapprove of those who function either too high or too low.

Motif synchronization involves this principle: accessing multiple entrainments across different life domains often defaults to the lowest common denominator.

When in Rome

The old saying goes, "When in Rome, do as the Romans do." However, what happens if you do not want to be a Roman? This creates a profound inner dilemma.

In ancient Rome, one of the biggest taboos was to claim that a person should pursue a higher calling beyond serving the empire or personal interests. Those who supported that idea faced harsh disapproval. Just look at what they did to the most famous advocate of this principle: Jesus Christ.

He was a life-altering—indeed, world-altering—experience.

What were the reasons for selecting Jesus as the Son of God to endure suffering and crucifixion? Christianity teaches that He was chosen by an omniscient God who preordained His fate. Was this a case of bad things happening to good people because God ordained it?

The crucifixion was "bad" for the man Jesus, but suitable for Christ—a spiritual catalyst for the birth of Christianity and, ultimately, the fall of Rome.

This prompts a complex inquiry: how can we determine whether the events that occur in our lives are intended or inevitable?

Science offers its disciplines to study cause-and-effect relationships. Religion provides moral laws (ten of them) from a Higher Power. Nevertheless, which "laws" should we follow to interpret meaning, purpose, and intentionality in unfolding events?

It's a question that collapses under its weight—impossible to answer fully, yet critical to raise. It highlights why some people seem blessed, while others suffer one misfortune after another, seemingly without reason.

A Matter of Timing

Was Jesus simply at the right place at the right time? Many Jewish men before Him claimed to be the Christ. Was it a matter of the idea's time finally arriving, after centuries of buildup through biblical prophecy? Jesus was born into a politically charged family lineage tracing back to

King David. Some historical findings (Discovery History Channel, 2005) suggest He may have been born out of wedlock and adopted by Joseph. This may have subjected Him to ridicule and bullying in childhood.

Despite these hardships, Jesus was gifted—a healer with sharp intuition and spiritual insight. He was born into the right family constellation, in the right historical moment, and perhaps in the right way (as an adopted child born out of wedlock). All of this set the stage for Him to fulfill a long-anticipated prophecy: that a Messiah would come to liberate the Jews from Roman oppression.

Jesus, the man—dealing with adoption, scorn, and marginalization, may have been entrained to fulfill this destiny through the life circumstances that shaped Him.

Historically, many people have claimed to be the Messiah. However, it was not until Jesus that all the necessary conditions came together perfectly. Was this the result of several long-term factors aligning, leading to the emergence of an individual with these characteristics?

Was it his unique combination of traits—his lineage, birth circumstances, inner healing capacities, and ability to reach the disenfranchised—that composed a motif destined for transformation?

If even one of these factors were missing—if there had been no prophecy, no tension between Jews and Romans, no adoption by Joseph—would Jesus have still become the Christ, the Son of the Christian God?

Synchronization and Critical Mass

Leaving aside matters of faith and discernment (which belong to the realm of individual experience), consider this: for any significant event to occur—be it a birth, graduation, atomic explosion, engine ignition, or even the courage to propose—certain critical mass conditions must be met.

If timing is everything, then synchronizing initial conditions is essential. Scientists have discovered that life itself depends on a precise, delicate balance: chemical compositions, electromagnetic intensity, Earth's distance from the Sun, the presence of a single moon, water cycles, carbon dioxide exchange, and more.

The emergence of life, as currently understood, is contingent upon a specific and limited set of conditions.

Such intricate orchestration might be attributed to omniscience, the laws of quantum physics, or the idea that the universe itself is a living organism, where life and death are simply phase transitions within that grand system.

As the saying goes, God only knows.

Without the right fuel mixture at the right time, a car won't start, a plane won't fly, and humans won't be able to process food or think clearly. Similarly, a car shifting from first to second gear needs to properly build up speed and energy before a synchronized shift can happen.

Although patterns and proportions differ, the core principle remains the same across all major transformations—whether you are starting a car, building a family, or founding a religion. Ensuring proper coordination of initial conditions is essential to achieving critical mass in all entrainment processes.

Could it be that the Second Coming is not a sudden event, but a two-thousand-year buildup? A slow accumulation of spiritual "RPMs" until we hit a new critical threshold—ready to shift into a higher "gear" of collective transformation?

Core Qualities, Probability Clouds, and Balloons

What is being suggested so far is that, just as Jesus, the man, may have been the right person at the right time to serve the right purpose, the shaping of our destinies greatly depends on how we are entraining at a fundamental level of synchronization, leading to critical masses of transformation from one level of functioning to another. Physicists refer to this as quantum leaps. They describe the atom as having a core nucleus (protons, neutrons, etc.) with electrons revolving around it in various orbital levels. These levels are simply probability clouds of energy within bands of possibility. Electrons need a critical energy level to move (quantum jump) from one level to another. They absorb energy when transitioning to a higher energy level and release energy when returning to a lower one. The frequencies and vibrations of atoms and substances reflect the activity of electrons jumping between levels. "Quarks" is used to name one of the fundamental sub-atomic particles. The word resembles "quirk," which is fitting given the complex and unique nature of the universe's functioning. (The universe has always seemed "quirky.")

Why "bad things" happen to "good people" might relate to their level of transformation, the energy required to leap, and the resulting entrainment that occurs in their lives. This indicates another level or realm of reality exists beyond conscious intentions, judgments, illusions, and fantasies of what each person perceives as right or wrong, good or bad, success or failure, moral or immoral. We often operate in an unseen realm where people, places, and things connect, and we only become aware of the consequences after they happen. It may be that events are less about being planned and more about being seeded, with outcomes unfolding only when the timing and conditions are right. For example, the FBI had reports claiming that terrorists could be trained to fly planes into American schools to crash into cities. This web of connections was so extraordinary before 9/11 that the FBI dismissed the report as beyond conscious reality and practicality.

It is important to recognize that, just like an idea whose time has come, each stage of entrainment has its own unique power, timing, and critical mass aligned with the patterns guiding our progress. However, there is a hidden reality of interconnectedness where anyone can experience or cause an endless variety of life-changing events at any moment and place. Part of this is because, indeed, anything is possible. Nevertheless, there is a deeper, even more profound truth about probability operating at the core levels of existence.

While I have spoken of each person as an individual with their own unique motif intertwined with multiple realities, a deeper truth might be considered: there are no such things as separate, individual, isolated units of people known as human beings. Instead, think of the core of all living existence as a single life force (Chi) from which we all originate—like branches and leaves of a tree growing from the same roots, or trees belonging to one forest. This is not just a philosophical or spiritual idea. The laws of physics that govern the universe explain how its components work together as a unified system. There is no single section (strings, percussion, wind) that makes up the entire orchestra; instead, its organization and connection create the music.

Humans seem like individual units with unique identities. However, every social scientist has noted that people cannot be fully understood without considering social contexts and connections. Imagine the human population as a giant blimp made of very flexible material. This entire structure can be reshaped into many different forms. Children playing with balloons love to twist, bend, and shape them into pretend forms like dogs, cats, or hats. Yet, no matter what shape the balloon (or blimp) takes, all parts stay as one connected entity. If humanity is seen as one big organism with many patterns, then each person is a single, unique design within that interconnected whole. This suggests that any part can be anything at any time. It's basically meaningless to talk about separate, individual people. When we realize that each person can play many "roles" or "hats" in life—as Shakespeare said, "all the world's a stage and each one of us plays many roles"—we get a glimpse of a "reality behind the curtain" of everyday awareness. We often misjudge others' true identities based on our perceptions. Still, at the core level of an organization, we see a reflection of ourselves.

This idea might seem purely theoretical. This observation indicates that our perceptions of others frequently reflect our characteristics. That is because at a deeper level, we are all part of one whole expressing itself through many unique facets. This allows us to connect to all possibilities of life-changing experiences. Our uniqueness comes from our traits, twists, and turns in the design structures derived from wholeness. The connection of our unique design remains with the whole, just as the subtle twists and turns in areas of a blimp (or balloons shaped like animals, images, etc.) serve as a backdrop, adding contrast and depth to the overall composition. Sculptors carve figures out of church walls (like Michelangelo in the Sistine Chapel), creating a series of figure-ground contrasts, where the raised figure stands out in relief against the background of the wall or ceiling, making the contrast essential to its existence.

Our uniqueness only increases the likelihood of some life experiences over others. We each have the free will to choose our path, but only if we are willing to take responsibility for our lives and make life-changing decisions that break us from illusions of safety and security. We may or may not see where our patterns are leading us. If we are willing to resist being intimidated by illusions of what seems overpowering or frightening—such as external authority, social expectations, or the belief that "... By challenging the mindset of "we have always done it this way," we reveal our distinct motivations and connect to a broader purpose. It might be like animal balloon figures untwisting and realigning themselves from tentative shapes and returning "back to the whole" with a "snap of insightful awareness"—as if a balloon figure quickly straightens from its twisted loops to its core. It could later reform into a more refined version or a different twisted design, gaining renewed energy from its return to its fundamental origins.

This shifting of levels—such as changing gears or orbits, like in critical mass—relates to realignment and intentionally adjusting one's lifestyle. Understanding interconnectedness is crucial because, in many ways, it also forms the basis of life-changing experiences. These shifts between levels of consciousness and energies of collapse and expansion reflect experiences of birth, death, and rebirth through transformative events. People engage with larger energy sources and evolve through different experiences. No matter how much effort we invest in resolving issues, there is always something beyond our current perception that we have not anticipated, considered, or deemed possible.

Life alterations involve the synchronization of our motives with effects that go well beyond what is expected or considered possible in our conscious world. There is a saying that "... there is nothing in the appearance of a caterpillar that would indicate it could become a butterfly." Life changes can happen unexpectedly and suddenly, coming "out of the blue." Because anything is possible, due to interconnectedness, and because we need a critical mass to shift from one level of existence (caterpillars) to another (butterflies), life-changing experiences are often surprising but inevitable events that help us reconnect with the core purpose of our existence.

Life's unexpected events can place us in moments of great significance. Major life occurrences can lead to unforeseen experiences with a profound impact. Whether it's during a resort vacation amid a tsunami, being an educator on the Space Shuttle launch on January 28, 1986, which tragically exploded upon takeoff, or canceling work at the World Trade Center on September 11, 2001, such events carry serious consequences. If we are fortunate enough to survive them, the lessons we can learn—and earn—are truly priceless. Why some live and others die, why some get a second chance to recover while others do not, all remain mysteries. However, the impact and gravity of these events stay with those who survive. Without the reality of death, life cannot be fully understood. By becoming more aware of our interconnectedness and reaching critical mass, we can recognize signs of transformation, challenges, and opportunities to improve our goals. These may be future memories, hinting at alternative paths of possibility, and urging us now to decide how we will shape our unique outcomes.

Life-altering experiences have the impact of reconnecting us to our roots at core levels. Near-death experiences, divorce, abandonment, relationship losses, and threatened long-term careers (consider the "bullet dodged" by Michael Jackson being acquitted of all fourteen charges in his child molestation court case) abruptly bring into awareness what we value and find deeply meaningful at the core levels of our lives. As one wealthy professional stated regarding the discovery that his daughter had survived the Indonesian tsunami, that everything else paled in comparison and seemed trivial in importance when compared to the survival of his child. Our ego of cognitive controlling is challenged to release its neurotic grip on our lives and surrender to gratitude for what we do have.

Why are we fascinated by courtroom dramas involving celebrities and their stories of tragic triumphs? It seems they connect us to the drama, uncertainty, and "rush" experience of challenging our "established" ideas of what is real and possible. Life-changing events shake our foundations and our motives for living (and dying). They confront us with existential questions of meaning and purpose. The end of a love relationship forces us to surrender to freedom, free will, and the idea that love is only genuine when freely given from within outward. We cannot love, nor be loved, simply by willing it to happen. While effort is always required, we cannot want "love" to be in the other person if it isn't already in their heart—or ours. We can only be the loving person we seek out there—in here first! Such a consciousness can create a synchronization with productive energy in our future—here and now!

Intriguingly, alternating movements between core levels of connection and those levels where we tend to function more independently reflect and are synchronized with the presence or absence of life-altering experiences. Just as we need sleep to be energized during our waking hours, we need to reconnect with our personal roots of core oneness (through meditation, prayer, mind-body synchronizations, etc.) to be able to function at peak levels of personal performance. Life-altering experiences pressure us to take the time and space and patience to deal with what's meaningful and purposeful if we have been ignoring this dynamic movement in our own lives. Without this dynamic movement of consciousness, it may not be possible to understand or identify the direction in which our various patterns of alignment are taking us. Checking our core values and priorities periodically can keep our individual strategies, goals, and objectives aligned with our unique motifs, and thus continued transformations.

Curiously, quantum mechanics refers to electrons as orbiting atoms as probability clouds, where the atom is more a wave that is everywhere and everywhen throughout that level. Only when it's measured does it collapse from a wave into a set particle of its own.

However, the uncertainty principle states that only one measurement of the electron—either its position or its momentum—can be known with certainty. The key point is that there cannot be an absolute observer; only varying degrees of subjectivity exist, and the observer can influence the outcome of events through measurement or observation. This is because our very act of "observing" an event involves an entanglement of "subjectivity," which affects what is being measured. We exist within a network of interconnections, inevitably engaging with various individuals, locations, and events at different levels. We all move through a space-time continuum of interconnected fields, maintaining alignment at the core levels of our unique motifs. This allows us to cross-check and adjust which entanglements to continue or stop. Understanding our universe's holistic or holographic nature is important, including bio-psycho-social-cultural-cosmological levels of functioning. We must break out of our "boxed-in" reality constructs to gain new perspectives without losing connection to our roots. Without roots, we have no wings.

Scientists (Grof, 1992) have stated that the universe moves as one. Interconnectedness (Bell) and the concept of wholeness, as described by Bohm (1993), are seen as aspects of our universe. The idea that there is oneness in the universe may seem confusing. Life situations appear to create tremendous diversity. Grof (1992) relates this condition to what he calls the holographic mind. He suggests that all boundaries are artificial in their frameworks. When individuals perceive themselves, others, or reality, they focus on defined forms, qualities, and characteristics, which exist on a universal continuum of varying figure-ground possibilities. Good people, bad people, aggressive, peaceful, friendly, animosity, etc., can be labels or areas of emphasis on a continuous dimension. How we set the measurement (how we label or frame something) makes it a fixed thing or object.

The holographic mind reveals a mysterious sense of wholeness that exists beyond the individual self. This feeling of completeness is bigger, deeper, and more inclusive of what has been and what might be. It crosses space-time boundaries and contrasts opposing realities (temporary versus long-term, part versus whole, living for the moment versus long-term investments, etc.). All of this suggests a mosaic of contours, roiling and forming boundaries that are defined arbitrarily. Reality is permanent—for now! If we could see reality through a fly's eyes, we would observe countless honeycomb-like cells. It's like watching several TVs side by side, sometimes showing the same image and other times displaying different parts of the same scene. The selves we perceive as separate can be thought of as coming through different TV screens or radio channels.

Yet, the borders and frames of each screen (or the radio station's frequency) can be removed, revealing the wholeness of a larger reality.

Entrainment of motifs is the unlimited possibility of formativeness that is representative of this larger-than-self wholeness. Enfolding, implicate realities (characterized by embedded electromagnetic field contours) permit human beings to entrain their formative motifs in multifaceted pathways. The many worlds theory in quantum mechanics suggests that multiple universes exist where all possible outcomes occur, highlighting the complexity of wholeness. Life-altering experiences are therefore entrained, formative outcomes representing one of many possibilities how we entrain with risk-oriented, traumatic experiences in the past, if not the repetitive present, involves unique combinations of events culminating in quantum leaps of catastrophes. A series of nodal points of change could be deemed catastrophic in their cascade of disaster following disaster. It may commence with a bad hair day and culminate in lawsuits, accidents, financial crises, and legal complications.

There is a recipe for disaster. To have fire, three elements are required: oxygen, combustible material, and ignition. Starting the day with inadequate preparation, hurrying due to tardiness, overthinking, which leads to mistakes, rapidly consuming breakfast, navigating through traffic hastily, reacting impatiently towards colleagues, and working at a speed that surpasses optimal performance contribute to instability, imbalance, and an environment of potential risks. Believing some event must happen immediately or dire consequences will occur if it does not (and there is no margin of error) sets us up for making mistakes by using simplistic solutions for complex conditions. Terrorism, cultural diversity, and managing national boundaries are just a few of such complex conditions requiring comprehensive, "out of the box" consciousness and action. That it is "now or never" creates confrontation politics in one's lifestyle. As anxiety goes past a certain optimal point, performance begins to drop. American politics seems to have a motif of getting into ambiguous conditions such as the war in Iraq, permitting extra-legal immigration, allowing healthcare to become expensive, and, for many, and of course, ignoring decades of oil dependency and social security for baby boomers. What interconnections do all these unrelated aspects seem to have in common? Could it have anything to do with permitting chaotic events to continue to evolve, such that the solution is that there is none? How does one stop an avalanche roaring down a mountainside at over a hundred miles per hour? Call a meeting! This will not stop the avalanche, but it will get you out of the way! Complexities such as the Iraq War are not unlike those of Vietnam in the 1960s. Once involved, it simply perpetuates itself. This pattern could suggest that continuous entrainment is present. What life-altering experiences are we already encountering?

We will now explore how to examine entrainment, multifaceted connections, and what models or paradigms can be employed in prevention and early intervention. Some self-help groups refer to this as bringing up the bottom.

CHAPTER 7

DEPTH PERCEPTION IN A MULTI-DIMENSIONAL UNIVERSE

Connect the Dots . . . Find the Monkeys

Life-altering experiences have been characterized thus far as

synchronized co-connections of coinciding events resulting from unintentional involvement (being present at the wrong place, time, and/or event), having unintended consequences. What makes something "wrong" are unwitting involvements that do not serve our needs at a certain time, place, or situation (being late for work when our partner wants to make a baby now, walking into the bank while it's being robbed, a daily habit of jogging in the park early morning, and being mugged). "Wrong" can reference unintended conditions and consequences interrupting our plans, agendas, or state of health (accidents, overwhelming financial expenses suddenly converging, just missing enough seniority to avoid being laid off from work, or saying the "wrong" thing to that special someone with devastating consequences). Our daily habitual motifs entrain with other asymmetrical habits/patterns of others, leading to many unintended consequences.

The perception of interconnected events, initially appearing unrelated, doesn't always have to be recognized after the fact, nor does it mean something is going "wrong" with severe consequences. For instance, years ago at an art expo in New York City, the famous artist Pablo Picasso wrote a check to the curator for services rendered. As was his habit, while waiting to write the check since the curator was late, Picasso would draw pictures on the back of his checks. These drawings, in effect, became artistic masterpieces by Picasso, which, when given to the curator, were worth many times the check's dollar amount. The curator's lateness, combined with Picasso's tendency to draw, was a fortunate event of seemingly unrelated factors, resulting in something going "right."

Often, we instinctively say or do something without a clear, logical reason, only to find it leads to a fortunate outcome. For example, we might take our umbrella to work on a sunny day "just to do something crazy," and then discover it was useful when it rained that evening. We might have unexpectedly called a friend or colleague and found out they had been trying to reach us with good news. What seems like luck, fate, serendipity, or a guardian angel often involves lucky "hunches" connecting unrelated events in an almost miraculous, helpful way. Our personal version of interconnectedness arises as a kind of consciousness from how we unintentionally create synchronizations. The resulting entrainment can take on a life or "consciousness" of its own, spreading like a complex mosaic that weaves its thread-like effects into the most intricate details of our lives.

The multi-dimensional nature of our reality (try to simplify it though we may) functions to connect and manifest themes, triumphs, and traumas in our lives, creating far-reaching ripple effects. Without understanding how we are connecting the "dots" of our mosaic consciousness, we might or might not "find the monkeys" in the tangled "jungle" (remember those children's placemats with puzzles and games, one of which was to find the hidden, embedded monkeys in the maze of chaotic dots and lines) of our life-changing experiences.

How the details of our actions connect with the emerging synchronization of our multiple and simultaneous interfacing motifs—which is a multi-dimensional connection—can be understood through the movie Babel (2007). The title clearly refers to the biblical Tower of Babel, where no one could understand each other because they spoke different languages. The film highlights the ironic, paradoxical, and shocking twists that arise from simple, seemingly unrelated acts. For instance, there is the Japanese father, a former hunter, whose wife committed suicide and whose daughter appears to be following suit, after he gives a high-powered rifle to his old Moroccan guide. The guide then passes it to a friend, who gives it to his sons, who test how far it will shoot.

They practice target shooting with a bus that has an American couple on board. The couple is on vacation, feeling distant from each other, having left their children with a Hispanic babysitter. The wife leans away from her husband just as the boy is testing the rifle, and she gets shot in the shoulder. The movie unfolds with complex, interconnected themes of 6th-degree of freedom, highlighting our interconnectedness, creating intricate mosaics. It powerfully shows how a simple action- like the boy trying to see how far the gun can shoot by targeting a moving object, which happens to be the bus with the couple- can cause ripple effects with life-changing consequences. Such events are only possible because their motives were already beginning to align- like the Hispanic babysitter, who cares for the children and had to take them to her relative's wedding because their parents are the busy couple. The firearm, originally gifted by the Japanese father to his guide, was subsequently transferred to the guide's associate. Ultimately, this associate's sons used the weapon to shoot the couple on the bus, an incident that prompted broader reactions from the United States.

The synchronization of passing the rifle from person to person resembles following the bouncing ball of an old-fashioned sing-along. There must be timing and synchronization for it all to work together. If chaos can be coordinated (call it new-age music), then the conflict caused by misunderstandings among all parties involved (the daughter was deaf and used sign language and handwriting, the Hispanic babysitter had difficulty communicating with the U.S. Border Guard because he saw her as an illegal, the police in the movie operated under a "guilty until proven innocent" mindset, and that hostility was consistent throughout) is evident. The rifle itself acts as a recurring motif. It's important to recognize that misunderstandings can serve as motifs with life-altering consequences, as shown.

There are multifaceted solutions involved (the husband and wife have to pull together and commit never to abandon the children; the sweet Hispanic babysitter has to leave the kids in the desert to get help and is accused of abandoning the children, which is a theme for all the children in the movie; and language barriers of both cultures and politics have to be surmounted through alternative, compassionate modes of consciousness). Learning to empathize with the framework of each entraining motif generated a higher consciousness of commitment for multifaceted compassion. Only then were fortuitous synchronizations of motifs available.

One final note about this movie is that the writer's first name is Guillermo, which just happens to be the same as the first name of the person who is typing this very manuscript. Synchronization occurs even when writing about it. Another aspect is that when I have tried to write this work faster than it was ready to be written (even writers can get impatient), something would happen to force me to slow down, or speed up, so that I could realign with the concepts that have come to me and are necessary to express. This even happened with my own computer, which stopped functioning in certain ways, forcing me to take a moment for more reflective thought, thus allowing for deeper self-understanding.

When "Wrong" Is About "Evil"

An important aspect of these experiential life "shocks" is the presence of evil as a contributing dimension. Evil, as well as forces for good, are not the conventional domains of science. Their inclusion in any analysis of this sort is considered unscientific and inappropriate.

However, people often assign descriptive labels to disasters, referring to storms, earthquakes, and acts of terrorism with terms such as "bad," "terrible," or "evil doers." Are there forces, energies, etc. in the universe, in our everyday experiences that involve entrainment with these dynamics (if indeed they do exist from a scientific point of view)? Are there evil forces I've entrained when glitches in my earnings, coupled with (read synchronized entrainment) increased expenses, increased family needs, and rising gas prices, all befall me simultaneously? Researchers such as Barbara Oakley (Psychology Today, December 2007) have studied what makes some people ruthless monsters, with special attention to a socially cunning, manipulative behavior known as Machiavellianism. In her book Evil Genes, she successfully intertwines family history with chromosomes, serotonin, and the amygdala. She describes how DNA, hormones, and brain structure may form their own axis of evil in several psychiatric disorders. There are implications of how this may have contributed to the behavior of Slobodan Milosevic wreaking havoc in the Balkans. She believes such infamous dictators manifest borderline personality i(family members, neighbors, bosses, etc.). Such an internal, formative axis of evil can entrain far-reaching synchronizations in the theatre of our global community.

Synchronization can align with an individual's natural creativity and social interest axis, centered at their core self-level. Scientists do not negate intuition, dreams, thought experiments, and "Eureka moments" of brilliant insights (the carbon benzene ring was discovered in a scientist's dream of snakes engulfing one another's tails to form a six sided ring; Einstein's thought experiments "riding light beams to the sun"; a French scientist floating in a bathtub suddenly getting a flash of insight regarding liquid density and buoyancy, causing him to go running naked out of his house yelling "Eureka"). Scientists say that over two-thirds of the matter and energy that make up our universe (they call it dark matter and energy) is simply unknown. What is known is that concentrated synchronization of motifs (internally and/or externally) can exert a formative "axis" of life-altering entrainment.

How should one address the concept of "evil" in this context? Real, imagined, too much possession, and satanic rituals in our music, food, and matter? Is this why Islamic fundamentalists want to annihilate the West—too much fast food? "Hell" (pardon the Biblical reference), we'll kill ourselves with high cholesterol diets and heart attacks before anything else possibly could. Let us explore "evil" as a possible construct in the operation of the universe as an actual dynamic as essential to existence as the four basic forces of the universe (gravity, electromagnetism, strong and weak forces).

It is important to establish the concept of "evil" in our universe before we can have an in-depth discussion. Therefore, a brief explanation of how physicists understand the essence and origins of our universe will lay the groundwork for "evil's" hypothetical role. Physicists (Lisa Randall, Neil Turok, Paul Steinhardt, and Burt Kushner, Discovery Channel, 2005) have said that there are eleven dimensions in the universe—ten spatial and one temporal. In the 11th dimension, we are all connected through a membrane of energy strings that are infinitely long and only one-trillionth of a millimeter thick (and that's at its widest point). This membrane is closer to each of us than the clothes touching our skin. The design consists of a donut-shaped torus with a smaller nested torus, resembling onion layers.

The 11th dimension, which resolved debates between string and membrane theorists over its number, contains infinite other membranes. These other membranes run through multi-universes, siphoning gravity (formative effects of dense matter designs) and thereby weakening this force, as compared to the other three forces (electromagnetic, the strong force holding molecules together, and the weak force holding atomic nuclei together). This can imply that we are entraining not only with formative synchronizations in our universe but in and from other universes as well. Is there no end to all this? I guess that is what infinite means. These other universes (each exerting a formative design influence), plus our own, are called the multiverse (Greene, 1998).

It is also postulated that, because these membranes wave and ripple, with the space between them so small, they undulate in colliding rhythms with one another. These rippling, waving undulations create singularities, "big bangs," and new "baby" universes with their own membranes. This is how physicists (Discovery Channel, 2005) believe our universe began and will end—endlessly recycle itself.

The ripples, waves, and their unique interference patterns (which is what waves do with one another) of "parent membranes" imparted themselves through their rhythmic "big bang" unto our universe. Such collisions account for the unfolding, asymmetrical, patterned universe in which we live. Motifs of these interference wave patterns ripple throughout our universe, permeating all levels of hierarchical existence (from the macrocosm of galaxies to the microcosm of cellular design). This can account for the asymmetrical effects of motifs, which are similar but subtly different variations of interference wave pattern effects permeating the organizational structure of our bio-psycho-social, cultural, and physical universe. This means that there is a congruence of asymmetrical effects (subtle variations of motifs) permeating the hierarchy of organized systems. The congruence of these effects reflects synchronization of motifs entraining throughout all levels of organized systems. Notwithstanding the scalar level of organization, whether within and/or beyond its boundaries, good or evil asymmetrical patterns of motifs will resonate with similar but subtle variations of their theme.

Our thoughts and beliefs shape what we can envision and achieve. The reverse is also true. On larger scales, what we observe in our families, communities, careers, country, international community, and even our concept of God influences how we think and believe. The opposite is also true here, since parts can influence the whole. Achieving this requires strengthening and aligning with our core purpose. Formidability is crucial with such holographic motifs.

Perhaps existence is an infinity of such unique, holographic, asymmetrical motifs conjugating. Two "parent" membranes banging together (would Sigmund Freud turn over in his grave?) create "baby" membrane universes regenerating themselves in ever-evolving, self-organizing forms.

Holographic means that every part is a miniature version of the whole, reflecting the same themes at all levels of organization. Therefore, the universe would form a web-like field of interconnectedness at multiple levels of organization. This would allow multifaceted motifs to conjugate within and between themselves in this web-like energy field, constantly giving rise to infinite asymmetrical variations of life forms and star systems, self-generating themselves. Entrainment may well be the nature of this web-like reality in the everywhere, everywhen (Atwater, 1996) and every universe of families of multi-verses.

Bell's (2005) interconnectedness theorem addresses entrainment at astronomical distances (both time and space). Einstein's thought experiment regarding "spooky action at a distance" describes the phenomenon in which pairs of electrons, even when separated by vast distances, exhibit correlated spins; specifically, when the spin of one electron changes, the counterpart instantly adjusts its spin to maintain equal intensity but in the opposite direction. Space is not empty. It is filled (read "composed") of supergravity closed string loops (Lee Smolin, 2001) energy networks reflecting formative, cosmic membranes. Consider closed-loop energy strings. This quantum field of universal energy has been referred to as non-zero energy or Higgs fields. The particles have negative energy.

This quantum "ocean of potential energy" stirs into mass or matter when particles move through it swiftly. This might explain how the patterns of formative waves or ripples from the "big bang" shaped galaxies—and even human beings—through acceleration fleets at the universe's origin. Discussions of comets seeding Earth with life (History Channel, 2007) suggest that deep space contains microscopic life. It is the formative seeding or entraining of formative processes. Einstein highlights that both particles and living organisms experience an increase in matter density and structural complexity as their acceleration increases, as described by his renowned equation: energy equals mass multiplied by the square of the speed of light. This limitation does not apply to photons, since they are massless particles.

Fish are observed to swim, while birds are observed to fly. It suggests that we all thrive within our own medium. Space is not empty, and time is not divided into isolated segments. Human beings are immersed and connected through web-like electromagnetic energy fields that interface with the psycho-social mind-brain-body. Previous research cited (Persinger and Einstein) indicates such connectedness, reminiscent of "spooky action at a distance," between people's consciousness and mind-control effects. Both positive and negative intentions can be entrained. Our human condition links our life stories through at least a six-degree interconnected synchronization. Perhaps this explains the popularity of soap operas and our fascination with the lives of the rich and famous. From the life of Princess Diana to the infamous Osama bin Laden, touching each other's lives from near and far can synchronize in uncanny, life-changing experiences.

Existence embodies transformational motifs of two "parent-like" entities (waving, rippling membranes conjugating with one another) synergizing to generate unique "offspring" universes. Physicists of membrane theory (M-theory) suggest that the asymmetrical design of our universe's spiraling galaxies, etc., reflects unique, formative wave and ripple patterns.

(Discovery Channel, 2005). They are imparted and embedded throughout the expanding universe, originating from the initial "big bang" (or conjugation). Could such formative patterning of our universe reflect a kind of "cosmic DNA" inherited from our "parent membranes"? This implies that, embedded in our human condition, there are both human and universal entrainments of synchronization.

Are these cosmic blueprints a form of universal "genome" reflected in the unique, infinitely varied, embedded formativeness of a holographic wave interference pattern? Does this mean that each human being is a unique, holographic motif expressing variations of these asymmetric, cosmic ripples? Quantum physicists say that light (matter is described as dense light) can be both a wave and a particle. How we construe and focus the consciousness of our motif or unwittingly allow larger-scale entrainment to do that for us influences how we measure our life experiences as a set thing or a flowing process of possibilities. When the wave function collapses into a particle, it transitions from a state of multiple possibilities to a more defined probability distribution.

We can find countless variations of this motif in our daily lives. Every decision, action, choice, or behavior shifts our potential possibilities into more defined and probable behaviors. Have the unique waves and interference patterns from the "big bang" been passed down and embedded into our genetics and unique DNA? Have they shaped (or have we become) who we are individually with our distinctive, signature motif? Are our choices and decisions aligned and synchronized with the evolutionary traces of these primordial, cosmic interference patterns? Is each of us a self-generating, differentiating system infused with the essence of our potential being, striving to unfold selectively? Do we need to align with people, places, and events to tap into the core of our "wave" potential and manifest our unique, "particular" forms—such as careers, relationships, love, and family?

If the universe behaves (and waves) as an organic entity (or being), then perhaps we might imagine that its complexity and mystery of wholeness could be reflected holographically through all patterning of formative waves throughout the universe. That would include (but not be limited to) that complex and mysterious organizing creature known as human beings. While much is known about how our mind/brain/body organization functions (including the human genome), science is far from proclaiming victory that knowing all this means knowing perfectly how each of us functions. There are epigenetic dynamics of formativeness, sensitive to entraining influences (stress, disease, autoimmune deficiencies, neonatal experiences, protein synthesis and neurotransmitters, human consciousness, etc.), capable of switching genes on and off. This is the dark matter of the human genome.

Evolution, both at cosmic and organic levels, proceeds through selective sequences from simple to complex design structures or motifs (simple elements such as hydrogen and simple organic amino acids to complex design structures such as gold made only in stars and human beings made in special environments like Earth). The evolution of stars, planets, solar systems, elements, amino acids, single-celled organisms, plants, animals, and humans all have at least one thing in common.

That common factor is that all of existence is governed by a cycle of creation and destruction. These are two aspects of the same coin of the universal realm. They involve the unpredictability of formative patterns that develop through dynamics of epigenesis. These feedback loops relate to the effects of thought and action that result in self-activation. Genes, described as "good" or "bad," can activate or deactivate in response to humans' short- and long-term experiences and choices. The formative patterns of entrainment resulting from our choices and actions, whether unconsciously synchronized from within or external influences, can "genetically" change our bio-psycho-social-cultural life experience. It can literally turn our lives on or off.

Call it good or evil, right or wrong, God or the Devil, moral or immoral. The prevailing principle across the universe is one of continual transformation: a process that involves creating a specific form, dismantling it, and subsequently reconstructing it in an improved manner within an ongoing cycle. There are infinite structures (or life forms) vying to come into existence.

When the timing, circumstances, and sequence of events align perfectly, a specific form may find the conditions right to emerge. Consider the dawn of humanity and the five-million-year history of hominid evolution. It follows a similar path. Even the existence of our planet and moon resulted from countless collisions that honed, shaped, and refined precise conditions, allowing you, me, and our offspring to exist. To reach this point, countless cycles of construction and destruction—breaking down, collapsing, decaying, and rebuilding—have occurred. How many life forms have appeared and disappeared? Each one has fought, battled, suffered, and died, laying the groundwork for the next stage of evolution. This is the dynamic pattern of epigenesis—a process of self-reorganization accomplished through synchronized feedback and reflective transformation.

Evolution, Entrainment, and Evil

Such a perspective is crucial as it creates a framework for understanding and enriching the dialogue about why destructive, painful, cruel, and terrible biblical Job-like disasters exist and will continue to exist in our evolving human experience. If we are all made of "stardust," as physicists often comment, then we and the stars are evolving together. We are born from a spark of creation, generate enormous energy, and produce highly specialized creations. Instead of creating complex elements like gold and iron, we create music, art, civilizations, cultures, and, of course, war! Eventually, like stars, everything and everyone burns out in a blaze of glory (or at least, we would like to think we will). For what may seem like forever, we each radiate our starlight (yes, some of us have brighter stars than others, but in the end, we all burn out).

Scientists say it can take millions of years for one photon to travel from the sun's core to its surface—it's that dense—and only 9.5 minutes afterward to reach Earth. Similarly, it can take years for a human being to bring out the best in themselves, but once they do (after years of training and discipline), they can radiate instantaneous brilliance (if one has been willing to make the journey).

However, the energy and creation of the stars involve destroying their raw materials, using themselves up. Clocks are ticking, resources are consumed, and evolution only gives us specific contexts that permit our existence. A coffee shop must close its premises at the end of each business day, ensuring proper reopening preparation. Each life must close, permitting a new one to open. Moreover, like stars, we each leave a legacy (hopefully something special).

Not everything that stars make is gold, silver, or silicon. Less attractive but equally necessary elements like carbon, iron, and sulfur are also generated. The "good" and the "evil" things men and women do live long after them. All events and experiences contribute to what is passed on to subsequent generations. Our mistakes, tragedies, limitations, liabilities, and vulnerabilities all assist the next generation in producing, evolving, and morphing in transformational motifs.

Evil manifests as terror in the horrifying events of 9/11. It appears as pedophiles kidnapping and killing our loved ones. It also shows as prejudice, justifiable rage, and revenge, like how 19th-century white Americans tortured and murdered Black Americans because they were "different" and seen as "inferior," "bad," and "evil." The complex, paradoxical effects of evil, often called "the dark side," are reflected in the tragic outcomes of Oprah Winfrey's great effort—her kindness in building a school for young girls in South Africa. Oprah has dedicated her life to protecting children from abuse. Sadly, the very people responsible for supervising the girls at her school were found to have been abusing them. Oprah has worked tirelessly to protect these children, but it remains unclear how such events occurred despite close supervision.

There appears to be an ironic aspect to generating corrective motifs when facing darkness and what could be called evil. When pursuing transformational experiences with dysfunctional motifs, there is always a risk of attracting the very issues one aims to eliminate. Firefighters get burned. Police officers are killed by criminals. Even Madame Curie, who discovered radium, died from radiation poisoning. Therapists can become "infected" with the toxic negativity of their clients during the recovery process. The effort to create a secure and empowering environment for the growth of young women can, paradoxically, trigger and reinforce some of the very challenges it aims to address. However, this phase will be brief if there is a strong, ongoing commitment to integrating formative themes in both school life and management.

This highlights a crucial issue: how integrated and embedded transformational motifs must be. Each person, community, neighborhood, region, gender, nation, corporation, and religion has a certain tolerance for differences. When this tolerance is breached, it is often vilified as "evil." The roots of evil are planted when this tolerance—while trying to live according to its motif—violates its alignment, seeming congruent (for example, when my neighbor drinks beer and I drink wine). Do the varying degrees and types of differences, beyond a certain point, amount to "badness" or even "evil"? America, as the world's leading democratic nation, is the land of tolerance. Yet, even here, prejudice, judgment, and intolerance still persist. Not without civil war, power struggles, revolution, and sacrifice—in short, "war"—has freedom to live one's own lifestyle been achieved. It is not absolute; it's only how it has been exercised so far.

The evolution of the universe, of Earth, and of Homo sapiens all involve competition (and cooperation) among formative entities for existence. Even in major religions (Christianity, Islam, Judaism), there is war and conflict for supremacy. What is the battle in Heaven (as described in the biblical testament) between Satan and God and His angels? This is the "big bang" of evil throughout the universe. The forces of light (good guys) battle those of darkness (bad guys), and God is said to be the Good Guy (or God) who permits it all because of free will and spiritual democracy.

Some people have ascribed free will as "each individual's God-given right to go to Hell in his or her way." This message of defiance, rebellion, pride, and so on sets us apart from oneness with God. This separateness is "Hell" in itself. It is much worse than not being accepted to the local country club or missing out on the black Visa card membership (which only celebrities have). This "Hell" would be much worse than being fired by Donald Trump or just missing becoming the next American Idol. I do not mean to trivialize the spiritual construct of Hell, but rather to suggest that human experiences of alienation, rejection, and separation can feel like "Hell on Earth." Family members who feel dysfunctional, scapegoated, victimized, left out, or unacceptably falling short of being perfect experience similar sensations of alienation and separation from the wholeness of family inclusion and recognition.

Conflict and competition, though sometimes unhealthy, link humanity's pursuit of spiritual union or connection with a higher power. However, evilness—from life-altering experiences—implies that acts or actions (terrorism, violence, emotional and/or physical betrayal, falsehoods, etc.) endanger our formative existence and its necessary network of connective, life-sustaining systems. Evil endangers our interconnection with any formative, nurturing network of family-like systems. Hell is truly separation from the God-network (faith, religion, family, country, or any network entity with which we identify and are rooted) that sustains our unique motif and way of life.

Evil, then, is that which threatens our connection to our source of power. It is also anything that diminishes our unique development's quality, integrity, and longevity. We collaborate well with people, places, and things that support, sustain, and enhance our sense of self, lifestyle, and guiding principles. We accept differences only to the extent that they do not threaten to undermine our way of life. This can include immigration issues, who our child marries, who we marry, plant closings in Detroit, Michigan, the length of teenagers' hair, the length of our wife's shirt, how big our car or house is compared to the guy is down the block, etc. Evil can be the unacceptable degree of difference perceived to threaten our way of life.

If you lived in Mississippi in 1963 and you were Black and wanted to ride in the front of the bus, you might question why so many white people were yelling and shouting at you for upsetting their way of life. How could such a simple, innocent act threaten so many people to the extent that it could place your life in jeopardy? What symbols and meanings might such a gesture impart to a 1960s white southern person? What connections and/or formativeness for that person's life motif could be perceived as threatened or undermined? A 91-year-old African-American woman, whose two friends were hanged in the South, described the racist hangings of the late 19th and early 20th centuries in America as the Black man's Holocaust. Remember, this is genuinely the greatest democracy in the modern world. What does that tell you about the rest of the world?

Is evil anything that is an altering experience for the worse? Most would say this is a positive alteration if we win the multimillion-dollar lottery. Nevertheless, many lifestyles have been ruined because the changes were so disruptive to that person's life motif that divorce, chemical abuse, and DUI arrests resulted for some. Is evil a sinister force, satanic in origin, deliberately wanting our "fall from grace" by antagonizing our resistance to some higher power so we will truly "go to Hell in our own way"? Pride, rebellion, self-doubt, the need to be greater than God, and the loss of humility are among the "sins" by which we may be condemned (read: "separated"). Separation on Earth can come in many forms—death, divorce, parental abandonment, job loss, etc. The concept of evil as a malevolent force that aims to sever individuals from their foundational origins is a recurring theme found throughout religious and spiritual literature. Even the "new agers," who expose the beautifully written (they say "channeled" through a spirit guide) Course in Miracles, refer to the concept of "ego" as illusions of control and artificial self-identity, separating us from universal mind, oneness, and wholeness. Fear, they say, is an acronym standing for False Evidence Appearing Real.

However, nature and human nature show that there is good reason to acknowledge the reality of fear. The facts of impermanence, change, and limited time are unavoidable. The fear of death exists in all civilizations, among all peoples, and in all intelligent species that understand what is happening. If evil separates us from our source of power to live and flourish, we should rightly fear evil's intent and purpose.

The evolution of the universe and its species, in all its formative manifestations (organic and inorganic), establishes impermanence and transformative change through life, death, and rebirth cycles. Whether you are a Christian or not, Jesus Christ's crucifixion serves as a universal motif of this generative, transformative life cycle.

American soldiers who die for our country are honored and revered. For those who perished in the 9/11 attack on the World Trade Center, it was the evil's manifestation, as they were innocent civilians victimized by sinister psychopaths driven by extremist fundamentalism. Such Islamic fundamentalism threatens my country, my way of life, and my values of human decency. I have discovered that there may be millions of people on this planet who see me and everything about my culture as evil, dangerous, and something to be feared and wiped out. These people may either be terrorists, support terrorists, or at least agree with them in theory if not in method.

So, how can this be? Are these people possessed by Satan or some evil demon?

Frankly, I believe that at least a few of these extremists are! However, countless thousands (or perhaps millions) believe that I and my fellow countrymen want to separate them from their roots, their source of power (or maybe even their heads).

What should we think about evil? Is it simply a matter of which side of the fence (or ocean or civilization) someone is born, raised, and rooted? Is evil such a construct that it is so relative that we can apply it in any context? I think at times, this might be true. For the most part, I believe there is a core source of evil throughout the universe that, while not a friend of the cosmos, may not be its outright enemy. I say this because evolution and life as we know it would not be possible without this fundamental destructive force. Without the Romans and their hunger for power and domination by any means—no matter how cruel, evil, or torturous—we would not have had the crucifixion of Christ, and therefore, Christianity.

I have (and I am sure others have also) wondered why the universe (and the world as we know it) operates in such a chaotic, nonlinear, downright painful way. While I do not know, I would venture a hypothesis: that the suffering and evil in humankind (as we frame existence) are part of missing the forest for the trees. Pain, suffering, and life-altering experiences blind us to the unfolding spirituality of universal purposefulness. Our pain, anguish, fears of non-existence, and sense of impermanence cause us to be immediately present in the here-and-now. For example, if I've been hit while riding in my car by a semi-trailer and I find myself upside down in my seat with the car on fire, I'm not going to sit back and contemplate the meaning of it all. I'm first going to do everything possible to save my life and the lives of my family and friends if needed. That's what I do. That's what I am. That's my job as a human being—to live. I'll ask questions later. This programming is deeply embedded at fundamental neurological levels.

The drive to optimize formativeness to its fullest ensures that the best qualities will persist for the next generation. An inherent instinct to protect those we care about is also deeply embedded within us. Formativeness begets and informs transformative processes. The universe, evolution, and life formativeness are about flow, process, and the exquisite diffraction of formativeness (mosaic complexities). It is about generating and evolving the right stuff, if you will. It is not about maintaining any status quo. It may appear as if we are spiritual cattle being culturally cultivated and harvested for our "best cuts of meat," feeding the next generation. Without evil, we could not achieve such magnificence. The suffering, cruelty, challenge, adversity, and overcoming involved in life struggles are the trials by fire that temper the metals to be utilized in future formative fashions. Humans are tool makers. We are also (spiritual) tools, lest we forget our roots. It is not that we will not suffer, laugh, struggle, and conflict with one another. It is rather that we (in every civilization and its occupants) hone and harness, in our dialectical tensions, ever more exotic, refined materials, tools, and qualities to further service the expansion of our legacy and universe.

But what, you ask, is it all leading towards? Great question! Again, evil presents itself with an... ah-yes, "evil smile"—a mischievousness that suggests we are still missing the forest for the trees. Evil is well... so evil! We believe we have a clear direction amid this ever-growing evolutionary energy.

What if the real "evil" is the illusion of the future, the past, or even the present? What if it's all about roots, wings, and how space-time curvature enfolds on itself infinitely? Evil creates illusions of separateness in time (living in the past, living only for the moment, anticipating better futures) and/or in space (I belong here but not there, I'm at home in one place but a foreigner, an outsider in another). The flow of space-time is a unification of interconnectedness where we are at the source of being everywhere and every when.

Fear and fixations of evil challenge us to overcome artificial limits in space, time, and identity. Each of us embodies the good, the bad, and the ugly. We are each in all the characters and identities in all times, places, cultures, civilizations, and configurations. How can this be? We are distinct individuals, separated by time, place, and circumstance.

The holographic universe and mind suggest that wholes and parts are interconnected at every level of organization. Hold a grain of sand in the palm of your hand and behold the universe with all its multiverses. Each human being is that holograph of infinite formativeness. We are each capable of being vast numbers of characters at our source. Every criminal could become a good policeman. As a child once said, "The more things change, the more they stay the same." The multiverse of our human nature is revealed in the challenge of life-altering experiences. These challenges are our trial by fire, testing the metal of our core character. How the inner facets of our core motif synchronize with the external context of chaotic challenge reveals the innovative resolution of our unique adaptation. It may bring out the best in us. It may bring out the worst in us. It may bring out an idiosyncratic, unique proportionality of our multifaceted nature. For example, if one were making pottery, the molded clay contains tiny iron-like bits of magnetite with small magnetic fields. Since the bits are randomly aligned in various directions, the pot has no overall field. However, when it is heated in a kiln and then allowed to cool, the small bits of magnetite uniformly align to the Earth's magnetic field, resonating into synchronization. The fire of the kiln released the magnetite from rigid fixation into a fluid form susceptible to reorganization by the larger context of the Earth's magnetic field.

Life-changing experiences stir multiple areas of our lives and personalities—such as desires, beliefs, expectations, daily routines, attitudes, ideals, and different ego states—often in chaotic and disruptive ways. When released from habitual patterns and usual ways of functioning, they become free to reorganize, aligning and synchronizing with the upheavals of their environment. After the initial chaos subsides, a new alignment with the theme of trauma and drama begins to form. For instance, a mother who lost her child in a traffic accident caused by an intoxicated driver might create an organization called Mothers Against Drunk Driving (M.A.D.D.) to prevent similar tragedies. The intensity of this experience causes a synchronization of motifs, bringing out the best in her. In the Columbine shootings, where the shooters had initially been victims of teasing and bullying, their violent actions reflected the darkest motifs. Challenges and hardships can heighten the potential for change, allowing a person to become a saint (Saul becoming Paul), a sinner (an abused child turning into a tyrant, Hitler, or radical extremists), or some mixture of both—shaped by the influence of the surrounding upheavals.

How we emerge from the initial traumatic disruptions of life-changing experiences can unintentionally lead us into intense adaptations of key formative patterns. Significant experiences test the ability of our core traits to maintain and boost their natural resilience. The degree to which our central motif is active or present during major life events may affect the chance of adaptive synchronization happening. Driven by the critical nature of trauma—such as the potential loss of a valued person, place, or thing, the inner core of one's unique motif naturally aligns itself inwardly. It is during this point of courage and healing that one's way of life begins to evolve toward creativity and functional innovation. Personal and interpersonal conflicts simultaneously tend to lessen. Consider how ordinary men and women step up to protect their family and nation under attack, achieving extraordinary acts of heroism. They clearly have a sense of purpose and dedication, aligning their beliefs and actions. Of course, there are other cases where a person's unique organizing motif is only partly accessed. In these situations, formative entrainment may develop unevenly. Such alignment often remains vulnerable to the destructive effects of trauma—like terrorism, sociopathic tendencies, and similar threats. Elements of a motif might need ongoing refinement, naturally adapting through creativity. Humans are more than mindless bits of magnetite. If only part of our motif interacts with the trauma during overwhelming experiences, its disturbances are more likely to lead us into unwanted complications without our awareness.

Life-altering experiences challenge us to connect with past events, discern and understand what happened, what it means, and how we can survive. Ultimately, they raise the specter of who or what is behind this. It is about our source, our roots, that allow us to sprout wings and fly. A fetus has an umbilical cord attaching it to its source, its mother. We move through many stages of development after birth, seeking continual connection from one life event to another. As we pass through the stages of our human development, we can only proceed as far as our connections to our roots will take us. Sometimes, we must bring our roots with us. It is called transplanting and genesis. This is especially important when dealing with loss and abandonment.

Our roots and wings come from, move through, and return to (head toward) our sources of origin. Misalignment of our roots and wings— where we deviate from our sense of meaning and purpose—can temporarily sever our connection to our life path development. We can no longer view evolution as we have lost this developmental connection. Evil obsesses us with fear, dread, terror, jealousy,

Blind sight is a condition where a person cannot see an object, is not conscious or aware of its presence, yet primitive brain pathways detect its motion. Discovery Channel (2004) described a case where damage to the visual cortex left a person unable to consciously see anything in the right visual field of either eye. Brain scans indicated that when he saw objects moving in his left-side visual field, completely different brain regions and pathways (including the prefrontal cortex) were activated. Individuals with this condition report acting and responding to objects outside their visual awareness in ways they cannot explain. Similar experiences are reported with patients who have split-brain hemispheres (where the connecting fibers of the corpus callosum are surgically severed in the treatment of epilepsy). Dr. Larry Weiskarff, a professor at Oxford University (Discovery Science Channel, 2005), reports on awareness. The other side of the page (registering on the right hemisphere) has words that stimulate the brain, but the patient will not be consciously aware of it (because of the split hemisphere). Such individuals, when asked to report and draw their experience (for example, when seeing the word "hourglass" with "hour" being on the left side of the page and "glass" being on the right), will draw a picture of an hourglass but indicate that they did not know why they did it.

Patients in such situations made up stories and fictional myths or rationales about why they drew the pictures they did (Gazzinga, 2005). When we make up stories or rationalize why we behaved in a certain way, we fabricate or bend the "truth" to fit the facts. In short, this is a form of self-deception or inadvertent lying to oneself. It may be compared to cheating at the card game of Solitaire. This can also be a way to reduce cognitive dissonance and maintain the illusion of some control and fixation of rationality. Could this be the seeds of "evil"? Certainly not in the malevolent, premeditated way.

Unconscious competence is advantageous, particularly for professional athletes such as tennis players who must skillfully react to serves exceeding one hundred miles per hour. They report only seeing the ball hit at a certain angle and then unconsciously (but competently, meaning learned, automatic reflexes) responding. This form of unconsciousness is a product of masterful learning, experience, and artistic motif.

Researchers (Dr. Patrick Haggard, University College London, Dr. Mike Gazzinga, and Dr. Benjamin Lippitt, Discovery Channel, 2005) report that much of our mind-brain activity is out of conscious awareness, involving unconscious or subconscious learning and programming. Think of things we do automatically, such as walking, driving a car, answering a telephone, eating a meal, or even falling asleep.

Researchers like Dr. Benjamin Lippitt (Discovery Science Channel, 2004) suggest that all mental processes originate from the unconscious mind. Every thought, action, and emotion is initiated unconsciously, and then we become aware of ourselves and the processes in motion. Brain studies by Dr. Lippitt (2004) show a half-second delay between neuron stimulation and our conscious awareness of it. The startling conclusion from this research is that we all live half a second in the past. We do not experience our environment (internal or external) as it happens instantly.

In line with these findings, Dr. Haggard (2004) studied decision-making and consciousness alongside Dr. Susan Greenfield. Researchers observed that, during decision-making trials, specific brain regions generated neural potentials approximately two thousand milliseconds before a decision and subsequent movement. Research suggests that decisions may occur before a person becomes consciously aware of them, raising questions about the level of control the conscious mind has. This buildup at the unconscious level indicates entrainment in patterned activities, problem-solving, and decision-making beyond conscious awareness. Is conscious free will, therefore, merely an illusion? If so, how can we explain deliberate, conscious choices to overcome pain and major obstacles, or Lance Armstrong's seventh heroic effort in the 2005 Tour de France?

Which comes first: the conscious decision to act on some goal, task, relationship, meaning, or purpose, or is it unconscious buildups from random acts that happen to form patterns and thereby predispose us to respond, making up fictional accounts as to why we choose it under the illusion of free will and control? The effects of conscious and unconscious influences, key motivations, and transformative experiences will be examined in detail later. The question of whether we are "organic machines" operating deterministically, entraining with life altering experiences, is an important and essential one in gaining mastery and empowerment in our lives. Social scientists and philosopher Dr. John Snow (2004) believes incontrovertibly that we all have free choice and will, even if we "choose" not to choose. The intricacy among these positions deserves full attention. We claim to have free will and choice, yet the extent of control we exert over our unconscious experiences and behavior is a matter of debate.

Studies of murderers' brains through positron emission tomography (Ripkin, 1994) indicated damage to prefrontal cortex regions, which involve impulse control. The psycho-social, impoverished background of the murderer was not a significant factor in some of these cases (Discovery Science Channel, 2005). Where impairment was demonstrated, courts gave murderers reduced sentences under diminished capacity defenses. The point here is not to suggest that we are not responsible for our actions. On the contrary, to maximize our functional capacities, it's important to realize that we can and are unwittingly drawn and entrained into life-altering experiences. Sometimes, we can be conscious, and at other times only partially or not. People who have suffered child abuse are unwittingly drawn into chaotic, intense, and enmeshing relationship experiences that unconsciously resonate with similar past abuse (sexual, financial, addictive, and/or fantasy idealizations). It's not unlike the moth being attracted to the light. This past-present resonance may be a human, down-to-earth experience of "spooky action at a distance."

Our unwitting participation in life-altering experiences can occur at multiple levels of resonance. It may be present in abusive relationships, resonating with past, "spooky," or haunting traumas of childhood. It may live in geographic, high-risk areas (Los Angeles and other cities along the San Andreas Fault). It may be a commodities trader in the World Trade Center (a symbolic target, apparently, to fanatical Islamic fundamentalists). The nurse, doctor, or firefighter may seek to nurture, help, or rescue someone in need only to find themselves the unwitting "victim" of a life-altering lawsuit. That femme fatale, romantic involvement from Europe, may have left you with the life-altering experience of AIDS. Being in the "wrong place at the wrong time in the wrong situation" is an entrainment waiting to happen.

These life-transforming experiences may be seen as accidental, political, unfortunate consequences (being at war), and/or just plain evil-inspired (the devil made it happen). Trauma and tragedy compel us to rediscover our essence, origins, and priorities. Most of all, it encourages us to become a student of the universe.

Cycles of Reverberation Communication

Perhaps a key to understanding consciousness is Dr. Greenfield (2004) proposed a theory about assembly neuron cells in the brain. She likens groups of nerve cells that operate as organizing assemblies in the brain to raindrops in water. When an external event stimulates our sensory system (hearing, seeing, or feeling something), it sends waves of rippling electrical impulses through groups of assembling nerve cells. Repetitive patterns of stimulation strengthen and reinforce selective groups of neurons to fire on and off sequentially and spontaneously. These neurons begin functioning together in assembled, resonant design structures (motifs). These assemblies of patterned, organized cells are uniquely designed in formative ways (motifs) to resonate with sensory input and generate behavioral responses.

Dr. Greenfield postulates that everything we think, feel, imagine, and decide to act on is a result of this ever-changing maelstrom of patterned brain cell assemblies. Consciousness is not located in any specific center or place but rather is a summation of the total effects of rippling, electrical patterning throughout various brain centers. The strongest, most intense of these patterns is what emerges from unconscious to consciousness, shaping how we define (and rationalize) our experience. Additionally, the visual cortex of the brain may be bombarded with millions of stimulated nerve impulses, but the retina may only be strengthened and trained to recognize 20,000 bits of information. We may be "in the dark" about unconscious entrainments that press, pull, and influence our thoughts, feelings, and actions at a sub-level of consciousness (which is why it's called subconscious or unconsciousness).

Studies on chemicals affecting these rippling waves of electrical patterning, which in turn affect consciousness and distortions, illustrate her theory. For example, a study completed by Dr. Vollen at a psychiatric hospital in Germany (2004) had subjects given small doses of catecholamine. Findings in consciousness distortion indicated enhanced mood, diminished response to external stimuli, and alterations in visual, auditory, and kinesthetic (internal sensations) modalities.

Dr. Greenfield's theory is that the drug reduced the strength of ripple waves from external stimuli by restricting their capacity to traverse internally. As a result, lower-intensity electrical ripple waves became perceptible due to reduced interference from external sources. In addition, the drug allowed new patterning of ripple effects to wave through newly reconfigured (transformed motifs) brain cell assemblies. Hallucinations and delusions subsequently became evident. Yet, the subject remained mentally healthy.

Imagine the conscious-unconscious cycle buildup that could entrain within and between individuals if such altered patterning or motifs were allowed to escalate to critical mass. During John F. Kennedy's presidency, the Cuban missile crisis with the then USSR (Soviet Russia) could easily have escalated to Armageddon proportions. The intense stress and trauma of such a situation could contribute to distortions, hallucinations, and delusions, potentially leading to the critical mass of thermo-nuclear warfare. In the novel The Guns of August, mutual distortions of threat are depicted, culminating in World War I.

If formative patterns in brain wave electrical stimulation influence conscious and unconscious entrainment, and if energy fields—both internal and external—can affect and entrain human experiences, then these factors may shape behavior and perception. In that case, we can understand how they might lead to unintentional, life-changing experiences. Suppose the brain-mind system consists of dynamic, transformative electrical wave patterns. In that case, it constantly produces electromagnetic fields in flux and can resonate internally and with external systems. This would explain how people, deeply and profoundly connected (e.g., mother and daughter), could influence each other at a distance without speaking. The Clark Johnson research project (2004) found EEG trace patterns provoked in a daughter simultaneously with her mother's visual perception of selected stimuli, demonstrating such entrainment at a distance.

Human Receivers and Broadcasters

When a nerve cell transmits an electrical impulse, it remains stationary. What moves is the flow of electrical energy traveling (depolarization) along the nerve and then electrochemically bridging the synaptic gap to the next neuron. The cell "lights up" with electrical current, then temporarily shuts down (the refractory period) to build up potential for the next stimulus. Groups of cells firing in synchronized patterns form cell assemblies of formative motifs flashing on and off sequentially, creating design patterns for brain-mind functioning.

Considering the electromagnetic nature of brain-mind synchronization of flashing design patterns, the screen of a standard television set has a remarkable similarity. It has small pixels (nerve cells) that flash on and off (firing and refractory periods of recovery), orchestrated by an electron gun guided by magnetism (organizing cell assemblies creating themselves through sensory input of guiding electromagnetic fields). Televisions are receivers of sight and sound—synchronized energy that we call (for better or worse) a program. An all-too-common question in many households might be, "What is on television tonight?" However banal that question has become, the time has come to ask ourselves: what is playing on the television screen of my mind tonight, tomorrow, and so on?

Unlike television, we send and receive synchronized sights and sounds that are programs to others and ourselves. We talk to ourselves subverbally at almost 1,500 words per minute. Our mental attention focuses like an electron gun on our mind-brain system. This leads to entraining formative neuronal assemblies, which can, in turn, synchronize our behavior with our mental focus. Understanding the formative, synchronized modalities of sights, sounds, and sensations— and their entraining influence (both on addictions to television shows and to ourselves and each other)—enables us to gain greater mastery in anticipating our participation in life-altering experiences.

Just as one might watch a violent movie, see repetitive seductive images, or be flooded with bargain sales at Wal-Mart, our mind-brain systems and televisions are becoming entrained. Different types of media can shape individuals' beliefs and attitudes. Selective purchasing behaviors create feedback loops between television advertisers and loyal viewers. The World Wide Web is a "television set" of global size that boosts entrainment to a worldwide community. That can be both positive and negative.

Our personal and cultural boundaries are closer (some would say nonexistent) than ever before. Financial, cultural, and military influences affect world politics in an instant. Entrainments transform faster in their looping back on themselves than ever before. If a politician makes a misstep, both extreme Republicans and Democrats often portray each other in divisive terms, sometimes drawing comparisons to Nazi Germany. In that case, it is instantly amplified and intensified in the media. 24/7 news coverage, the World Wide Web, and the capacity to amplify distortions, misunderstandings, and escalating tensions create a tightly entrained design structure.

What U.S. soldiers in Iraq do well, do poorly, or do not do at all is immediately seized upon by the Arab world, many times in the worst distortion-enhancing motif. Both individually and globally, the entrainment of formative motifs, distorted and skewed out of alignment, can create synchronized evil through all levels of organization. In the computer Internet era, it is called a virus.

Divided We Fall, United We Stand

This could serve as a mantra for our nation. It also suggests how change and transformation can happen, for better or worse. If we keep tugging at the loose threads of a sweater, that single thread might eventually unravel the whole pattern. The integrity and coordinated functioning of fundamental patterns and design structures—from neural systems and individual cognition to societal organizations and nations—depend on overall coherence and harmonious integration. However, existence is inherently dynamic and constantly changing. Coherent design structures enable evolution to produce both familiar and new offspring across generations. Ultimately, water movement along its natural, winding course defines a river. The rate and manner of change—gradual or sudden (evolution or revolution; genetic development or mutation)—determine whether the change is truly transformative or poses a risk to a species (though not to life itself). One person's evil spirit motif might be another's salvation motif. The asteroid that wiped out the dinosaurs 165 million years ago may have seemed evil to them, but it ultimately saved Homo sapiens and opened new opportunities for beginnings.

We must examine life-changing experiences from various perspectives, including mastery of our conscious and unconscious patterns of transformative themes. Existence, creation, and recreation all involve shape, form, and motif design structures—both organic and inorganic. Has it ever occurred to anyone that organic and inorganic elements (simply life consciousness and unconsciousness) are all part of the same family, just at different levels of hierarchical organization? The elements of the periodic table are as harmoniously connected to exotic substances as notes of music are to a Beethoven composition. Are the metaphors of inorganic and organic universes just a coincidence, or do they imply a more profound interconnectedness?

Up to 95% of our universe consists of dark matter (25%) and dark energy (70%). No physicist currently knows this darkness, and its nature remains unclear. Curiously, the human dark matter and energy of our subconscious mind also make up 95% of our motivating mutuality and human universe. This parallel connection with the universe deserves further study.

The next chapter examines accidents, natural disasters, and events significantly impacting lives. Are they all merely variations of one another, or is an accident just an accident? If one mistakenly puts the decimal point in the wrong place on their income tax return, is it part of a larger entrainment or simply a singular event? Sometimes a cigar is just a cigar (even though it irritates many people when smoked). However, singular events can, in themselves, be devastating and life-altering. Is the nature of such events one of striking out of the blue, suddenly and dramatically, without rhyme, reason, or warning? The foundations of these questions, their dilemmas, and the quandaries surrounding them are challenges of future explorations ventured forth in the following chapters.

Chapter 8

Causality, Evil, and What Matters

Profound, traumatic experiences compel us to reevaluate our perceptions of reality and challenge conventional wisdom.

Key existential questions that emerge when faced with shock and trauma are who we are, what our life is about, what we are trying to achieve, and why.

Central to these experiences are urgent questions about how such shocking events could have happened—9/11, the Madrid and London train bombings, life savings lost in corporate scandals like Enron, the sudden onset of serious illness, or the risk of losing a lifetime of work, to name a few. Critical questions also arise regarding the impact of these events. What will be possible in the future? Will there be a future? What are the chances of continuing life as we knew it, instead of facing an unknown, alternative lifestyle? How willing are we to adapt as needed?

The quest to understand these and many other questions about the nature of life-changing events—what they consist of, what we are made of, what caused them, and what might cause them again—resides at the core of every suffering soul. Various multidimensional sources could be explored as potential answers. These include aspects of conscious versus unconscious dynamics, active or passive lifestyles, consequences of personal choice versus fate or destiny, accidents and coincidences versus unwitting synchronicities of nature and/or human intuition (such as conspiracies), acts of biblical proportions (God, the devil, divine intervention or providence, effects of parallel universes, etc.). Sometimes, we wonder if we are cursed, or if gremlins, the bogeyman, or the green fairy are behind it all. What role does evil play in our experiences of life-altering events? Are we under attack from evil or Satan, or are we being punished by God for our sinful nature? Are we facing modern-day tests of faith, like Abraham being told by God to sacrifice his son and then being spared by divine intervention? Or do we resemble biblical Job, subjected to endless suffering to test the pride or sinfulness that may arise from believing we know what God wants? What factors contribute? How do we handle the unknown, chaos, and shocking uncertainty?

Some argue that no one can truly know, so why bother trying to understand? Just accept it and move forward. This mindset creates a problem with repeating mistakes. If we can't learn from what happened, how can we prevent it from happening again if it's too hard to understand? The other extreme is attempting to be omniscient and know everything. Good luck with that! Maybe Robert Louis Stevenson was right when he described man's nature as an ongoing struggle between good and evil in the classic novel Dr. Jekyll and Mr. Hyde (the evil side that "Hyde" is overshadowed by the healing light).

Is this where the evil, thematic "Hydes" hide within the bright shadows of good people like healers, ministers, teachers, doctors, lawyers, and others? Can such shadowy parts align and synchronize with life-changing events? Is this what contributes to abuse, violation, and its self-perpetuating cycle?

To answer such questions, it is crucial to explore more deeply the issues of uncertainty and human nature. We are born with dispositions, potentials, and temperaments that interact selectively and mutually within ourselves and our environment. This lifelong selective interaction begins in self-reflective and self-fulfilling ways. Regardless of the type and level of temperament and disposition a child is born with, the way they manifest depends on their development and interaction within a broad range of contextual factors. Unique temperaments and resilient or vulnerable constitutions interact with psycho-social-cultural variables of enrichment or deprivation, shaping lifestyle patterns. The specific contribution of these internal and external variables combines to form the experience of self at any moment within a person's lifestyle.

Such a congealing of multi-variable synchronization can be seen in Sid Caesar's life. Raised in the northern, hilly part of California, Sid's working mother assigned his older brother to babysit him during the day. As entertainment, the bored older brother would take young Sid to the top of a hill, secure a rope to the axle of a carriage, and attach the other end to a telephone pole. He would then launch young Sid in the carriage down the hill toward a busy intersection. Sid was saved when the carriage reached the end of its rope, just short of the dangerous intersection. As an adult, Sid Caesar became a famous entertainer, but he mysteriously disappeared for 20 years. Later, he was interviewed on television and explained that he had been recovering from alcoholism. He said he could never understand why he always felt out of control and used alcohol as self-medication. After learning what his older brother had done to him as a child, he realized how synchronized and entrained his lifestyle had been with such malevolence and looming danger. Although he did not blame his alcoholism on this, he recognized how it had permeated his life.

Each person has free will. However, unwittingly aligning with self-limiting and negating patterns creates shadows of uncertainty and doubt on our resilience and ability to change. Free will functions only when we are aware of the choices we truly have. Traumatic events can influence and distort how a person perceives and interprets meaning, potentially causing their behaviors and routines to follow harmful, unconscious patterns.

The uncertainty principle means no universal formula for predicting how each person will respond to trauma, as everyone reacts uniquely. This is the beauty—and the duty—of one's free will. This motif of how one chooses to respond constitutes the inherent uniqueness of the core self. Unfortunately, such inherent uniqueness and resilience may be ignored and overlooked in the smoke and mirrors of life-altering synchronization. This is not to say that the probability of how human behavior may be expressed has no basis in principle or design. Instead, the uniqueness inherent in each person can rise above their biology, which is the "nature" of their biology.

Uncertainty can foster creative, moment-to-moment innovations of expansive, epigenetic motifs. Unwitting traumatic synchronization entrainments constrain innovative expansion motifs, supplanting them with motifs shadowed in distortion.

The goodness and badness of behavior are always personal choices, but they never occur in isolation and can be influenced by context more than we often realize. The sum and formation of each person's self-awareness are shaped by and shape the synchronization of context. In other words, we are responsible for exercising the epigenetic muscle of our character development. We do this by grappling with and engaging in the vortex of context synchronization. It is our subjective interpretation, which is our unique motif of self at work. For better or worse, it can unknowingly influence our lifestyle (Adler, 1954). Struggling with good and evil is resistance training that strengthens our unique wholeness, epigenetic selfhood. It reflects the level or position where we move ethically, morally, and spiritually. This process is influenced by, and influences, the wide range of inner and outer contextual variables operating in our lives.

The Address of Self: Contextual Coordinates of Location in Space-time sending a letter to someone's home address requires writing important details specifying their name, house number, street name, and so on, as well as confirming that the address is up to date. Similarly, locating a person's core self—their "psychological" address—involves tracking dimensions of place and time, particularly concerning the "inner birth" of core consciousness, from the moment one becomes self-aware.

Tracking or delineating the motif of one's evolutionary journey— benchmarking life-altering events and nodal points of change—reveals where one's consciousness resides in the present. A person's current core consciousness is shown by how effectively their central theme responds to present challenges. How much has your core sense of self developed in response to current challenges? To what degree has the synchronization of these challenges compromised the formative consciousness of one's core self-motif?

Such a degree reflects hidden or compromised aspects of one's core self-motif. It may reveal the impact of negative, life-altering experiences embedded in a person's journey. The interaction of contextual variables during phases of entrainment shapes key traits of a person's core consciousness over time. A person's temperaments and dispositions can be influenced in many ways by these interactions with contextual factors. Additionally, there is always the "inner context" or "inner space," which involves our beliefs, interpretations, and subjective experiences, all of which contribute to the overall synchronization of our context.

How we synchronize and entrain with current psychosocial events—regarding work, love, friendship, etc.—can greatly influence our quality of life. The moral and ethical focus of a person's motives at any given moment is shaped by selective triggering events that generate recycling entrainment.

For example, consider a child who suffers physical abuse from a family member, which persists over time and contributes to borderline personality disorders in later self-development stages. In that case, their "address" is the totality of their entrainment. There may be a tendency to entrain with abusive, anger-provoking, or abandoning experiences, recycling previous triggering patterns. This can lead to splitting people and events into black-and-white categories—good or bad—and can synchronize with contextual variables in ways that sustain, attract, and entrain ongoing life-changing experiences.

This may manifest as difficulties in forming or maintaining relationships, changes in self-identity, involvement in higher-risk relationships, symptoms of depression, shifts in thought processes, and tendencies toward self-destructive behaviors. In short, it's a life-altering experience likely to recur. The development of goodness or badness (the Dr. Jekyll or Mr. Hyde split in identity) creates a contextual recipe for what might be called the perfect storm. When combined with current triggering events and exploitative external environments, maladaptive internal alignments can lead to a perfect storm of disastrous, life-altering experiences.

If we treat each person with kindness, love, and empathetic respect, we can expect that the capacity for goodness will be prioritized in an adult's lifestyle. However, no matter how perfect one tries to be in parenting during formative years, inadequate consequences for misbehavior, value conflicts, or a lack of understanding can persist in some families. Even with ideal parenting, triggering events and exploitative environments continuously challenge tendencies toward negativity.

Each child has a unique signature of temperament and disposition, seeking to express itself adaptively throughout life. However, human beings will, despite their best efforts, operate with faulty logic (Adler, 1954) that can remain hidden—the birth of Mr. Hyde festering like an open wound for years in the child's life. Themes such as power, revenge, and feelings of inadequacy may influence work, relationships, personal growth, and spiritual development.

Therefore, the inherent limitations of human reasoning can make people vulnerable to manipulation by unclear external influences. Goodness and evil result from formative, developmental experiences. People are rarely born inherently evil or as angels. If goodness — caring about oneself and others' rights — can be developed during childhood, then the same applies to bad behavior or evil (acting on desires without considering others' rights).

Entrainment of goodness is like building muscle, where children learn to choose ethical and moral actions over immediate gratification or harming themselves or others. Meaningful and purposeful acts of goodness can become a standard to strive for. However, the dark side, Mr. Hyde, lurks within us to varying degrees, causing dissonance, turmoil, disturbances, and feelings of resentment, guilt, powerlessness, depression, and potential for mindless rage.

Seeking others to blame, acting out in torture, and persecuting others become outlets for the day. They create the illusion that some twisted sense of justice is being served by punishing a dehumanized "other." The hidden darkness of mistaken logic and schemas harbors past and present wounds and transgressions, seeking retribution as "just desserts." We develop aspects of goodness, badness, and unattractive behaviors, usually within normal limits. However, because we have not fully evolved and cleansed what hides within us, we remain vulnerable to being pushed too far, tempted too much, and feeding unhealthy fantasies, addictions, and impulsive needs for gratification, regardless of consequences.

Even without being sociopaths or psychopaths, we can still commit harmful acts. To start a fire, three things are needed: oxygen, fuel, and a spark. Similarly, for evil behavior to happen, there must be: 1) indulgence in self-gratification or perceived self-preservation, 2) a space or setting to act out planned behaviors that harm oneself or others, and 3) some provocative energy to reach a critical point or threshold.

All these factors will be mitigated by the degree to which the individual is formatively developed and entrained with goodness for its own sake.

We are always responsible for some level of formative development, and we must strengthen this muscle of morality and ethics to the degree we are capable.

Social science and leadership studies show how role models—or their absence—affect the conditions that lead to bad or evil behavior. Research indicates that normally decent people can be strongly influenced to act in ways that go against their usual sense of goodness and propriety. Situational factors, such as seeming to approve of abusiveness or lacking structure, can bring out the worst in them. This worst includes abuse, punitiveness, hostility, and the potential for murderous rage.

Consider the Abu Ghraib Prison near Baghdad, Iraq. American soldiers abused and humiliated prisoners and were later convicted (e.g., Chip Frederick) for their crimes. While these soldiers may not have had perfect childhoods, they were not inherently evil monsters. Instead, they were put in uncontrollable positions of unchecked power over prisoners whom they perceived as dehumanized. This psychosocial context—enabled by military conditions—brought out the worst of human tendencies and a desire for power.

Studies conducted decades ago at Stanford University discovered similar tendencies in relatively good people, showing their capability to impose cruel, overpowering behavior on those in dependent, vulnerable conditions.

Indeed, leading good people into bad behavior can be seen as an example of a bad experience happening to a good person.

Consider that a "good person" is a normal, non-pathological individual. It does not mean a highly self-actualized, high-functioning human being.

While no one is entirely immune to psycho-social conditions, there are thresholds of transformative, ethical consciousness where maturing mastery of moral and emotional intelligence can better resist such entrainments.

One example of such high-functioning synchronization of consciousness is a hero like John McCain during the Vietnam War, who chose to stay with his fellow prisoners of war rather than return home without them.

Everyone has a mix of strengths, weaknesses, and untapped potential. This can make us vulnerable to syncing with the prevailing psycho-social conditions around us. Some researchers (Zimbardo, 2007) have compared good people to good apples in a bad barrel (i.e., social or military conditions). It's also important to remember that there is always some imperfect, underdeveloped part of the apple that can resonate and align with the bad barrel.

We are not robots, wholly controlled by social conditions, but we are also not invulnerable to them. We have already been in many barrels long before encountering the "Abu Ghraib" in our lives. The fact that good people do bad things is a consequence of bad things happening to good people. Unintentional conformity is a psycho-social and cultural reality that must be addressed and controlled. Even the researchers who design such inhumane experiments—or those who create military training environments—are themselves like apples in barrels, creating more bad barrels into which more good apples will be entrained.

While the entire social context is greater than the sum of its individuals, each person—composed of their selective, interactive experiences—can influence the others around them. There's an old saying: "If you meet the Buddha on the road, kill him." while this may sound sinister, it serves as a warning that a single leader or expert can mislead and deceive the whole. Each of us holds a complete self within. There are many parts or potentials inside each person—the good, the bad, the ugly, the lover, the hero, the villain, and others—shaped by countless selective interactions with complex psychosocial conditions throughout life.

The degree to which everyone matures in moral will—through self-responsibility for growing up—raises their threshold for self-correcting behavior under harsh conditions.

Countless reports describe acts of loving, altruistic behavior from people across the country helping victims of Hurricane Katrina. However, there are also thousands of fraudulent claims—some estimates as high as $200 million—where individuals tried to exploit others' tragedies. Dr. Lynne Tan, M.D., a psychiatrist from Montefiore Medical Center, explained how people, during chaos and a lack of accountability, can act selfishly. It is like leaving one's house wide open for the taking.

In situations like disorder, selfishness, or blind obedience to authority, people may be pushed toward negative or hostile actions. Understanding and gaining proficiency in our entrainments can be a valuable process. Especially if "being average" makes one dangerously vulnerable to such exploitative entertainment.

It is important to distinguish evil from simply something bad happening. Experiencing job loss or a vehicle malfunction relates to outcomes and performance. Unless malevolent entities cause such things, they can be considered unfortunate events—perhaps inevitable—but not evil in and of themselves.

Evil here is seen as the egotistical drive to do—and keep doing—whatever one desires, no matter how it affects others, because it only benefits oneself. This also includes actions framed as good intentions, like claiming war saves lives, regardless of whether that claim is true. Hidden motives (Mr. Hyde's motif) behind such justifications might include revenge, power, sadomasochistic pleasure, or simple self-gratification disguised as fundamentalism.

Harmful actions can come not only from violent or destructive behavior but also from conflicts between positive intentions, such as different religious beliefs in the 21st century. Is evil behind this? Or is there another principle at work in our lives beyond moral values? In other words, is there truly a Lucifer Principle? Before answering such broad, complex questions, let us first address more

Local self-related issues include self-deception and dishonesty.

Why We Lie

A researcher, Dr. Thompson (2007), explained how deception with malicious intent can be detected through the brain's Machiavellian modules. People naturally sense what others are doing using built-in mechanisms for detecting deceit. What might seem like mysterious "mind-reading" or psychic ability is a function of neurological modules—templates or cell assemblies—that help us "know" (even unconsciously) whether our interactions are authentic or deceptive.

When we make eye contact or communicate verbally, these Machiavellian brain modules can eerily detect unspoken information. For example, individuals undergoing psychoanalysis are often able to deduce specific personal characteristics of the therapist, despite the absence of direct disclosure and facing away from the analyst during sessions.

This human ability to match, mirror, and synchronize unconsciously can lead us to unexpected, even shocking, actions in relationships. People often share deep, personal truths with complete strangers—on trains, planes, or walking down the street—simply because of a nod, an "uh-huh," or a receptive gaze. If these strangers happen to be unscrupulous sociopaths or predators, the danger increases.

Paradoxically, these same Machiavellian modules that help us detect deception also make us vulnerable to being detected. Like radar, we can observe and assess how we monitor potential threats. In quantum physics terms, we become part of what we observe. The way we observe and frame an experience helps shape its nature. We are subjectively involved in what we observe.

Our experience of the world—both external and internal—interacts reciprocally, pulling us into itself through entrainment. It's like fishing for sharks, only to be dragged into the water with the catch. There is no strict "doer" or "receiver"—only the mutuality of entrainment.

This creates a chaotic complexity that, if not interrupted, can evolve into a critical mass with life-altering effects. Quantum-level transformations can occur at such junctures. Being in the wrong place at the wrong time—like the World Trade Center on 9/11—may sometimes be an accident waiting (or preparing) to happen.

Despite multiple warnings from intelligence sources, the 1993 WTC bombing, and known terrorist threats (including from Osama bin Laden), a critical mass was reached without a conscious, coordinated response. Our unconscious Machiavellian modules failed to emerge quickly with the clarity needed to connect the dots.

However, significant entrainment effects do not always appear on a global level. They can happen during common moments in daily life. Many relationships can fall into destructive patterns of enmeshment. Caring deeply for someone—mainly to prevent their suicide—can become risky for both people involved. I recall a situation where a man, trying to help his female friend avoid suicidal thoughts, became so emotionally connected that he fell in love with her. As she improved and gained independence, he became more demanding, controlling, and needy. The pressure he placed on himself and her grew so intense that both ended up in the hospital. His attempt to save her almost destroyed both of them.

Learning to be honest and open in our interactions with others requires a fearless moral inventory. As the saying goes: To thine own self be true, and it must follow, as the night the day, thou canst not then be false to any man.

Motif and the Lucifer Principle

The Lucifer Principle suggests that violence and aggression in human nature promote order and complexity in life. From the smallest microbes to massive social revolutions like China's Cultural Revolution, evolution seems to necessitate competition among organized entities to develop more intricate systems (Bloom, 1995).

Bloom draws from MacLean's (1973) concept of the triune brain— reptilian, mammalian, and neo-cortex—highlighting biological roots of aggression, war, and emotional group bonding. He suggests that collective human behavior (what he calls superorganisms) acts competitively and often violently to ensure the propagation of children, genes, and ultimately, group survival.

In addition to individual genes, Bloom identifies memes—cultural belief systems—as socially inherited blueprints similar to interpersonal "genes." He explains how belief systems such as Catholicism, Islam, Protestantism, communism, capitalism, rock and roll, and even the hippie movement compete for survival and dominance. Often, this competition is justified through ideologies that rationalize the mass destruction of those who are "different." For example, Bloom mentions how Muhammad reportedly taught that in the name of Allah, the world was divided into the faithful and the infidels, leading to holy wars marked by cruelty, devastation, and death.

The Lucifer Principle, as outlined by Bloom, is founded upon five core concepts:

1. Self-organizing entities (replicators): These include genes and production systems that create outputs capable of making others obsolete.
2. Superorganisms: Collective entities made of individual components.
3. Memes: Self-replicating clusters of beliefs that shape civilizations and cultures.
4. The Neural Net: A web-like collective consciousness that influences emotions and behavior.
5. Pecking Order: Dominant hierarchies in both animal and human societies.

Throughout his work, Bloom depicts nature as a battleground where life forms—whether chemical, microbial, human, or cultural—struggle upward toward higher levels of organization, often via violence and destruction. He even explores how biological factors like hormone regulation and the immune system support such evolutionary battles.

He insightfully highlights that evolution is fundamentally about developing increasingly complex order. At both the genetic (biological) and memetic (cultural) levels, self-organization and propagation are at play. Bloom focuses on how individuals fit into larger systems— superorganisms, hierarchies, neural networks—but in doing so, he overlooks critical differences between people and cells within an organism.

For example, while he acknowledges that living cells serve unique roles within an organism, he also fails to grasp the depth of individual human complexity fully. Unlike cells, people are not fixed components. Everyone has a distinct ability to shape themselves. Joining a group activates certain aspects of this motif while others lie dormant. Just like germ cells have the potential to become many things, so too do individuals. When a person becomes overly specialized or confined, it can lead to stagnation and even spiritual or psychological death.

Humans are not easily fitted into fixed group roles like parts of a machine. Our individuality requires us to engage flexibly with various systems, groups, and affiliations. For example, a rock band's drummer might also be a practicing Catholic, a single parent, and a spiritual seeker. How can such a person ever fully belong to just one group? It's like solving a Rubik's Cube—finding balance across faces, colors, and axes. However, this complexity remains modest when contrasted with the distinctive characteristics inherent in each individual soul.

Indeed, evil exists. But it is not inherent. It appears when an individual's motivation is tightly suppressed—reduced to mindless, repetitive conformity that erases personal consciousness. Evolution favors complexity, integration, and growth. Variations and mutations—whether genetic, cultural, or spiritual—drive evolution forward. A child is created from the combination of two distinct genetic sequences. When difference is excluded or suppressed, stagnation and death quickly follow. Look at what happens in breeding and genetic uniformity.

The same applies to culture. Memes that allow offshoots, branches, and innovations last much longer than those that are rigid. America's multiculturalism is a strength that stands in stark contrast to the dullness of closed, totalitarian societies. Evolution depends not on static forms but on formativeness—a dynamic, evolving potential within individuals, cultures, and the universe itself.

Formativeness is not fixed—it grows, reshapes, and renews. Each person's motif is inherently formative in its unique expression and the differentiated roots from which it emerges. The future unfolds from today's motif, evolving as time passes into tomorrow's complexity. Even in violence and war, what we often interpret as evil may reflect primitive limitations in our ordering systems.

After the Big Bang, only particles and atoms existed—primitive structures with few options for ordering. As complexity increased, atoms combined into molecules and elements, allowing for an exponential growth in creative potential. As formativeness expands, so does our sacred potential for spiritual evolution and higher consciousness. In this light, evolution may even favor spiritual capacity as a biological advantage.

Violence and aggression are simply basic tools—primitive ones. Cooperation, synchronicity, and conscious fusion provide richer opportunities for creating refined, highly organized superorganisms. Interestingly, researchers (Ramachandran & Blakeslee, 1998) have identified a region in the left temporal lobe, sometimes called the God-spot, which appears to mediate spiritual experiences. When stimulated, especially in conjunction with limbic and frontal cortex areas, it triggers kindling, forming new neural pathways through which spiritual experiences may resonate.

The soul's spiritual blueprint is woven into these psychoneurological patterns. As people deepen their sense of individuality and cultures embrace diversity, the need for competition and violence might decrease. Michelangelo once said that he carved away the marble to reveal the statue of David inside. According to Bloom's framework, this might be seen as destruction, even evil. But for the artist, it was an act of sacred unveiling.

When Native Americans hunted buffalo, they used every part of the animal out of respect for the sacredness of life. There was no waste, no competition, just a spiritual act of coexistence.

So it is with motifs: nothing is wasted. No part of us is without meaning or purpose. Motifs unfold holistically, forming connections across levels, groups, and dimensions. Like a zygote becoming a body, we grow not by competing with ourselves or others, but by cooperating, allowing each part to become what it is meant to be.

Complexity and intricacy are not signs of chaos but marks of a sacred, involutional movement—a deepening spiral of meaning within life itself.

Motif vs. Fixation

When genes or memes become fixated and rigid, formative evolution— both individually and globally—is thwarted. At such points, the spirit or spirituality embedded in religious or cultural ideals can become obsessive and perverted, manifesting as harsh and cruel violence.

Psychopathology, in this sense, is the loss of formativeness in evolutionary motifs. This is the real evil: not darkness as an external force, but the internal collapse of growth and possibility into reified rigidity. The inherently formative nature of the universe—an ordering, evolving system—seeks to transcend and transform such fixations.

Cultural memes, when distorted or taken out of context, can turn into harmful obsessions and warped perceptions. Adolf Hitler's rise to power in Nazi Germany was driven by twisted memes of supremacy, targeting the vulnerabilities of an oppressed and impoverished nation. His delusional obsession with superiority led to the synchronized destruction of both himself and his nation.

In complexity theory (Hackett, 2007), the dynamics that allow an idea, culture, or individual to rise to prominence can also trap them later, hindering further growth. In simple terms, a cultural movement (like the 1960s revolution) may form in response to specific needs (such as the Vietnam War draft). However, once that situation changes, the original structure can become outdated. When the draft ended, so did the driving force behind the revolution. If the movement extends beyond its initial stage and becomes rigid, reified, and inflexible, it might eventually act as a tool of repression.

Like a cancerous evil, it mutates into an entraining addiction, devouring the very vitality it once sought to empower. Synchronization turns into entrancement. This entrancement of fixation has given rise to global phenomena such as fundamentalist terrorism (e.g., Islamic extremism and the attacks of 9/11). But it can also unfold in smaller, more personal contexts—such as in our schools, communities, and neighborhoods.

The Virginia Tech massacre, in which 33 lives were lost (32 murders and the suicide of the perpetrator), illustrates the dangerous potential of suppressed rage exploding in an unsuspecting environment. The tragedy was worsened by numerous ignored warning signs over the span of a year. CNN reported that the shooter had been referred for treatment, separated from at least one class due to extreme content in his writing, and described by roommates as socially withdrawn and verbally uncommunicative.

The video manifesto he sent to NBC revealed a terrifying level of rage and vengeful hostility. Although a clinical assessment would be necessary for certainty, his behavior appeared psychotic—possibly paranoid and delusional. His language reflected literal, fundamentalistic thinking. He seemed to believe that well-off students had insulted or rejected him, and that such perceived transgressions demanded revenge. Even though no documented act of rejection occurred, he interpreted their status alone as justification for violence.

This dangerous potential for psychotic-like, paranoid projections— directed at others solely because of their psychosocial attributes—is eerily reminiscent of the thinking behind the 9/11 attacks. Both are examples of how evil can emerge through entrained entrancements.

The tragic irony is that simple, innocent acts—pursuing education, enjoying a certain lifestyle, participating in a campus community—can unwittingly synchronize individuals with an untreated, unstable person entrained toward destruction. Without knowing it, we may become part of the very entrainment that culminates in evil.

We often believe that minding our own business keeps us safe. But this illusion of separation and personal safety is misleading. In truth, our very existence is interwoven with others in a de facto interconnectedness. We are continually being enjoined into countless potential entrainments— whether we realize it or not.

As technology develops, patterns of unconscious synchronization become increasingly complex and progress rapidly. The potential for unforeseen and dangerous synchronizations intensifies. Thus, maturing our awareness of motif—our core consciousness and spiritual patterning—becomes vital. Doing so offers a multidimensional, mosaic-like map of our possible entrainments.

Even in the most ordinary moments—walking down the street, shopping for groceries, chatting with a passerby—we must remain attuned to the energies we sync with. As the following story illustrates, the subtle act of entrainment is always happening.

It has been said that a thousand-mile journey—such as recovery often feels like—begins with a single step. In this case, it began with cherries.

One evening, I went out for a quick "trip" (which turned out to be exactly that) to the local grocery store. I was in search of a few fruits for dessert and briskly passed the cherry stand on my way to pick up some red seedless grapes and strawberries. As I walked by, I noticed a man sorting through the cherries. Something about the situation—and the man— made me feel uncomfortable. A sense of subtle discomfort was present in the environment.

So, what did I do? I went out of my way to explore it. I am uncertain of the reason; however, it may have appeared to present a challenging, outstanding issue that required resolution. Did curiosity kill the cat? I didn't even want cherries. Still, I walked over to the cherry stand, examined a few pieces of fruit, thought the whole thing was silly, and returned to my original goal.

Leaving the fruit section, I had to walk past the cherry stand again. As I approached, I saw the same man again—this time in the aisle next to the cherries, walking toward me. As we passed, I suddenly felt my feet slip. I lost my footing and slipped on a pile of cherries that had been scattered across the floor.

My focus on the man, my unease, and the distraction of the situation pulled me out of present awareness. I lost complete control of my balance. I did what can only be described as a "lovely ballet spin in the air," then landed—hard—right into the pile of cherries. I sprained both hands trying to break the fall, suffered whiplash from the jolt to my neck, and bruised my right knee.

I walked to the store manager's counter, where they applied ice to my hands and interviewed me for a customer incident report. As the manager was finishing the report, I saw the man at the checkout line. I waved him over and asked if he'd be willing to act as a witness. I could see the cherries sticking out of his bag.

He agreed, wrote out a statement about my fall, signed and dated it, and included a phone number. He commented that he had seen the cherries on the floor and knew it was a hazard. Then, with a wry, condescending tone, he added, "Better you than me." And just like that, I realized what had drawn my attention to him from the start—his attitude. Somehow, I had sensed something disdainful, and I had felt compelled to test it out, to confront it. Later, when the insurance company tried to reach him to verify the event, they discovered his identifying information was invalid.

Had I ignored the whole thing—had I simply noticed the moment without fixation or preoccupation—would I still have fallen? Would I now be in physical therapy, which was the direct result of the incident? Why didn't I just let it go? Why did I feel the need to test out an ambiguous, uneasy situation—one that ultimately proved itself to be negative and disdainful?

Was this an entrainment with the shadow side of human character? Was it about ego? Insecurity? Is there a requirement to provide evidence or substantiation? Was it evil entraining evil? Or was it the universe—God, my unconscious, synchronicity—conspiring to teach me a lesson by landing me, quite literally, in a pile of cherries? Certainly, it was educational.

There were, perhaps, many lessons buried within this strange and slightly comical misadventure.

These are just a few of the questions we ask ourselves in the wake of unfortunate events—no matter how trivial or how life-altering. (What if the fall had been worse? What if I'd been permanently injured?) From a professional standpoint, these instances can be regarded as particular examples illustrating the fundamental conditions necessary for any event to materialize.

Whether it's rainy weather in Spain, the Boston Red Sox winning the World Series, stubbing your toe, getting out of bed, or changing the oil in your car, all events require certain conditions to be met. The right balance of variables—psychological, physical, circumstantial—must align or the event won't occur.

For example, performing an oil change on your vehicle requires both the appropriate motivation and necessary resources. Without both, nothing changes. Perhaps in some alternate universe, the car changes its oil. Maybe a genie appears, or a green fairy does it for you. Alternatively, maybe someone else gets tired of waiting and does it themselves.

This reminds me of the classic joke: How many therapists does it take to change a light bulb? Only one, but the light bulb has to want to change. The same is true for us. Events happen when the conditions for change are just right in the proper amount. Ironically, the more we connect with our true self, the easier this becomes.

When unfortunate events occur, we tend to seek specific causes. People often seek to assign responsibility to an individual or factor. We assume a designated "doer" or ego is behind the wheel. We default to black-and-white thinking: either something external controls us, or we are entirely in control.

This attribution of causality to the ego—the "I" that makes things happen—can obscure the more profound truth: our decisions and actions are often co-shaped by internal and external forces we don't fully understand. What, then, influences our "controlling ego"?

All-or-nothing thinking can blind us to the resonance between inner and outer forces—how they synchronize into life-altering events. Their synergy transcends free will or fate, creating a unique fusion—a kind of existential "marriage" of influences.

In this way, the selective synthesis of self and circumstance becomes more than the sum of its parts. Once formed, this life-altering synchronization self-assembles and self-perpetuates. In such a context, the debate between free will and determinism becomes a moot point. Change only becomes possible through transformation of the synchronization itself.

Science has revealed so many factors that shape us—brain chemistry, DNA, socio-cultural pressures—that it borders on delusional to believe that our ego alone governs our fate. However, history shows us examples of individuals who transcended even the most embedded limitations— Victor Frankl, Lance Armstrong, and countless others—who transformed oppressive circumstances through sheer courage and spiritual depth.

The next chapter will explore such cases. The discussion will demonstrate that concepts such as control, destiny, and determinism are best understood not as objective external realities, but as internal narratives shaped by context and perspective.

So ask yourself: What are the conditions required to change your car's oil? What specific agent or internal force initiates the act? What are the supporting elements—money, time, space, motivation? What influences you—mileage, habit, guilt, weather, your spouse? Furthermore, how much of it is you, and how much is everything else?

Even self-organizing systems—fractals, living organisms—need an initiating spark. In cloning, scientists must apply an electric pulse to set the process in motion. So, what sparks us? What gets us to stop procrastinating, to act, to change? Who or what holds ultimate authority in this context?

Of course, sometimes strange things happen. Someone might mistake your car for theirs, change the oil for you. Or your car breaks down, gets towed, and a stranger repairs it. Causes—whether singular or a complex web of factors—synchronize into a threshold-crossing moment, like lightning striking during drought, sparking a forest fire.

These synchronizations manifest as physical events. Just because we don't see them doesn't mean they aren't there. Perhaps they're like dark matter or dark energy—unseen forces shaping the visible world.

Like the tip of an iceberg, we only perceive the surface. The real depth lies below. And perhaps it's there, in the silent synchronizations beneath awareness, that true power resides.

We often search for a simple cause to explain pain. What was the underlying factor that led to this cause? What sparked the lightning? And what caused that spark?

What's the cause of all causes?

And what caused me to write this?

Statistical probability may bring us to 99% certainty—but never 100%. The more we seek a single cause, the more a-causality reveals itself. That, at least, was Jung's (1962) contention.

Science (as do many of us) works within given sets of conditions, environments, and presuppositions. If I'm speeding on an icy road, I have a high probability of losing traction and control of my vehicle's direction. Assigning cause and effect makes sense only when contextualized.

Life-altering experiences challenge our conventional wisdom of contextualization. These processes encompass a wide range of complex variables and require innovative approaches that challenge conventional perspectives. What if the weather is clear, the road smooth, and I'm driving responsibly—yet I end up upside down in a ditch? If there are no other cars near me, my vehicle is functioning properly, and I'm alert and sober, I'm at a loss to locate cause and effect.

While we may think we've covered all the "bases" in determining what could be affecting us, there is often more to any given experience than meets the "I." Such is the nature of life-altering experiences.

What entrainments have unwittingly resonated with me (or I with them) may lie far beyond my conscious comprehension. The process I believe I control expands in directions beyond my schema of expectations. My sense of self-efficacy is threatened. Without this internal sense of control, I feel vulnerable, chaotic, and victimized. Do I need therapy? An understanding of existentialism? Chaos training, flow, surrender, prayer—what?

There are causal dimensions to all experiences, but only when contextualized—through statistics or other frames of reference, constraints, and identified variables. Science and religion each strive to explain life's mysteries in their own ways. But beyond the causal dimensions of contextualized experience lie Life-Altering Experiences (L.A.E.): the a-causal mysteries of life.

So, what of my "war" with the cherries? Let us explore the alignment of just what conditions were required for these events to unfold. It may be suggested that what operates at one level of organization (e.g., physical laws of cause and effect) may metaphorically resonate in congruent ways at higher levels of complex organization. This concept calls into awareness the theme of holographic principles discussed earlier.

First, there had to be some attraction, draw, or stimulus—physical hunger and an ego agenda.

Second, there had to be action or response to this stimulus to reinforce it—walking toward the fruit stand, an increase in ego-driven adrenaline.

Third, the stimulus had to match or resonate with my being on dualistic levels—physical and psycho-physiological.

Fourth, there had to be an arena, a space and time—a stage—for these conditions to play themselves out.

Fifth, a detailed sequence of steps was required through which an escalating threshold or critical mass could be reached.

Sixth, there needed to be a climactic, cataclysmic event to culminate the experience—the cherry on top of the whipped-up dessert, if you will.

Seventh, there had to be reflection, recognition, and realization of the cascading crescendo of events to truly feel their impact.

Eighth, quiescence is required to reset the space-time frame and allow the process to repeat.

How do we answer the question of what caused my fall? The answer(s) come from multiple dimensions: my choosing to act on inner sensations, the existence of my inner life and associated senses, and external factors— like the number and type of people present, store conditions, and especially the slippery floor covered in cherries.

Do we consider it all just an "accidental" accident—one of those fluky things with no pattern or intention? Or do we go the other direction and claim destiny, fate, or divine providence? Could this dimension include evil or satanic entities just waiting—tempting me to "fall" from grace? (I certainly didn't fall with any grace or style!)

At the risk of "begging the question," am I just making something out of nothing? Now we approach a question that just might be answered. If all space contains non-zero energy, it represents unused potential for creation. The instant this energy is tapped, structured into some patterned design (motif), it ceases to be potential. It has transitioned from a state of non-existence, representing potential energy, to a manifested state characterized by coordinated energy forms corresponding to specific quantum gravitational wave frequencies. This dense space is known as matter.

Our human universe (psycho-physical-social/cultural field or matrix) also transforms nothing into something by applying potential energy, turning it into entrainments—manifest design patterns. This means we can always create something out of nothingness (no-thingness). If we make a big deal out of it, then it becomes one. What we allow ourselves to be drawn into becomes the unwitting big deal.

Based on earlier statements, the universe and everything within it experience movement, transformation, and change as interconnected systems with many possibilities and patterns. Statistics describe these patterns as combinations and permutations (groupings of numbers, with or without order, like telephone numbers). The number of possible combinations and permutations in our universe is so immense that algorithmic calculations are required to estimate a total.

My cherry fall was a unique, entrained arrangement of multidimensional variables, aligning themselves through a process of proportional selection—filtering people, places, and events through an organizing motif. Any number of scenarios (almost infinite) were possible. The outcome was carefully coordinated in all aspects, resulting in a seamless sequence that brought me to the grocery store floor.

While the outcome was completely unexpected (as life-altering experiences often are), the manifestation required synchronized holistic assembly from multidimensional sources—a motif—well before its occurrence.

Think about the simple act of turning on your car headlights. You need to believe the time and conditions are right for them to work. The electrical wiring and headlamps must function properly. If you have a passenger, they should not distract you, whether playfully or annoyingly. Your mental and physical states must also be in good shape to handle the "simple" act of turning them on.

You could keep listing the specific conditions needed, but what really stands out is a thematic motif that organizes these various resources. For example, if you're having what's commonly called a “bad hair day”—a cowlick, a jammed bathroom doorknob, a ringing phone just as you leave, and a garage door that won't stay closed—you might notice a pattern. Faulty functions surround you. This motif can, but doesn't always, match other events like your car breaking down or headlights refusing to turn on.

The causal factors are not the exclusive domain of psychological dynamics. They are, like all multidimensional sources, always present. While we will explore what specific causal factors may have generated this motif, for now it's important to emphasize: the synchronization of multidimensional sources is an entrainment—an assembled design pattern, or motif—that can thematically resonate for better or worse in your daily experience.

That thematic motif was operating when I did my “dance” on the grocer's floor. But don't take my word for it. Think for yourself.

Describe an event that happened to you today—whether ordinary or unexpected, a fluke or not. Be a creative observer. Is it possible to spot multiple instances of synchrony involving different people, places, and elements that were perfectly balanced—like a motif—such that any small change in one variable would have prevented the event from occurring? The “cause” was the presence of just-right conditions shaped by organizing motifs. When synchronized into entrainment, events can happen without an obvious cause or purpose. It is our collective creative consciousness that gives them meaning and purpose.

I recently attended a seminar on how entrepreneurs need to design business plans and cultivate specific, nurturing environments of networked resources. They were advised to seek a niche that fulfills a previously overlooked need in a product or service area (like fashion design for large-sized women that doesn't look like it's for large-sized women, "fat" chance of that! Just kidding). The point is: to build a successful business, as in anything in life, there must be awareness of how to synchronize a holistic assembly of related variables, precisely combined and sequenced in a proportionally balanced pattern.

As I said earlier, for any event in life to manifest, there must be an entrainment of assembled design patterns moving as one unified motif. If this is observed in business and science, as well as in discussions about environmental themes related to significant historical events (Parts I and II), it may also be relevant to transformative life experiences. Just because we don't see it coming doesn't mean it's not on its way—to a theater of operations near you!

So, what of the roles of evil, destiny, divine intervention, killer asteroids, and random audits by the I.R.S.? How do they factor into the precise, proportional balance of motif variables that manifest synchronized, life altering entrainments?

In seeking answers, it helps to remember that each of us is embedded in multiple layers and spheres of influence, what could be seen as a hierarchy of organizations. These include our own physiology and psychological lifestyle, our family of origin, present family systems, the communities we live in, our careers and coworkers, our sub-cultural and cultural identities (including religious and spiritual practices), and the broader regional, national, and global dynamics of identity, politics, and socioeconomics.

This general hierarchy reflects our human global collage, yet there are even more systems of hierarchical organization that imprint on us— geological, regional, and global weather systems, ecological systems involving other life forms, and cosmological systems of planets, galaxies, star formations, and perhaps even parallel universes.

Scientists tell us our universe is undergoing accelerating expansion from every point in space. Counterintuitively, there is no "center" to the universe. Since Copernicus revealed that Earth wasn't the center of the solar system, science has continued to decenter humankind from its imagined cosmic throne.

The mind-blowing number of influences in our lives seems to make chaos inevitable. Yet chaos theory suggests a hidden interconnectedness across all systems (e.g., the butterfly effect: a butterfly flaps its wings in South

America and alters weather in the American Midwest). Human beings can choose, though not exclusively, whom they engage with—who they work with, marry, or befriend. Still, many of us simply follow our patterns, life histories, and long-term habits. Where we live, whom we marry, and the careers we pursue are often heavily shaped by our family of origin, culture, psycho-social environment, and level of personal development.

All this said, the seeds of influence are often planted in our psychosocial programming—from early lessons about what it means to be a man, a woman, successful, or a representation of the "American ideal." We face age-appropriate behavioral challenges within the context of our psychosocial culture. For example, during adolescence, we are invested in making impressions, rebelling against authority, following trends, experimenting with identity, and striving for independence and "coolness." It's a stage characterized by intense self-discovery and separation from family systems, asserting autonomy while dealing with the pressures of responsibility. And of course, this includes experimentation (sex, drugs, and rock 'n roll).

Oddly, adolescence seems to recur throughout life—midlife crises, for example. These lifestyle phases are nodal points of change, where people are especially vulnerable to influence. At these moments, hierarchical layers of influence—from families, communities, hormones, psychological needs, and sociocultural pressures—exert entraining motifs that can culminate in life-altering experiences.

Teens and young adults may rush into starting families or marrying to make up for issues in their family background or due to peer pressure. This often leads to midlife crises, where 35-year-olds have affairs because they never experienced a true adolescence or the chance to explore themselves independently. Recovering lost youth seems to be a common pursuit nationwide.

Like Russian nesting dolls—boxes within boxes—we carry generational knowledge and trauma within ourselves, only to pass it forward into the next generation.

So, does this suggest divine intervention, evil temptations, or destiny? While I believe these forces can exist, I also think that the seeds of life-changing experiences are planted across many layers of influence, often years before they come to fruition, bitter as that fruit may be.

We can modify the blueprint at any point. If we are willing to reconfigure our current participation in life-changing patterns through intentional synchronization and new awareness, fresh motifs can emerge in this and future generations. The future is re-entering our consciousness now, even as we speak.

To illustrate how negative patterns can be planted years in advance—where evil and darkness are truly cultivated—consider post-World War I Germany. The German population faced high inflation, widespread unemployment, national humiliation, and deep despair. This created fertile ground for the roots of evil to take hold—what is Adolf Hitler, if not that?

Germany's cultural legacy once symbolized strength and vitality. Its loss of these qualities made it more vulnerable to Hitler's illusions of the Aryan Superman Race. Hitler manipulated the German mind by embedding a motif of racial superiority, tapping into a desperate consciousness searching for meaning, power, and blame.

Blaming the Jews became a psychological escape valve: "I'm not inferior; it is the Jews who are to blame for Germany's downfall." Ironically, historians note that what enabled this entrainment of evil was the humiliation Germany faced from the victorious powers—how their dignity was undermined after the war set the stage for Hitler's rise.

Was Hitler the Anti-Christ? Was he evil incarnate? While those answers are tempting, perhaps even more disturbing is how the world itself was entrained with the precursors to evil—how nations appeased Hitler by offering him land, which only emboldened his ambitions.

In 1948, Israel was declared a nation by the United Nations, a direct response to the Jewish people's need for protection from another Hitler. Fast forward 50 years, and we find ourselves in the ongoing Middle East crisis. Who could have predicted that German inflation and unemployment would resonate through decades into suicide bombings, biblical prophecies of Armageddon, and 9/11?

Chaos theory discusses the butterfly effect. But what about seeding motifs—narratives, beliefs, energies—that influence generations and entire cultures, leading to global, life-changing experiences?

If the seeds of evil (and goodness) can produce far-reaching effects, then this principle can also apply to each of our lives. Entrainment doesn't only happen among humans; it can also synchronize with non-human phenomena.

A-Causal Motif

The occurrence of life-altering experiences is an event that happens when past conditions have been proportionally (with precise balance of variables) synchronized through selective motifs. Suppose we realize that everything in the universe—people, places, things, time, space, the cosmos, all qualities of good, evil, etc.—is about formativeness and synchronizing motifs. What "causes and effects" each of our lives is pure design. It is the just-right conditions enabling its manifestation.

If the Devil wins and drags all of humankind into Hell, it will only happen if the right conditions supporting this design are allowed—partly by mankind—to exist. If good is to triumph and we all go to Heaven (well, maybe not everyone—but that's a design feature in itself), then the necessary conditions must be in place for this outcome to occur.

We are co-creating architects of our lifestyle designs. Problems and solutions in our life experience revolve around how we're designing and blueprinting the architecture of our personal, interpersonal, and transpersonal configurations. If something isn't flowing smoothly in some or all of our life areas (work, love, friendship, etc.), consider the design of your approach, beliefs, and strategies. There's an adage: If you change (rearrange) one grain of sand on the beach, then you've changed the order of the universe.

Motifs are limitless in their potential for formation—possible arrangements of configurations. Each potential configuration (known as a life form) seeks its own specific combinations and permutations to come into being. If the conditions were ideal for all to appear, they would.

According to Barbour (1999), some scientists propose that all possibilities and moments exist simultaneously. Our physical experience of relative time and space is an illusion created by selective wave functions in classical, linear physics. Similar to motion pictures, when still images are displayed in rapid succession under appropriate lighting conditions, they are perceived as continuous motion. This critical fusion frequency affects our perceptual and cognitive construction of the universe.

Barbour suggests that what comes into being and is physically experienced as concrete reality is the collapse of quantum wave potential into a fixed form or particle—a kind of critical flicker fusion frequency has been reached (the level of oscillation at which a rapidly flickering light appears constant). This collapse creates the physics of our universe with the illusion of an "arrow of time" having a beginning, middle, and end.

Think of watching a videotape movie: if you only have the "play" function available, the action can only move in a one-way arrow of time.

While we needn't delve deeply into quantum physics, such underpinnings suggest that under the just-right conditions, anything— person, place, or time—is not only possible but pressing to come into being. Could this pressing be the hallmark of evolution?

Life-altering experiences that seem to come "out of the blue"—where we misperceive emerging forms—suggest hidden, even inherent orders and degrees of formativeness. They are difficult to perceive and configure because they are embedded in multi-level dimensions.

Human beings are pattern-seeking creatures. We strive for familiar consistency in our lives. Some degree of predictability involving the cause and effect of our efforts—our careers, families, relationships—provides continuity in our evolving sense of self-identity. A predictability infused with the flexibility of formative possibility can sustain us through all stages of growth and development. Our brains crave patterning—a healthy balance of expectation and surprise—for stimulation, function, and the enrichment of higher faculties.

Symmetry, as evident in beauty, art, music, poetry, architecture, and even human physical features, exemplifies the presence of pattern and form. In relationships and jobs, we say things like, "It's a good match," or "Things just aren't clicking anymore." Alignment—physically, mentally, emotionally, behaviorally— requires patterns of symmetry, form, and design.

These unique patterns of alignment are a kind of motif—but only one form among many, each with its own signature.

The process of creating "forms" represents a central theme, emphasizing the interplay between similarity and innovation within a distinct, asymmetrical equilibrium.

What we call evil, a curse, a jinx, or "a cloud hanging over our heads" is a patterned set of motifs that, like all motifs, presses for the right conditions to manifest. Many times, what we call "evil" (excluding 9/11) is a form of positive disintegration—a break from old forms seeking renewal. When disintegration happens without transformation or supplanting, that's what we mean by evil.

Curiously, scientists have said that the shape and design of the universe today is a manifestation of the asymmetrical patterned motif created almost immediately after the Big Bang. The arrangement of stars, solar systems, and spiral galaxies exhibits asymmetrical patterns throughout the cosmos. Even the microwave background radiation—the residual from the titanic battle of matter and antimatter—is part of this. While they annihilated each other, the slightly greater amount of matter left behind created everything we see today.

The life-altering experience of that very beginning was that the game was rigged: there was slightly more matter than antimatter. Consequently, the result of the conflict between opposing forces was effectively predetermined. How could the good guys lose under that design motif?

Look into your own life. See how where you are today may reflect life orchestrating motifs set in motion from the moment of your personal "Big Bang" at birth. We are all born in the same universe. It doesn't matter what part of the design we get. The game is rigged for all of us to win—if we create the just-right conditions for our unique motifs (which keep pressing to be manifest) to activate themselves.

We are people, not gods. So we don't just create; we are also incorporated in other motif creations—multiple hierarchies of organization. The battle of formativeness among pattern-seeking humans wages vigorously at all levels. It also rages in non-human formativeness—ecology, cosmos, asteroids, comets, economics, disease, death, volcanoes, tsunamis, and more. We need to increase our consciousness of who is entraining whom, or what.

The distinction between 3½ pounds of brain tissue and 3½ pounds of stone lies in the potential for cognitive processes present in the human brain, which has yet to be fully measured. Life-altering experiences have a universal denominator for all of us: they challenge us to create—out of actual needs to survive and thrive—increasingly complex design motifs of formativeness. Moreover, it starts with our unique motif. Existence is continually evolving, creating itself.

Trauma, tragedy, and suffering are the sparks which motifate growth of self, of culture, of the universe, and beyond. What we consider flaws, challenges, weaknesses, and even resourcefulness are all about the emergence of a never-ending process of multifaceted, enriching formativeness. It's the familiar surprise that provokes transformation.

Motifs entrain our own perpetuation, demise, and—hopefully—rebirth. Evil, destiny, bad luck, slips, falls, accidents (large and small)—these are constant destabilizers pressing both human and non-human formativeness (planets as well as people) into being. We invent myths, legends, heroes, and their archrival villains—to keep our conscious minds busy, distracted by illusions of purpose and meaning. It helps us justify the, at times, insanity of existence (and all that came before or will come after). However, these processes are essential in creating conditions that support life.

From the personal stress of maintaining careers and relationships, to making mortgage payments, surviving illnesses, organ transplant needs, famine in Niger, and global terrorism, there exists a multitudinous, endless cycle of formative pressures pressing for manifestation.

Even the evil and egotistical selfishness of warring governmental administrations, who stockpile hunger-relieving grain and supplies away from famine-stricken regions, manifests formativeness for their existence. A brutal, ugly reality of the universe is that what enriches one motif's manifestation can destroy another. Whether it's a wanton desire to destroy or what in war is called "collateral damage," the killing of innocents—all of it reflects motifs. Evil, fate, accidents, even beneficial uncertainty (where not knowing the outcome may increase prosperity for some motifs, if not for all—these are the challenges of evolution.

This is not just my hypothesis. It is a matter of existence (and yes, interpretation). Those that survive and thrive do so through the evolution of formativeness. It is not at all clear that human beings are the centerpiece of the universe—but we may be one mighty quantum leap (albeit one of many) in the formative nature of the cosmos.

Why Do Some Suffer More?

It has been said that each of us has our own cross to bear. Why some suffer in one way—physical loss, pain, abandonment—while others endure emotional suffering, may be more a matter of the motif each of us is seeking to manifest, and how it attracts and interacts with multiple levels of reality.

The personal reality of our life experiences is intense, gripping, and fully engaging us in the here-and-now moment of conscious living. Whether it is pleasure, pain, or joy, fully living in the moment is where creation and formativeness manifest. Life-altering experiences often provoke intense fear, anxiety, and loss of control. A father's heart surgery, a missing teenager in Aruba, growing old and alone—all provoke reassessment and awaken consciousness about the nature of life and death and their potential meanings and ramifications.

The limbic system of the brain is aroused. Emotion infuses thought and action. Awareness of one's existence in the present moment serves both as an ongoing process and as the outcome of its pursuit. It is not about questions, answers, or dialogue. It is about generating and manifesting formativeness in complex cognition, Supreme Court discernments, and lifestyle mastery over fear and trepidation. The "purpose" of it all has less to do with some absolute answer to our lives, and more to do with the unique formativeness we manifest through the life of our motif. Heaven, Hell, God, and the Devil are all concerned with the manifestation of formativeness within domains that themselves are manifestations of formativeness. Whether we exist as individuals or as parts of larger formative systems, the evolution of formative systems remains fundamental.

Our contribution to this earthly plane could be measured by how we expand and enrich design motifs. Such a contribution goes beyond what is simply good for humanity, specific civilizations, cultures, or neighborhoods. We consume cattle and other life forms to survive—so they must die. That is the hierarchy of species and evolution. Stars burn out so their newly formed chemical compounds can nourish the next generation. Parents sacrifice their lives so their children can thrive. Are human beings, as a species, spiritual cattle being "fattened up" in the traumatic fires of life-altering experiences to forge new and complex materials of formative consciousness—preparing the way for the next species to evolve?

One of my old college professors once theorized that computers would become the next stage of human evolution. After all, what would the development of pure intelligence look like in the 21st century? Imagine the development of a computer chip—its ability to exponentially increase information processing in yearly cycles.

Is it evil, sin, or simply human impulsiveness—acting out our neediness—that tempts "good" people to cheat on taxes or spouses, manipulate others' altruism for personal gain, gamble, drink, use drugs, or commit crimes? When are we the perpetrator, the victim, or the rescuer? Don't we play many of these roles at different points in our lives? Understanding how we cycle through these roles and patterns can offer deep insights into the complexity of our personal stories, family origins, and lifestyles. It can also reveal motifs and their stages of development.

Psychosocial conditions provide insight into the internal factors that influence human behavior and development. However, humans can also de-contextualize and re-contextualize what they choose to sustain and create. The motif of motifs is one of epigenesis—shaping how we create our own development.

Many life-changing moments come from misalignment with our own unique pace and timing. Driving well above or below the speed limit on an expressway can have serious consequences, especially when large vehicles like 16-wheeler semitrucks are nearby. Whether you are a 20-something filmmaker or a seasoned lawyer with 40 years of experience, growth involves moving into the next personal stage of development. Trauma might be being asked to direct a full-length feature film with no prior experience, or mistakenly thinking that, after decades in legal practice, all cases are the same. Such assumptions can cause serious mistakes, possibly even leading to wrongful convictions of innocent people.

Whether raised in a dysfunctional family with abuse and addiction or scarred by multiple divorces, learning to love, trust, and surrender into a healthy relationship can itself be a traumatic, life-changing experience. The rock musical Jesus Christ Superstar once said, "It is easy to be hard." Learning to embrace tenderness when raised in a war zone—literal or emotional—is an act of fortitude during formative years, demonstrating some of the highest human qualities.

Many of the world's religions speak of sacrifice and giving one's life for another. When Christ died on the cross, the impact resonated worldwide. It wasn't just religious—it represented the highest form of influence that elevates humankind toward awakened consciousness. Although Christ said His kingdom is not of this world, His impact was—and continues to be—deeply rooted in this world of transformation. It signifies influence, not just for a person, place, religion, or philosophy, but for creation itself.

One of the fundamental principles of Western democracy is the idea of freedom of expression within a culturally diverse society. Formation—how structures are created, maintained, and evolve—is upheld by the rule of law. Democratic societies exemplify cultural motifs that encompass diverse design systems. The strength and impact of such societies rely on how much they permit and support various forms of expression. Similarly, the more developed, detailed, and organized a motif is in any network of motifs, the more influence and dominance it holds within that system.

A motif becomes more dominant when it incorporates multiple dimensions—ideas, emotions, behaviors, events, and even anticipated outcomes. These motifs start to "entrain" or influence those that are less developed. In other words, more complex and structured motifs exert a gravitational pull on others, shaping them. From Einstein's contributions to physics to Karl Rove's political strategy for President George W. Bush, those with the most developed formativeness tend to have the most influence and control.

This explains why people often become deeply affected when they are exposed to highly intense and organized life events or systems. These "life-altering experiences" reflect a vulnerability to the strong shaping effects of these powerful formative structures.

In one example, an American Jewish news commentator interviewed an American Islamic magazine writer. The commentator asked why moderate Islamic leaders had taken so long to oppose fundamentalist terrorism publicly. The writer explained that Islam lacks a centralized religious authority, such as a pope, and is more like Protestantism, with multiple decentralized leaders. The commentator responded, "So there is capitalism and democracy in your religion." This exchange revealed how the dominant democratic-capitalist framework influenced and shaped the Islamic writer's explanations and comparisons.

This principle applies across many fields: politics, religion, law, gender dynamics, and more. Whatever person, group, religion, or political entity holds the stronger, more complex, and interconnected motif can influence or "entrain" others around it. This idea is not limited to human interactions; non-human factors also have an impact. For example, geologists have traced humanity's evolution from Africa over the last 200,000 years, showing how environmental changes—climate, geology, and continental drift—have shaped evolutionary development.

Non-human forces also continue to shape human behavior today. The performance of our cars and computers, solar flares, variations in light, environmental toxicity, and natural disasters like floods or hurricanes can all affect our emotional states, beliefs, and behaviors. These occurrences can influence our understanding of timing, objectives, and daily habits. People living in areas like Florida or California are familiar with how the motifs of hurricanes, earthquakes, and droughts shape their daily lives.

Those with more developed and resilient internal motifs—structured beliefs, values, coping skills, and personal meaning—are better equipped to endure and adapt to these powerful external influences. The ability to preserve formativeness, rather than revert to rigid belief systems or fundamentalism, is key to resilience and growth.

Individuals who overcome significant challenges—whether physical illness, disability, trauma, or loss—often demonstrate high levels of resilience. Olympic athletes, for example, exemplify this by their ability to consistently perform at peak levels by connecting with their core selves and aligning with their most fundamental patterns of development.

Tragedies like the Oklahoma City bombing serve as stark examples of how life-changing events force survivors to reorganize and reshape their lives. The motives of the perpetrators might be called evil, irrational, or unjustifiable, but the impact of these acts is undeniable: they disrupt life, meaning, and values. Survivors are left to reconstruct their reality, establishing new patterns of understanding and purpose in response.

This reconfiguration usually shifts individuals from concrete concerns like survival or safety to more abstract values such as patriotism, love, or purpose. In this way, traumatic events can prompt growth by forcing people to develop new frameworks of understanding. However, "evil" itself can be viewed as a destructive motif that aims to challenge or undermine the completion of other motifs. It is not only harmful; it is deformative—opposing the development and integrity of cohesive structures.

The imbalance between matter and antimatter defined the beginning of the universe itself. There was slightly more matter—

allowing life to emerge. This suggests that life, at its core, is about what "matters." Our response to life-altering events reveals our values—what we believe truly matters.

In this context, darkness symbolizes what has not yet been integrated or aligned with freedom and diversity of design. It can be seen as a corrupted form of formativeness, one that resists cooperation and seeks control or destruction. These forces challenge us to grow, transforming what we value and how we organize our lives.

Madame Curie, for example, dedicated her life to extracting purity— distilling tons of material to isolate radium. While this was a scientific breakthrough, it also led to her death from cancer due to radiation exposure. Her story illustrates the double-edged nature of purity: the pursuit of truth or clarity can be noble, but it can also expose one to powerful, dangerous forces. Even noble discoveries can have unintended consequences if not handled within a balanced framework of responsibility.

Grief and loss, such as those experienced during the Oklahoma bombing or the 9/11 attacks, catalyze formative learning. The emotional and physical losses lead to new meaning-making processes—expressed through patriotism, remembrance, and the resolve to carry on. These abstract values are only meaningful because they are grounded in physical reality—the people and places we have lost. Matter (in the form of people, structures, and land) is transformed into energy (in the form of values, meaning, and purpose).

This raises the question: why do such extreme events need to happen to trigger profound growth? Maybe it's because of how our universe is created—both physically and metaphysically. Einstein's formula for converting matter into energy ($E=mc^2$) shows that small amounts of matter can release enormous energy. This idea also applies metaphorically, suggesting that minor changes in life can lead to significant psychological or spiritual development, especially if those changes are part of a well-developed personal motif.

Losing relationships, careers, youth, or health disrupts the balance of identity and meaning. Retirement, for example, can cause a loss of self-esteem, purpose, and daily routine. However, re-establishing these elements in new arrangements can lead to the development of new roles and identities. For instance, the collaboration between Bill Clinton and George Bush after their presidencies to assist tsunami victims shows how crossing political lines can create a new, more unified purpose.

While Einstein's physical constants stay fixed, human development does not. Each individual's life follows unique patterns, and the way people interpret experiences and pursue personal development varies from person to person. Every person's change results in varying degrees of loss, matter, and energy.

Motifs are never exact replicas of one another. Like fractals or tree rings, they are similar but never identical. Our personalities, memories, and relationships evolve in familiar but ever-changing ways. True individuality means constantly recreating ourselves in response to life's changes, within the shifting proportions of what matters.

The transformation of lost "matter" into "energized" formativeness represents the evolution of motifs into new life forms. This involves converting significant loss into life-generating qualities. The void created by loss energizes space and time, allowing for the creation of new motifs that are imbued with meaning. As we experience the absence of a loved one, we come to understand their impact and legacy, often carried forward by their offspring. Life is the preservation of motifs of formativeness. Through this process, physical loss is converted into energy, maintaining the essence of the motif in non-material, synergistic form—what could be called "spirit."

At a funeral, I heard a colleague's friend reflect on the timing of a loved one's passing. She said, "He always left just before a new project was about to begin." She remarked that while his physical body was gone, his essence lived on in a different form. Her words made me realize that she continued to resonate with him, extracting his essence beyond his physical presence.

This process of transforming physical loss into formative energies involves refining the essential qualities of a motif into purer forms. It resembles Madame Curie's quest for radium. She and her husband processed tons of raw earth ore, and one evening, in a moment of desperation, Madame Curie noticed a faint glow in her laboratory's darkness. What remained from the ore was a thin film of pure radium, only visible in total darkness. Similarly, in life's darkest moments, the shift from matter to formiveness reveals itself.

As we evolve, matter gradually transforms into a form that becomes more distinctive and less reliant on physical substance. The idea of rebirth after death, as described by poets and philosophers like Fritz Perls, involves turning physical structures into unique, less material-dependent designs. As we grow, our understanding and experiences need less physical material to grasp their reality.

Physicists like Rupert Sheldrake suggest that fields of energy, consciousness, and formative force exist beyond physical matter. We observe this in phenomena such as the phantom limb experience, where individuals who lose a limb may still feel sensations as if the limb is there. After the 9/11 tragedy, large white spotlights were used to mark the locations of the twin towers, symbolizing the preservation of the buildings' formative energy even after their destruction.

Similarly, the physics of black holes suggests that while the material form of a star may collapse, its information—its formativeness—is preserved. This illustrates that the motif of matter persists, even when the physical form is destroyed. Motif is the conversion of material losses (money, power, loved ones, etc.) into the essence or meaning that persists beyond the material form.

This transformation does not occur without struggle. Such transitions require significant conflict, hardship, and personal growth. Long-term recovery from addiction or overcoming other personal challenges often involves painful processes that reshape individuals and enable them to reemerge as more complex, evolved versions of themselves.

Transforming physical matter into productivity demands strong motivation, usually sparked by life-changing events that cause deep emotional or physical reactions. Our brains activate fight-or-flight responses, providing the energy needed to confront challenges. Overcoming these obstacles often results in remarkable achievements and personal growth.

Without life-threatening adversity, what motivates people to dedicate themselves to larger causes like war or societal struggles? They devote significant resources, including money, personal dedication, and effort, to efforts that represent abstract values such as patriotism, safety, and justice. As life goes on, we often move from focusing on material achievements to expressing our values through more abstract, qualitative things like creativity, beauty, and meaningful relationships.

Survivors of life-changing experiences often notice shifts in consciousness and values, resulting in a greater appreciation for life and a clearer understanding of what truly matters.

Being in the right or wrong place at a specific time can sometimes seem like pure coincidence. Only God can see such matters from an infinite perspective. Still, we can recognize the influences operating on levels below infinity. The capitalists appear as ignored warnings—such as the rise of anger among terrorists against America's capitalist monetary system, symbolized by the World Trade Center, and those in power, like stockbrokers, traders, and CEOs. The ability to manage multiple frames of reference, both simultaneously and sequentially, can be overwhelming, much like how parallel computers handle complex tasks. However, a lack of imagination and communication difficulties within complex intelligence centers can prevent us from spotting these threats.

Retrospective analysis, or "Monday morning quarterbacking," is sometimes used to review major events. During periods when the U.S. government was involved in complex political affairs, such as the impeachment proceedings concerning President Bill Clinton, attention and resources were diverted from addressing external security threats. This misalignment of priorities allowed entrainment to set us up for disaster. Suppose President Clinton had responded with the same urgency to the 1993 World Trade Center bombing or the 1998 intelligence reports regarding Osama bin Laden's terror potential. Might he have acted more preemptively? The shuttle incident in 2005 indicates that, despite progress in risk management, issues concerning cost-cutting and quality control at NASA remain present, although their impact has lessened. Although awareness of potential risks is important, entirely preventing issues necessitates eliminating detrimental entrainments from the formative process. In these moments, only enlightened action can truly make a difference.

Evil, in this context, is the force that seeks to prevent the full expression of unique motifs. As previously discussed, what is considered evil to one may be seen as holy by another—one man's meat is another man's poison. However, true evil goes beyond mere survival instincts. It distorts motifs, preventing their inherent uniqueness from coming to fruition. Therefore, we must be careful in identifying what is genuinely evil—it is not simply competition or conflict, but a desire for absolute power and control, which inevitably leads to self-destruction. History has shown this in the case of Adolf Hitler and his successors. From fundamentalism to anarchism, intolerance remains the root of all evil. When the ambitions of one culture or group violate the boundaries of another to the point of mutual destruction, it is a form of evil. The question remains: how close can we get to this threshold without crossing it? In today's globalized context, cross-border migration between Mexico and the United States and the export activities of corporations both contribute to the transmission of cultural motifs across regions.

Respect and wisdom must guide our interactions in these situations. Terrorism presents the alarming threat of future life-altering events. In the following chapter, we will explore ways to enhance our ability to adapt from multiple personal and global viewpoints. This will help us foresee, prevent, and steer choices toward more positive outcomes. If we don't deliberately re-educate ourselves away from the past, we risk repeating it. Time travel can be described as reordering events that remain within an ongoing present.

Life will prevail over evil. I believe that synchronizing tolerance for different motifs will emerge, but only when integrity and respect for formative processes become the highest priorities for everyone involved. Major disruptions may occur before this event. This will become clearer in the next chapter. The unwitting connections of life-altering experiences can catalyze tremendous changes in our formative evolution, not only in this domain of reality but also in others, including after death. However, such transformation may not occur without active engagement in the processes of life, death, and what follows. Developing empathy, rather than only sympathy, is necessary for personal growth. And in that process, one learns to appreciate meaning in the diversity of living and beyond. As Fritz Perls once said, "To suffer one's death and be reborn is not easy." Without the integrity of unique core motifs generating formative synchronizations, the challenges of the next evolutionary level will be formidable.

CHAPTER 9

REVEALING MYSTERIES OF LIFE ALTERATIONS

The Emperor's New Clothes, The Naked Ape, Beauty and the Beast

Comedienne Gilda Radner's character, Emily Litella from the popular late-night show Saturday Night Live, used to reflect, "It's always something," referring to the experience of being alive.

Ms. Radner later passed away from cancer. Life-changing experiences are the "Always Something" of life, occurring with sometimes uncanny timing and synchronistic patterns. Phrases such as "never get too comfortable" and "expect the unexpected" reflect a type of sentiment that suggests life's uncertainty and unpredictability.

If quantum theory correctly identifies existence as being based on the probability of possible outcomes rather than certainty, then our real-life experiences of there always being something to deal with could not be different. The universe's mysteries—shrouded by illusions (or delusions) of everyday cause and effect, and linear reality—reveal themselves in the chaotic beauty of uncertainty.

Embracing chaos and its many possibilities is, ultimately, an unavoidable realization. In many ways, this is a powerful source of formativeness, expressing itself in endless, evolutionary reconfigurations of design structures (motifs).

However, we can become so fixated on the illusion of cause-and-effect "button pushing" (we hit the remote and our TV is affected) that we fail to understand or appreciate the complex linkages involved and how they operate. This can keep us from being open to innovative possibilities for living our lives. It can even contribute to anxiety and depression by falsely believing that all is lost if our "buttons" don't work the way we believe they should.

Advancements in quality and living standards can boost our comfort zones and provide some predictability. However, every gain in modern technology also brings greater uncertainty. We live in a time of post-9/11 terrorism, constantly changing global political alliances, and new technological challenges arising from increasing worldwide complexity—what some call the "global village" dynamic.

At the same time, there is a need to identify effective resources that can address the complexities of global issues. From groundbreaking advances in stem cell research (controversial as it may be), to discovering the origins of the universe, to Mars missions, global warming, missing honeybees, and looming energy shortages, there is a constant effort to find greater order within the ever-growing chaos.

This pursuit might be like chasing the horizon: the more we learn and grow, the faster and larger the universe (and our world) appears to expand. Physicists have discovered that the universe is expanding at an accelerating rate. The Hubble constant, which measures the rate of this expansion, is currently estimated at about 70 kilometers per second per megaparsec. For every 3.26 million light-years a galaxy is away, the expansion rate increases by 70 kilometers per second because of the expanding space around that galaxy. The farther a galaxy is, the faster its space expands. The idea of rate differs from speed. While speed refers to distance traveled over time, rate involves a proportional comparison between different quantities. For example, according to the Hubble constant, the farther a galaxy is, the faster its rate of expansion, showing a proportional relationship. For each megaparsec, or 3.3 million light-years, or three billion trillion kilometers from Earth, the universe expands an additional 73.3 kilometers per second. To make things even more complicated, fluctuations in matter density during the early universe have further changed this proportional rate based on distance.

Additionally, space is not the only aspect of our universe that is expanding. Scientists and educators have also discovered that human knowledge is expanding at an accelerating rate, doubling itself exponentially in progressively shorter periods across all fields of human endeavor. Today's innovations are often obsolete within years, months, or even weeks.

Artificial intelligence could someday match human intelligence, making the distinction between "artificial" and "real" irrelevant.

It feels like an ongoing contest, trying to master life's experiences only to realize that no matter how much power humanity gains, "it is always something else". Life mastery remains just out of reach. As the poet Robert Browning wrote, "A man's reach should exceed his grasp, or what is a heaven for?"

How should we approach these ongoing mysteries and challenges? While each of us must answer that for ourselves, Socrates provides a hint. This Greek grandfather of all philosophers stated: "Know thyself, and thou canst not be false to anyone else."

Many life-altering experiences may result from an overall lack of in-depth understanding of one's core self or underlying motivations.

Remember that other "ancient" philosopher from the '80s, Buckaroo Banzai, who said, "Wherever you go, there you are." While this line came from a cult Hollywood film, it suggests that wherever we go in our life's journey, we'll find familiar life-altering entrainments we've previously synchronized with. Without re-synchronization, those previous patterns can reach a tipping point, creating chaotic alterations.

Willpower, faith, prayer, Vitamin C, mega doses, being a Republican, a rock superstar, or even "The Donald" (as in Trump) are all useless without a fearless, moral commitment to know thyself.

Our participation in an experience influences it; we shape our observations and are simultaneously shaped by them. Motifs naturally influence and are influenced by pure formative qualities, emerging as intentional configurations. Engaging in community service, giving rather than receiving, and being purpose-driven—all are admirable qualities. Examples of these formative qualities can be seen in language patterns across various dialects as well as DNA coding. Organizing shapes and designs of motifs provides an informational structure in the design and coding sequences of DNA and its peptides. Peptide sequences are systematically arranged based on defined patterns, which are determined by the structural motifs inherent in DNA. These peptides form an alphabet-like arrangement, conveying meaning and coded information derived from the organizing patterns of motifs, without which they would be indecipherable and dysfunctional. The fine-tuning of functional proteins generated by the DNA molecule is achieved by intricately arranged amino acids, with their placement guided by the design patterns of motifs. The precise placement of amino acids in the protein enables it to bend and shape itself into the correct pattern to function properly, creating cell structures for the organism. The protein molecule supports its primary role of building essential tissues in the organism. The sequence of amino acids combines in just the right permutations, allowing the protein to adopt a specific shape and form that becomes functional and instructs the cells of the body to produce meaningful biomolecular interactions involved in forming tissues, cell walls, bones, muscles, nerves, and more. Without the guiding structural format of DNA and its epigenetic sequencing, the likelihood of these combinations occurring by chance would be very low. This fine-tuning of specific functions and regulatory operations is directed by organizing motifs within the DNA itself, which require formative organizing functions for DNA to maintain its self-organizing capabilities within our bodies. The information is encoded in the structural design of organizing motifs, without which the coding patterns would be indecipherable. The very structure and nature of motifs constitute the information that organizes and facilitates fine-tuning at the mind-body and spiritual levels.

The geometric space between word meanings is quite similar across languages, such as in the comparison of the words Queen/princess and Mother/daughter. The formative space of these word pair similarities is asymmetrical, serving as motifs throughout languages. Such formative, geometric space configurations could act as a "Rosetta Stone," providing a universal template for translating and communicating between different languages and people. Consider the configurations of bioelectromagnetic studies, which reveal four body organs, tissues, and DNA emitting subtle fields of vibrational energies influenced by our thoughts, emotions, and behaviors. Our vibrational signature reflects our geometric ratios of shapes, designs, and motifs that may be healing or harmful to our health. We have crystalline structures in each cell that, when vibrating at various frequencies, alter the crystal's geometric shape and emit electromagnetic wave fields affecting our health, growing bone lattices, and helping to heal cancer cells. This can alter our DNA. Motifs are geometric formative design fields representing our Self-Signature vibrational field matrix, which can promote health and wellness. Generating a 528 Hertz vibrational frequency could be as effective a painkiller as any medicine. The world consists of vibrational patterns of harmony. By attuning to them with our unique signature motif with greater integrity, we can attain quality synchronicity in our health, sense of purpose, and intimacy of relationships.

However, our inner, subjective, unconscious motifs shape and influence our intentions, which in turn affect the quality of our experience. Consequently, our inner intentionality becomes shaped and formative. Motifs can be a double-edged sword of creation and destruction. This power requires us to stay true to ourselves, or we risk falsehood in our ability to shape reality. Effective development involves carefully refining artistic truth, aligning with one's identity, and encouraging unconditional self-acceptance. Resonating with one's self-signature of the inherent motif is what unconditional self-acceptance is all about!

Within the best qualities of you and me, the worst also exist. The good, the bad, and the ugly (like in the old Clint Eastwood movies) are still present even in the "holiest" of priests, rabbis, ministers, CEOs, healers, and others.

Someone from a recovery group once said that not knowing himself was like trying to clean his kitchen with dirty shoes. No matter how much he wanted to serve others or do "God's work," he realized that without addressing his issues, he could only help others as much as he could help himself stay clean and true to his Motif. These dynamics are interconnected and reinforce each other; helping others brings reciprocal benefits as well. But ignoring one's core self in the name of service risks unleashing the "beast" lurking behind the "beauty" of good intentions.

Hurricane Katrina devastated New Orleans, leaving millions homeless. The storm's destruction was reflected in the widespread looting among people—and in the failure of government agencies like FEMA.

There are at least two "battlefronts" in dealing with life-altering experiences (though certainly more exist): the chaos of the external world and the chaos of our internal world. Resonance from within our core is often activated, more than we realize, by something external.

A moth isn't to blame for being attracted to light, nor is the light bulb that fries it. The real "evil," if you want to call it that, is the ignorance that hides these attractions—pretending (like in The Emperor's New Clothes) that some noble truth is being revealed when it's just a lie and the emperor is naked.

Mature moths learn to avoid flying into deceptively beautiful yet deadly lights. Leaders in areas such as family, government, or work can sometimes spread misinformation by sharing persuasive but misleading stories that appeal to the public. If we do this, we risk trapping ourselves in a never-ending cycle of serious consequences.

Are we exercising free will — or just believing in the illusion of freedom, caught in the determinism of our habits and conditioning?

What internal chaos—doubt, uncertainty, or attraction to false authority—draws us toward the burning light?

Complicating our understanding of reality is the phenomenon of simultaneous multi-framed or multidimensionality! It refers to the ability to observe a single experience from multiple perspectives at the same time. A simple example is a figure-ground illusion: sometimes you see two faces, and other times a vase. When you perceive both at once, you may be moving toward unity with unconditional self-acceptance of this multiplicity!

In more nuanced situations, siblings may view the same parent very differently—whether as loving, neglectful, strict, or unfair.

What indicators can be used to determine if an individual is exhibiting rude behavior? Do we take it personally or see it as just part of their usual behavior? Do we tend to react the same way to everyone? Two people rushing to use a postage machine might see each other as rude, nervous, aggressive, or simply unaware.

Life events are like Rorschach inkblots. What and how you perceive is what you get. Building mental strength to see multiple interpretations of an event expands our creative ability to resynchronize, adjusting our responses based on feedback from real-world consequences.

This improves our ability to achieve healthier, life-changing outcomes. If we are ruled by doubt, insecurity, impulsiveness, trauma, or rage (from within or from others), we can easily be pulled into negativity.

The capacity to understand the diverse aspects of experience is dependent on both emotional and cognitive development, often referred to as emotional intelligence.

As we grow from childhood to adulthood, our interpretation of events changes. A 10-year-old boy losing a sibling will perceive that loss very differently than he would at age 60. We can revisit trauma later in life with greater understanding and integration.

A child who shows uneven lines at age six may perceive them all as the same length. As an adult, that same "child" reflects on the past and recognizes their unevenness. We "see" or perceive our timeframes with different perspectives as we mature, especially if we stay flexible or formative in our lifestyle.

This principle is fundamental to many forms of psychotherapy: healing early trauma through more accurate and formative reinterpretation. As we age, this ability improves—at least in theory. What we lose in physical agility, we can gain in wisdom.

Neuroscientific research supports this—many brain development programs for seniors aim to increase neural networks by exercising pattern recognition and flexibility in developing the formativeness of capacitation. This reflects a multi-framed, multi-formative universe.

There are at least 8 million people in Chicago. Each one carries their own values, careers, family structures, political views, and hobbies. Each person interacts with others through a unique lens.

The "six degrees of connection" theory suggests that every sixth person a Chicago resident meets is connected to someone within their network. These evolving webs of human connection form crucial networks—capable of fostering opportunity, love, or transformation. However, they can also be abusive, manipulative, or destructive.

In the end, the mysteries of life alterations lie not just in what happens to us, but in how we perceive, respond, and resynchronize our inner world with the world around us.

Interactions involving different types of entrainment happen between people, regardless of whether they are aware of these processes. Our increasing ability to understand the complex connections in our personal and social lives is essential for strengthening our free will to influence outcomes in such a universe. The universe involves not only exploring how our interactions shape its structure but also understanding the elements that appear in life, which can greatly affect personal and professional results. What we bring into our lives reflects our potential or untapped abilities in some way. We might not realize who or what we are, what we attract, are attracted to, or what seeks to attract (or attack) us.

Much of what we consider life-changing isn't just about what we deserve but also about the unique patterns of growth that shape how we understand ourselves and others' development. As lawyers and judges are well known for saying, "ignorance of the law is no excuse." In contrast, the universe is even less forgiving. If I jump from a plane with a badly folded parachute, gravity will pull me down regardless of my character. There's an exception to this: if we believe we do not deserve or do deserve specific outcomes, that belief will also influence how we develop concerning results.

Suppose I am a pilot flying a commercial jet, a stockbroker, a New York commuter on a business trip leaving Boston, or a firefighter, among others. In that case, my life and the lives of my fellow Americans are in serious danger on the horrific morning of September 11, 2001. Who could have imagined such a terrorist attack happening on American soil? Many of Tom Clancy's books, Hollywood movies about airplane hijackings, and terrorist bombings of American embassies and the World Trade Center in 1993 may have foreshadowed what was to come.

The idea that foreign terrorism on American soil was just fiction before 9/11 created a sense of disbelief that such disasters could occur. This limited way of thinking acted as a form of denial to protect our collective consciousness. Our perception of reality shapes what we see as causes and possibilities. We rarely see events in our lives as caused by magic, fairies, or genies because that is viewed as beyond responsible understanding. However, when we hold rigid, narrow views of what's possible, we block ourselves from seeing new opportunities and remain unaware of what might be possible. We often don't realize our own blindness. This doesn't mean we should believe in mythical legends or fantastical creatures, but it does mean we need to recognize—for our survival—that in the real world, anything can truly happen.

The saying that truth is stranger than fiction suggests that reality's power is much greater than what our cautious, practical minds allow us to see. Life can feel overwhelming when unexpected events—like a partner leaving, losing a job, or facing health problems—make us feel like things are spiraling out of control. We struggle to find causes and explanations and seek a sense of meaning and purpose in our lives. As discussed earlier,

Cause depends on context, and to understand what is operating, one needs to "draw a fence around" the phenomena of experience. This allows for proximate causation, which involves attributing cause to a specific factor—an agent, entity, or mechanism responsible for the event (a field in which forensic specialists excel). We may seek a schematic design that provides enough cohesion to explain such events. If our schematic or "fence" is drawn too tightly, we might experience a sense of causality, feel out of control, or panic. With enough presence of mind—or consciousness—we then look not only for some agents of cause and effect but also for ways to expand our fence. This involves thinking outside the box. However, it is more about reconfiguring one's consciousness. Such efforts require a willingness to be imperfect, a suspension of rigid insistence on being right, and an openness to mystery. This becomes a resource for our expanding consciousness and capacity to shape our experiences, generating innovative connections within our core motif.

The tragic event of 9/11 was initially linked to the destructive influence of fundamentalism. It was also blamed on the failure of American intelligence agencies and their limited ability to connect crucial clues, such as ignored secret intelligence reports known as "Able Danger," in real-time. How do we define the boundaries of such a vast area? Transforming our personal and national understanding from fantasy to reality creates significant stress and energy for change. This energy encourages powerful transformation, expanding our limits and the range of possible foundational setups. Resynchronizing core themes becomes achievable. Webs of cause and effect, operating in the moment, form instantly as a mosaic of possibilities. All of this stems from engaging with the mystery. This applies both internationally and personally. The predictability or foreseeability of an outcome is influenced by the extent to which boundaries or reference frames are broadened to consider additional possibilities. Think back to when we were children, trying to count the number of monkeys, boxes, or triangles hidden in complex puzzles. The more intricate our multi-layered frames, the more characters we could identify within them.

Our search for "causes of causes to effects of effects..." (referring to nested loops within loops of cause-effect mosaics) can encounter multiple ways in which events may unfold. Our effort to determine what synchronization of assembled events leads to a specific outcome is like piecing together a puzzle where the pieces are constantly changing shape. A recent example involved the father of an African American son on trial for shooting a white teenager who had come to the father's house with friends to protect the son from a potential rape of a white girl. The controversy on both sides shows multiple ways this could have been prevented. However, the deep-rooted racial overtones, especially in the South where the event took place, colored an overdetermined event (one that could have been prevented at many points) into a sudden, life-changing incident. The shooting happened between two parties who each believed they were acting rightly. Racial stereotypes influenced the event, which seemed unrelated but had a significant impact. This stems from the motif's proportionality—how skewed perceptions, timing, and psychosocial factors align to drive chaotic events uniquely. Carefully analyzing these embedded motifs is essential when dealing with the future of such life-changing events.

Predominance, Timing, and Synchronizations of Motif

Motifs have features that help with understanding. Key to this complexity is the adjustment of subtle proportions—forms that emerge from the possibilities of shape-making. Escher's figure-ground reversals showcase these detailed proportional relationships, with one configuration contrasted against its opposite. We need to observe how formative proportions of forms blend, interact, and separate, conveying potential alignments of events. These can be seen as conditions that generate formations of possibility, future timelines.

We can predict the "future outcomes" (along such sequenced timelines) of continuing our strategies in shaping our lifestyles, up to a certain point in time. This varies depending on how broad our boundaries are. The extent to which we can expand our "enlightened time cone of proximate cause" affects our ability to foresee the future. In fact, such extensions create a future consequence to "remember"—as if looking back from the future to the present in different future scenarios—in helping us choose a course of action. These "future memories" help us view the "now" (the current situation) as if we have "already experienced" (déjà vu) the future moment. Acausal future realities retroactively returning "to the present" have been observed in quantum-level experiments involving variations of the double-slit experiment, which detect photons as waves and/or particles.

Life-changing experiences challenge our perception of time. Time is the actual unfolding of specific, unique patterns of development. For example, figure/ground reversals illustrate the Arrow of Time! Depending on how light beams strike a revolving strobe, the phase shift creates the illusion of rotation backwards while the car moves forward. Motifs involve phase shifting by emphasizing how different design configurations relate proportionally. Time exists and emerges through the synchronization of these design structures, forming the syntax of time. Remember how Escher transitions from fish to birds by gradually emphasizing one design over the other, fading into a new timeframe. Time is about synchronization. The dominant proportionality of a person's main motif influences timing and the kinetic timeline of events. The Time Motif is an illusion that functions as reality through synchronized timing. The motif of synchronization becomes the primary timing process in life-altering moments. Think of a flower opening in morning dew, a ballet dancer leaping and spinning, a DNA molecule unfolding to build the fetus, or the universe expanding with billions of spiral galaxies (or a used car salesman who won't go away!).

Ironically, skilled marketing professionals can project future "need creations" to generate demand for their supply. How do you think you and I developed the "need" to have a cell phone, computer, Blackberry, etc.? Experts in foreign relations (the Middle East conflict, dealing with China, trade deficits, border control, or lack thereof) can project alternative, formative scenarios into the "future," already embedded now in the timing of present synchronizations. Strategies and policy implications depend on understanding what configurations will be formed from current policy positions. The timing of those configurations makes the future now—it's already happening, even as we speak. The Bush policy of invading Iran was theoretically a formative move to democratize the Arab-Islamic world. Whatever its merits, the formative configurations of cultural transformation are its outcome, now. Mastering our personal lives involves understanding the formative patterns that could develop in our real-world futures. If we do not achieve this through raising our consciousness, we might unknowingly align with future events that could be difficult to recover from. Elevation is the ability to see above perceptual barriers—ego, habit, neediness, demanding, etc.—that blind us. How can we see the future around the bend in the road? God gave us sight through the eye of formative imagination.

The "Blink" of an Eye

Examples of perceiving and interpreting future trends from current evolving design structures (or motifs) are given in Malcolm Gladwell's Blink: The Power of Thinking Without Thinking (2005). He explains the idea of "thin slicing"—quickly understanding the main designs of what's happening through pattern recognition of unique signatures.

He explains how, during World War II, army intelligence couldn't decipher the meaning of German Morse code but could identify what was called "FIST" pattern recognition. They found that each German Morse code sender had a unique pattern or signature. Each signaler transmitted dots and dashes with distinct rhythms, spacing, and combinations, creating a personalized pattern. Recognizing the "FIST" of each operator helped track their movements and, in turn, the German military forces.

This ability to access unique signatures through "thin-slicing" is also mentioned in Gladwell's discussion of marital relationship research. Psychologist Dr. John Gottman, for example, can predict the likely outcome of a couple's marriage within minutes. Like the FIST construct, Gottman looks at a couple's frequency, intensity, and proportion of positive to negative messages. This signature pattern—the "DNA" of the couple's marital interaction—serves as a reliable indicator of how the relationship will develop without intervention. It seems to be a predictor of which couples are at risk of divorce (Carrere & Gottman, 1999).

Curiously, "thin slicing" happens more through intuitive pattern recognition at an unconscious, felt-sense level than through verbal-linguistic analysis (Klein, 1998; Dodson, Johnson, and Schooler, 1997). Visual memory taps into rapid pattern recognition by cutting through large amounts of verbal data—getting to the core signature of an event, phenomenon, or life-changing experience. Jonathan Schooler (1993), in Thoughts Beyond Words, explains how critical words and analysis often overshadow insights gained from recognition. Could such dynamics have contributed to the "blind sight" and intelligence failures of 9/11? Could they also explain why we sometimes miss obvious signs in our personal lives—where we're "too (verbally) smart for our own good," blind to the "writing on the wall" and the signature patterns that could signal life-changing events?

Learning to focus on what truly matters is essential. Gottman (1999) explores the essence of marital interactions, filtering out irrelevant details and highlighting key signature cues. Essentially, he makes a decision based on intuitive intelligence—unconscious competence—about the core of a situation.

This intelligence isn't about IQ scores but reflects a seasoned maturity—someone who has "been there, done that," and recognizes the signs and symptoms of emerging syndromes. We see this type of expertise in predicting weather patterns, climate change, economic trends, health outcomes, parenting effects, and more. The list goes on.

The end of the world was once predicted to happen in 1963. That prediction clearly failed to understand key patterns—or, if it did, timely interventions were taken. Interestingly, this occurred during the Cuban Missile Crisis, when the world was really close to nuclear disaster. Since then, new predictions—such as Biblical warnings, the Book of Revelation, etc.—have appeared. I've read from various sources that the new date for the end of the world (as we know it) is now 2012 (History Channel, May 20, 2007). Hopefully, my next book on revisionist pattern recognition will be published in 2013. I'll have more to say about this in about eight years (assuming my pattern recognition hasn't gone off course or been erased by then).

1. Gottman's thin-slicing predictions are largely based on four constructs of marital interaction:
2. Defensiveness
3. Stonewalling
4. Criticism
5. Contempt (which he believes is the most critical)

Much of Gottman's work is a formative derivation of earlier research by Paul Ekman (1978), who studied muscle movement in facial expressions to identify emotions. He found that he could detect who was feeling what and even who was lying by observing one of 3,000 possible combinations of facial movements. Ekman developed a taxonomy of these muscular configurations, known as Facial Action Coding Systems.

By the way—have you noticed how human beings create codes for codes, then turn those into meta-codes? This hierarchy of grouping and regrouping (as in induction and deduction) is exactly what we do with computer programs. One computer can code for another. When it enhances the system, it's called an upgrade. When it degrades the system, it's called a virus. In that case, the computer has "caught a code" (pun intended), and we must "purge" the system. Likewise, we will later explore the need to purge traumatic events from our self-signature motif to prevent degradation of our own human being.

Returning to Ekman's system, he states that facial expressions accurately reflect the configurations happening in the mind and brain. In other words, the face mirrors what is occurring internally. Facial expressions generate neurological information flow through the autonomic nervous system. A reciprocal micro-expression involves the orbicularis oculi muscle and is usually seen when a person is genuinely smiling. Its absence indicates falsehood. The fusiform gyrus in the brain is involved in this involuntary facial expression.

Note the subtle proportional variation—so small, so nuanced, yet so significant—in how meaning and reality are framed. Coding, formativeness, and motifs resonate internally, externally, and interpersonally.

The Forest for the Trees – The Epiphany

The ability to intuitively—almost unconsciously—understand the implications of core pattern recognition (at a heightened level of awareness) requires a strong connection with one's sense of self and the signs that indicate it. Shock, anxiety, and panic are not usually what put us in the best state of consciousness to identify and get to the heart of what is happening. However, shock could be used to jolt someone out of and into different states of consciousness, for better or worse.

The resilience involved in finding the "eye of the hurricane," where everything is calm at the center of chaos, seems crucial during times of impending, life-changing events. Firefighters, car accident survivors, and those recovering from cancer—to name a few—all appear to have tapped into inner reserves and resources. These often originate from meaningful, early-life experiences, though not always. Sometimes, individuals can identify core aspects of their character that serve as sources of focus and motivation.

Maintaining self-awareness, concentration, and composure amid emotional challenges or societal difficulties allows individuals to access resourceful and empowering states of mind. These conditions allow for quick and automatic pattern recognition. Could this centered state be what we call "surrender," as if standing in the eye of the hurricane?

At the speed of light, there is no space or time—only the eternal now. However, that does not mean training and experience do not matter. You do not wait until you are thrown off a sinking ship to learn how to swim.

Over a decade ago, I saw a stockbroker and his wife in marital therapy. During one session, they explained how he had lost more than sixty thousand dollars in less than a week. On Monday, his stock dropped twenty grand. He stayed invested, hoping to make back his losses. As it fell further, he grew more desperate. By the end, he had lost sixty thousand. He was shocked and anxious, and his wife was upset about the hit to his reputation.

He admitted he did not know how to "cut his losses." He had lost control of himself. "I could not stop myself," he confessed, throwing good money after bad. Many people caught in addictions—alcoholism, drug abuse, gambling, toxic relationships, eating disorders—know this hellish conundrum of losing control over their behavior.

When we skid on ice, slamming the brakes only makes things worse. We might understand this logically, but instinctively, we panic. Our midbrain fight-or-flight response doesn't leave enough time for our inner wisdom to kick in and prevent us from doing something stupid that we'll regret later.

This shows a lack of awareness of the precursors, entrainments, and patterns that come together at critical moments. Have you ever heard intelligent, successful people say, "How could I have done something so dumb?" Upon reflection, I recognized that this was not an instance of ignorance, but rather an example of entrainment manifesting as a lack of understanding.

We are not talking about simple human error. This isn't just missing a free throw in basketball. It's about figures like President Bill Clinton, Kobe Bryant, Martha Stewart—people who have done incredibly stupid things. They ignored the full scope of their entraining patterns. This is perceptual tunnel vision focused only on the must-have experience.

Say what you want about morality and ethics. These are high-minded ideals—but where do they go when a minister publicly says we should "take out" the Venezuelan President Chavez? When challenged, he said he meant kidnapping. His cover-up made him look worse.

The same applies to President Clinton's "I did not have sexual relations with that woman," or Martha Stewart's obstruction charges. When we're slipping on life's ice, our instinctive reactions—primarily to hide our "errors"—become the real test of character. Isn't that what the Garden of Eden was about? We're always facing that damned tree and its fruit.

Learning to cut our losses is one of the first steps in potentially preventing life-altering chaos before it reaches a critical point. The more we resist (meaning: deny or ignore) what we have already helped create—whether intentionally or not—the more likely that chaos (in its worst form) will take control.

Paradoxically, resistance is a form of resonance. It signals our unintended participation in speeding up the very experience we're trying to avoid. You can see this in politics. Resisting terrorism makes sense—on the surface. But fighting shadows without removing the root of terrorism is dangerous.

If terrorism arises from oppressive governments, whether internal or external, and from the fixation of fundamentalist rage, then cultural liberation becomes crucial. Arresting psychopathic terrorists is necessary, sure. But not every terrorist fits that description. Eliminating Al-Qaeda and the Taliban is vital. However, forcing American democracy on vastly different cultures, which see us as part of the oppressive problem, only makes things worse.

The Iraq War isn't just a fight against terrorism—it's a battle over how to combat it. False stories about weapons of mass destruction, Iraq's supposed ties to 9/11, and nuclear threats were examples of denial and distortion, echoing the chaos we say we are fighting.

This war might have even boosted terrorist recruitment, worsened threats from Iran and North Korea, and overlooked the Sunni-Shiite division. We tried to force different cultures into an American mold—as if all we had was a hammer and every problem was a nail.

Utilizing intuitive, visionary thinking requires brutally honest self-inventory: what's real, what is innovative, what is necessary for formative growth? That is how you enable rapid cognition—deep insight into core motifs for transformation, not impulsive reaction.

You need to let go of how you think the world should be. Hold onto your energy—your restraint—long enough for a new perspective to develop. That is what genuine think tanks are for. You must understand your unique dynamics before you can connect meaningfully with the world beyond your shores.

In our personal lives, the focus should be on formativeness—our unique self-structure. One of the greatest dangers to this self-structure? Feeling so worthless and undeserving that we deny ourselves.

We aim to please others and seek their approval, yet secretly reject any positive people, places, or things. Deep inside, we don't believe we deserve them. Realizing that you do exist—as a unique, complex creation with vast, untapped potential—is an eye-opener. It could even be the key to breaking a terrorist's fundamentalist conditioning.

Accessing your motif can lead to quick shifts in thinking. However, first, you must recognize the disconnect between your lived experience and your core self. That means noticing the deviations, the contrast effects, and the moments that could turn into life-changing chaos.

It is important to dispel any misconceptions you may hold about yourself, such as "I am not good enough" or "I am not necessary." Living for the approval of others blinds us to the power of self-approval. Rebellion without growth is just self-sabotage disguised as freedom.

How do you explain this to a suicide bomber?

I believe people find it more difficult to receive than to give. Receiving a gift involves accepting it and acknowledging its value.

One of the main causes of selfishness is our failure to value what we already have. Money, love, or success cannot increase self-love. Instead, we seek new sources of stimulation or satisfaction. When the initial excitement fades, we go back to feeling dissatisfied with ourselves. We keep chasing it—that's addiction. Tolerance develops, and we fail to see where our pursuits are leading.

Life-changing experiences often involve reckless, unwitting involvement—sticking with what does not work. Yet we do not see the sharks circling.

Victims of terrorists, serial killers, and drunk drivers often had no clear warnings. Nonetheless, intuitive cognition may continue to offer protection, provided there is a willingness to remain receptive to it.

The Arrow of Time

We live in a reality where cause (yesterday) leads to effect (today), which then influences feedback (tomorrow). However, what if today is the result of what will have already happened tomorrow? (Yeah, that is future perfect tense.)

This isn't about rewriting physics—it's about widening the scope of "proximate cause." Getting stuck on the same stairs repeatedly, often feeling low energy, dealing with ongoing exhaustion, and observing that people nearby seem tired could all signal a developing issue. Maybe today's events are consequences of a systemic future cause.

Just because we haven't experienced the future yet doesn't mean it's not already happening. A tree in the forest still falls—even if no one is around to hear it. That moment might be part of a design pattern from the future that occurred earlier.

Our coordinates in space-time align differently. Although what we refer to as "the future" has yet to occur, its underlying design sequences may already be in place. Maybe I've already had a heart attack somewhere in one of those sequences. But that's just one possible path. There are many.

Time isn't fixed. It's subjective and relativistic—just as Einstein said. Carl Jung's synchronicity theory highlights that not everything in the present is caused by the past. Sometimes, events align in ways that defy probability.

That gap in probability—the .05 or .01 significance level—is where the "acausal" sneaks in. Not predestination, but the weaving of multiple potential tracks across all time frames.

The specific track I choose—toward or away from that heart attack—reflects my free will. However, have I mastered the forces shaping what I decide to will? These forces—my habits, my traumas, my inherited temperament—can be influenced by the future design sequences I'm already entrained with, right now, in the "passed days of tomorrow."

This confusing mix of free will, determinism, and life-changing experiences arises from the endless, multi-dimensional design patterns. They appear as a mosaic of interconnected, shaping motifs. Being in sync with a specific set of design patterns—like tracks or paths—reflects a resonance between part of my motif and that path. If I do not choose a new "track or pathway" (meaning a new design sequence), I end up choosing—or am forced to choose—my heart attack, which on this "track" has already happened in my "future."

These infinite design sequences are unfolding configurations, diverging or radiating "back" to us from (not to) what we call the "future" (pardon me, Steven Spielberg). If we can thin-slice—using "link and rapid cognition"—to warning events and pre-cognitively grasp their "future causes," we might be able to prevent and retrace our life-altering entrainment. Rapid cognition, intuition, and early warning detection of paths leading to and being pulled by life-changing events can be understood as the future "causing" itself in the present. What we call future outcomes are wholes—sum totals greater than their parts—or gestalts of formative motifs.

Think for a moment. When you visit an old classmate from grade or high school, you might notice they have become more like what they already were (core motif). The acorn turns into the oak tree. We express this from the perspective of time's arrow moving from past to present causality. However, we could just as logically say—through a configured (figure/ground reversal) consistency—that the gestalt wholeness of the oak tree's motif "caused" or attracted the acorn toward its becoming, its inherent nature from before birth. So, which came first, the oak tree or the acorn?

I believe the nest (as in nested loops of embedded design structure) potentially already exists. How you "slice it" determines—like fate or determinism—the arrow's flight path. Does the past cause the present, freely chosen as it happens, or is it determined by destiny, or some integrated version of all the above?

Sometimes people describe themselves or mishaps as "accidents waiting to happen." Is this a reference to some "future" whole gestalt or life-altering motif waiting, pulling, or causing the present to shape itself into such a future?

The devastating impact of Hurricane Katrina (category 4, with 145 mph winds) destroyed the Gulf states of Louisiana (including New Orleans), Mississippi, and Alabama. The accompanying flooding of New Orleans (caused by a 100-yard levee breach) and thousands of stranded residents resulted in tragic loss of life, property, and infrastructure. Was this an "accident"— even though it was a natural disaster—waiting to happen?

The early warning signs, often precognitive, date back to 1927 with major flooding and storms. Over the next seventy-eight years, repeated warnings, damaging storms, FEMA predictions, and expert articles consistently described how such a disaster was an "event" waiting to happen. In the days before Katrina, evacuation orders were issued. Still, the poor, the ill, and many others who did not believe it would be "That bad" remained. After the Gulf's tsunami hit, everyone realized the "perfect storm" had struck America's southern coast.

As if it wasn't bad enough, government agencies took five days to start any meaningful relief effort. This situation didn't require speculation or urgent action since the necessary information had been available for a long time. It became clear that the problem was real, not hypothetical. One of the main reasons people ignore problems is their tendency to bury their heads in the sand, denying that the future is already here. It is "already happened," and ignoring the warning signs only leads to crashing right into it—over and over.

Future Paradoxes Past

There is genuine confusion about what these time frames—past, present, future—are and where they are. The ancient Greeks described the future as existing in the seed of birth (the acorn containing the complete future image of the oak tree motif), a concept they called entelechy. Alfred Adler (Ansbacher, 1954), one of Freud's original students (or seeds), depicted the individual as goal-oriented and purposeful from a very early age. He explained how rules of apperception (the design shaping one's worldview and long-term direction—what he called lifestyle) are formed before the age of five.

Cosmologists have shown that the geometry, relationships, and internal dynamics of galaxies were established at the Big Bang. We observe this in how the universe expands uniformly in all directions. Space itself, along with all stars and planets within it, expands as a coordinated whole.

The future's location and its role in influencing significant events are subjects for consideration.

Watching a movie from start to finish, we perceive a rapid sequence of projected images that reflect off the screen into our eyes. As kids, we might believe the images come directly from the screen itself. Adults recognize that these are sequences displayed by a projection device. There is nothing behind the screen—just emptiness. But motion feels real—an object changing or 'moving." What we call motion is a subtle wave of continuity, frame after frame, beyond conscious awareness. It's an illusion created by the brain's selective synchronization of still frames.

Let me be clear: I'm not describing fate, determinism, or destiny as unavoidable. It's not that reality has to be a certain way. I'm saying there are signature motifs in all reality that are, by definition, formative— embedded patterns seeking their own expression. Whether that nature "must" be that way is beyond this discussion.

We always have choices. Nothing is pre-determined in the sense that a specific outcome is inevitable. We are not objects in motion, but waves of motif capable of multiple directions. These synchronizing motifs are unique embedded identities of formative matter. Each of us is a unique identity of formative matter. The future, then, could be understood as sequences of formative design—existing in what we call the past—and projected as a self-fulfilling prophecy into what we call our future.

Intriguingly, what we call our future may actually be the unwinding of the movie of our life. Once the reel has run out, become explicit, and finished, we call it death. It has unraveled, unfolded, and returned to the beginning gauges of formative influence. This describes the reduction of an implicate order design, characterized by increased disorder, entropy, and zero energy. This paradoxically becomes "before now" or past. The explicit manifestation—what we typically call "the future"—is, in this view, actually our past.

These implications are intense. If the future is the past in terms of unraveled sequences returning toward zero-ordered randomness, then we have paradoxical processes unfolding simultaneously.

Three Tiers

To understand how the directional flow of design sequences and matter formation can happen in both directions, consider the following: For example, in the case of a salmon, its unique formative designs are established at conception and are encoded within its DNA. Genetic and epigenetic motifs are also encoded. Your future development is already set in implicit form. The future exists at the start of your physical life—what we often call "the past." However, DNA is viewed as sequencing, and its unfolding over time to create the salmon suggests that re-sequencing it in a different temporal direction is possible. Cloning already exists, so what if it were reversed? The DNA seeds of the salmon could be replanted and sequenced differently, potentially creating a new fish adapted to a different environment. Usually, that might be considered an amphibian. Ironically, humans were once amphibious. Who is to say which came first, the chicken or the egg, the frog or the man? Although I know this is brainstorming and conjecture, remember: time, sequencing, and motifs all carry multiple creative interpretations when they are not fixed or final.

It is like pulling a strip of movie film starting from the end and unwinding toward the beginning. The programming of your life's design potential is already set at the subconscious level. From that point, your design (entelechy) begins unfolding "back" toward its physical expression. The paradox: the more ordered the physical form becomes, the less potential remains in its original design. Yet, the more formative learning the salmon acquires, the greater the learning for the next generation of salmon. Our DNA could be redesigned and passed on to the next generation, helping salmon learn how to avoid predators like bears while swimming upstream!

You notice this when someone reaches their maximum height or shoe size, or when they exhaust their current mental capacity. While literal formality may seem to be achieved, the potential for design remains limitless. As individuals grow in physical and mental maturity, their ability to access and harmonize deeper aspects of their innate formative processes increases.

To use a metaphor, we return to that ocean not with buckets but with boxcars—capable of holding exponentially more. The future is Today. Our future is shaped by connecting our early experiences with the identities we develop over time. We see this in neuroplasticity: the more you use your brain, the more capable it becomes. Tomorrow arises from the present future we create each day.

The way individuals are motivated influences the direction of their future. This is the free will of destiny. This is the destiny of free will. This process is generative: mature forms expand their capacity for growth. This is how rejuvenation occurs, both mentally and physically. At the same time, we express selective variations of our formative pattern. The variety and complexity of these expressions are shaped by our interactions, which are influenced by both conscious and unconscious choices.

If you're a salmon, you begin your journey by releasing your full potential. The story of your life unfolds through contrasting images: earlier generations of salmon and their egg-laying patterns, the connection between your internal rhythms and external events, such as your timing when swimming upstream while bears hunt downstream.

You develop scales, fins, quirky-looking eyes, a mouth, go through adolescence, and all the other fishy stages salmon experience. During this process, your salmon-ness (entelechy) becomes clearer through specific environmental interactions. These physical signs mark your movement (the arrow of time) from a past (the moment of physical conception), through a present (where you are now), toward a physical "future" (where all salmon go—ironically, back to where they came from—to their original spawning grounds—back to their future, and their previous potential for development).

Assuming you are not eaten by a bear while swimming upstream to your origins, roots, etc., you will lay eggs, die, go to salmon Heaven (if you have been a good fish—choosing epigenetic, core motif alignment), and in doing so, generate new futures of design potential that, in their generations, will unwind and undersign themselves from the complete wholeness of formative motifs back to the past of their origins (zero ordering potential and rejuvenation).

The other interpretation of time refers to a process that moves backward from the future toward the past, which is described as having zero ordering potential and relates to the formative characteristics of an entity. This may seem like a confusing, unthinkable, or unimaginable concept. The theologian Martin Buber once wrote that every I–Thou encounter was destined to become an I–It (objective thing) encounter, and that renewal was always necessary to rejuvenate the phenomena of I-Thou-ness. In a sense, once the life-formative aspects of each person (or fish, if you will) have exhausted their rejuvenated formations, it cannot continue to exist as anything but a thing (no, not John Carpenter's monster Thing). The time clock runs backward (from future to past) at the level of embedded formativeness because its progress into physical form is its regression away from its origination source, where it was a complete design gestalt.

It's interesting. I understand that even the Bible contains a phrase that echoes these contrasting arrows of time: "...mourn the birth, celebrate the death." While somewhat dramatic (I wonder if salmon possess a higher power), the reference to leaving one's foundational origins—home, embedded designs, source or roots of one's unique being—and beginning the journey of life emphasizes the two stages of formation and being formed. When one thing ends, another begins.

Once the potential for formation (the completeness of design possibility) begins to manifest into physical form, some doors will open while others will close. The zygote is a single-celled, fertilized egg. As it starts to divide and differentiate, it loses some of its plasticity (the stem cell's ability to develop into any specific tissue or organ) as it commits to a particular biological growth path. Some flexibility in formation is inevitably lost during cell differentiation so that a unique human being can be born and thrive. Someone once said that death begins at birth, to which I would add: "You cannot leave home without it" (the projection of formation design potential to light your way).

The third level is our unique motif—originating from our formative years (okay, from mom and dad, but we already knew that)—and it influences everything we think, do, interact with, and what interacts with us. We look to what we call "our future" in everyday reality and notice (if we are truly observant) the visible projection of our formative motif in our daily actions, choices, and decisions, as well as in our expected future. Perception results from reflecting or refracting information that was present from the start. Our formative years are our origin, which contains our future from the very beginning. Because of this, I call this third level the embedded nows of the arrows of time. No matter where you go, your unique formative expression remains. It's always there—even "now" as you read this, before you read this, and after you read this (regardless of the direction your formative journey takes when you read this).

When you understand who you are and how you develop on both basic and complex levels, you'll also understand who you are in the present. Life-changing experiences become embedded in our life paths because they, in some way, resonate—partially or fully—with the unique foundational features that emerge (or are about to emerge) in our real-world experiences. Chaos has an inherent, underlying order, just as every form of order exists alongside boundaries that blend into chaos. Small cumulative changes can spread through a system, causing structures like flood barriers to break down. Just observe what happens when a hurricane hits New Orleans and a once-civilized community descends into chaos. Drop a pebble into a pond and watch the ripples expand outward and bounce back from the shore. Now, drop a series of increasingly larger pebbles, and chaos becomes possible. The tipping point of chaos in life-changing experiences creates waves of design patterns moving back and forth in synchronized, moment-to-moment interactions.

Wholeness Moving as One Entrainment

We do not move through our lifestyles in isolation. We naturally intertwine in groups (small or large), with our synchronizing resonances that constantly attract, are attracted, merge, diverge, and emerge in a sea of altering sub-groupings. Our families, work colleagues, neighborhoods, coffee shops, bookstores (even Hooters-type places) are just a few of the sub-groupings—pools of people, roles, scenarios—with which we can and do entrain. That some may lead or evolve into life altering experiences is only a matter of time (whichever arrow you'd like to use or follow). This is one of the clues—a symptomatic class of indicators—that pre-frame the oncoming life-altering experience.

Are your eyes, ears, and pre-cognitions open and receptive to how you are moving, negotiating, entraining, synchronizing, and pursuing critical life themes that may unwind themselves right in front of you? Clusters of events, thematic connections, a coherence of typical people and/or relationship encounters, beneficial (or not-so-beneficial) accidents, slips, miscues, etc., all can signal and allude to types of indicators—what is coming if you follow or continue.

There are time waves, like quantum gravity waves, moving through the timeline of our lives. Past and future curve around each other in space-time (six of the eleven dimensions in superstring theory are multi-shaped energy loops, curving inward like instruments of an orchestra, resonating endless particle formations in infinite synchronizing motifs—The Elegant Universe, PBS). Focusing on the present moment can help individuals prepare for upcoming events and allow past habits, if maintained, to remain consistent with future circumstances. The challenge is how to get ahead of the curve of our timeline—to choose our destiny before experiencing it. To do this, recognizing that the future is now allows us to accelerate in time, so that we are there to meet the curve on which we may already be traveling.

Free will is a natural muscle that gets stronger with practice—making choices to continue or change ongoing patterns. Unknowingly accepting questionable patterns will, if repeated, become our destiny. Working on increasing the ability to shape our internal and external worlds is part of exercising this muscle.

There are certain phenomena of entrainments that can help us. For example, a sudden focus on a specific music genre like jazz, rekindling interest in playing an instrument such as the piano, or a curious clarity in visual or auditory perception—experiencing sharpened nuances and receptivity, as if perceiving a bright, crystalline chandelier. Additionally, you might notice the walk, grace, or style of someone passing by. You could be startled by the golden glow of metallic wings hanging from a chain around her neck. Out of the blue, you start a conversation, and she explains they were a gift from a friend (angel's wings) who passed away a year ago. An inexplicable connection exists between your observation of her—as if she moves angelically—and her wearing angel wings to symbolize her loss of her friend.

Then she tells you she is unhappy living with her parents while her husband lives hundreds of miles away—and you find out she is suicidal.

Here comes another intense, transformative moment.

(What is that old song that echoes the mantra: "...here it comes, another 19th nervous breakdown"?) It seems interesting that thematic qualities— depending on one's perceptual filters, slices of perspective, or however one defines figure-ground structures—reflect unique, organizing principles for such entrainments.

Are these phenomena just random acts of probability? Acts of God (or evil)? Or could they be something fundamental to the existence of our universe?

As discussed throughout this work, matter and energy (gravity, electromagnetism, strong and weak forces) exhibit inherent patterning and resonating properties of organization and entrainment. Formative signatures originating from the Big Bang, amplified by accelerating expansions (energy, intensity, vacuum space, galaxies moving outward in all directions), demonstrate such holistic interactions. These operate as embedded principles of organization at all levels of existence.

This does not aim to endorse a purpose or inherent meaning in existence (God only knows what that might be). Instead, it supports the idea that formativeness, with all its implications, is a fundamental aspect of existence and our daily lives. It explains entrainments across the streams of time.

The remarkable implications of formativeness in our personal lives are that we can never operate in a vacuum of emptiness. Whether we are in a large crowd, a small one, or alone, we are always interacting in some way (for better or worse) with other people, places, and events. The shrinking world of a global village is evident. Yet, such interconnectedness has been an inherent property of formative organizing principles since time immemorial. Formativeness in one's unique motif influences many tracks or life pathways at once. The way we pace ourselves, our patterns of thought and attitude, mood states, and behaviors constantly align and re-align with those people, places, and events that are also unfolding in parallel resonance to us. From how we drive our cars to how we carry on conversations and meet similar people dealing with issues close to our own, these are reflections or refractions of such entrainments.

Have you ever noticed how many friendly people you meet when you're in a cheerful, confident, upbeat mood? It's not that you make others happier; rather, you tend to filter and choose those with a similar outlook because you have already connected with them in some way whether past, present, or future. People can also sense our negatives, such as intolerance, agitation, fears, and anxiety. Have you noticed how animals can pick up on fear in humans—and are more likely to attack because of it? Fear can trigger aggression.

We shape our future by choosing what we send out, project, and spread. Be careful about what you wish for, as you might get it. However, it is not always possible to be fully aware of the signals we emit or the cues we respond to when trying to resist, avoid, or change them. What acts as a variation of other functions may be complex entanglements of unintentional involvement. I would call this participation at non-conscious levels. We are pulled and pull others by various people, places, and things in many ways or through different traps. An individual's career choice, like pursuing a role as a real estate agent, affects these traps. A real estate agent specializes in understanding local markets, neighborhood trends, and the pricing of different types of houses. These are examples of traps. If the real estate agent works six days a week, nine hours a day, marriage, family, and physical health may suffer. These, too, are traps.

The point is that no behavior happens in a vacuum. There is always some context or condition it connects with, a pathway or track that gets triggered. If left unchecked, these can develop into core aspects of our lives with serious consequences. I know what happens to my lawn when it isn't cared for. Think about neglecting our health, relationships, family, careers, and more. You might say you are very diligent and familiar with these areas. However, even the most attentive gardener faces weeds, insects, drought, and so on. Many husbands are surprised to discover, after years of a good marriage, how unhappy their spouse has become. The signs were there, but they did not notice them. Though they have eyes, they are unable to see. As Emily Dickinson once said, "I could not see to see" when suffering from an illness that kept her from perceiving what was coming. The illness of tunnel vision or ignorance—ignoring the details of holistic interaction—places blinders on our understanding, leading to entrancing and entraining problematic involvement.

"Chunking up," as in the phrase to see the forest from the trees (the big picture or sequence of unfolding movie frame designs to see what ending it's leading towards), is crucial in reading the signs of future life-changing experiences arriving on the tracks or pathways we have unwittingly chosen to follow. From our one true love of a partner to our one true passion in life, are we aware of the multiple ripple effects with which we are setting things in motion? Today's popular career choice can become tomorrow's dinosaur (tool and die makers in auto assembly plants are now being replaced with computerized robots; an oversupply of MBAs; pilots with 25 years of experience being laid off because of major airline bankruptcies, etc.). The partners we entrust can influence or devastate our future lives for years to come.

It has been said that America has been in a war against terrorism for over Fifteen years went by unnoticed until the devastating impact of 9-11. Matthew Lippman, a terrorism expert at the University of Illinois, Chicago, said on August 19, 2005, that many warning signs of 9-11 were clear. However, due to the legal structures in place at the time, the information could not be received or understood. Rigid patterns in government and personal life hinder our ability to adapt to new information that could warn us of upcoming dangers, potentially leading to consequences if we continue on the same entrenched path, even if we are unaware of it.

It is not the subjectivity in our unique motif that threatens us with life-altering experiences. Instead, it is the false illusion that the paradox of what makes us wonderfully unique—our subjectivity, our passion, etc.—reflects absolute reality, separate from the larger system of interactive entrainments. We must learn how to come up for air (emerge from our own personal and national self-involvement) and recognize the multiple possible pathways of entrainments, as well as which ones we have unknowingly chosen. Accessing our unique motif requires stepping beyond fixed, rigid assumptions and beliefs. It challenges how we perceive unfolding realities and alternative futures. It also fortifies and exercises the muscle of our free will.

This is not about Monday morning quarterbacking (looking backward with "could haves" and "should haves"). Instead, it is about "Tuesday afternoon" (I like to sleep late), wake-up calls, and how my previous life experiences could be setting precursors for my future. However, I need to be, at times, brutally honest about what I am up to or not up to in how my attitudes and actions are asking for a winning or losing life-altering future—now! The way I play, the intensity of my participation, and the presence of genuine desire and skill are all telling or warning signs of what games I am playing with myself, my life, and my colleagues.

Coming to terms with my free will and my willingness to observe what I am doing in my entrainments allows me to navigate the arrows of time. From the future back to my own future shaped by past potentials, I need to exercise mastery of determination (not determinism) to make healthier choices in my entrainments. Recognizing my hidden, embedded, and disguised entrainments is crucial. The key points are: 1.) realize that you can head down a dangerous path without knowing where it leads, 2.) practice fearless honesty about how self-involved you might be, 3.) understand what you are projecting and creating for your future, 4.) commit to practicing decisions that boost flexibility and honesty (creative, innovative, out-of-the-box, etc.), 5.) challenge yourself to engage in activities that are comfortably uncomfortable (and, of course, legal and moral), and most importantly, 6.) resolve to break any sense of entrained determinism in your lifestyle.

Everything we do is a choice. The range of options and real-world opportunities for reorganizing and reintegrating different patterns are substantial. Exercising freedom of choice demands effort and time. Mastering one's lifestyle—perceiving, modifying, and committing to reassembling innovative patterns—is about building the muscle of formation. This is the true breakfast of champions.

Life-altering experiences challenge the process of strengthening innovative creativity. Without the passion of blood, sweat, and tears (I also enjoy their music), humans will not engage in differentiating formative motifs. If we can challenge ourselves before or during life's unfolding events, we might prevent or at least reduce their impact. Then we can understand these life changes—perhaps as catastrophes—that are serious but not deadly. It is crucial to realize that this universe constantly recycles itself through birth, death, and rebirth. The universe doesn't revolve around humanity; instead, humanity revolves around and through the evolution of the universe. In the final chapter, entropy and the evolution of life-changing experiences will help explain that there might be an answer to the question, "Why do good things happen to bad people, as well as bad things happen to the goodness in us all?" What drives motivation?

For now, it may be helpful to review the tragic behavior at the Abu Ghraib American prison, which was used to detain enemy combatants during the Iraq War. The abuse inflicted by some American soldiers—such as sexual abuse, inhumane conditions, and acts of humiliation—on Iraqi prisoners of war illustrates how decent soldiers (not sociopathic or psychopathic) can become caught up in the excesses of personal power and the tacit approval of military authorities. As the authorities looked the other way, the soldiers' sense of unrestrained power—fueled by unchecked and unaccountable oversight—became self-perpetuating. This cycle intensified as their act of abusing power motivated them to do even more. Ultimately, this escalating pattern of abusive entrainment reached a tipping point, where the abuse was carried out solely for its own sake.

Social psychology studies (Zimbardo, 1971, and Stanley Milgram's research on obedience to authority) have demonstrated how tacit approval of authority can entrain normal, healthy individuals into ways of thinking and acting that are aberrant and exploitative. It is not so much a battle of good versus bad people, as research demonstrates. Rather, it reflects the plasticity, formativeness, and entrainment capabilities inherent in human nature. Goodness or badness is not a fixed quality; it is more an exercise of unwitting choice. A simple example of this can be seen in how motorists accelerate or decelerate depending on the absence or presence of a policeman. Most people make unwitting choices based on contextual entrainments as criteria for their behavior.

The challenge has been understanding how to internalize a sense of moral or ethical behavior within an individual as something that is inherently right for its own sake, rather than because of external sanctions or threats from authority figures. As will soon be shown, bad or evil behavior results from a combination of factors. Normal individuals do not necessarily possess a highly internalized sense of right and wrong for its own sake. Instead, most of us tend to act in psycho-social situations based on contextual cues that we have become conditioned to respond to. This can lead to unintentional choices, such as indulgence, self-gratification, excessive acting out, or inappropriate obedience to authority. These deviations create a disconnect between our core self-motif and our behavioral choices. Such a mismatch is what one might call bad or evil.

The research conducted by Zimbardo in the early 1970s randomly divided groups of student subjects into prison guards and prisoners. Since each group was allowed free rein with no formal guidelines, the role-playing naturally developed into "real" behavior. Those acting as guards became increasingly focused on challenges to their authority. That is, as the pseudo power of prison guards was challenged by rebellious prisoners, the guards took these challenges personally. They became invested in and identified with proving and asserting their authority. This dynamic emerged even when there was no genuine authority to assert. The prisoners, in turn, became increasingly identified with being defiant and rebellious.

These shifts from role-playing to real scenarios indicate a significant change in consciousness. The sense of self becomes tied to distorted motifs, impairing and twisting the individual's unique identity. The motif of formative influence is now heavily restricted. As this loss of motif formativeness occurs, mental and behavioral symptoms may emerge. The metaphorical image of the soldier is transformed into a concrete, reified form. An altered state of consciousness involves merging role-playing into a tangible and solid reality. Such a change in perception indicates entrancement. It represents a distinct form of entrainment. Such involuntary entrainment led to life-changing experiences of mental, emotional, physical, and sexual abuse by pseudo-guards toward pseudo-prisoners. The constriction of this synchronization became so severe that it required stopping the research within a few days.

Stanley Milgram conducted a study on obedience to authority that produced notable results. He showed how ordinary, healthy people could be pressured into administering painful electric shocks to innocent victims whose only crime was failing a simple test. The willingness to obey authority, even when it conflicts with personal ethics and morals, demonstrates the powerful influence of social conformity. When a person over-identifies with a distorted part of a psychosocial system embedded with cultural norms and values, the lines between reality and illusion become blurred. This confusion arises between free will and fatalism, where the ability to act according to one's core self becomes entrained due to conflicts or aversions to the surrounding context. The individual's sense of self conflicts with external influences, especially those exerted by figures in positions of authority. This can lead to dissociated states of an Altered Sense of Self experienced as "not me"! It may then feel like being taken over or compelled to act in risky ways, feeling out of control, and behaving involuntarily.

It is essential now to access your unique core motif to rebuild your ability for reality testing. This requires space, time, and a shift in your moral compass. It involves clearing your sensory filters to achieve an unaltered, unbiased view of what you hear, see, and feel. This is where the motif becomes invaluable. It provides "fresh" eyes for perceiving and interpreting your world from an unprocessed, non-adaptive, non-programmed standpoint. The self-actualization of the scientist or artist within all of us enables innovative, refreshing perspectives.

It is important to establish the need for personal accountability. The criteria for justifying one's thinking and actions should be rooted in what is genuinely right and aligned with that unique core self. At this point, such alignment effectively becomes synchronization of self. Therefore, this can be seen as a form of self-entrainment.

We all have free will and choice. The problem is thinking and believing that we are exercising choices when, in fact, we have been seduced or induced by illusions and authorizations which emerge from questionable, selective interactions. Politics, religion, social, and family environments need to support the integrity of the individual being true to him or herself. We need to learn how to master the consciousness of our own unique synchronization of motif to discern whose rhythm we are entraining. Henry David Thoreau alluded to this over a hundred years ago when he said that each person moves to the beat of a different drum. The challenge here is the recognition that our personal best or rhythm can be unwittingly entrained into a skewed symphony (or synchronization), taking us off our "beating" track. As such, what at one time may have appeared as our unique resonance now becomes subsumed or entrained into a skewed distortion of ourselves. Being ourselves now could amount to "being" alien to the core, a unique alignment of our motif.

Motif's Unique Design as a Technology of Core-Self

Identifying and refining your unique motif serves as a deep well of strength from which nearly unlimited resources can be drawn. Just as a professional athlete mentally and visually rehearses, imagines, and practices complex skills, it is equally important to master alignment with your core self. This requires understanding your boundaries and the subtleties of your core identity while managing potential psycho-social influences. Developing the ability to navigate this landscape would make the challenges faced by professional athletes seem insignificant by comparison.

It is probably no surprise to anyone that setting personal goals and objectives throughout life is important. These should be based on the unique makeup of one's core self. The more precise the articulation of the refined nature of one's unique character motif, the more enriching and empowering the achievement of one's goals will be. Nothing is more disappointing than spending years training and studying in fields misaligned with what one truly desires deep in their heart.

Knowing our unique core self and the special gifts and talents embedded therein is not an easy task to accomplish. Paradoxically, it is the misaligning effects of life-altering events that challenge us to review, explore, and mentally rework what it is we want for our lives. The trauma and passion of these events move us to articulate our unique core selves in ways that may previously have been unheard of. God and the devil are both in the details. By clearly defining the desired standards of design within our relationships, families, recreational activities, and other life domains, we are able to make more informed and thoughtful decisions. The greater our precision and articulation of our unique motif of core self, the more empowered our resilience and integrity for self-righting behavior.

It's the detailed expression in precise formative terms of how we think, feel, act, and synchronize that fuels our empowerment of ourselves. We need to identify, prioritize, and align (regarding our unique pace, tempo, and patterning of themes with people, places, and things) with our core motif. For example, what qualities do you prioritize, and in what structure and proportion regarding areas of work, love, and friendship? Where and how do you want to live, and what psycho-social environment? What psycho-social-cultural qualities resonate with key target areas in your life that align with your core self-motif in mental, emotional, and physical ways?

Such inquiries and their emphasis guide you toward developing strategies to showcase your unique abilities in meaningful and empowering ways effectively. It's about learning, through your life-changing experiences, to pay selective attention to how you uniquely relate, entrain, and interact in the process of being your core self. You may find yourself repeatedly entraining in unhealthy relationships, seeking others to provide excitement and the rush of high drama. Learning how to choose and mentally rehearse healthy ways to fulfill that need for yourself can save you a lifetime of painful entrainments. To emphasize one's unique expression of a motif is to understand the details of one's cognitive and sensory themes. These configurations form the foundation by which we learn the art and science of synchronization with our core self-motif. Improving your ability to express your motif's subtle nuances aligns with what could be called "Being Yourself in your own, idiosyncratic fashion." "To thine own self be true, and thou canst be false to any other man."

CHAPTER 10

TIMELINES AND THE "ARROW"

Analysis of Significant Experiences

The construction of arrows of time tiers assumes an almost limitless capacity for motifs to form. Interestingly, the more randomness and disorder are infused into experiences, the greater the potential for new shapes and patterns to develop. This is because losing a specific form or design "breaks down and opens up" more opportunities for fresh shapes and patterns to appear. For example, cracking an egg (simply breaking it open) allows for multiple outcomes—omelets, scrambled eggs, egg salad, ham and eggs, and even green eggs and ham, as in Dr. Seuss.

The human zygote (fertilized egg cell) "breaks down/opens" and develops, forming into differentiating cell groups that eventually become a human being after nine months. Remember, however, that breaking the symmetry of formative potentials means these "futures" of design will specifically differentiate into one set of forms, thus excluding other possibilities. In these conditions, the potential for form is diminished. The paradox, as will be explained, is that these actual forms themselves carry "seeds" of new, renewable future designs. This "planting" arises as these new forms work together in a dynamic synchronization of their motifs.

Volcanoes, earthquakes, and hurricanes bring about massive chaos, destroying cities, communities, and both physical and psychosocial structures. Tragedies involving loss of life, property, and financial devastation challenge the status quo, compelling humans to step up and rebuild with newer, more resilient designs, even under the harshest conditions. The reconstruction of Europe after WWII, along with the rise of America as a global power following the Japanese attack on Pearl Harbor, exemplifies the phoenix rising from the ashes of destruction. Breaking an ice cube into crushed ice increases the surface area, which can cool drinks more efficiently and allows for easier sipping through straws. At the quantum level, reality "breaks" down to the Planck scale of 1.6 x 10 to the minus 35 centimeters.

All substances, whether human or nonhuman, are made up of layered design structures both within and beyond themselves (similar to the metaphor of Chinese boxes nested inside one another). From molecular structures to advanced communication systems and the human genome, coding within coding and design within design are fundamental aspects of existence and formation. The more disorder there is within set, formal design structures, the greater the potential for inherent formation to emerge, be unleashed, and surpass what existed before. This reflects the nature of humanity, the Earth, and the universe overall.

As our embedded formative processes develop over time in our lives, what we imagine as projections of our future (commonsense reality) may only be a limited or partial display of deeply complex formative potentials. These capabilities may be realized through positive disintegration, a process encompassing both elements of breakdown and subsequent breakthrough. Adolescence, turning thirty or forty, midlife crises, developmental life stages, and similar experiences can all serve as examples of breaking away from the old and releasing new formative qualities that are present before us and embedded in our lifestyle, psycho-social context, and universe. What shapes our perspective, our overall perception of formative experience, depends on our subjective emotional commitment at any given moment.

Suppose my development task is to pass a college exam in English (to serve my long-term goals of graduation and career development). In that case, I might meet with other classmates, study in libraries or coffee shops, and stay up many hours into the evening. It could open me to new connections, discussions of study strategies, and even dialogues about why the purpose of my efforts, as well as my underlying values and beliefs, matter. To pay for the course, I may need to take on various part-time jobs, interact with situations and people I would not have encountered before, and deal with the stresses and anxieties of rising to the challenge of passing English exams. Learning involves experiencing the nuanced details of the process in manageable "chunk" sizes that demonstrate how each motif unfolds successfully, similar to learning to play the piano, which involves fingering techniques and tapping through the keys. The formativeness of motifs is essential in music.

The entrainment may provide access to individuals who can assist me in managing stress and relaxation through the use of medications. It could cause me to adopt the use (or abuse) of certain performance-enhancing drugs to attain my goals. Unwitting participation with alcohol and drugs to cope with one set of entrainments could draw me into another set of entrainments. These would certainly open me up to new formative possibilities that could be devastating to my current lifestyle or motif. Yet, they would bring to light my needs, insecurities, and embedded formative identities of who I was, am, and could become.

Unexpected entrainments can certainly test the multifaceted strength of one's character. They can also reveal hidden identity functions within self-transforming constructions and beliefs about who I perceive myself to be. However, it is the subjective, emotional entrainment that evokes and provokes the mobilization and emergence of embedded design structures. The driving force behind unfolding these potentials is my personal engagement with my unique emotional involvement. This process is primarily experiential and nonintellectual, yet it challenges one's mind, body, resources, and wisdom. The motivation for change, therefore, mainly stems from the entrainment of my motivation—my unique emotional involvement—in interactions with people, places, and/or events. My unfolding, implicit future (embedded in my shared reality from the past) can be influenced by the entrainments in which I may unknowingly participate. These entrainments tap into, release, break down, and open embedded future design structures already encoded in our past (shared reality). When these embedded future design possibilities are activated and released through entrainments, they are projected back from our physical future (shared reality) into the present moment as destiny, fate, kismet, etc.

Entrainments with people, places, and events also suggest our connection to our own aroused, triggered, and projected future physical reality. For example, I might be conditioned to see myself as Donald Trump, John F. Kennedy, or Albert Schweitzer. Still, what I'm meant to be is as much a projection and internalization of entrainment representing selective perception as it is concrete reality. In short, I've become so captivated by my own projected visions from embedded designs of potential futures that I now believe "now" is what the "future," common-sense reality must be. However, this may be only one of many unfolding possibilities. In other words, what seems like our destiny coming from the future are actually entrained choices from potential futures occurring in what we call our past.

Life-altering experiences generate enormous amounts of psychic, emotional, and physical energy. While such bursts of energy can spark growth, they can also cause negative, paralyzing, and debilitating effects like overwhelming anxiety, panic, and eventual depression and hopelessness. Belief in and premature conviction that a life-changing event (such as disasters, disease, disability, death, etc.) is irreversible and catastrophic tend to fixate perceptions and shape beliefs about reality. If you were among those in the Twin Towers during the horrific 9/11 tragedy—whether as a worker, visitor, or emergency responder—you would notice various kinds of entrainment happening. The series of synchronized events involving financial and business leaders in concentrated areas like the Twin Towers (a symbol of American capitalism) attacked by militant Islamic fundamentalists demonstrates entrainments of resonant events. The involvement and synchronization of firefighters, police, and emergency workers also reflect these entrainments.

The grouping of synchronizing events is quite obvious because of the themes or motifs of American capitalism, financial centers, culture clash, terrorism, and Islamic fundamentalists. Life changes likely result from a corresponding convergence of events leading up to a critical mass of the 9/11 events. The challenge in identifying the unique, uncommon pattern of such an event cluster is to see its origin as a coming together of potential that shape the future, which synchronize and pull into the present. This pulled-in "present" comes from a shaping future that, according to our usual timeline, is located in what we call the "past." The "future" in our common sense timeline can be seen as the unfolding past of previously set future design potentials that were already drawn in.

The chaos of 9/11 illuminated numerous accounts of heroism and courage among civilians as well as civil servants. A severe, life-altering event highlights the unpredictability of survival outcomes among individuals. At the same time, no one knows why in any absolute sense, constructs of entrainment and synchronizing motifs offer at least some light on the phenomenon.

Some who worked in the towers escaped unharmed, but tragically, others did not. Newspapers captured images of people holding hands, jumping to their deaths, trying to escape the pain of burning flames. Their chances of surviving depended partly on the floors where they worked. This was because of the height at which terrorists directed the jetliners into the buildings. The assignments for individuals on different floors were based on complex plans made years earlier.

For example, to be located on the critical floors above the fires immediately after the impact of the planes, one would have to consider numerous variables. These could include (though not limited to) choosing a career in business and/or finance, residing in New York City, New Jersey, or a nearby area to allow for a commute downtown, working in a business within the towers, going to work that day without delays, staying at work long enough to experience the attack, having an office above the floor where the planes hit, the terrorists' flight training, their strategic assault on the towers, how passengers and crew on the planes handled the terrorists' takeover, and so on.

These are some of the many variables that interact to create a synchronized resonance of embedded organizing motifs, influencing people, places, and events. Motifs can lead to multiple outcomes. Emerging motif outcomes are intuitively indicated by an increasing noise of seemingly unrelated events that organize themselves through patterns of chaos, similar to fractals. In the case of 9/11, the uncommon factors in these unfolding sequences of events were multi-dimensional entrainments of time motifs. The concept of time relates to the sequencing and structure of unfolding events. For there to be a sense of time, there must be a perception or illusion of change from one discrete event to another (as in the sequence or pattern of a dancer's steps).

There is a resonant "timing" or proportional distribution of interval events, such as steps, that are grouped, ordered, and sequenced, which entrain these unfolding steps or events. The distinctive proportionality of this resonant timing is its recognizable signature rhythm of a motif. The motif in music orchestrates this entrainment of seemingly unrelated events. It is the motif that functions as the "conductor of time." Such a motif might exert its formative design energy in a way that geometrically shapes space-time continuums and the structure of associated electromagnetic field currents. Einstein described a similar phenomenon called frame dragging, where the movement of light and/or matter can change the design contours of the space and time through which it moves. Interestingly, Dr. Ron Mallet, a physics professor at the University of Connecticut, is using this principle of frame dragging with spiraling laser light beams. The aim of this innovative research is to create the world's first time machine capable of transporting subatomic particles backward in time. This emphasizes the potential power of motifs as formats.

This formative congealing of multi-dimensional, sequenced events is orchestrated as a motif of family processes, each characterized, to varying degrees, by asymmetrical timing. That is, there is just enough resonant timing with variation to complement the overall orchestration of life-changing events coming to a head. Imagine multiple streams of water trickling and converging at the delta head of a river. While not perfectly aligned and slightly off, there is enough asymmetry, or "slight imbalances" of entrainment, so that the timing of flowing water organizes its self-motif into the whitewater rapids of life-altering experiences. The asymmetrical timing of water troughs and overlapping wave peaks contributes to this effect. Light waves of time may also flow in similar ways.

These motifs are urgent for existence as a life form or entity. When the balanced presence of similar design forms resonates as a whole — when a unique, critical mass of recurring formative designs supports and reinforces each other, increasing their frequency and strength — then the motif of life-changing experience appears suddenly. Enough levels of formativeness for that life-changing event (like 9/11) now make a critical mass more likely. Formativeness can also refer to how data converges to create meaning in language and computer processing. It is similar to the culmination of giving birth or the end of a complex journey from one part of the world to another. What makes this setup deeply important is that it challenges the very foundation of our perceived existence.

Ideas about how formative designs come into being have been suggested in Dr. Rupert Sheldrake's work. His theory of morphogenic fields states that when an idea, concept, or skill is practiced enough times (such as when a hundred monkeys learn to wash sweet potatoes in the ocean to make them tastier), a special energy field called a morphogenic field is created. This leads to the learning of that particular idea or design becoming common within the species (monkeys around the world suddenly find faster and easier ways to wash sweet potatoes to improve their flavor).

The point is that formative concept designs are not just about learning or knowledge acquisition; they are about creation, existence, and life-changing experiences. The 9/11 horrific tragedy (like many life-changing events) is the culmination (or the proverbial last straw that broke the camel's back) of a buildup of formative events, reaching a critical mass that allows the perception and shaping of the critical or catastrophic event to occur. There is an old joke about how many therapists it takes to change a light bulb (none—the light bulb has to want to change). Events change only when they happen and when their preconditions are met. Dr. Sheldrake suggests that at least a hundred instances of learning a concept must occur (like a hundred monkeys learning to wash sweet potatoes) before a morphogenic field is created, which facilitates general learning within that group. The strategic timing of events is crucial in creating impactful, formative motifs. Attaining certain levels of synchronization criteria may be necessary to generate the formation of motifs. The buildup of synchronization occurred before the unfortunate event. It's as if the sense of the "future" is happening in the present, lighting up the event before it has occurred. The arrow of time may move in different directions if we pay attention to the new formation of motifs unfolding before our eyes!

There have been many terrorist attacks on the United States before 9/11. Although hindsight offers perfect clarity, it is clear that terrorists' activities showed a pattern leading up to major events. These include the 1993 World Trade Center bombing, the attack on the U.S. destroyer Cole, threats from Osama Bin Laden, and portrayals in movies and books of terrorists hijacking commercial jets, which culminated in the pivotal events of 9/11. One U.S. State Department official hinted that 9/11 was not a question of "if" but "when."

It was only after enough past incidents — which suggested that a specific type of life-altering event was imminent — converged and resonated with one another, their timing aligning to influence each other profoundly. The question is: Is this phenomenon merely a coincidence of resonance (past), or is there a larger overarching design coordinating these events?

Such accumulations can also happen on an individual level. I remember meeting a business executive leaving his office, and I asked for directions to Union Station in Chicago. He kindly guided me and, during our interaction, began sharing details about his personal life. His main approach was to bend over backward, comply, and overextend himself to tolerate others' disrespect and self-centered behavior. This ingratiating attitude kept him on edge, never knowing if he could maintain others' approval, fearing rejection and abandonment. He was experiencing a growing list of losses: losing his father (whom he could never satisfy anyway), the expensive and painfully unavoidable consequences of his irresponsible spouse, and his attempts to self-medicate the pain through affairs and gambling. These issues led to a life-changing dilemma. If he did not set boundaries, establish clear expectations, and define his own life goals separate from his family's demands, he would face significant emotional and physical difficulties over time.

At thirty-five, he reached a crucial turning point in his development. External events became more intense, highlighting the crisis: he had to stand his ground—define his core values—or risk being swept away by cycles of anxiety and depression, endlessly chasing illusions of control, perfection, and peace. The convergence of recurring themes—patterns emerging and increasing challenges to maintain stability amid mounting losses and reckless behavior of others—led to a transformative experience. His marriage, extended family, and health all declined, threatening his lifelong strategy of maintaining an illusion of home, family, and togetherness. The accumulation of these themes into a critical mass challenged him to trust his own learned, intuitive sense of who he was as a guide to navigate the external signs of what he calls success. He needed to strengthen his organizing principle of taking charge—seizing the moment and series of moments he had been learning and preparing for during the first three decades of his life.

He could reshape and redesign his physical reality by starting with his core motivation instead of yielding to external pressures; he instead fueled his efforts from his central motif. He thoroughly evaluated his lifestyle in line with his guiding principles and adopted new methods for self-assessment and goal setting.

What determines which formative designs can enter, in part or in whole, is their unique balance or prerequisite conditions. Life forms can only exist in this world if environmental or contextual conditions support their formative motifs. Dinosaurs perished (they did not do well with meteors), while mammals prospered as the environmental conditions were uniquely altered to support one life form over another.

Similarly, modern human beings, nations, cultures, politics, and conceptions of God are among the countless formative designs vying to enter our physical reality. It is similar to how America admits immigrants through its borders. Certain standards and criteria must be met, such as quotas, law-abiding behavior, and physical health. Illegal immigration is often unofficially tolerated when there is demand for workers. This is seen as a "win-win" in some cases where cheap labor benefits both sides, but it also has flaws and can lead to cultural conflicts. Formative influences also seek entry on international levels, like the contrast between democracy and autocratic government. For example, America's effort to introduce democracy into Middle Eastern Islamic theocratic nations illustrates a formative life form trying to enter a new universe—one that manifests differently because of distinct cultural contexts.

The subtle nuances and differences within similar ways of life, such as democracy, and between them, like East versus West, show how small variations can lead to significant results. The genetic difference between a chimpanzee and a human is only about three percent, yet that small variation results in profound differences. Likewise, minor differences in perspectives on issues like abortion, influenced by age, cultural values, and political beliefs, can produce vastly different outcomes.

What allows a formative design entity to manifest over others is the degree of precedent forms that have come before it. These forms evolve in refinement, with each stage entraining on the previous one. For example, the evolution of human beings is built upon the bipedal humanoids that came before. Life-altering events can be seen as the manifestation of formative designs pressing for existence, dependent on the degree of evolution of the previous forms that lay the foundation for them. This is the critical mass effect, wherein certain life-altering events emerge when sufficient accumulated effects reach a tipping point.

Examining the effects of entrainment and the directional aspects of time is relevant for studying major life events. Take, for example, the common experience of buying goods on credit. With interest rates on unpaid balances ranging from 18 to 27 percent, a $1,000 balance at just 18% paid with a minimum payment of $20 could take over ten years to settle, resulting in total payments many times the original amount. Living this way could lead to a financial crisis, causing bankruptcy, lower living standards, and strained relationships. If someone is raised in a family marked by financial struggles, this cycle could end in complete financial collapse. It is often seen that economic disparities tend to grow, with wealthy people increasing their wealth while those with fewer resources face bigger challenges.

Contextual effects of generations passing down financial habits (whether liabilities or assets) set the stage for inevitable life-altering events. This extends beyond families to the geophysical state of the planet. After decades of environmental damage, the year 2005 was recorded as the hottest year on Earth in modern times, marked by rising temperatures in the Arctic Circle. Such effects of global warming will inevitably lead to life-altering events.

Consider the shutdown of oceanic thermal flow channels due to rising freshwater levels from melting Arctic ice packs. This could lead to a sudden, catastrophic shift in global ocean currents, creating an "on" or "off" scenario, which could result in an ice age. Such events are not instantaneous but are the culmination of synchronized processes spanning over vast periods.

This same concept of synchronization applies to human life. Just as several factors influence weight loss (metabolism, gender, age, culture, emotions), many different motifs impact significant life-changing experiences. Whether it's a personal crisis or a global environmental event, these factors align in such a way that, when the critical mass is reached, a tipping point happens.

Our personal lives are constantly syncing with people, places, events, and situations. Timing is crucial. We are always aligning our thoughts, emotions, behaviors, and intentions with the inner and outer worlds we experience. Whether navigating traffic or adjusting our conduct in professional settings, we are continually working to sync ourselves with our environment. This process of synchronization reinforces itself, sometimes leading to success and other times to tragedy, but it is always evolving.

For example, teenagers who associate with the wrong crowd—like drug users, alcoholics, or criminals—might fall into a cycle of entrainment that leads them down dangerous paths. Similarly, idealizing a partner due to a need for attention and love can result in unhealthy, life-altering relationships. Entrainment isn't always about addiction; it's about how we sync with the world, which influences the outcomes we encounter.

In politics, similar patterns of synchronization are at work. John F. Kennedy's election in 1960 resulted from multiple intertwined factors—religion, economics, television, regional issues, and even the Mafia—that aligned and coordinated in a way that led to the election of America's first Catholic president. Timing, context, and the synchronization of various forces contributed to this transformative event in American politics.

It has been acknowledged in many documentaries that, without the influence of the underworld (such as Sam Giancana and Chicago-style politics, where each person is encouraged to vote and vote often in the same election), events might have played out differently. Ironically, when Kennedy took office, his brother, Bobby Kennedy, then Attorney General, aggressively targeted Mafia figures. Could this be a case of one biting the hand that feeds them? The tragic assassination of President John Kennedy in November 1963 led many to believe that, at some level, underworld influence was involved as a response to such a possible betrayal of loyalties.

Whether such scenarios are valid remains debatable. Yet, the accumulation of life-changing events in the so-called Kennedy Curse—the assassination of Bobby Kennedy, the death of their firstborn, Joe Kennedy, in World War II, and Ted Kennedy's apprehension about running for president—could have origins in their father's past. He was a bootlegger in the 1920s and '30s, amassing a fortune through illegal activities. The profound experiences of President John Kennedy and the accompanying losses may have derived from their father's illicit pursuits in money and power. What is that phrase? "The sins of the father may be visited upon the son."

Life-changing experiences have a future rooted in past origins, unfolding over time. If not modified, they fall back to our usual view of the "real" future. Yet, the key pattern of synchronized entrainment is a done deal—a future design embedded in our perception of past time, unfolding in our real-time future. We are only destined or fated if we choose to keep such synchronizations with these embedded future patterns stemming from what we call our past.

Consider your transformative experiences and analyze the recurring patterns of intricate themes that emerge from familiar contexts, culminating in a significant and impactful event. Think about the disorienting, foundation-shaking effects these experiences might have caused: teenage childbirth, the death or divorce of a spouse you believed was lifelong, a career ruined by a lawsuit, and so on.

There is an illogical pattern in entrainment where schemas of motifs connect and merge. These mergers or entanglements seem to defy logic and even the laws of nature. What physical principles determine the organization of these different individuals, locations, and objects into a unified series of synchronized events that could potentially lead to transformative experiences? For example, why was New Orleans, Louisiana, struck by both Hurricane Katrina, the most devastating hurricane in history, and killer tornadoes in the same season? Or why do jurors, called to jury duty from all walks of life, often come together (in most cases) to deliver either innocent or guilty verdicts? They somehow organize, synchronize, and entrain into one movement. Discourse, dialogue, debate, criticism, compliance—diverse perspectives examining evidence from nuanced viewpoints—this is the "cacophony of the new symphony" of harmonious entrainment.

The seemingly illogical order of unrelated events leading to life-changing experiences might seem confusing and bizarre. However, if our "past" is a future design and our "future" is the outcome that unfolds from the past back to its origins, then we have it backwards. Imagine looking at your handwriting through a mirror reflection. Reading the reflection reverses the order of the words and letters. This creates confusing and illogical connections. Not only are the letters and words unrecognizable, but the beginning of the sentence now appears as the end, and the end appears as the beginning.

If our timelines were reversed in a similar manner, with our current lifestyle mirroring a distorted version of the past and future, it could explain the chaos we experience when faced with life-changing events. Reading the reflections of what we believe are the messages of our lives may be distorted mirror images of errors in syntax and reversals of past and future, cause and effect.

For example, watching a Shakespearean play like Romeo and Juliet for two hours involves engaging with a work that has been fully scripted and prepared before the performance begins. By the end of those two hours, the future shape of the play has unfolded before the audience, tracing back to its origins, where the script has exhausted its plot development. The actors in the play are not creating a new future but rather acting out a collection of existing forms already shaped by the author, namely, Shakespeare. If one of the actors improvises in some way, they have altered the foundational design of these accumulated forms, crafting a new ending that still reflects variations from its beginning. The point here is that the future ending previously laid the foundation for the motif of the play in terms of setting the characters and schematic context. In this way, the future of the play's motif predetermined how the beginning, which we call the past, was going to happen. Hence, it is future formativeness that synchronizes the past to occur, not the past causing the future! It can be argued that life is not a predetermined script, and individuals have the freedom to shape their future according to their aspirations. However, our ability to create our future depends on how and with what we are already synchronized in our lives! I believe we are free to choose, but the caveat is that if we are already caught in risky patterns, we may not realize what is unknowingly influencing our choices. Some researchers suggest that our decisions are made in microseconds at the subconscious, synchronized level before we are consciously aware of what we are going to choose! It's not about willpower, fate, or demonic control! It's about our organizing formative motif that functions mostly in the unconscious realm of inherent organization. This is an integrated organic matrix—mind, body, psycho-social-biological-genetic, and spiritual! We are the matrix, the complexity that we so readily project onto our environment, in which we unwittingly participate! Indeed, it's not the spoon that bends, but our minds that bend! We could become more mindful and thereby awaken from our plays and dreams to experience the full artistry of our creative motifs' formativeness! What if you created your arrow of time and trusted your intuitive creativity? Just imagine!

On a sunny day, you might have an intuitive urge to take an umbrella to work. On your way home, it starts to rain, and you're surprised to realize how purposeful your umbrella has become. You have successfully moved away from a mistaken interpretation of cause and effect in your life. You sensed the weather that day and understood the design of the future's features for that day. What seemed illogical and out of place was actually quite consistent with the future of that unfolding design already set in your past. Could you start with how your day is meant to end? Could you finish your day by realizing that you are only just beginning? That is, how do you want your day to flow if you project your outcome from the start and trust the guiding pattern to lead you?

When it comes to the outcome of sporting events, one often hears the phrase "Monday morning quarterbacking," referring to the 2020 hindsight of what should have been done at the previous Saturday afternoon's football game. However, the time to intervene in any sporting event or challenge is to shape the future design synchronizations of a winning pattern before the game is played. What happens during a Saturday afternoon football game is the unfolding of past and future design synchronizations that already script the outcome. As my high school football coach once said, how well the team practices Monday through Friday already sets the stage for Saturday's result. By the time Saturday arrives, the synchronization of entrainments has already been established, making it highly unlikely to avoid certain inevitabilities. Our involvement in shaping the future influences what occurs before it happens. It's not about fate or destiny; it's about our subjective participation in the motif of future formation, which creates the illusion of tomorrow as spontaneous when we have already unwittingly scripted a fait accompli.

Our tendency to see our lives through external reflections rather than recognizing the active dynamics we participate in stems from a decline in our subjective involvement in shaping forces. While we value objectivity, losing our sense of subjectivity leads to errors in perception and interpretation of cause-and-effect patterns in our lives. A diminished sense of self as a tool confuses and restricts us perceptually, hindering our understanding of how past patterns emerge from formative plans into life-changing experiences.

It is the accumulation of precedent forms from various facets of motifs that support their existence. For example, the diversity of jurors, each with their own perspectives, can significantly influence the outcome when they collaborate and reach a consensus, affecting the defendant and everyone involved. These facets may stem from literal, metaphorical, or seemingly chaotic events that come together to cause life changes. For instance, a refrigerator's fan malfunction, a heartbeat irregularity in a person over 50, a washing machine clogged with socks, and a car needing an oil change—all happening within a month. It seems the man over 50 was showing signs of heart and stroke issues, which could indicate his "motor" needing clean oil (olive oil, fish oil, Omega-3s, etc.) and concerns about clogged arteries (tubes) caused by cholesterol (socks). If left unchecked, these events could build up to a critical point, leading to a sudden, life-altering event.

Life itself, the flow of events from one moment to the next, is an ongoing process of entrainment. Each moment is a coordinated ensemble of countless elements—people, places, things, atoms, quantum particles and waves, planets, stars, galaxies, universes—all synchronized and perfectly choreographed to happen simultaneously. Whether crossing the street, waking up, driving to work, waiting at the bank, or searching for a parking spot at the grocery store, people perform these everyday tasks with attention and routine. These activities occur at the same time. Daily routines like crossing the street, waking up, commuting, waiting at the bank, or finding parking at the grocery store are carried out with focus and precision, reflecting a consistent level of attention in our everyday lives.

Observe crowds, traffic jams, or shoppers on Christmas Eve. The ongoing patterns relate to matching and pacing of distinct motif patterns. For example, one must get up to speed on the highway (matching the flow of traffic). When President Bush appointed Condoleezza Rice to his second-term cabinet as Secretary of State, she had to get up to—or already be at—speed in the configurative, political thinking style of the President's platform. Different aspects of each person's individual motif match, mirror, pace, or even lead and fall back in service of the whole, connecting with similar points of the overall development.

What we may not realize is that the application process is an ongoing, moment-to-moment activity that flows and ripples through our daily experiences. The impacts of our fantasies, wishes, needs, appetites, and personal integrations all influence how this daily matching and pacing process naturally aligns with the organizing flow of ensembles.

Life-changing experiences can result from these natural connections. For example, when President George W. Bush supported democratic elections in Palestine in 2006, he overlooked experts who warned that Palestinians might vote for Hamas, a terrorist-affiliated group, which could threaten the core concept of democracy itself. When the elections occurred, Hamas did indeed gain control of the government with 61% of the vote.

When the formative process turns inward, it can cause a dangerous escalation of chaotic events that may become life-changing experiences. Transforming democratic processes into terrorist and tyrannical paths undermines the very foundation of reality, causing shocks that disorient our perceptions. However, such a profound event—like alienating international financial support for Palestine—took time to develop. The sequence of moment-to-moment events was cumulative, with the chain of occurrences traceable back to the Clinton administration. Consider the relatively liberal and unconventional behavior of the then-President with his intern, which led to massive political upheaval and the rise of compassionate conservatism, ultimately helping George W. Bush get elected twice as president.

The Horrific Tragedy of 9/11

The tragic events of 9/11, along with earlier terrorist attacks like the 1993 World Trade Center bombing and the USS Cole bombing in the Middle East, were pivotal moments that increased the urgency of the War on Terrorism. The series of preemptive strikes against terrorism eventually led to the strategy of promoting democracy in the Middle East. However, these actions sparked a cultural clash. Experts warned President Bush to be cautious of the paradox that democratic elections could result in the rise of tyrannical terrorist groups taking power. This warning proved true during the Palestinian elections, when Hamas was elected. One must be careful about what they wish for, as it may come in an unexpected form.

The Life-Altering Twist

The events described could not be predicted using a logical, reality-based view. What cause-and-effect link could there be between President Clinton's misconduct with an intern and the unprecedented Palestinian democratic elections, which oddly resulted in a terrorist group being elected? Is this similar to the chaos theory's idea, which says that when a butterfly flaps its wings in South America, tornadoes and weather changes happen in North America's Midwest? It's often said that every sixth person you meet knows someone you already know (the six degrees of separation theory). This interconnectedness suggests complex connections both among people and within their relationships. Additionally, it implies that we are connected to the non-human world—physical objects, the timing of events, and being in the "right" or "wrong" place at the "right" or "wrong" time, depending on your view.

The twist of life-altering events happens when seemingly unrelated events (people, places, things, etc.) interact in connected and illogical ways. These resonances create motifs that reflect each person's unique essence. These motifs are not limited to humans; they exist in all forms of life, both human and non-human. Each person's motif interacts with others, much like facets of two diamonds fitting perfectly together. These design structures—schemas in our minds, relationships, and life events—align and mirror parts of each motif's ratio with another.

For example, interactions with authority figures in the workplace can trigger specific dynamics between individuals that influence future outcomes. These sequences may result in a promotion or termination. However, we do not exist in a vacuum, and what we display at work can be affected by outside factors like harmony or stress in our personal lives. For example, the physical or emotional health of a loved one can impact our behavior at work, which may also be influenced by stress from the authority figure.

Over time, these repetitive cycles can gradually spiral out of control without us realizing it. Each encounter with an authority figure might leave lingering confusion, misunderstanding, or resentment. This cycle of dissatisfaction can escalate into workplace aggression, sometimes called "going postal." Introducing healthy variations, similar to a mobile with different bell lengths, can help restore balance. In relationships, reducing the frequency of confrontations with authority, shifting focus, and trying different communication methods can create asymmetry, reducing the severity of these potentially destructive cycles.

The distorted balance of motifs, when combined with another person's subtle motif, can create a tangled web that, if not addressed, may turn inward and significantly impact life. It's important to understand that each person's motif is unique. For instance, one person might react to work-related interactions by reflecting inward and focusing on their thoughts, while their supervisor might emphasize social interaction.

This mismatch in communication styles can cause dissonance, misunderstanding, and feelings of alienation. If these distorted cycles are not broken, they can lead to serious, life-altering consequences.

The Chaos of Entrainment

The chaos of entrainment increases in a cumulative, self-reflective way. The lack of open-ended dialogue, including playful exchanges, sharing information, and even misunderstandings, gradually limits communication. This intensifies deadlocked misunderstandings that could lead to a life-changing event, such as losing a job or career, with serious impacts on a person's lifestyle.

Time is a series of resonating patterns from moment to moment. The eras, generations, cultures, and environments into which we are born shape and enhance certain aspects of our complex motifs, while diminishing others. What pre-birth motifs influence where, when, how, and under what conditions we are born is a question that occupies theologians, philosophers, and visionaries alike. Nonetheless, the multifaceted coexistence of diverse entities on Earth—both human and non-human—interacts in an interdependent, unfolding matrix (ecological, bio-psycho-social-geo-physical). In a sense, we move as whole ensembles, each maintaining its uniqueness within the broader whole.

Life-Altering Events and Their Synchronization

Life-altering experiences represent a special case of synchronizing motifs that coalesce in critical mass, shaking us to our core. We are often astounded by the acausal connections between seemingly unrelated events. For example, missing a commuter train because the alarm clock didn't work could be seen as part of a larger chain of interconnected life events. This interconnectedness extends even to the brain's neural networks, where millions of neurons stimulate one another via neurotransmitters. It's been said that the combinations and permutations of these neural connections are more numerous than the atoms in the known universe.

Dr. Susan Greenfield (Discovery Channel, 2005) suggested that life events act like raindrops in a pool, creating ripples of activity in the brain. When certain events occur, they stimulate various brain regions, generating waves of electrical impulses that ripple through the brain, with the strongest waves reaching consciousness. These waves are both affected by and affect external life events.

Dr. Larry Weiskopf (Oxford University, 2005) compared the brain's functioning to a cathode ray electron gun, controlled by electromagnetic fields. Life events trigger different electromagnetic fields in the brain, influencing and being influenced by shifting patterns in those fields. These patterns can change our perceptions, stress levels, and even cause mind-altering experiences such as pain or drug effects.

Synchronicities and Life-Altering Experiences

Synchronicities—events that seem unrelated but are actually deeply connected—often lead to life-changing experiences. These events might appear as accidents or coincidences, but their combined effects grow stronger over time. For example, a politician might rise to power, face criticism, and eventually be indicted. Similarly, someone struggling with addiction might hit "rock bottom" and have a life-altering realization.

Synchronicities represent the ripple effects of entraining motifs that gather energy, intensity, and power if left unchecked. Our awareness influences whether we permit or interrupt these events and the potential consequences they carry.

The Arrow of Time

The arrow of time comes from our experience of sequential change—an endless variety of arrangements that shape our reality. Life is made up of a chain of events that, when looked back on, may seem to move with purpose or direction. Time can be seen as a form of entrainment, where patterns align across different levels, both through conscious and unconscious processes.

In this broader view, we are not just passive participants in life but active co-creators of the patterns shaping our experiences. Our decisions, actions, and interactions generate ripple effects that reach both forward and backward in time, influencing our current awareness and choices. The future can influence the present, and choices made now can potentially impact events that happened in the past.

When people find themselves in desperate situations, they often make promises to a Higher Power, vowing that if they survive, their lives will change. For example, a lawyer was out boating in the Atlantic Ocean and was thrown from his boat. He prayed for help, and a partially inflated helium balloon floated his way. When that didn't work, he prayed again, and a piece of driftwood came to him. After 8 hours of struggle, fatigue and exhaustion set in, but he kept praying. Finally, a helicopter appeared and rescued him. It turned out his boat had run aground on an island beach, nearly causing casualties. The boat was traced back to him through his brother. This lawyer's life was permanently changed. If he betrayed his commitment to a new life, he risked facing the dangers of his past coming back to him in the present or future.

Swimming upstream, parasites can quickly sync with wave ripple frequencies. People like alcoholics, drug addicts, drama queens, and workaholics—if they break their current commitments—find themselves rapidly transported back in time, reinfecting themselves and falling deeper into the same cycles they tried to escape.

In life-changing experiences, we are never separate from the past or future because both exist in the present moment. All possibilities for transformation are always accessible. Our wave-like ripples of motif consciousness select, filter, and manifest reality. To change that reality, we must first alter the cellular assemblies of our motif-creating consciousness. Consciousness is fundamental to the universe, and it forms unique motifs that attract, create, and unintentionally participate in multiple synchronistic events simultaneously.

For example, when we see a spinning car wheel, we can change how fast it looks like it is moving by adjusting the frequency of light waves reflected from it. Mechanics use this idea when testing and analyzing car engines. By increasing or decreasing the flicker rate of the light waves, we can match the peaks and valleys of the wave to the spinning wheel. The closer these peaks and valleys match, the higher the frequency appears, and the faster the wheel seems to turn.

We may not realize that our awareness of motifs shapes and emphasizes aspects of our daily experiences, intensifying and reinforcing them until they become a tangible reality. Recognizing that we actively help synchronize our realities is the first step toward changing the patterns we follow. This process enables us to reshape our future.

I knew a woman who constantly felt unloved, unappreciated, and abandoned by her family. Raised by an emotionally distant mother who repeatedly relied on her for care while neglecting her emotional needs, this woman spent her life feeling inept and unappreciated for her efforts to help others. Eventually, she realized she had been trying to mother others the same way she was mothered—hoping to fix her mother through her actions, to finally receive the love and nurturing she lacked as a child. She had been waiting for irresponsible and unloving people to accept her, which kept her feeling abandoned. She understood that changing her mindset was possible by surrounding herself with supportive people, which helped her in her recovery and self-care.

Clues to recognizing our synchronization motifs and life-changing entrainments involve subtle, non-tangible connections between people, places, things, and events. These connections often appear through recurring themes and motifs. You may observe:

Attracting individuals who may have unconventional backgrounds or characteristics, including those with criminal records or experiencing disorientation.

Sudden episodes of illogical behavior, such as anger, aggression, or self-harm.

1. Unexplained financial losses or demands—sudden losses in business accounts, job terminations, rising bills, or taxes.
2. Physical health changes—such as skin conditions, glandular issues, or emotional shifts that reflect physical ailments.
3. Delays or procrastination in reaching goals—such as ongoing setbacks in relationships, long waits at stores, or stalled progress in education, career, or personal ambitions.

These entrainments often signal impasses or bottlenecks, where our actions and resonances with these motifs can trigger life-changing crises—such as depression, impulsive behavior, missed opportunities, or setbacks in personal and professional growth.

Connecting with motifs across different levels—whether through people, places, or events—may seem illogical or unscientific. However, these synchronizations reflect the inherent wholeness woven into our universe. The idea that nothing exists without resonance with motif groups suggests that, instead of everything happening for a reason, it occurs because of the resonance of entraining motifs. The "why" often arises from a critical mass of previous forms leading to a significant shift in current reality.

Our perception of time affects how we experience significant events. Our choices generate ripple effects that alter reality, influencing both the past and the future.

Our decisions produce ripple effects that alter reality, influencing both the past and future.

Einstein suggested that surpassing the speed of light could, in theory, reverse the arrow of time. Similarly, a parasite in the Amazon Jungle, like a salmon returning to spawn, can adjust its oscillations (torque and curvature) to move faster than the flow of time. Just as someone might walk on water or dance on wave crests, these Einsteinian-like ideas of time travel blur the lines between past, present, and future.

Changing our motifs and aligning our consciousness with transformative ensembles requires releasing ego attachments and shifting our perspective from conventional reality. Carl Jung, the Swiss psychologist and former student of Sigmund Freud, suggested that cause and effect are never absolute; there is always a small percentage of experimental reality that remains indeterminate. Meteorologists, for example, can predict hurricanes with high accuracy, but they cannot determine their exact timing or path with 100% certainty. Introducing additional variables increases the unpredictability of outcomes.

This paradox in entrainments shows that, while we can narrow down options, the complexity of variables prevents total control. Trying to achieve this is like aiming for the horizon; no matter how hard we try, it stays forever out of reach. In this uncertainty, there is potential for acausal events—the future influencing the present or past.

I believe the fundamental building blocks of our universe and personal realities are these entrainments of formative motifs. If thoughts, ideas, and constructs are things—neuro-electrical magnetic fields influencing physical manifestation—then our universe exists holographically within and among us. Understanding how mind-body synchronization resonates through our lives empowers us to create new realities. Recognizing this enables us to change our timelines, opening up possibilities that might otherwise seem inevitable.

Grains of Sand and the Universe

Changing a single grain of sand on a beach affects the universe. How could that be? Years ago, during a high school football practice, I found myself face-to-face with a 375-pound offensive lineman. I weighed 210 pounds. When the ball was snapped, something inexplicable surged through me, propelling me into a collision with this massive opponent. After the dust settled, I saw him lying on his back, his nose bleeding. The coach was astonished; my forearm had lifted him off the ground.

The impact was so powerful that I went on to play first-string defense for a state-ranked championship team. That moment triggered a series of events: an Ivy League football scholarship, graduate school, and ultimately my career as a clinical psychologist. That single event fundamentally changed the course of my life. It was an intense burst of awareness, creating a unified theme that shifted my path.

Such moments of reconfiguration are embedded in each of our lives, often called luck, kismet, or divine intervention. They are the almost imperceptible shifts that ripple through time, altering our course. These moments shape the trajectory of our lives, for better or worse.

Like the sands of time, transformation requires subtle changes at nearly imperceptible levels. For example, it is possible to observe unusual behavior from a neighbor. Although these actions may seem harmless at first, they can ultimately signal more serious issues. Recognizing these shifts, these patterns, can be vital in protecting our well-being.

If you are driving home and, through no fault of your own, get hit by an uninsured motorist, resulting in devastating injuries, this can also be a life-changing moment. While not always predictable by cause and effect, these events happen through interconnected patterns that lay the groundwork for change.

While driving, we focus on projecting our path hundreds of feet ahead. Past developments influence the landscape ahead and also affect what comes after. For instance, the hill in front couldn't exist without the lower terrain that precedes it. Context is everything. Removing the hill alters the context, like moving a grain of sand in a pattern, and changing what is before it as part of a larger wave, filter, or strobe-light effect.

When one changes the current and/or upcoming arrangement of contextual motifs, what keeps appearing before it also shifts. Where the head goes, the body will follow. The front end of a car can't avoid bringing its rear end along. What it hits in the future will influence the past experiences it carries. What President Richard Nixon did in the Watergate scandal cast a shadow on his later accomplishments, opening political doors to China. Indeed, it slowed his "door-opening" policies in foreign affairs when his future presidency was ended by his pressured resignation from office as President of the United States.

Something as simple as a golfer's follow-through after the club hits the ball influences the ball's launch angle. Therefore, follow-through is crucial for maintaining past or previous achievements. Our daily lives, together with Einstein's curved space-time shaped by matter, density, and light's energy frequency, operate as an interconnected system. The entire landscape of our lives is orchestrated in perfect harmony—even during life-changing moments. How is that possible?

Harmony in Dis-Harmony

For anything to exist, it must be time-synchronized in a common motif. Have you ever noticed that when you seem to be in a relatively peaceful state of mind, your environment also reverberates in an entraining, synchronizing support? Occasionally, when writing a complex passage with interrelated and uncertain elements, the surrounding environment mirrors these complexities through simultaneous noise and disturbances. During the process of integration, external distractions decrease and internal structures become more cohesive.

Perceive how, in an accident involving two or more cars, they must align in some synchronized pattern of time, space, and configurations, or they will never collide. Accidents in this context involve alignments and synchronization motifs, indicating resonance in speed, angle of direction, and points of contact. What we call "accidental" relates to our conscious, human will or ego-driven intentions. Just because something may not be consciously chosen doesn't mean we and others aren't syncing in some rhythmic, coordinated follow-through that draws us into a series of life-changing events. There's that very odd saying that the best-laid plans of mice and men (and computerized machines as well) often go astray.

Projection in a direction indicates that multi-dimensional interfaces are considered functional in any area of operation. Mediators refer to perceiving the world with "soft eyes," noticing the spaces between points and the background or contextual field. Zen Koans relate to the sound of one hand clapping and the sounds of silence. These and other acausal phenomena evoke concepts such as ensembles, holism, embeddedness of eleven-dimensional universes, and the interconnection of matrices at quantum levels of consciousness and reality.

Human life on Earth involves participating in different levels of reality organized by hierarchical events. Positive or negative attitudes, moods, perceptions, beliefs, and actions can inspire, destroy, nullify, or create wondrous or disastrous life-changing events. Recognizing the impact of critical mass effects, acknowledging our interconnectedness, and avoiding self-centered views can lead to significant expansions in vision and perspective. These changes can happen anytime or during any transition within the space-time continuum. Adjusting to the ongoing sequence of interconnected motifs reveals noncausal influences in forming fortunate timelines, which are essential to our core identity. The idea of self becomes cohesive and aligned when engaged within the context of extraordinary, unconscious awareness. When we are in these flow-like states (Csikszentmihalyi, 1992), optimal performance becomes achievable. We experience higher formative energies, which grant access to altered states of consciousness and transformative realities.

There is a strong connection between altered states of consciousness and life-changing experiences. One can cause the other. Traumatic, abusive experiences in childhood, war, natural disasters, etc., can shock and disorient people into altered states of awareness, perception, and parts of the subconscious. These parts can reappear in a person's life both as causes and effects, or as recurring traumas in their lifestyle.

For example, a 43-year-old divorced man who endured physical, mental, and sexual abuse from ages 4 to 9 experienced recurring trauma and disruptions in his adult relationships and parenting efforts. His constant refrain was, "There just aren't any good women out there anymore!" Both his mother and wife had died from self-inflicted harm. He didn't cause these tragedies. However, these experiences became ingrained in his pattern of trauma and drama. The effects of childhood abuse contributed to similar patterns in his adult life, with core themes aligning with those of others who share vulnerabilities like weak boundaries, a fragile sense of self, and internalized negative and distorted beliefs.

The cyclical nature of altered states of consciousness and transformative experiences exemplifies multi-dimensional patterns of how motifs function across multiple levels of entrainment. These cause-and-effect (or chicken-and-egg, acausal loops) of entrainment are synchronized by motifs—repetitive themes and behaviors that are configured together. Such future-oriented, formative design is what gives rise to life-changing experiences. We are not gods, nor are we leaves helplessly blown about by the winds of fate. There is a notable degree of co-determinism in the relationship between individuals' destinies and unusual experiences.

What sets of altered states are we unknowingly creating and being shaped by as we move between the external world of people, places, and things? The cycle of altered states of consciousness (ASC) and life-changing experiences (LCE) builds its pattern, connecting mind, body, and psychosocial-physical events into synchronized groups. Crucially, it is important to recognize that both time and physical objects are part of these groups. The traumatized 43-year-old was prone to accidents, bad luck, illness, and repeatedly being in the wrong place at the wrong time. He seemed like someone who walks through life with a cloud over his head.

No, he is not cursed (though he certainly felt that way). Instead, he was caught in a network of synchronizations emerging from an influential future of unrecognized motifs.

Alterations in his ASC and/or his LAE could resynchronize and entrain new operational motifs. Achieving such transformative changes requires mastery of optimal flow experiences related to core self-other motifs. Unfolding matrices of self-other entraining motifs help in attending to and accessing the core loops of an individual's artistic motif. The issue with ASC resulting from abuse and/or LAE, or LAE emerging from traumatic ASC, is their mirroring and magnification effects on each other. Transforming this timing pattern involves asymmetrically arranging core self-motifs to trigger unfolding, creating ideal conditions for re-synchronization. LAE can then be shifted through motif re-synchronization by surrendering one's sense of self and reality to a larger, higher, or asymmetrical constellation of self–other motifs.

It's like discovering that the ugly duckling syndrome is actually the beautiful swan, unknowingly surrounded by ugliness because it believes it doesn't deserve better. When someone feels ugly in a comfortable ASC, they tend to identify with other ugly ducklings. Even worse, these recurring themes mirror physical realities and natural disasters, which happen at the wrong place and time. Mastering core self-awareness and addressing asymmetrical motifs can break the cycle of the ugly, destructive ASC and LAE. It's important to note that LAE can cause shocks and disorientations that promote altered states of consciousness (ASC). Like volcanoes, they have the potential to rejuvenate environments and sometimes improve the overall quality of life. Those who have experienced illness, natural disasters, financial ruin, wars, and so on often say, "if it did not kill them, it made them stronger and a better person." Senator John McCain of Arizona, a POW in Vietnam for five years, shows how such experiences can lead to personal transformation.

Mastering motifs of core self-ensembles involves discovering our innate, inherent, unique patterns of how we think, move, feel, sense, wonder, pace, and lead our lives. Understanding our speed, style, character, attributes, and introversion-extroversion temperament, among others, creates new resonance and synchronization in aligning these motifs. Each of us operates with a distinct, asymmetrical (slightly skewed, off-balance) combination of attributes and idiosyncratic qualities. Recognizing and mastering our sense of unique self—uncovering the inherent tendencies of our core character beyond psycho-social adaptation—enables new synchronicity, an improved ASC, and optimal LAE to develop throughout our lives.

CHAPTER 11

LIFE-CHANGING EXPERIENCES THROUGH MULTIDIMENSIONAL CONSCIOUSNESS

"The time has come," the walrus said, "to speak of many things, of sealing wax and sailing ships, of puppy dogs and kings." – Through the Looking Glass.

Motifs are unique, organizing structures growing upon the recurring, self-organizing themes of an individual's repetitive thematic thought, emotions, and behavioral themes, incorporating unique psychosocial events, drawing upon experiences of places and events that are intricately connected in a hierarchy of nested mosaics, like Chinese boxes within boxes. Imagine TV soap operas, spanning decades, with recurring, asymmetrical variations of ensembles within ensembles of interconnected plots and subplots, scenes flowing through moment-to-moment events and complex dilemmas. Each frame of the drama forms its own ensemble of interconnected shots or scenes. Regardless of frame size or sequence, the interpersonal dynamics of synchronized ensembles unfold in a seamless harmony of interwoven motifs.

Each of us moves in synchronized harmony—within ourselves, among others, and with the universe at large—reflecting unique combinations of coordinated events at every level of existence. Each group of people, places, and things moves as one, coordinated both internally and across larger or smaller organizational units. It's similar to planets orbiting the sun in different ratios, or solar systems and galaxies moving together to form clusters.

Imagine a group of people inside a vehicle, all moving together with the car. As the car progresses through traffic, it lines up with others around it. During rush hour, waves of cars can cause a traffic jam, where they come to a standstill, like a "parking lot" of stopped vehicles. This unity happens in varying degrees of synchronization, just as different levels of syncing exist across the hierarchies of reality, from the infinitely small (quantum mechanics) to the infinitely large (the macrocosmic universe).

Someone might wonder how such harmony can exist in a world filled with terrorism, child abuse, torture, diseases, and death. Harmony doesn't mean that our world is perfect, moral, or personally satisfying. It means that a network of connected variables operates in synchronized timing. When tragedy occurs, like an accident or loss, it results from precisely synchronized events and factors.

Consider the case of a married executive who had an affair. When his spouse discovered it, the emotional stress triggered a heart attack, sending him to the hospital. The consequences affected his entire life, leading him to leave his job, move, reassess his priorities, and face the "death" of his marriage. This event prompted deep self-reflection, revealing distorted beliefs about love, success, and nurturing. His affair was an expression of synchronized harmony, shaped by embedded motifs, waiting for the right conditions to surface. Similarly, favorable opportunities arise when the right events align.

These synchronized ensembles of motifs—people, places, and events—align perfectly in timing. They can occur anywhere, from restaurants to workplaces, depending on how unlikely factors coincide. Take, for example, the daily commuters who form bonds over time, even though they have never met before. How is it that strangers can develop strong connections so quickly? This happens because we project and resonate with compatible traits, creating neurochemical bonds that can lead to romantic entanglements. However, not all outcomes are positive, as the intensity of these synchronized interactions can produce both good and bad effects.

Synchronization of experiences can also lead to fortunate events, such as winning the lottery, where the right people meet at the right time. These events often display patterns similar to fractals, revealing underlying order within apparent chaos. Here, we begin to observe the emergence of asymmetrical motifs in unpredictable, acausal ways, much like weather forecasts. This level of interconnectedness encourages us to expand our consciousness into higher, multi-dimensional states of awareness. Life-changing experiences push us to broaden our understanding and expand our perspectives, enabling transformation and growth.

Take, for example, the man who had to cut off his arm to survive after being trapped by a fall in the mountains. This situation required a major shift in mindset, involving a choice between losing his life or sacrificing his limb to live. The fabric of our interconnected life patterns is in harmony, following its own design. It's not about whether the world was "meant to be" as it is; it's simply the way things are.

Transformation happens by re-synchronizing our motifs. Every change—no matter how small—can shift the course of the universe. In our lives, we need to recognize when to adjust our patterns or risk merely stirring the sand without true transformation. Our behaviors and emotions are influenced by both conscious and unconscious forces, including early childhood experiences and societal influences. Yet, it's our personal, unique interpretation of these experiences that shapes who we are.

People are often influenced by external events and interactions with others. If we didn't sync with them, our existence as we know it wouldn't be possible. When faced with unpredictable situations, we need to learn to manage these dynamics. Whether merging into rush-hour traffic or dealing with trauma and loss, we are uniquely connected by patterns shaped by our early selves. The challenge is to expand our multi-dimensional awareness and align with our true core, which embodies the art of being in harmony with our natural selves.

For instance, when Hillary Clinton aligned with her core self during the New Hampshire primary, she spoke from her heart and inner strength rather than trying to win an office. This alignment empowered her and deeply connected with voters. Despite predictions of her losing, her victory was an acausal event—an outcome of perfect harmony.

The synchronization dynamics also play a role in high-stakes situations. For example, consider a jury deciding a verdict. Each juror must synchronize with others, processing evidence in their own way. But a "hung" jury, where they cannot reach a consensus, is also a form of perfect harmony, as it requires twelve individuals to agree to disagree in their own unique ways.

Madness and Transformation

The incorporation of future designs within systems such as family, community, and culture creates distinct synchronizations. However, when these patterns challenge the rules of engagement, disorientation and shock can occur. Consider the worker whose field becomes obsolete after decades of dedicated work, or the tool and die makers replaced by robots. These life-changing shifts challenge our established synchronizations, pushing us to develop new patterns of action.

In the same way, aligning with a political figure or supporting a cause means associating ourselves with the results of their actions. Every decision we make closes some doors and opens others. While we may not always "deserve" the outcomes we face, we are, in a way, in perfect harmony with them.

What about madness, psychosis, and artistry? Often, creative problem-solving requires thinking "outside the box." However, how do we break free from our ingrained patterns? Consider the collapse of the Tacoma Narrows Bridge in the 1940s, which was caused by the rhythmic walking of crowds. The more people tried not to synchronize with each other, the more they did, leading to disaster. Similarly, when we try to "think outside the box," we often fall deeper into the patterns we aim to avoid. Achieving liberation involves shifting our focus, embracing non-self-identities, and exploring altered states of consciousness. This is where "madness" and "artistry" collide, revealing hidden parts of ourselves.

Many prominent figures—Einstein, King, Van Gogh, and even dictators like Hitler and Milosevic—were able to think "outside the box. Though their societal impacts varied, each person exhibited similar patterns affecting themselves and others. The difference lies in how they used their creative or destructive potential.

The transformation we undergo might be akin to an "artistic-like madness," a shift in consciousness that can either benefit or harm humanity. It is a process of recognizing our interconnectedness, embracing the uniqueness of our standard themes, and understanding how our actions echo through the fabric of existence.

The Artistic Motif of Unique Proportions

How do we uncover our own "mad, artistic genius" self of motif? That wild, energetic flare of loving, robust brilliance that resides within all of us, even the seemingly mundane and simple. There is a dedicated commitment to constraints, embracing a passionate artistic vision nurtured through rigorous self-discipline, meticulous attention to detail, thoughtful design, structured planning, and intricate, complex architectures. It all reflects "madness of geniuses".

Our distinctive distribution of motifs leads to powerful, surprising, and sometimes daunting results. Showcasing our individuality demands careful and deliberate effort, tailored to our developmental stages and lifestyles.

Children and adolescents enjoy experimenting, playing, and exploring. However, they need wise parental guidance and supervision to nurture and develop their emerging talents properly. Achieving this balance of creative direction is a challenge that goes beyond the scope of this work. Recognizing the specific traits of our self-motifs requires a unique set of skills.

Golden Proportions Of Our Unique Motifs

How can one recognize members of their family? Children do not look exactly alike. Even identical twins are not perfectly identical. Although they may share up to 60% of their DNA, this percentage does not mean they are completely genetically identical. In families, resemblances can be seen in eye structure, facial shapes, movements, gestures, temperaments, voice patterns, and more—the family system of motifs among relatives shares common but not identical traits. Similarly, the unique combination of personality traits within each family member is like a family itself. Each person carries within them an internal family constellation of attributes and characteristics, each with its own proportional "recipe."

Making a cake requires a recipe with the right proportions of ingredients like sugar, flour, milk, and butter, along with proper mixing and baking times. This concept of balanced ingredients and following a step-by-step process is similar to how self-motifs develop within each person. Healthy and wise parental guidance is crucial to support this process. However, children are born with inherent qualities that can develop on their own, even without parental guidance. If they are prematurely exposed to overwhelming social situations, they may experience a sudden, life-changing event (teenage pregnancy, drug addiction, etc.).

Cakes won't bake themselves and require a chef to make them. Children will want to grow up, however. Yet, without guidance, they could go quite "mad" (or rageful) if left to their own devices, not knowing how much "water, flour or butter" to add to their own "mixture" of self-motifs. Sometimes, the "madness" that occurs is a way "out of their boxed-in-ness," as it may come from the trapped box in which they already live.

The unique proportional balance of their core motif will continue to drive expression, regardless of how inappropriate the child or others might mistreat or mis-parent them. Like a plant buried under concrete, it will bend and reshape itself to break through the concrete. The way or path of its expression reflects its motif. However, this may not fully reveal its true potential.

What is an example of this specific proportionality in design? How about yourself, the one reading this? Let's explore and see what you discover about yourself that makes up the "recipe of you-ness." Reflect on your unique self as you consider the general areas of unique proportionality.

The motifs show proportionality in both their schematic and structural designs. This includes an individual's unique set of proportions, such as facial and body features like bone length, and the size and shape of cheeks, jaws, head, arms, and torso. It also covers thought patterns regarding their intensity, frequency, divergence, convergence, tangential aspects, and more, along with emotional temperament, movement style, speech, pacing, leadership behaviors, and interpersonal style—all of which reflect their ability for multi-level entrainments. The specific proportions of an individual's motif enable selective compatibility and alignment with various people, places, and events. For example, the pace and gait of a person's walk, the level of abstraction in their thinking, and their use of inductive or deductive reasoning will proportionally match and mirror those with similar proportions.

(and personalities). Additionally, differential entrainment happens when different ratios match. For example, if I take one step and another person takes three, then I am entrained with that person at a 1:3 step ratio. The same idea applies to rates and styles of thinking, expressing, acting, and so on. Suppose I have one comprehensive idea or thought that includes three smaller concepts from my partner. In that case, my main idea has absorbed the other three beneath its hierarchy of organization and abstraction. How far ahead or behind the "curve" of one another's thinking or understanding—partly or wholly—reflects the capacity for multi-level entrainments with multiple people, places, and events. This could be a factor in causing unexplained coincidences.

Recently, while waiting for a friend, I did some paperwork in a restaurant I had only visited once before. While waiting in my booth, I overheard a conversation behind me and learned that a colleague was discussing a potential meeting with a client. The timing, reason for visiting this restaurant to find comfort and prepare for an upcoming meeting, and concurrent activities all align.

There is a perfect balance in all forms of entertainment. A certain ratio of congruence often links motifs together. This is possible because of their unique and separate proportions. As our experiences become more detailed, our patterns of motifs grow more distinct. It is a result of aging, gaining skill in our careers, or refining our details that, coincidentally, unpredictable life events are more likely to happen. They are also more probable when we remain open, flexible, and adaptable in our perceptions, allowing hidden patterns of chaos to emerge within structured, causal groups. I started my career after meeting a psychiatrist in a self-serve restaurant, with whom I had previously done an internship. As he walked down the restaurant aisle, I asked if there was an open position at his mental health center, considering the favorable conditions for a transformative life experience. Three months later, I was working as a trainee in their residential alcoholism program. Over the past thirty years, this has significantly contributed to my clinical career, training, and expertise.

Ensembles of entraining motifs appear at key points of change and self-transformation, such as early childhood, adolescence, early adulthood, midlife crisis, the mature and golden years, and the end of life. The unique, individual proportions of these motifs asymmetrically repeat themselves as fractal chaos patterns that become increasingly refined, prolific, and complex over time. Changes in consciousness result from the interaction between significant life events and altered states of awareness. The chaotic and frame-breaking redefinitions caused by catastrophic external events align with, influence, and resonate with internal altered states of consciousness during these vital moments of change and self-growth.

The awareness of transformation must recognize that "good things" (beneficial, personal experiences) can and do happen to "good people." As widely acknowledged, the opposite also occurs. I believe one of the main factors shaping how we perceive life-changing experiences is our rigid perceptual filters that insist people, places, and events "must" be a certain way; otherwise, life feels catastrophic, dangerous, and traumatic. This doesn't mean that natural disasters like Hurricane Katrina and the Indonesian tsunami are caused by rigid filters (although some rigidity may stem from poor warning systems and unpreparedness to recognize such realities). An owner of a South African farm complained about rocks emerging in the soil, which interfered with planting and harvesting. The farmer eventually decided to sell the farm and leave. The new owner, with a fresh perspective, realized that the "rocks" were diamonds!

In the previous chapter, I discussed concepts of time related to time travel experiences. At one point, I used an electronic calendar that could be programmed through December 31, 2100. Beyond that date, the calendar would move "forward to the past" (instead of "back to the future"). Thank you, Steven Spielberg. That is, moving beyond that date would automatically "flip" or "loop" the calendar forward, "back" to January 1, 1900. Scientists say that space-time curves around itself. Imagine traveling eastward from Chicago, Illinois, U.S.A., to the Greenwich Meridian. The closer you get to it, the later the time zones become (New York City is one hour ahead in the "future"). When moving east across the Greenwich Meridian time line, the new day begins on the eastern side of the line, marking the start of a 24-hour period that aligns with the previous calendar day. Time travel is said to occur in Einstein's world by traveling faster than the speed of light (as space-time reconfigures one's movement to loop around the curvature of the past-present-future-past continuum). Intriguingly, scientists have found that space (our universe) expands faster than the speed of light, "looping our universe" through space-time curvatures.

Personal travel through one's timeline reflects the physics of our universe. While we may not be able to go back to our past and change what "actually" happened, we can access new historical roots of our sources—such as early childhood, cultural neighborhoods, and family or social connections—to enrich and empower our present and future opportunities.

Consider the parasite traveling upstream in the Amazon, the salmon returning to its spawning grounds, and the forward movement through time. In our daily experience, as we move forward in harmony with our unique formative motifs, we can resonate "faster than light" in "no time at all" with "being ourselves" throughout our entire timeline. Wherever we go, have gone, or will go, we are there when aligned with our unique motifs. Bending time and space, and following the continuum of our unique motifs' curvature of time loops, allows us to journey through our own distinct time.

I knew a carpenter who had endured physical and emotional abuse as a child and could see the vintage beauty and worth in old furniture that others overlooked. He was skilled at using tools to "smooth out" the "rough edges" of antiques. He also could envision future artistic and restorative projects in his home, which reminded him and brought him "full circle" toward future encounters with his "past" childhood experiences. This involved smoothing out rough edges in his family relationships—conflicting parents and guilt-ridden, harsh,

Cutting-edge critiques of shame-based experiences in his family. His rummaging through other people's "garbage and throw-away furniture" propelled him into future encounters with "past" experiences. Resurfacing furniture and salvaging objects became his talent, helping him reconnect with lost identities over time. He had been learning to travel "in no time zones" at all, "faster than the speed of light," recovering lost parts of himself by using his unique motif of "soften edges," resurfacing damaged goods (damaged goodness), and salvaging artifacts (personal salvation of lost souls) on his life's journey. This person instantly resonated, reverberating with his unique past experiences of rebuilding and renovation as he "traced back" his forward projections to his origins.

The future "light waves" of unique motif projections provide access to the origins, sources, and subjective experiences of the whole self—our core awareness. A car's headlights not only illuminate the road ahead, revealing its shape and direction, but also display the current position and starting point of the vehicle. Recognizing the contours and patterns of past, present, and future pathways fosters a sense of wholeness and interconnectedness. In this way, immediate access to the resources and origins of the "past" becomes possible, allowing individuals to align with themselves—and others. Empowering resource states are achieved by "riding one's future light beams" back through personal time, space, and emotional states, enabling a more precise alignment with one's unique self and motif.

Einstein imagined riding a light beam to the sun to better understand aspects of relativity. Similarly, each of us can "ride the light beams" of our future projections, but in different ways. We can ride, retrace, and reshape the forward wave of our formative movement and the contours of our future paths. How does one ride future projections in reverse, contrast, or juxtapose? By completing the formative contours of future events through multi-dimensional historical perspectives. This involves developing an awareness of patterns in daily events and understanding their meaning and consequences from various viewpoints. With this perspective, one can see how minor deviations, if left unchecked, can grow into major destructive forces—like cracks in a dam that lead to rupture or breakthrough, depending on one's view.

Riding the future's waves back in time refers to a multi-dimensional, meta-level "wave of the wave" phenomenon. The synchronization of emotional and experiential events (traumatic or not) moves in waveforms—unique peaks and troughs, varying intensities, variable frequencies, and dilution patterns. The "wave of the wave"—its meta-pattern of alternating high and low—has its signature or motif. This code-like configuration allows movement—dancing across the peaks— in all directions and dimensions of time and space. Capturing the design patterns between lifestyle highs and lows, between events of traumatic challenge or strange synchronicity, allows the emergence of meta-level, formative "wave of the wave" motifs.

You don't need bipolar or borderline conditions for such cyclical patterns to happen. Chaos theory looks at similar ideas: tipping points, feedback loops, thresholds (like global warming, glacial melting, carbon emissions). The "wave of the wave" describes non-linear, acausal events that build up in layers of energy across different parts of a person's life—physical, biological, psychological, familial, communal, and societal.

During multitasking—such as talking on the phone, writing, gesturing, driving, and watching the clock at the same time—mild trance-like states can occur. Energy builds up and flows from physical actions to psychosocial effects and then to altered perception. In these states, perception itself might change, creating opportunities for new transformative behaviors—like reframing, taking risks, and trying new things. What initially seems chaotic may, upon reflection, reveal underlying patterns.

Chaos theory uncovers the hidden order in what appears to be randomness (e.g., 1:3, 3:5 ratios), forming the beautifully asymmetrical fractals of nature—and human behavior. Each person's "wave of the wave" ratio creates a unique, motif-like pattern, serving as a gyroscopic alignment for self-identity. During altered states of transformation, new problem-solving pathways emerge.

Focusing too much on future goals can sometimes diminish recognition of past achievements and divert attention from current priorities. Still, there is a deeper "wave of the wave' connection that links past, present, and future arrangements. The idea of the "future" can lead us to revisit our past, including memories of joy, teenage struggles, and a renewed appreciation for what we have always had but never fully noticed.

The complexity of core self-phenomena becomes condensed, enveloped, and epi-structured—self-organized around each person's unique motif. This journey through personal motif trajectories—toward one's past—resembles circumnavigating the globe or navigating curved space-time. Like

Columbus sailing west to find the east, it's akin to going up and down an escalator—an experiential reversal through resonating motifs. This "non-mirrored image reverse" (James & Woodsmall, 1988) enables traveling upstream in the river of time via a complementary "wave of the wave" frequency, realigning one's motif across the lifespan.

A carpenter's skill in refurbishing old furniture mirrors his "non-mirrored image reverse wave" of completion—a return to his roots and becoming whole. His future develops from his origins—his planned future is connected to his past, which can be understood by tracing his practical reality back to its fundamental theme. Expanding his awareness of timelines resynchronizes his nested, combined motifs.

Scientists observe that traveling at light speed contracts time and stretches space—lower frequency and longer wavelengths. Although we don't achieve those speeds, trauma (like a near-miss on the highway) can trigger accelerated mental processing. In seconds, the mind rapidly considers options, making time seem to stretch. A person's life may "flash" before their eyes. This kind of time-travel through experience and emotion, condensed into seconds, can lead to epiphanies—insights about the overall impact of one's life journey.

In these heightened states, consciousness operates at a higher level. It's "fifth gear" processing—where one cycle of thought can be equivalent to five in normal circumstances. Synchronization accelerates. Time feels compressed and expanded at the same time, and intuition often becomes more acute.

Future Memories of Life-Altering Experiences

We may catch glimpses of the future through flashes in the chaos of the present— reflections of our past projected into tomorrow. Melting glaciers, droughts, wildfires, and mudslides are echoes of our future coming back from the arrow of time.

Psychics are believed to foresee the future through intuition, but in fact, everyone can experience intuitive insights that span past and future moments. For instance, consider a married lawyer having an affair while involved with someone else—an emotional triangle with unavoidable consequences. You don't need to be psychic to sense what those choices will lead to.

Flashes, patterns, and associations that do not display a direct cause and effect may nevertheless serve as indicators of significant events. We might not always notice the signs now, but they are revealing themes of what is to come.

Exploring how our projected future, influenced by time compression, fits into extended waves of lived experience helps us understand key events within our timelines. If major life events occur every 5–7 years, can we expect them to happen again in the future? What patterns come together to produce hidden, life-changing results?

Consider someone with a gambling addiction. Every 4–6 weeks, a recurring pattern occurs: money on hand, late-night restlessness, lack of companionship—leading to casino visits and financial ruin. The pattern is transparent and somewhat predictable. However, many life-changing events happen "out of the blue": terrorist attacks, infidelity, victimization, betrayal, and job loss. These are harder to predict.

In such unpredictable areas, detection relies on observational skill. Like a detective, we need to follow clues—whether they are simultaneous or related events, recurring themes, stories from others, media reports, or experiences within our social network (six degrees of separation). Gestalts, or complex patterns that stand out against life's background, often indicate larger trends that can lead to real outcomes.

For example, layoffs at major companies, rising energy costs, a friend's job struggles, global outsourcing, and your growing interest in foreign cultures—all these factors can lead to a life change: working abroad. Suddenly, your dream life could turn into a nightmare if you get kidnapped by extremists while on assignment.

Imagine this: you attend an all-male university, go home for the summer, and your sister convinces you to go on a blind date. The woman becomes your wife, leading to an abusive divorce seven years later. You later reconnect with your old girlfriend and discover that your mother blocked her calls, misleading her into thinking you were with someone else. The pattern repeats: isolated schooling, family pressure, ignoring red flags. The cycle continues.

Now, years later, your child faces the same "stay or go" dilemmas you once did. You decide to stay home for your grandchild or because pursuing opportunities abroad is no longer feasible. Meanwhile, your mother and sister are traveling the world. You are still at home.

And the beat goes on.

Motifs of future design have thematic resonances beating in their signature waves, projecting themselves onto the days of our tomorrow.

Our future is now! Tomorrow is the realized past of the future designs we envisioned before tomorrow. The structure of time is the sequencing of motifs in our future plans. The alternating sequence of time asymmetrically revisits itself through unique variations on a common theme, creating recurring patterns. The repetition of past, present, and future may reflect selective time waves forming repeating patterns. The human experience of time as concrete realities is based on the selective perception of the syntax of time.

Yet, as this syntax of time turns on itself in endless cycles, the repetition of past, present, future, and "past" again within holistic time—where all time frames are interconnected in a circular way—suggests the future can influence the past. Therefore, the "passed" yesterday might very well be the "future" of tomorrow, which just arrived today! How's that for overnight delivery?

The syntax of time shapes your reality. It involves aligning the manifestation of thematic motifs in your life. These recurring themes match the timeline of your life, guiding your interactions with different groups of people, places, and events. You may encounter people who remind you of your themes as they ask whether they should stay at home, travel the world, get married, settle down, or stay with their family of origin.

You may experience boredom, depression, or anxious agitation—impulsively acting out your stuck dilemmas through unhealthy, risk-taking behaviors such as alcohol use, drugs, unstable relationships, or jumping from one distraction to another. Complications with civil, criminal, or career-damaging, life-altering events could arise. Thematic motifs might repeat themselves in irregular, asymmetrical, or varied forms. However, the formative nature of their motifs continues to influence and trigger a series of life-changing events.

It is important to recognize that you might impulsively take a vacation—flying to some "hot spot" in the world—and become hijacked by terrorists. The randomness of passenger selection on hijacked planes shows a clear pattern of recurring designs. Wanting a trip to a "hot spot" at a specific time depends not only on the driving forces of your lifestyle but also on the current interactions between people, places, and things. Impulsiveness attracts more impulsiveness.

There are many options and possibilities in life. Whether turning left, right, or going straight at any intersection, the decision can be influenced by the driver, traffic levels, road conditions, or the passengers. Who boards a plane headed for disaster—and who avoids it (such as in illnesses, accidents, or the financial collapse of mutual funds in which one is or isn't invested)—I believe is affected by the perfect harmony of multiple motives that may unknowingly come together in a person.

Entrainment in Our Bio-Physical Universe

Just as we are only six degrees of separation from knowing one another, we are also that close to influencing and connecting. We also interact with non-human patterns in nature, physics, solar storms, changing electromagnetic fields, chemistry, natural disasters, and our ancestral genetic history. In short, our behavior is heavily shaped and driven by many interconnected factors.

Adding to the complexity is the level of consciousness (intelligent awareness) we bring to our various entertainments. Perfect harmony exists in our everyday universe — from the balance of physical forces that hold matter, the planets, and us together, to natural and personal disasters. What is the perfect harmony for psychosis, post-traumatic stress disorder, volcanoes, fires, hurricanes, or global warming? Both beneficial and disastrous outcomes require a precise recipe tailored to each situation. These forces include human consciousness.

How we choose to calibrate our thoughts, ideas, constructs, and beliefs influences the quality of our entraining motifs. For example, when matching energies, note that the absorption of helium and beryllium atoms aids in forming carbon (which is vital to our existence). However, since the lifespan of the helium atom is very short, rapid absorption cannot occur without perfectly aligned energy levels.

Similarly, our consciousness is influenced by and interacts with psychosocial, physical, and natural forces that exist both inside and outside of us. The consciousness we emit, project, and shape seamlessly blends with many patterns of motif ensembles—whose possibilities are nearly endless.

My perception, cognition, and consciousness arousal coordinate and are coordinating selective interactions between myself and my world to produce the entrained phenomena I call reality synergistically. In this way, we each create (and sometimes feel created by) and re-create instant, innovative timelines of new pasts, presents, and futures.

The passengers aboard the 9/11 hijacked 747 planes were tragically caught up in various motives—work, family visits, entertainment, diversion—and most importantly (for this writing), with the terrorists, who matched just enough to guide the group toward a completely different, tragic ending. The intelligence community's numerous warnings and failures to connect key information indicate either a lack of awareness or an unwillingness to consider crucial details. It was difficult to accept the unbelievable nature of such an event. It was like asking the authorities to believe that aliens from another planet were planning to attack New York.

Ironically, it was aliens from another planet—another world known as Islamic fundamentalism—that attacked us.

Life-altering experiences often accelerate a person's motif imbalance. The amplification of subtle motif nuances through runaway feedback both fuels creative potential and hastens life's end. Revitalizing a motive involves designing new structures that are formative and focused on the future. As the saying goes: "What does not kill us makes us stronger."

When a person's motives are constantly challenged, bombarded, and stressed, resilient process-activation mechanisms are triggered. They can no longer operate in a "business-as-usual" manner. When Martha Stewart went to prison for obstructing justice, her financial and entertainment empire faced temporary jeopardy. Her personal, financial, business, family, social, and physical conditions all experienced a ripple effect.

She was thrown "back" upon herself—forced to rethink, re-vision, and reprocess who she was and what her empire meant in light of her legal, life-altering ordeal. She had to "loop through" a personal transformation of her lifestyle. In her effort to protect her financial interests, she engaged in a series of actions that kept "turning back" on themselves—amplifying asymmetrical deviations that challenged her to either expand her consciousness or face collapse.

The uneven nature of these experiences creates escalating, uncontrolled positive feedback loops that strengthen specific aspects of one's motif. In Stewart's case, her quick thinking and independence—traits that made her refuse insider trading to protect her empire—were heightened. If these traits go unchecked, they could have led to her downfall. Instead, she adapted.

Under normal circumstances, life involves both symmetrical experiences that maintain balance and asymmetrical encounters that challenge it. A healthy life requires a balance of both. When asymmetry becomes too extreme, pushing us toward exaggerated expressions of our unique patterns, significant events are likely to occur. Like a mobile hanging from a ceiling, a healthy life needs balanced asymmetry.

Understanding the asymmetry within our motives helps us access and break free from runaway feedback loops that could lead to chaos. Conscious transformation and awareness of multi-dimensional motives—before they take control—is a mark of human excellence. While life may seem unpredictable, the power of asymmetry lies in its subjective nature—residing in the "mind's eye" of our consciousness.

Quantum mechanics teaches us that the observer influences uncertainty. However, this uncertainty is not always negative. It reflects the formative nature of consciousness—the process of entraining, synchronizing, and shaping harmonies with people, places, and events. If we remain unaware of our consciousness, we experience chaos. But if we awaken to it, we connect the dots and understand how we co-create our distorted, life-changing experiences.

Choosing to exercise awareness means reconnecting with everything around us. A study by Masaru Emoto (as featured in What the... Is Going On, Channel 520, March 2005) illustrates this. He attached written messages—blessings, love, thank-you notes—onto jars of distilled water. After leaving them overnight, he photographed them with a dark-field microscope. The resulting molecular formations varied greatly depending on the emotional content of the messages. If simple thoughts can influence water, and human beings are 90% water, then the quality of our thoughts deeply affects us.

The structure of the brain and mind consists of networks of neurons. Our associations — such as love, pain, joy, sadness — activate specific neural circuits. As the saying goes, "neurons that fire together wire together." Repeated experiences strengthen these neural pathways. Emotional repetition causes the midbrain (hypothalamus) to release long-chain neuropeptides that trigger bodily states — like anger, sadness, euphoria, and lust.

In this way, our thoughts and emotions, though intangible, physically shape our brain and body. Over time, repeated emotional experiences become ingrained patterns of physiological arousal. Addiction, for example, is often caused by repeated neurochemical "highs" linked to specific memories or patterns. Our brains create motifs—neural templates—that make it difficult to break the cycle without conscious effort.

When these learned motifs become linked to destructive patterns, they can trigger life-altering events like alcoholism or drug dependence. These neural motifs organize ideas and actions into groups, forming complex patterns of unconscious activity. As the saying goes, "we have met the enemy, and it is us." Our unconscious awareness unknowingly connects with people, places, and events, constantly shaping our visible life motifs.

Addiction, when left unchecked, can spiral into destructive feedback cycles. What is needed is a broader awareness of one's inner motifs—a guiding consciousness that aligns our choices with healthier patterns. This kind of recovery re-trains us to reconnect with our true self-motifs.

Our attractions and repulsions operate through associative consciousness, similar to how natural laws govern physics. The concept of co-creation—how we shape our world and are shaped by it—is still in its early stages. It's not about blame, guilt, or innocence, but about accepting responsibility through higher levels of conscious awareness within ethical frameworks.

The traumas and trials of birth, childhood, adolescence, and adulthood can fog our understanding of who we truly are. Mental health involves being aware of ourselves — even if we can't always understand, we can recognize our feelings. If we can't yet "think what we are thinking," then we need to "sense what we are sensing." Awareness of our distorted consciousness can inspire change.

Honest, fearless moral inventory reveals how our attraction and repulsion dynamics shape our life-changing experiences. Respecting our intuition and honoring the emotional "horizons" that signal new frontiers helps us bridge the gap between suffering and growth.

However, a key caveat: some life-changing experiences—such as the death of a loved one, a serious illness, or violent trauma—bring intense pain. After tragedies like 9/11, people worldwide felt shock and confusion. The feeling of losing control raises questions that often do not have immediate answers.

In such moments, there is no room for guilt or blame. The focus should be on regrouping, reassessing, and strategizing with urgency. It is too late to dwell on what might have been done. Recognizing the initial condition without engaging in hindsight criticism acknowledges both the limitations and strengths inherent in control.

The aim of this work is to explore and expand consciousness without assigning blame or guilt. Loss affects not only the immediate circle but also people worldwide, as seen in international reactions to events like the 2004 tsunami or Hurricane Katrina. These events show that we all live within interconnected, multidimensional patterns—and we each influence one another and the planet.

The emotional energies released during trauma—such as losing a child, experiencing war, or through senseless accidents—access powerful altered states. These states, like controlled explosions, require creative innovation. This is where artistic motifs come into play: our innate creative sensibilities often allow survivors to transform their suffering into growth.

"Losing one's mind" might be necessary to unlock one's creative instincts. Turning trauma into growth is about the victory of accessing and utilizing our natural motifs—re-training ourselves for a new life path.

Trans-formativeness refers to the creative ability to define, redefine, and reshape boundaries—personally, nationally, and culturally. For example, the U.S.-Mexico border debate is not just about policy but also about identity and formation. The proposed amnesty for millions of undocumented immigrants has broad support: from the Catholic Church to companies like Walmart and Nike, each with a vested interest.

However, what is transformative for one group might seem deformative to another, such as African American communities fearing economic displacement. Groups such as nations and communities use politics, war, and alliances to ensure their protection over time.

These coalitions of life engage, synchronize, and resonate through diverse motifs. Communication, both internally and externally, is complex and often shaped by various factors, some of which may not be immediately clear.

Communication and exchanges among and within political parties, lawyers, judges, court cases, and legal precedents (with precedents being a form of law itself) operate on many levels simultaneously. In a court case, there may be exchanges concerning the actual charge or allegation. At the same time, there might be discussions about the procedures used to communicate those allegations. Later, meta-level exchanges arise—debates about which procedures govern what can or cannot be exchanged. These spirals or "wobbles" of multi-layered communication and interaction can become motifs themselves. As a result, they may develop a "life of their own." We might call such an entity a motif manifesting within the rule of law. This concept is fundamental to the country's identity. Therefore, the important debate over appointments to the Supreme Court remains highly significant.

Within these meta-level "wobbles," there are multiple embedded strategies and factors. These can spiral toward a critical tipping point, triggering new patterns. For example, in court cases, violent criminals like Al Capone were convicted of nonviolent offenses (such as tax evasion), effectively stopping the formative development of their lives, careers, relationships, and lifestyles. Any prolonged activity, if not periodically reviewed, may eventually require adjustment.

We know that the Earth rotates daily on its axis. Less well-known is that this axis itself also rotates or "wobbles" every 27,000 years. This phenomenon is called precession. Activity at one level influences change at higher levels, much like shifting gears. You can't perceive the Earth's axis of rotation unless you first recognize that the axis exists. Similarly, reorientation requires prior orientation—this is the core of the "wobble" of change.

The "hyperspace drive" from the old Star Trek series fictionalized this idea, illustrating how the movement of space itself (rather than through space) can shift to depict multi-light-speed dimensions. Our emotional lives follow similar patterns. As our lifestyles change, they often "wobble" into a spring-feverish meta-state—mood swings that intensify and spiral inward. Manic and depressive cycles can develop, sometimes escalating into suicidal crises. Notably, spring has the highest rates of suicide attempts, likely because of its emotionally energizing forces. Still, it is also a season of rebirth, renewal, and mating rituals—a paradox of life emerging from chaos.

Motifs emerge in these powerful deviations, these meta-level disruptions in entrainment. It is at these disorienting, transformative thresholds that life-or-death changes occur.

Moving to a higher level—a "fifth gear" of functioning—depends on going beyond the plateau of our current lifestyle. It may require us to let go of old identities, reframe core beliefs, and rebuild the structure of the self. Aging and maturation challenge us to extract and elevate wisdom, leading to deeper values and meanings.

When I drive past a cemetery by the highway, I think about the lives buried there. Who were they? What did they aim for? What legacies did they leave behind? Are they aware now, watching from the "other side," looking forward to renewal as much as reflecting on what was?

When I was a senior in high school, I would often look out the library window, wondering where I would be in ten years. Ten years later, I found myself outside that same school, looking in—remembering the young man I once was. In that moment, time seemed to fold inward. Past and future merged into a single "now." It felt like reaching the summit of a mountain and being greeted by someone who had already completed the climb.

This analysis thoroughly examined my future self, exploring key questions and suggesting possible solutions. When we die—when we pass through that "window"—will we look back at ourselves living here, trying to connect the nonlinear dots of time and experience? Is Jim Morrison truly on the "other side" of The Doors, not just buried in Paris? Will I, one day, connect with myself from beyond a cemetery fence?

We hold multiple layers of love, emotions, and experiences. Each layer builds on the one before it. Life-changing experiences serve as windows—portals—into different parts of ourselves. They call us to evolve throughout our lives, to create something new from what we've been through. We might not yet see what we already understand. By opening ourselves to our beliefs and feelings, we lay the foundation to shift, grow, and transform.

Artistic expressions can explore themes of transformation. When we think, feel our emotions, and act on our choices, we create new motifs. The more we reflect, the more powerful our motifs become. To truly understand ourselves, we sometimes need to step outside of ourselves. Still, we must stay connected to who we are becoming—aligning with the potential for self-creation and global awareness.

Listening to jazz provides a perfect metaphor: a drumbeat sets the foundation, a guitar adds a syncopated layer, and a saxophone dances above in counterpoint. Together, they form a complex yet cohesive whole. Life and communication involve multiple interconnected layers that build gradually. In family dynamics, when someone experiences a breakdown or breakthrough, it often happens at a systemic crescendo. The victim-perpetrator-rescuer triangle intensifies until it flips, transforming the entire relationship dynamic.

Sometimes, loss disrupts this system—a breakup or a death. The absence of that guiding figure destabilizes everything else. It can lead to a breakdown or a wild shift in ideas and emotions. I have seen spouses pass away within years of each other, their lives too intertwined to separate easily. If life does not "spring" forth again, death can become the dominant theme.

Life-changing events are not isolated moments. They follow natural, recurring patterns that erupt, evolve, and regenerate energy—like volcanoes reshaping the earth. Coalitions of consciousness—on issues like immigration, border security, and national identity—serve as social motifs that can erupt with equal force.

Imagine a cue ball hitting a rack of billiard balls. The complexity of torque and angular force is so great that no one can accurately predict where each ball will go. This is similar to the chaos that happens after a world-changing event like 9/11. One form of protection (against terrorism) conflicted with another (border security). Motifs collided and bounce in unpredictable directions.

Tensions like these rarely resolve neatly. More often, they reorganize—approaching a new tipping point, flipping the system from one state to another. Peace and war oscillate in dialectical harmony, constantly challenging our balance. The evolution of altered states of consciousness (ASC) intertwined with life-changing events (LCE) spirals endlessly, gyroscopically, seeking balance through new pattern configurations.

Success often follows adversity. This is the butterfly effect in action—subtle shifts in motifs altering the universe in profound, mysterious ways. Effectiveness flourishes in asymmetry, defined by a harmonious imbalance. Asymmetrical motifs are crucial for innovation. This unique "imperfection" sparks creative adaptations and new meanings. It is this motif-generating force that fuels resilience, abundance, and evolution.

Asymmetry isn't a flaw—it's a reservoir. It fuels altered states that promote epigenetic evolution and human consciousness.

I believe that life-changing events happen independently and follow nonlinear patterns, going beyond cause and effect. Space and time are interconnected: slowing down time stretches space, twisting time alters the arrangement of that space. Events blend into each other. Time speeds up. Moments shrink. Chaos erupts.

Frequently, understanding occurs retrospectively, not due to hindsight bias but as a result of interpreting different moments as parts of a chronological whole. Sometimes, we get answers to questions we have not yet learned to ask. As children, we wonder how the world works. As adults, we explore expanding fields of mystery. The wisdom of life's mosaic lies in knowing what we do not yet know.

Our consciousness may be able to bend time and space through how our motifs synchronize with reality. Distorted motifs lead to distorted experiences. However, from that chaos, new configurations of reality emerge.

In business, there's a saying: "Ready, fire, aim." Act first and adjust based on the results. This demands self-trust, not reckless impulsiveness. Imagine the idea that time flows from the future to the past instead of from the past to the future. Our roots are our wings. We are challenged to create futures now, which ripple backward and reshape the past—time loops. Flashbacks become previews of what is to come.

Life is a Rorschach test—each of us interprets the inkblot differently. From chaos and ambiguity, we find personal meaning. When we tune into our rhythm (thank you, Henry David Thoreau), we often discover the very tools we will need tomorrow. It might be tripping over a hammer in the garage one day—only to need it the next.

The Great Fall

Writing this chapter was a lengthy and emotionally immersive process. At one point, I had to pause to attend to some urgent financial matters. I met with my accountant, who had just gone through a life-altering event. He had experienced a severe fall in his garage, breaking his thigh bone. A metal plate was inserted, but the only available screw was too long. He spent three months in the hospital.

His fall, it turns out, may have saved his life. He had been overmedicated for hypertension because of inaccurate blood pressure readings by a physician's assistant. The resulting electrolyte imbalance had gone unnoticed. If he hadn't fallen and been hospitalized, the doctor said he would have died within two weeks.

By a strange coincidence, his wife had recently started a new job that offered comprehensive health insurance—just in time to cover nearly half a million dollars in medical bills. He missed work (which he hated), received attentive care from his spouse, and may now get a settlement from a malpractice lawsuit that could fund his retirement.

He laughingly called it "The Great Fall"—unaware of how fitting and layered that metaphor was—the synchronicity of it all—the stream of motifs and outcomes—felt orchestrated by something greater.

CHAPTER 12

EPIGENESIS: ASYNCHRONIZATION IN ASYMMETRICAL MOTIFS

We all possess a wide range of talents, resourcefulness, and unique quirks. We are, in essence,priceless. However, mastering our lives can feel like putting a five-year-old in the cockpit of a 747 jetliner. Our potential for empowerment is great; yet, we often feel overwhelmed by the complexities of our own lives. I have known many talented financial brokers, brilliant at managing large sums of money, yet often squandering most of it with a similar brilliance of self-nihilism.

They, like many of us, have been overwhelmed by the challenge of learning how to manage their lives and how to "get off the ground and fly to great heights without crashing and burning." True self-mastery is being in harmony with our consciousness. Epigenesis is the process of learning how to wisely control the flow of choices that influence the selective design of how we use our consciousness.

Similarly, our DNA contains generative genes that selectively turn other genes on and off, producing the right type of protein at the right moment. Likewise, our consciousness has self-regulatory, self-generating states of expanded awareness and arousal. These states intentionally shift our immediate focus of awareness in the present moment (the "protein" components of our reality), thus shaping the design elements of what appears in our figure-ground consciousness—the prominence of one configuration over others, most of which demand our attention at that time. The subtle, proportional design elements (such as ratios or weighting of variables like visual, auditory, kinesthetic, and dispositional temperaments) involved in selective perception and reality construction reflect motifs at quantum levels of organization.

Imagine a motion picture projector capable of controlling which frame or combination of reality scenarios will flash, for how long, and in what sequence or structure. Epigenesis is this motion picture projector— expanded consciousness of consciousness, or Meta consciousness—of our mindful attention across all levels of awareness. It embodies the idea of self-creation through its own designed framework. This self-projection requires true alignment with both our internal and external realities. Mastering our consciousness involves subjectively stepping into and "owning" our unique self-motif at these heightened levels of awareness. Not only do we become "one with the ball," but we are also empowered to be "on the ball" in mastering the quality of our consciousness.

The mastery of consciousness and life-changing experiences come together when our relatively organized and controlled daily reality clashes with the sudden, devastating impact of chaotic, 9/11-level disasters. Our sense of mastery over consciousness can turn into a sense of mystery about consciousness—how can one ever overcome such trauma and chaos? Our courage and survival instincts are tested as we try to create and control order from chaos, especially when chaos seems to have temporarily taken over our lives.

It is important to recognize that underlying patterns can exist in chaotic situations, along with unpredictable elements within structured systems. All order is only approximate, as imperfection and asymmetry are embedded at its core (like the leaning Tower of Pisa). Chaos manifests as its expression. It is called "hidden" only because of how subtly its design is woven into the sequence of unfolding events. Its irregular, aperiodic qualities make chaotic patterns difficult to identify. Like a tsunami, its hidden nature can suddenly cause a major impact without warning. Hidden chaos is experienced as disruptive, interruptive, and eruptive to any established status quo—even chaos itself.

Chaotic-like expressions exhibit asynchronous timing, marked by subtle irregularities that create wobble effects from the interaction of multidimensional motifs. This reflects the asynchrony of people, places, and things (including our changing states of consciousness), which unevenly (asymmetrically) contribute and eventually cause deviations that unbalance any dynamic system. That's why the phrase: "the best laid plans of mice and men often go astray." It's always something that throws us off course, off plan, or off scheme. We may not see it coming. Paradoxically, it is this acausal, over-determined (multiple causes) chaos that enhances our ability to transform through close encounters with life-changing experiences. It introduces epigenesis into our capacity for innovative re-synchronization.

In recounting the accountant's ingrained motifs of "hidden" chaotic ordering, even here, uncertainty appears.

This capacity for innovation comes from the layered complexity of our inner selves—an intricate structure of nested motifs that resonate at different levels of consciousness. These motifs, woven together through threads of experience and perception, form the foundation for our understanding of self and reality. However, much like a symphony with discordant notes, the interaction of these motifs can create moments of deep dissonance. Yet, it is within this disharmony that the potential for transformation lies.

Life-changing events often serve as catalysts, shaking the foundations of our established patterns and forcing us to confront the chaotic beauty of our existence. During these moments, the lines between order and disorder blur, pushing us to reassess our innate abilities for resilience and adaptation. This is the essence of epigenesis—the power to rewrite the story of our inner themes, aligning them with a greater awareness of our potential. Through this process, we don't just survive chaos; we transcend it, transforming it into a stage for self-discovery and growth.

The accountant became angry and aggressive about his life situation, entering a heightened state of agitation and taking out his frustration on clients by overcharging them. This caused a series of disruptive, interruptive, and explosive consequences: stress, client resentment, and ultimately, a career-threatening loss of income.

There is a chaotic entrainment of unique motifs where the hidden order of chaos itself becomes chaotic, asynchronized into an unbalanced balancing of deviations in the way deviations had been occurring.

This dynamic interaction between epigenesis and chaos reveals the deep potential for human transformation, shedding light on pathways to re-synchronization that go beyond traditional understanding. When we face life-changing events, we are often pushed into a space where usual coping methods fall short, and the complex weave of our consciousness must adjust, reconfigure, and grow. It is during these moments of upheaval that the seeds of innovative self-realignment begin to take hold.

By recognizing the subtle patterns hidden within chaos, individuals can access their natural ability for epigenesis, unlocking new opportunities to reorganize their lives. This process requires not only greater awareness of personal themes but also the courage to face the irregular shapes of one's experiences. Through this confrontation, we gather the pieces of disorder and transform them into a clear narrative that reflects our evolving selfhood.

Such transformations expose the paradoxical nature of chaos as both a destructive force and a creative catalyst. The balance needed to manage this duality comes from the complex layers of our inner structure, providing a stable foundation for realigning the themes of our consciousness into harmonious unity.

Life-altering events involve the imposition of unbalanced timing (asymmetrical timing of aperiodic events). Imagine building a leaning tower of Pisa on top of another leaning tower, and then again on another, endlessly. As each is constructed upon the other at opposing angles, the overall design's asymmetry becomes more pronounced. Increasing the degrees of angularity boosts its asymmetry, eventually leading to chaotic tipping points and the collapse of the structure.

The accountant faced challenges not only with managing his physical disabilities but also with dealing with unpredictable mood swings and altered consciousness. These factors made it harder for him to keep a consistent and organized workflow over different periods and events.

His mood swings resulting from altered states of consciousness, along with those of others he interacts with, create irregular time intervals in his daily coping, further disrupting his adjustment to life-changing events. His unintended efforts to compensate increase his inherent imbalance, pushing it toward a "tipping point" of change. His pursuit of "balancing points" in such asynchronous states is a response to the new uncertainty and chaos that disturb his usual routines. Finding balance or centering involves managing the misalignment caused by shifting consciousness states, such as mood swings, emotional arousal, agitation, anxiety, fatigue, and malaise. Resynchronization requires accessing his ability for epigenesis, which opens up a range of innovative ways to realign himself for self-transformation. He needs a new method for this synchronization, using nested motifs.

The complexity of human beings is reflected in the synchronization of consciousness that emerges from one's unique, layered motifs. This is the core of epigenesis: the ability to create new configurations of behavioral patterns. Because our fundamental motif is embedded within unique, multi-layered, nested loops (like Chinese boxes within boxes), our ability for selectivity and plasticity in reshaping, remodeling, and recrafting innovative behaviors is supported. We can choose to turn synchronizations into different response patterns when faced with life-changing experiences. We start the process of analyzing and recognizing how our unintentional choices impact these outcomes, followed by a reassessment of our identity.

The capacity for reflective consciousness is essential for effectively navigating complex experiences. This "observer within" holds the key to untangling the chaos of asynchronous states, giving us the chance to step outside the storm of internal conflicts. By nurturing this detached perspective, we develop the capacity to examine the interplay of our nested motifs without being swept away by their currents. It is here, in the calm of observation, that we begin to recognize patterns—not as fixed entities, but as fluid tapestries that evolve with our changing awareness.

From this perspective, transformation is less about enforcing order and more about embracing the natural balance within chaos. The process of changing states and resonances requires coordination, not to eliminate inconsistencies, but to integrate them into a developing balance.

The interplay of epigenesis and chaos constantly challenges our understanding of balance, often revealing truths that are beyond immediate logic. Like a kaleidoscope's shifting patterns, the motifs of our consciousness reorganize themselves under the influence of introspection and external pressures. These reorganizations are not just responses to life's turbulence; they are active recalibrations that enable us to rethink the structure of our being.

As the accountant wrestled with his growing complexities, he inadvertently revealed a universal truth: chaos, when acknowledged instead of fought, becomes a fertile ground for growth. His efforts to find balance, despite several missteps, demonstrate the broader human effort to create order from disorder. It is during the process of confronting these uneven patterns—like leaning towers balanced precariously—that new ways of thinking emerge, reflecting the dynamic and ever-changing nature of human consciousness.

This delicate balance between chaos and order is neither simple nor predictable. It urges us to explore the layered aspects of selfhood, to identify the motifs that resonate most deeply, and to develop a consciousness that extends beyond mere survival. By engaging deeply with the asynchronous rhythms of life, we not only adapt but also grow, creating new facets of identity that honor both our vulnerabilities and our strengths.

We are the conductors, empowered by the understanding that we are both the creators and inhabitants of our inner landscapes. These complex patterns of internal change represent the delicate balance that humanity constantly seeks amid its layered chaos. The cycles of disorder and realignment, like waves on an ocean, echo through our experiences, prompting us to reflect deeply and seek harmony. Growth involves more than just facing disruption; it requires actively engaging with change, understanding complex challenges, and using these experiences to foster innovation and build resilience.

In this dynamic process, the architecture of selfhood becomes a canvas for the interplay of fragmentation and cohesion. Each thought, emotion, or reaction contributes to shaping identity. By recognizing the fluidity of our nested motifs, we move beyond the rigidity of preset pathways and embrace the transformative potential inherent in every interaction with our inner and outer worlds.

The challenge is recognizing that chaos isn't an external enemy but a close part of ourselves that shows the depths of our consciousness. To truly engage with this truth requires both humility and bravery: humility to accept life's natural unpredictability, and bravery to rethink the patterns that influence how we understand ourselves and our connection to the world.

We reinforce our self-identity through how we interpret our experiences. This core motif of selfhood serves as the foundation for our lifestyles—our leaning towers of Pisa—being built. It creates layers of awareness: motifs of motifs of our central self (like nested Russian dolls), forming patterns within patterns in organized hierarchies.

Think of actors who play many roles, their sub-personalities within sub-personalities creating complex, unique mosaics of characters. Imagine people pretending to be others, meeting others pretending to be someone else, only to realize they are all the same people talking to themselves. Remember, these hierarchical organizations of the core self are not uniform. They are asymmetrical and vary in their levels of intensity, depth, and relevance in the altered state the person might be in. Expanding our awareness of nested pattern motifs in thought and action helps us "chunk up" to higher gear ratios of alternate synchronization.

An increased awareness of our perception can sometimes cause the feeling that time is slowing down, as if we are processing multiple moments quickly one after the other. (In a car crash, everything seems to move in slow motion as quick, fragmented snippets of altered states of consciousness form.) This "chunking up" of larger pieces of information broadens the "wave" of our space-time consciousness, helping to realign it.

We cycle and recycle through different levels of consciousness many times during the day. Entrainment and asynchronization of changing states of consciousness during life-changing experiences create chaos in a person's unique pattern. Often, these are a-synchronizations that reflect on our unintentional interactions with people, places, and events. These interactions create meaningful life patterns. No one is an island. We unknowingly connect with our multiple inner selves (intrapersonal) as well as our external social selves (interpersonal).

The idea that consciousness can influence reality has been supported by many studies, including one from 1993 in Washington, D.C. ("What the Bleep... is Going On?" Channel 520, 2005). Four thousand people meditated to lower the murder rate in D.C., and after 90 days, police reported a 25% decrease.

Recognizing our motifs of altered states of consciousness is essential for enhancing our lives. Humans can think internally at about 1,500 words per minute. Are we sending ourselves messages to live—or to die? Just like in Roman gladiator days, where Caesar's thumbs-up or thumbs-down decided a fighter's fate, are we giving ourselves 1,500 words-per-minute subliminal thumbs-up or thumbs-down self-talk? We need to learn to master and become experts at owning, creating, and rewriting (if necessary) our motifs of changing states of consciousness. Such mastery can help us prevent unconscious entrainment in our lives. In a universe full of endless possibilities, mastering personal choice is evolutionarily advantageous. It is widely accepted that thoughts can have a real impact. What is clear is that we are not only the writers but also the editors of what we choose to include—or delete—from the motifs of our consciousness.

Chaos fuels more chaos in asynchronous patterns of conflicting motifs once critical points are crossed. I knew someone whose recovery from addiction improved from daily abuse to just once or twice over six months. This person struggled with surrender and isolation, reaching a tipping point roughly every 90 days. At these key moments, the pain of staying sober felt heavier than the painful consequences of relapsing. Even success can create challenges: maintaining fulfillment while avoiding stress. This is a common issue in addiction, where life purpose depends on having something to recover from. Even if there is a "cure," the chaos of lacking that thing can leave someone lost—and vulnerable to relapse. How is that for the chaos of chaos? The motif of recovery contains an inherent asymmetry.

This recovering individual cycled through unpredictable periods marked by isolation, control issues, and fear of abandonment. He experienced ten to twelve shifting states of consciousness within just a few days—paranoia, anger, hurt, self-soothing, depression, rage, defensiveness, rationalization, denial, and distorted beliefs about losing his sense of identity. It's like racing thoughts that disrupt sleep, or a child too excited to sleep until they finally crash. This surge of chaos led to a relapse. He rejected support groups and friendships that could have helped him let go and simply be himself. This chaos prevented him from receiving the nourishment needed for healthy connection and transforming ego control into artistic expression.

As he learned to pay attention to, recognize, and develop "self-empathy" with his cycling altered states of consciousness, he discovered his "observing ego" as a subjectively separate part of his relapsing self. He realized that his sense of "detachment" was a key meta-motif in the sequence and proportion of altered states that "set up" relapse.

Interruption, disruption, and eruption are key elements in both relapse and recovery, as well as in crafting transformative patterns. Changing even a small detail on the beach shifts the universe's formative energy. The highest form of creation is consciousness of spirit expressed through human states of being. The ability to access and regulate states of consciousness serves as a fundamental base from which the development and growth of self-structures emerge. What falls must rise or move back through time. It creates an endless spiral of wholeness—our emerging oneness with the universe, including people, places, and events. Just as cutting a curve out of a winding road by driving straight through finds the center "I" in the hurricane of life-changing experiences, grounding us in oneness with the universe and its challenges, transforming isolation into omnipresent connection.

To foster the emergence of "I-ness," aligning with our core motifs is crucial. This strategy improves effective entrainment while reducing the intensity, duration, and frequency of involuntary entrainments that can lead to significant experiences.

Multi-dimensional Viewing

The ability to perceive and imagine entraining motifs of complex realities depends on the synergistic capabilities of our mind-brain-body system. For example, depth perception depends on binocular vision. Seeing the same object from slightly different angles (visual signals from both the left and right eyes hitting our visual cortex with slight variations) prompts our brains to create a cohesive, three-dimensional mental image.

An image is created through non-localization, where different parts of the brain process various attributes and qualities of an object—such as size, shape, color, brightness, horizontal and vertical orientations, proximity of figures and dots, foreground, and background—and then combine them into a unified, cohesive image.

When visual stimuli from the left and right eyes differ slightly in angles, activating different parts of our brain responsible for various attributes and qualities, the image we perceive results from neural integration. The more diverse the viewpoints (such as moving around the object and viewing it from different angles) and the more qualities we access (like sensory details including sights, sounds, textures, smells, tastes, and others), the better our ability to perceive multiple dimensions of any object or reality.

In *Groundhog Day*, Bill Murray's character repeatedly relives February 2. He encounters the same people repeatedly. Interestingly, with each repetition, he sees them in slightly different ways depending on the situation. There is an annoying insurance salesman who initially irritates him. The second time, he punches him. By the third time, he understands and learns—and eventually hugs and embraces the man.

Each day repeats, and he perceives a new facet of the "same day" with softer eyes and changing angles. What is changing is his perspective on his perspective. He creates a shifting context of how he perceives himself in contrast to himself with each passing, daily repetition. As his history "keeps repeating itself," he learns something new—so it becomes a "new" repetition each time, with a deeper, richer understanding of meaning and value.

In this way, he learns to accept, enjoy, love, and be present with what he previously called "difficult people." Many aspects of his own character proved to be the real challenge. Only then does he begin to move forward. His ego had blinded him to how his perspectives perpetuated his misery. His multi-layered view became an integration of various sensory inputs from the same repetitive day (Groundhog Day—seeing his shadow-self, if you will), creating an unavoidable feedback loop of how he kept "running into himself"—manipulative, exploitative, and egotistically demanding.

Repeated life-changing experiences build up until reaching a critical point, leading to significant transformations. They expose us to multiple sensory inputs from various (often unrelated) parts of our lives. It is through this ability to view things in multiple dimensions that we grow, emerge, and gain the power to see how intricate our entraining motifs can fully operate.

Indeed, it is by integrating the many aspects of how we think, feel, and behave under stress, as well as how we manage conflict, loss, abandonment, and intense emotions in relationships, that we shape the motif of our self. Such transformation requires honest, personal self-reflection—to face our demons and tame our dragons. Otherwise, life might just "drag on." (Sorry about that.)

Life-altering experiences challenge our multi-dimensional perspectives to expand, innovate, and discover unique, previously unseen vantage points. The process of letting go, which involves freeing oneself from traditional frames of reference and orientation, can be achieved through practices such as meditation, prayer, and trance-like shifts in consciousness.

This process of multi-dimensional viewing goes beyond just sight. It also shapes how we understand and deal with events, relationships, and our interactions with the world. By accepting the complexity and variety of perspectives, we open up the ability to see life's detailed patterns and connections, which often go unnoticed with a rigid, one-dimensional view. Basically, this skill of incorporating diverse sensory and emotional inputs fosters deep personal growth, helping us understand the layers of our own minds and others' with more subtlety and compassion.

For example, the recurring patterns in our experiences can be seen as opportunities for gaining deeper understanding rather than just being repetitive. As we encounter familiar situations in new contexts, our ability to view them from different angles improves. This shift, similar to the layered image created by our visual cortex, clarifies parts of ourselves and our surroundings that were previously unnoticed. It is through this process of observing and re-observing that change happens, helping us break free from the repetitive traps of unconscious patterns.

Significant life experiences can sometimes cause drastic shifts in our perceptions, which may initially feel overwhelming but can lead to greater understanding or new insights. This is where transformative breakthroughs occur. If "it does not kill us," it can leave us renewed and stronger.

Several non-chemical, mind-expanding techniques are available to help open consciousness without waiting for a life-changing event. In addition to those already mentioned, another method is photoreading, which involves shifting focus — for example, concentrating on objects 12 inches from the nose and then moving to objects 3 feet away. This technique allows us to see the background of an object—its context—by changing our focus. The object itself is then perceived with "soft eyes," enabling us to view its surrounding field. This creates an almost binocular, double-visioned image that is blurred and slightly superimposed.

These recursive experiences are similar to how binocular vision works, where slightly different inputs from each eye combine to create a sense of depth and clarity. Just as our visual cortex merges diverse signals to form three-dimensional images, our mind also weaves together multisensory inputs from repeated life experiences to develop a richer, more detailed understanding. This repeated process of blending different viewpoints challenges rigid preconceptions, opening new pathways to awareness and personal growth.

You can try this yourself: hold your finger 12 inches from your nose. First, look at your fingers; you should see just a single digit. Then focus on a point two feet behind it—you'll see "two fingers." It's like seeing the forest for the trees. This perceptual shift enables the visual cortex to receive the whole image directly and immediately.

This technique allows reading at speeds up to 25,000 words per minute because the light signal goes directly to the visual part of the brain. The main challenge is accessing and converting that data into a conscious, usable form. That's the essence of formativeness—to bring complex, multi-faceted forms, patterns, and designs into conscious awareness.

It is essential for both personal growth and the evolution of global culture that we loosen our deep-rooted and persistent perceptions of reality. The first step is being receptive to the world of possibilities with "soft eyes." As Shakespeare said: "There are more things in heaven and earth than are dreamt of in your philosophy."

Such alterations of consciousness—using techniques like multi-dimensional entrainment, enrichment, and absorption (e.g., fixation, opening, accessing)—allow our mind-brain-body-sensory system to perceive and understand acausal events. This empowerment can greatly help in disrupting unconscious entrainments that might lead to catastrophic outcomes. In "911" terminology, "connecting the dots" means understanding how seemingly unrelated phenomena are interconnected in complex, multi-dimensional ways.

The core of this transformative journey is understanding that rigidity in perception is often the biggest obstacle to growth. As humans, we tend to prefer patterns and comfort zones, creating frameworks that help us navigate life predictably. However, these frameworks can become inflexible, turning into prisons of thought and behavior. To free ourselves, we need to engage in ongoing self-examination, much like peeling an onion, to uncover the deeper truths beneath superficial understandings.

This recursive self-exploration often reflects the dynamics of a Möbius strip—an endless loop where beginnings and ends merge, and what appears to be a single-sided surface reveals its depth upon closer inspection. From this view, personal transformation is not a straightforward climb but a winding journey through repeated experiences that deepen our understanding. Each cycle provides a new opportunity to challenge assumptions and broaden our awareness.

Additionally, this process involves building resilience and adaptability. Life's paradox lies in its apparent contradictions: security comes from flexibility, and clarity often arises from ambiguity. By embracing these paradoxes, we learn that breaking down rigid frameworks doesn't cause chaos but instead reorganizes our inner landscape. This is where the concept of "soft eyes" becomes vital—not just as a metaphor for perception but as a guiding principle for navigating life's complexities.

The Groundhog Day technique effectively breaks through rigid, fixed fundamentalism. Repeating the same experience from multiple perspectives within self-perpetuating feedback loops causes rigid, literal perceptions to dissolve.

In the movie, Bill Murray's character repeatedly faces the despair of his same old reactions to the same old events. Only when he experiences a change in his sense of self—where the events won't change until he does—can he move forward. Each of his days feels like "déjà vu"—already seen or experienced, but never finished because of narrow, one-sided thinking. It wasn't so much a rerun of an old movie as a repeat for him to discover something he'd already seen but not yet truly understood.

Transformation only occurs when he lets go of his ego-driven control and narrow perspective.

This cyclical journey of self-awareness and transformation often uncovers the layers of our deep-seated patterns. These patterns, like fractal designs, repeat across different areas of our lives, presenting both challenges and opportunities. The key is to recognize when these patterns act as tools for growth and when they become self-imposed limitations. In this context, the concept of "soft eyes" becomes a way to explore the interconnectedness of our experiences, helping us see the wide web of relationships that shape our reality without falling into tunnel vision.

A broader perspective allows us to see the subtle interactions between our intentions and actions, along with their ripple effects. This insight also opens the door to seeing paradoxes as opportunities for growth. In this space, contradictions aren't obstacles but invitations to explore further and question the assumptions behind our perceptions. The balance of rigidity and flexibility becomes a dance, where moments of surrender lead to meaningful breakthroughs. By allowing patterns to dissolve and reemerge, we realize that chaos isn't the enemy of order but its foundation — the fertile soil from which new structures grow.

This insight calls for a shift in mindset from control to curiosity. Curiosity, after all, acts as the bridge connecting us to the unknown and uncharted areas where our deepest potential resides. Through a lens of curiosity, even the most confusing challenges become opportunities for exploration and discovery. The practice of "soft eyes," therefore, goes beyond mere observation—it becomes an act of aligning with the rhythms of life itself, embracing the unpredictable and ever-changing fabric of existence.

As this openness deepens, it becomes clear that transformation is less about changing who we are and more about discovering who we have always been. In this process, we gain the courage to confront the unknown parts of ourselves and engage with the asymmetry that underpins our existence. This asymmetry reflects the idea that no single moment, action, or thought can fully represent a person's entire identity. Instead, it is through the interaction of these moments, their echoes and variations, that our true essence emerges.

This recognition motivates us to actively reflect on our story, considering how our recurring themes influence our interactions and the environments we build. It encourages us not only to observe but also to participate in shaping our identity, refining and redefining ourselves through purposeful choices.

His feelings of helplessness and hopelessness were illusions—products of rigid, literal thinking and fixed perceptions. Paradoxically, he needed to focus on his obsession with fundamentalism to lead him to "give up" the old ways of thinking. Embracing a broader, higher source of multidimensional motifs became essential.

Such personal transformation demands sincere self-reflection—fostering a calm, visionary response that goes beyond typical reactions to the so-called "difficult people" of the world. Interestingly, our core pattern instinctively loops and feeds back on itself—the results of our designed action patterns—in an unbalanced way.

This transformation process also reminds us that our patterns, although deeply ingrained, are not fixed but living expressions shaped by the interaction of our inner and outer worlds. Each recurrence and cyclical pattern offers a valuable opportunity for careful evaluation and the development of informed perspectives. It is during this reflection that breakthroughs happen, allowing us to move beyond rigidity and into the expansive potential that flexibility provides. In this view, balance is not a static state but a dynamic equilibrium where contrasting elements interact and mutually reinforce each other.

This view considers self-similarity as the idea that identity isn't fixed but includes a range of expressions that can change. These expressions, like echoes in a canyon, reflect our core self while showing variations that might have gone unnoticed before. From this perspective, being oneself is less about sticking to a perfect ideal and more about accepting the natural changes that come with being human. Each change, instead of being a deviation, helps us discover new parts of ourselves that strengthen our sense of identity.

As we examine this intricate dance of motifs, we start to see how our growth ties into larger patterns in life. These connections, though subtle, serve as meaningful gateways to a deeper understanding of ourselves and the world. Recognizing this interaction gives us the confidence to embrace complexities and paradoxes, viewing them not as contradictions but as complements that enrich our life's tapestry.

This feedback demonstrates how our lifestyle-influenced behavior patterns affect us, showing up in areas like work, love, and friendships. As a result, a person can't completely detach from certain parts of their identity.

Due to inherent asymmetry, an individual can approximate their ideal self-identity but will never fully attain it. Some variation might occur in quality, theme, expression, or features. Paradoxically, to be oneself is to resemble oneself (self-similarity) but not to be identical to one's self-concept or ideal.

The idea of recurring motifs and personal growth also relates to how we perceive and interact with the world around us. It's not just about internal change but about an ongoing conversation between our inner stories and external realities. This repetition influences how we interpret experiences, promoting active engagement where patterns evolve over time instead of remaining static. It's like the fractal beauty of nature, where each repetition is detailed, unique, and contributes to the bigger picture.

In this context, the idea of "soft eyes" becomes even more important — not just as a metaphor for perception, but as a deliberate way of observing the world with curiosity, openness, and a willingness to be surprised. From this perspective, we see that even the most ordinary things can hold deep insights. Engaging with our environment in this way creates a framework for making connections between different moments, helping us find wisdom in everyday life and see the extraordinary within our daily routines.

As we improve our observational skills, we start to see how choices, patterns, and motifs influence different parts of our lives—whether in relationships, work, or personal goals. Each interaction becomes an opportunity to align with the larger motif shaping our lives, helping us refine, improve, and unify parts of ourselves that were once fragmented or hidden. This should not be viewed as a problem; rather, it is an opportunity.

Our self-concept and identity never fully reflect our true essence. Self-identity is a set of traits and characteristics centered around a core theme. This explains many paradoxes. For example, when someone tries too hard to be themselves, it can seem unnatural. But when they do something effortlessly, they are more likely to stay true to the natural flow of their core self's resonance.

Our identity is made up of unique traits within our pattern. On this journey of self-discovery, we encounter not only the harmonious aspects within us but also the conflicting forces that disturb our balance. These contrasts, whether as internal conflicts or external obstacles, serve as catalysts for personal and professional growth.

Reconciliation demands courage and self-awareness, which involve honest reflection on our identities.

This exploration encourages us to understand the complex nature of existence, recognizing that our inner world is as intricate and full of contradictions as the outer world. Here, the concept of motifs goes beyond individual identity, shaping our collective stories and societal structures. These common patterns, passed down through generations, help form our views on morality, progress, and how everything is interconnected.

As we examine these motifs, we are drawn to the art of discernment—a practice of distinguishing what aligns with our values from what undermines them. This discernment is not a fixed judgment but a flexible adjustment, guided by empathy, introspection, and a willingness to grow. Through this perspective, transformation becomes less about fixing imperfections and more about accepting them, allowing the imperfect to coexist with the aspirational dance of authenticity.

This encourages spontaneous creativity. When someone appears different, they might be tapping into an overlooked or undeveloped part of their personality.

This leads us to explore the nature of our inner structure—the complex network of values, beliefs, and instincts that make up our being. Inside this structure, motifs serve as both signposts and mysteries, influencing our choices and reactions while pushing the limits of our self-awareness. They are dynamic frameworks that change through interaction and reflection, uncovering the layers of complexity that define our consciousness.

Aligning our inner motives with external realities requires intentional effort—a willingness to confront our shadows and accept the light that guides us. Through this process, we learn to turn vulnerabilities into strengths, transforming weaknesses into assets. Power, survival, ego, and dependence are no longer obstacles but parts to acknowledge and develop as we build resilience.

In doing so, we get closer to understanding the limitless possibilities life offers. These possibilities are not random but are deeply connected to the interaction between our inner worlds and external forces that influence them. The world acts as a mirror reflecting our motifs back to us, helping us see patterns that resonate with the core of our humanity, as well as those that challenge or destabilize it.

We cannot not be ourselves—regardless of what we do—because we are the ones doing it (assuming we are conscious and not physically forced). Even in a trance, free will exists—we cannot be made to do something that contradicts our values. Even in experiments testing authority and abuse potential, there are exceptions. We are vulnerable to our motives and the range of possibilities they encompass. We can be unwittingly entrained if our "resin vulnerabilities"—power, survival, ego, neediness, etc.—have not been mastered through new synchronization of consciousness.

Transformation of motifs is not automatic. So, where do evil, malevolence, Satan, the Anti-Christ, Armageddon, etc., fit into this idea of formation? What about cruelty, torture, pain, innocence, "getting away with murder," genocide, sadism, and psychopathic deviance? If we live in a universe of infinite possibilities, maybe it is time to cite an American icon—Clint Eastwood—who said the universe is made up of

"The Good, the Bad, and the Ugly." While not a scientific or religious framework, it captures a fundamental truth. Each of us can embody all three roles.

The concept of good and evil, along with how they manifest in human actions, forms a complex pattern of neural signals and motifs. As we learn more about morality and deviance, we see that these ideas are deeply connected to our brain structures. The interaction between our instincts, feelings, and reasoning creates a complex harmony that can either work together or conflict, depending on the situation.

Evil and malevolence are better understood not as external forces but as expressions of unresolved patterns within neural networks—patterns shaped by trauma, unresolved impulses, or systemic influences. These imprints form patterns that, if left unchecked, can lead to destructive behaviors. Yet, amidst this chaos, there is hope for change. Awareness and purpose can rewire these neural patterns, leading to a shift from destructive tendencies to healthy growth.

Similarly, the question of innocence and vulnerability highlights the fragility of our inner structures. Whether through societal conditioning or personal experiences, themes of pain and cruelty challenge us to recognize these patterns not as fixed labels but as opportunities to reshape the neural pathways that influence our reality.

Every person has three brains: 1) reptilian, 2) mammalian, and 3) neocortex. We can engage in cold-blooded (reptilian)

acts of violence. We are warm-blooded, emotional creatures—with animal cravings, desires, and fight-or-flight responses. Additionally, we have an advanced cerebral cortex—enabling higher consciousness, executive cognitive functions, and spiritual connections to a higher power (however we define it).

Each of these "brains" embodies a motif—our "good," "bad," and "ugly" not only exist in the world but also within us. Recognizing our unique motifs of good, bad, and ugly can greatly help us understand what we might unintentionally attract.

As Rev. Jerry Falwell once said: "We are all sinners."

Entropy, Quantum Leaps, and the Geometry of Gravitating Motif

The life patterns that form the basis of our diverse motifs operate at the lowest energy level of stability. So how do we learn to handle new, disruptive, life-changing experiences that "shake up" our highly organized, low-entropy, alert lifestyle? It seems that much can be understood by looking at the geometry of our brain's neural network and its pattern of energy shifts—what physicists call "hills and valleys."

John Hopfield, a physicist, explained in 1982 (Kaku, 1997) that the neurons in the brain are similar to atoms in a crystal lattice. Atoms can spin "up" or "down," among other ways. The complexities of the combined or sequential spin pathways can influence the motif contours and the electromagnetic structure of the lattice. Hopfield suggests that neurons are interconnected (networks of motifs) in different energy states of "fire" or "not fire."

Hopfield's theory suggests that both atoms forming a lattice and neurons forming the brain's neural network function similarly in a quantum solid state. That is, neurons (like atoms) would "fire" in a way that minimizes the energy used. Therefore, learning in the neural network resembles a rolling ball that flows from "hills" (neurons capable of firing) to "valleys" (neurons already fired or not firing due to energy constraints). The "ball" represents the current learning experience. The topography of "hills" and "valleys" in the neural network depicts the learned pattern—the motif uniquely engraved into the network. These pathways of patterned topographical geometry ("hills" and "valleys" of firing/non-firing neurons) become etched or "grooved in," like worn paths winding through dense woods—creating unique motifs.

The geometry of these topographical motifs reflects the minimum energy needed for this learning pattern to become embedded in the neural network. It demonstrates the unique design of quantum energy fluctuations linked to that learning motif. The lattice and the neural network thus serve as matrices of interconnected fields of motifs created by quantum-level energy fluctuations.

The stable, low-energy, and low-entropy state of this highly ordered pattern can be disrupted by life-changing events. In other words, chaos increases entropy, which pushes the "ball" of learning and coping not from top to bottom (hill to valley) but from bottom to top, toward higher energy states.

The interaction between our neural motifs and the fabric of multidimensional reality shows a deep bond between the inner and outer worlds. Just as our brains shape patterns of energy across hills and valleys, the universe itself weaves gravitational motifs through a complex dance of dimensions. These connections imply that the motif is a universal principle—not only limited to our neural networks but resonating throughout the vast structure of existence.

In such a scenario, the "ball" of learning could "roll up" the neural "hill" if the entropy caused by chaos provides enough energy to overcome the natural resistance.

Indeed, this is exactly what occurs when increased energy flow causes chaos and broadens random possibilities, including greater disorder. The entropy of life-changing experiences accesses not only more energy but also additional dimensions of reality.

In 1992, physicist Jim Smolin proposed that string theory, which suggests that subatomic particles are energy strings that shape gravity, involves eleven dimensions within our four-dimensional experience (one in time and three in space).

This interplay between chaos and order creates a vivid picture of how life-changing experiences can serve as catalysts for growth. Just as the neural network's energy shifts embed new patterns into our awareness, these disruptions reflect the cosmic dance of forces that shape reality itself. They act as portals to deeper levels of existence, pushing us to adapt, grow, and reshape our mental and emotional worlds. Navigating through complexity improves our understanding of reality, enabling us to access opportunities that once seemed out of reach.

He describes this new integrated theory as M-theory (M = membrane), where an infinite number of energy membranes (parallel universes) collide and interact, creating new universes in this 11th dimension. Physicists have hypothesized that gravity's relative weakness compared to the other three fundamental forces in our universe is because of its ability to transfer between multiple universes, including the possibility of inter-universal leakage both into and out of our universe.

This interconnectedness between neural motifs and universal principles reveals an intricate dance where our internal systems mirror the workings of the cosmos. The pattern of motifs in the neural network aligns with the broader story of existence, where energy flows shape the structure of galaxies and gravitational forces. These parallels prompt a reassessment of the boundaries of individuality by integrating both the microcosm and macrocosm within a well-balanced relationship between order and chaos. Life-changing moments become not just disruptions but also parts of the universal rhythm, helping us access deeper energy and insight. Through these transformative experiences, we move beyond mere survival and connect personal growth with the vast mysteries of the universe.

Since acausal entraining motifs are multi-dimensional, it's clear that intense quantum energy fluctuations both create and are shaped by life-changing experiences. Even Carl Jung (1992) stated that 5% of the probability scale lies beyond traditional cause-and-effect predictions. Could this be the quantum fluctuation of energy "rolling up" the "hill," defying gravity, common sense, and our usual understanding of cause and effect?

Einstein proposed that traveling faster than light could fundamentally change the shape of space and time, so what appears like "forward" movement might become "backward" in time. Moving faster than the speed of light distorts the shape of the frequency wave so much that, beyond a certain "trigger point," a phase shift occurs. This is similar to the stroboscopic effect observed with a spinning car wheel, where increasing speed makes the wheel appear to spin backward as the car moves forward. However, this effect extends beyond just the visual; it involves a refraction of phase shifts in light waves, which alters their sequence and influences how reality manifests in that phase. It broadens our perception of the spectrum of visible light beyond the familiar linear cause-and-effect understanding.

This intricate connection between energy shifts and multidimensional existence paves the way for a deeper understanding of both personal and cosmic transformation. Periods of disruption not only break established routines but also serve as crucial opportunities for personal growth, revealing previously unseen potential within individuals. As neural patterns adjust under entropy's influence, they develop, creating new pathways that provide insights into our place within the universal web of existence.

This complex interaction highlights the strong potential for change that comes from chaos itself. When life's turbulence disrupts the neural network, it causes recalibration and encourages the mind to explore parts of existence that were previously hidden by inertia. These periods of upheaval can serve as catalysts for further exploration, motivating investigation into aspects of consciousness where new patterns may form. Here, the balance between order and disorder becomes a crucial process for growth, opening pathways that lead to greater awareness and resilience. Although these experiences might seem chaotic, they act as triggers for breaking old patterns, making room for new frameworks of understanding and adaptation.

This interaction between neural motifs and universal forces highlights the elegance of adaptation—an ongoing process of recalibration that goes beyond linear boundaries. Although chaotic, disruption creates opportunities for growth in new ways we couldn't access before. These transformative energies open new paths, both within the mind and throughout the fabric of multidimensional reality, showing that the chaos we face isn't just random but a meaningful invitation to explore the complex structure of existence.

As we face life-changing moments, they prompt us to reshape the core of who we are. The chaos within these experiences acts as a pulse—an internal rhythm that aligns our inner turmoil with the universe's order. Every shift in mental focus reflects larger patterns, linking individual experiences with their broader social environment. Through this perspective of interconnectedness, we can begin to recognize the transformative power of these moments, turning pieces of instability into clear tapestries of growth and insight.

Since space-time is curved and shaped by relative speed and position, changing velocity will alter the pattern of a person's phase shift. However, the opposite is also true: changing the configuration of a person's phase shift could seem to change their velocity.

What all this indicates is that life-changing experiences reshape the core of our lives through dramatic shifts caused by tipping points. These experiences "push" the "ball" not downward but upward the neural hill—against the natural slope—accelerating our coping mechanisms to the speed of light and beyond. We can intentionally alter our lifestyle through conscious re-synchronization of our connections. Acceleration redefines space-time. It is about reconfiguration, not speeding up.

This intricate relationship between chaos and order takes on a new dimension when seen through personal stories and their connection to cosmic laws. Consider how moments of deep disruption can activate hidden parts of the self. These disruptions not only form new neural pathways but also reflect the cosmic collisions described in M-theory, where universes interact and evolve. Likewise, human consciousness responds to the entropic forces of life—reorganizing, adapting, and ultimately rebuilding its sense of identity and purpose.

Such transformative phenomena rely on the idea that stability and instability are not opposing forces but complementary ones in the development of existence. Just as energy fluctuations can ripple through space-time, creating new dimensions of reality, our emotional and cognitive landscapes reflect this dynamic interaction. When we allow ourselves to embrace disruption, we unlock the potential to reshape the templates of our identity, enabling growth that surpasses linear patterns. Through these shifts, the boundaries of individuality blur, revealing connections to universal motifs that link us to the larger web of existence. The recalibration of self does not merely adapt—it integrates, weaving fragments of chaos into coherent stories of resilience and insight. These moments are invitations, not obstacles, to explore the deeper architecture of being—an architecture that merges the microcosmic intricacies of personal growth with the macrocosmic rhythms of the universe.

What is hyperspace but the movement of pieces of formative space?

As mentioned earlier, when your car is traveling at 80 mph and about to collide head-on with a semi-truck, it is the speed of your decisions and the multidimensionality of your life that flash before you—like a bolt of lightning striking the core of your being.

William Shakespeare wrote in Hamlet, "There are more things in heaven and earth, Horatio, than are dreamt of in your philosophy." In response, I agree that this statement is true. It's wise to open the mind's eye, soften our hardened hearts, and reach further to understand the mysteries beyond the surface of time, space, and the illusions of our reality.

Transformative experiences may not always give us a full view of what lies beyond or let us see clearly through existing barriers. However, they expand our perspective—opening windows and doors to new possibilities. They can feel like a fresh spring breeze clearing away the old cobwebs of stagnation or like a Kansas twister that lifts you up, spins you around, and rolls your "ball" over the hill or past the hump of stability. What is on the other side of time and space, when and where you come back down "from being up there," is the destination of your life's theme.

Her motif of low self-esteem formed the complex foundation for her pain and misery. Her natural self-concept had been dulled and hindered in its growth and confidence by absorbing motifs of manipulation, false promises, and the core belief that love equals pain—and that pain is how love is given. Such schemas resemble traits of borderline personality disorder. They are also quite common in many relationships.

This person's self-image of multifaceted worth and dignity was intrusively damaged by repetitive, traditional patterns—such as maternal dominance that conveyed guilt, worthlessness, and misplaced responsibility to others. The tangled loops of maladaptive motifs "flipped" her into a mindless, repetitive subjugation in intimate relationships. From this state, she "meta-looped" herself out through passive-aggressive, self-

(and thereby relationship-) destructive, clingy, demanding-withdrawing behaviors.

By learning to focus on her consciousness-changing, multi-dimensional perspectives of her unique patterns, she was able to identify subtle differences in her emotional and belief distortions related to her roles in relationships. She can more clearly distinguish between misperceptions, distorted beliefs, and healthy perspectives when rebuilding appropriate relationship behavior.

For example, she was empowered to understand how her need for approval and affirmation acted like a "carrot on a stick." No matter how hard she tried or how much effort she put into pleasing her partner, his approval—and to her, his love—was always just out of reach.

She realized it wasn't about being "perfect" enough. It was about refining her artistic motif of appreciating the beautiful, valuable human being she already was—and is. To do this, she needed self-approval and an internal frame of reference. She learned to step into her motif, sensing herself instead of relying on the mirror image reflected in the eyes of external admirers (whom she tested).

Despite facing instability and isolation due to abandonment, she developed a strong sense of integrity. Her new structure reinforced her belief in herself as a valuable, lovable, and self-validating person who deserves loving relationships.

Multiple perspectives arise as contrasting juxtapositions when self-motif templates are layered over intrusive, maladaptive motifs. Until these internal self-organizing templates—or structural designs of motifs—are reconstructed, the individual remains vulnerable to potentially destructive, life-altering experiences.

Rebuilding one's self-esteem and self-worth is essential for changing potential patterns that affect important life experiences. Without this process, negative behaviors can emerge in areas like career, finances, relationships, and physical, emotional, and spiritual health.

As computer programmers often say about faulty coding: "garbage in, garbage out." If someone engages in maladaptive patterns that can create intrusive, negative, and numbing effects on their core self-motifs, life-altering patterns may become more likely, intense, and complex.

Could this be a factor in the lives of people we know—some of whom seem to have the "worst" or "best" luck for no apparent reason? The formative influence of one's self-esteem motif can even be reflected in their annual income.

For example, at financial seminars, participants are asked to rate their self-esteem and how well their current income reflects their perceived worth, using a 100-point scale for each. Not only are these ratings typically very similar, but when they compare what they think they should earn to their actual paycheck, the ratings are also found to be quite alike.

There is a clear link between what people believe they deserve and what they receive. Just as water naturally finds its level, the results of a person's efforts are influenced by their sense of self-worth.

An important caveat to this assumption is that the "self-fulfilling prophecy" of our self-esteem's motif is not about our true worth or deservingness. Instead, it involves the entrainment effects of how we may unknowingly shape and construct the motif of our self-esteem—forming mental concepts and beliefs about our worth and value that influence the structure of that motif.

People go through different events in their lives, which can shape their sense of identity and beliefs about themselves as individuals.

Depending on the individual, self-esteem patterns can form in ways that lead them to accept and adopt self-negating treatment. For example, children and adolescents who experience verbal, physical, sexual, and/or emotional abuse may unknowingly develop self-esteem behaviors that align with and support harsh, painful, shame-based treatment. Lower thresholds for shock and surprise—along with a tendency toward overstimulation and emotional numbness—are some of the structural features that may be involved.

Such motifs of diminished self-esteem accept, tolerate, and may even justify their abuse, deprivation, and longing—unmet needs. Potentially life-changing synchronization is occurring within these design structures.

The motif of diminished self-esteem lacks a core sense of self-structure rooted in unconditional self-acceptance. Such a motif of self-construction promotes resilience when facing disappointment and helps individuals persevere through adversity. Patterns and configurations that foster resilience and high frustration tolerance are essential qualities often present in motifs of high self-esteem.

Finding a sense of meaning and purpose in one's life is essential for thriving. It results from a mutually reinforcing, reciprocal interaction between themes of self-creation and psychosocial frameworks. Motivation stems from the alignment between an individual's core drives and the characteristics of their specific psychosocial environment.

Uncommon Denominators of Core Motifs

Consider, for example, the woman inspired by Oprah Winfrey to develop a body-shaping product for women—known as Spanx. She connected with Oprah's creative solution of cutting the feet off pantyhose when wearing sandals. This woman "flipped" the perception, reimagining pantyhose as "body hose" designed to firm and tighten the entire female figure. One year after this inspiring idea, her initial $5,000 investment grew into a $1,000,000 company. She chose the "K" sound in Spanx because of its positive associations with celebrities, jokes, songs, and success.

Her distinctive motif combined various artifacts and variables into a deliberate design. She viewed Spanx from multiple angles: footless pantyhose, the slimming impact of hosiery, Oprah's entrepreneurial influence, and her own needs as a woman. Aligning one's self-motif with different elements in one's psychosocial environment allows the coordination of seemingly unrelated people, places, and things—lacking any traditional common feature—into a coherent and meaningful pattern. This captures the essence of a motif: uniting different aspects of life into a single, unified pattern. These unique connections create a distinct personal motif, much like the intricate web of relationships in a soap opera.

Motifs of self-esteem can be a double-edged sword. For those who have experienced varying levels of abuse, the core motifs can become "frozen" in time and space. Maladaptive, artificial structures—alien to the nature of the core self—overlay and attach to them, creating the illusion of lacking a true identity. Low self-esteem, often a result of trauma, distorts these motifs and gives the impression of emptiness or a lack of identity.

Contextualizes the sense of self-core. That is, it places the individual in a deficient, non-nurturing situation where survival depends on centering life around the sadistic gratification of others.

Such motifs lack a true center of core self and become distorted, which disrupts the asymmetrical design that serves only as an extension or residue of a "significant other's" sadistic self. In severe cases, this can lead to serious personality disorders. More often, individuals with such motifs face unrealistic limitations and inhibitions in their pursuit of success. The very structure of their motif is self-limiting, directly originating from an unstable or absent core foundation.

Alignment of Core Motifs

Architects and engineers know: the taller a skyscraper is, the deeper and stronger its foundation must be. Similarly, for an individual to reach the highest levels of personal success and fulfillment, there must be a strong connection to the roots of one's core self-motif. The degree to which this alignment is established and maintained determines how transformative life experiences can become into life-enhancing ones.

Life-changing events will happen regardless. Whether they are viewed as good or bad mainly depends on how aligned a person is with their core motivations. Winning the lottery might seem luckier than surviving a terrorist hijacking, but a person's internal alignment affects how they interpret and emotionally respond to these events. For example, someone with low self-esteem might be devastated by sudden wealth, leading to addiction and isolation. Conversely, a person who aligns with a mindset of high self-esteem could become a hero, risking their safety for the greater good (e.g., Flight 93 during 9/11).

Motifs shape our experiences. The saying "thoughts are things—so be careful what you think" feels more accurate than we might realize. Thoughts, beliefs, and affirmations can connect seemingly unrelated events into life-changing patterns. These patterns can be positive or negative. Like spotting a hidden monkey in the greenery of a jungle maze, our cognitive and emotional motifs can reveal surprising details and link them into life events. This is true for both brilliant innovations and destructive failures. That's the power—and danger—of aligning with motifs that are central to the self. Misalignment can be disastrous.

Multi-dimensional viewpoints help us understand the importance of shifting consciousness and realigning when necessary. Recognizing when our actions match or do not match our core motives can offer valuable insights. As the old saying goes, "To thine own self be true, and thou canst not be false to any man." It's essential to assess how our thoughts, beliefs, emotions, and actions align and make adjustments as needed. This fine-tuning enables us to move toward healthier, more fulfilling life experiences. Depth perception expands our perspective.

Ethics, morality, spirituality, and religion are all higher-level domains that—at their best—provide access to a deeper alignment with the core self. It's important to focus on the essence of reality and the universe as a source of creation—not as fixed structures, but as the ability to shape, influence, deshape, reshape, and sometimes let go of form (i.e., death). From theological conflicts in the 21st century to the rise of the internet and its billions of formative entities (people, programs, portals), our world is increasingly an interconnected web of information systems. Both content and context are expressions of formation operating at different levels of organization.

Logical levels refer to how information is organized hierarchically by abstraction. For example, individual phone numbers (content) are part of the larger category of a phone directory. Confusing a member with the whole class creates a paradox.

The dynamic interaction between core motifs and the broader psychosocial environment is like an artist composing a symphony with seemingly discordant notes. Each experience, whether it is a memory, challenge, or opportunity, can influence personal development. When people learn to harness these different threads consciously, they unlock the ability to shape their lives beyond conventional logic. Static forms or fixed paths do not limit this mosaic of transformation; instead, it is driven by the natural fluidity and adaptability of the human spirit. Through reflection, recalibration, and deliberate action, one can cultivate motifs that resonate deeply with one's true self, fostering both personal growth and collective harmony.

Groucho Marx's joke—he would never join a club that would have him as a member—is a humorous take on the self in conflict with its sense of inherent identity as a motif. This is a motif of Groucho identifying himself as a self-negating reflection of "to be himself is to simultaneously not to be himself"! He could keep pondering this identity question until it causes him stress, or he could reach a level of self-awareness where he accepts the different parts of his changing sense of self, enjoying his cigar and a smile. It also shows how loops and paradoxes can appear in systems of self-reference.

Formativeness is a hierarchy of classes, extending infinitely—design structures nested within other structures. If the class of formativeness is limited to a fixed set or object, it risks collapsing into paradox and losing its ability to generate new forms. Conversely, it can evolve into higher-order, multi-dimensional formations—meta-levels of formativeness. This accurately describes what occurs during the internet's information explosion. Digital participants (bloggers, servers, websites) are not just static forms but dynamic agents that create and recreate other entities.

Think about a room in your home. Change the lighting, your sitting position, or your viewing angle. These minor adjustments alter which features stand out or fade away. Picture the room itself transforming with each shift in perception—based solely on frequency, light, or point of view. This "fifth-dimensional" perception, which alters time and space, allows for the reconfiguration of space and form, suggesting endless possibilities for shaping reality. In such a world, our multi-faceted motifs operate within a multi-dimensional universe of constant change.

If formativeness is ever turned into a rigid construct—worshiped as a fixed idea—it loses its ability to generate new ideas. It might even become harmful.

It is no surprise, then, that multi-dimensionality "leaks" into our four-dimensional world through life-changing experiences. Even when we are shocked, there is often a sense that something intense was coming. As Emily Dickinson wrote: "I see that I cannot see." Sometimes, when we close our eyes, we see more clearly with the "inner eye," which guides us to love, awe, and the universe seeing itself as a web of home, family, and interconnectedness.

We each possess a unique wholeness. Still, we are all connected. In this world of people, places, and events, we can learn to choose our adaptable flow by seeing with "soft eyes" — the eyes of inner transformation. As we follow the bouncing ball of lived experience and learn to recognize the shapes and patterns of our motifs, we begin to understand how to align these transforming motifs as our guides through the mysterious landscapes of our interconnected lives.

The Future Design Has Already Come to the Now That Creates It, And Is Created By It

As we explore the complex relationship between fluidity and the evolving fabric of human experience, we often encounter challenges that test our ability to accept ambiguity. These moments require us to surrender to the interconnected web of life—a willingness to look beneath the surface and examine the unseen forces shaping our existence. Whether through deliberate reflection or spontaneous insight, our ability to adjust our perception is essential to our ongoing consciousness.

Here, synchronicity and serendipity act as guiding forces, offering glimpses into the deeper structures of reality. Like threads woven through the loom of time, these phenomena remind us that our lives are not isolated events but part of a complex design spanning past, present, and future. By learning to identify and understand these occurrences, we can align our internal patterns with external circumstances, which may lead to increased awareness and understanding.

Often, the future, made up of interconnected, sequenced events that are multidimensional, reaches us before we arrive there. Symbols, signs, and phenomena—like receiving a call from an old friend we were recently thinking about, or taking a different route to work without a clear reason and discovering our usual route was closed—happen without obvious causal or logical links.

In this fluid realm of change, we see the deep connection between our inner patterns and the outside world. This ongoing dance between how we perceive ourselves and the patterns we encounter in life urges us to look beyond surface appearances and engage with the subtler forces of existence. Change begins when we realize that our choices, whether intentional or instinctive, are part of a larger story woven from interconnected strands. These strands, often unseen, connect us to a network of experiences and insights that extend beyond the immediate and lead us toward a greater understanding of ourselves and the world around us.

At the heart of this idea is resonance—the belief that our thoughts, actions, and perceptions vibrate in harmony with the universe. This resonance helps us tune into the signals around us and decode the hidden messages in our daily lives. As moments of synchronicity happen, we see that life isn't just a series of isolated events but a rich tapestry woven with many layers of meaning and influence. This understanding encourages us to move away from overrelying on logic and control and instead embrace the mysterious and transformative power of life's unpredictability.

When we align our inner motifs with the larger currents of existence, we open the door to higher consciousness—a realm where intuition and creativity go beyond rigid rationality. Here, humility serves as a bridge to complexity, allowing us to accept the vast interconnectedness that shapes our being. In this deep humility, transformation happens: a shift that redefines our understanding and aligns our perception with the ongoing evolution of our collective and personal motifs.

This is not about believing in psychics or mysterious forces (though I was impressed when the Governor of Georgia gathered spiritual leaders to pray for rain, and it rained a few days later). The 11 interconnected dimensions of space-time suggest that mutual influence takes place across various levels, including past, present, future, human, and nonhuman, spanning from the very large to the very small.

This goes beyond the familiar chaos theory metaphor of the South American butterfly whose wings are said to cause rain in South Dakota. It also addresses the scope, depth, and complexity of interconnectedness—likely far beyond what our current ideas can grasp. As Shakespeare said: "There are more things in heaven and earth, Horatio, than are dreamt of in your philosophy."

We can drive ourselves as "Battie," flapping our wings or spinning our wheels, trying to control our lives. However, when we expand our consciousness to include the illogical, the unexpected, the creative, even the unconscious or intuitive, we create space for transformation. Yes, praying for "rain" in our lives has value. Doing so allows ego consciousness to surrender to a broader humility in the face of complexity.

Aligning our intuitive awareness, including anticipation, empathy, beliefs about intrinsic worth, and commitment to personal values, requires consistency with core guiding principles. This alignment involves acting with integrity and maintaining ethical standards, even when no one is watching. These are just a few ways we begin connecting with higher consciousness and the acausal realities that influence our lives.

Attunement, Entrainment, and Self-Projection

Being open to what enters our awareness enhances our consciousness. We can choose whether to engage with whatever captures our attention. At the same time, this awareness helps us see what we might be unconsciously attracting or projecting. It reveals that we, too, are doing some "wing batting" of our own.

Taking time and intentionally making space for what is awakening within can change the course of a life-changing encounter.

This ongoing conversation between the inner self and the external world highlights the powerful influence of our core motifs. These motifs, shaped by our values, experiences, and subconscious projections, do more than just define who we are — they act as filters through which we perceive life's complexities. If these inner connections are out of sync, we might face recurring problems or unexpected opportunities that impact our choices and relationships.

The interaction of attraction and projection encourages us to consider the unseen forces shaping our lives. It makes us ask whether we are intentionally attracting experiences or unknowingly pushing them away. What might seem like coincidence can often be traced to the subtle vibrations of our consciousness operating within the fabric of existence. It is said that if you want to uncover the secrets of the universe, think in terms of energy, frequency, and vibration—a quote by Nikola Tesla, 1944. He was a Serbian-American engineer, futurist, and inventor; many regard him as a genius comparable to Thomas Edison. Tesla noted that we are bombarded with frequencies of negativity and conflict, as well as enthusiasm and harmony, and that the material world manifests from "solid" frequencies. While this idea about vibrational energy, reality, and manifestation is not new, it is crucial to remember that our motif desires, when aligned with our unique character structure and performative artistry, generate vibrations of a highly effective, actualizing form. These are delicate, fine-tuning frequencies based on our motivations, which require cultivation, mindfulness, and disciplined practice to develop. Shock, trauma, and other disruptions destabilize our organizing motifs with disruptive, toxic negativity and conflict, vibrating through our mind, body, spirit, and soul. As mentioned throughout this manuscript, the shape, design, and formative structures guide and carry the information and coding that influence the quality of our reality. Suppose we fail to discipline and develop our motifs' shape, design, and encoded nature. In that case, we become vulnerable to a barrage of frequencies, vibrations, and energies that fracture our harmony and synchronization, leading to a lower quality of life. Most of us are not raised to discover our unique, signature vibrations—our architecture, shape, designs, and motifs—since we are constantly bombarded with conforming and disharmonic energies that clash with our core nature. However, as we grow in any culture, ignorance is no excuse for neglect. Law enforcement will not punish you for neglecting your artistic or personal talents, but life's consequences can be even harsher than legal penalties. Life may be cruel and unfair; still, neglecting our unique, self-organizing design motifs may be the cruelest blow of all. It deprives us of the richness and creative abundance for which we were meant to live and thrive. When we are out of sync with our motifs' vibrational frequencies in areas like work, love, friendship, and spirituality, we are implicitly self-limiting. Our unique artistry in any field depends on understanding our motifs to attain the success and abundance we deserve. We may not fully know who we are or what we can do, and we might feel like impostors. In truth, feeling like an imposter often stems from not recognizing our actual abilities and qualities, despite being capable beings. This lack of self-awareness does not exempt us from responsibility; instead, it empowers us to change our perspective and take responsibility for modifying our patterns in pursuit of growth and authenticity.

We are always connected to something: a person, a place, or an event. We are part of what we observe and what observes us. Fortuitous events can serve as a barometer for what our future designs have projected into the mirror of our tomorrows.

The reality is that "bad things" happen to "good people." Being a good person doesn't prevent internal self-images, traumatic memories, or unconscious visuals filled with shame, darkness, or despair. The way we shape and understand ourselves—our self-esteem and our feelings of success or failure—is the core pattern we project onto the world. This projection connects us with the very experiences we might unconsciously seek or fear.

The Power of a Projected Motif

Many dedicated and skilled individuals, including business professionals, politicians, and laborers, struggle internally with self-destructive expectations and persistent emotional trauma.

The motifs we hold are adaptable; they shift with self-awareness and intention. When we carefully examine the subtle patterns of our thoughts and actions, they often reveal hidden stories that influence how we engage with the world. These stories can act as a mirror, reflecting both our fears and hopes. By becoming aware of the motifs we unconsciously project, we can adjust them, aligning our inner harmony with the outside world.

This recalibration often requires us to confront uncomfortable truths about ourselves. It involves embracing vulnerability and breaking down defenses that protect us from perceived judgment. In doing so, we create space for growth, allowing new patterns to develop—ones that feel more authentic with our evolving selves. The process isn't without challenges, but it offers the opportunity for deep transformation, altering our relationships, careers, and inner worlds.

Their projected motifs continue to produce strong synchronizations. I know a successful businessman, now the CEO of a Fortune 500 company, who can never forget the poverty he came from. Despite his achievements, he had many affairs, socialized with influential people of questionable character, and took risky decisions that nearly wrecked his marriage and career. I believe all of this was his way of trying to validate a fractured sense of self-worth through flashy clothes, high-status connections, and money as a distraction from deep shame and feelings of inadequacy.

This dynamic interaction between conscious and unconscious motifs influences the patterns of our lives. When our internal projections are validated by external events, it can feel like luck or, on the flip side, like persistent bad luck. A key step in breaking out of cycles of self-defeat is recognizing and adjusting these inner patterns to match healthier projections.

However, such work requires honest self-awareness and a willingness to confront uncomfortable themes that may lie beneath the surface. These themes often surface during moments of crisis, when the tension between our idealized images and real-life experiences becomes unavoidable. These disruptions provide an opportunity to reevaluate the fundamental patterns that shape our actions and decisions.

Often, this starts when external events mirror our fears or fantasies. Whether it's the unspoken belief in one's worth or a persistent idealization of unreachable dreams, these projections can create self-fulfilling cycles. By intentionally examining these patterns, we can break their hold and choose to focus on themes that reflect our true aspirations.

Eventually, his risky choices led him to influential individuals with similar illusions, who later aimed to destroy him. His turning point came when he confronted his distortions, his inability to distinguish fact from fantasy, and realized that small adjustments in his "design features" could change his life.

He learned, for example, that entraining a fantasy, like having an affair with a prostitute and imagining it would turn into a long-term relationship, was a key part of a pattern of heartache and betrayal. He realized that his "bad luck" was influenced just as much by his entrainment as by any external factors. He had been creating his distorted pattern, unconsciously aligning himself with destructive affirmations of unworthiness.

The Harmony of Projection and Reflection

In this way—and in many other ways—there is always "perfect harmony" in life. There is always resonance between the motifs we entrain and the realities we face. Whether in sickness or in health, for better or for worse, till death do us part—we project motifs, and they are reflected back to us, even when the motif is "perfectly" neurotic.

Many of our challenges stem from losing our sense of identity and the boundaries that define us, which in turn break down. We have multiple layers—ranging from our core beliefs and self-image to external behaviors and styles (introversion, extroversion, etc.).

Many mistakenly believe a boundary is a rigid barrier between oneself and others. Boundaries are dynamic patterns that shape identity. Gaining or losing boundaries reflects the multidimensional construction of our projected motif design. We recognize ourselves by our boundary configuration, just as we recognize the borders of a country like America. However, unlike a map, a human's boundaries are fluid, capable of expanding or contracting within a healthy range. That balance indicates a mature motif.

Compression, Role Distortion, and Cultural Intrusions

Significant others—parents, peers, culture, biology—may violate or distort parts of our fluid boundaries. When entire themes of self-development are squeezed into compartments or roles (e.g., "the smart one," "the athlete," "the caretaker"), we confuse a part of the person with the whole of their self. To say a child is born a quarterback or pianist—even if true—only captures a fragment of the full complexity of that child's unique design.

Many interpersonal, political, and cultural conflicts originate from one person or group imposing their preset template on another. These impositions are often oversimplified and fail to recognize the depth and complexity of the other's motives. When someone, like a parent or partner, reinterprets or distorts someone else's behavior into a guilt-based expectation—e.g., "If you loved me, you would call me daily and shop with me weekly"—they risk constraining the other's boundary identity. This kind of relational compression leads to "un-heavenly" entrainments. Formative Design in Law, Culture, and Meaning-Making

How many cultural "framings" could be applied to the horrific events of 9/11? The same applies to public trials, like the O.J. Simpson case. The determination of guilt or innocence often depends on a lawyer's ability to present and organize the facts into a persuasive narrative systematically. The jury's verdict depends on how well that presentation fits their internal framework.

Legal battles, much like life itself, are won not only with facts but through the skillful use of design. The most well-crafted, impactful motif often determines the outcome. The next time you seek a lawyer, consider not just their credentials but also their ability to grasp complex legal concepts and build a compelling case.

This connection between projection and reality emphasizes the inevitable cycles of harmony and disruption in human relationships and societal dynamics. Boundaries, although flexible, act as frameworks that shape the main themes defining individuals or groups. However, these structures are constantly influenced by external forces—such as cultural norms, interpersonal expectations, or environmental factors—that often compress or distort the natural complexities of identity. Themes develop from the interaction between personal perspectives and established narratives, with their significance shaped by how they evolve over time.

The fight for uniqueness amid external pressures often sparks innovation, as individuals or groups look for ways to stand out. This process reflects the challenges faced during early growth, where identity becomes a flexible idea shaped by internal beliefs and external validation. It is in this space of contrast that many of life's most important experiences happen, showing the complex balance between pushing away, pulling in, and adjusting.

Our ability to resist, assert, and empower our own development depends on the "best fit" adaptation related to our unique motif's asymmetry. Evolution shows adaptive resourcefulness across many species. For instance, the skunk has such an "asymmetrical odor" that it resists being integrated into group living. Adolescents also display asymmetry to various degrees. Blowfish, porcupines, turtles, and others each have distinct, alarming asymmetries in their design that prevent them from being preyed upon. However, this does not mean that evolutionary processes will stop driving increased uniqueness and innovation as survival strategies. Even the U.S. military recognizes the powerful, evolving role of asymmetry in designing its stealth bombers. The multi-dimensional aspect of asymmetry enhances resilience and adaptability, helping living beings survive and thrive.

Since many languages have their own unique structures, there exists a meta-language—often called a language of languages—that has its own "family" of coded meanings and constructs. Syntax, subtle nuances, word combinations, and wordplay all shape the layered meanings of ideas and constructs. Concepts like love, freedom, and surrender are linked to groups of similar processes, each with its own nuanced meanings and purposes. These features are part of specific design structures within motifs. For example, the construct of 'coldness' has over 80 nuanced meanings in the Inuit language. The idea of "Word" acts as inspiration—a vital breath of life—representing the endless creative force of

The paradox of asymmetrical motifs in life forms is that aspects of their uniqueness both attract and are attracted to similar qualities in others through a dynamic resonance of entrainment (Frankl would attract and be attracted to other prisoners who held similar beliefs). Because no two unique motifs of people are exactly identical, groups of similarities can only "lock in" to a limited degree of fit before subtle differences between individuals establish a boundary.

This is a double-edged sword: when balanced correctly, it can create intimacy and harmony. This is evident in couples and/or families where there is a complementary balance of similarities and differences at just the right level. Partners may both need to address issues with overbearing, intrusive mothers. However, one person might experience total immersion (boundary compression) in unprotected exposure to parental demands and see it as "normal." The other might adopt roles to avoid such immersion, having been raised by parents who could detach—perhaps even playing one controlling parent against the other.

The downside of asymmetry in entraining motifs is the difficulty of separating oneself from these combined entrainments. Since similarities between partners' motifs can never be perfect, but are still very intense in their boundary immersion, there must be "room and space" for individuality to flourish.

This dynamic balance of compression and expansion appears not only in personal relationships but also in larger systems of meaning and adaptation. Consider how individuals and groups navigate their unique motifs within societal structures. These motifs often reflect the paradox of outer conformity and inner divergence, setting the stage for both innovation and conflict. Sometimes, the struggle between asserting individuality and meeting societal expectations drives growth, pushing us toward greater self-awareness and collaboration. This delicate balance highlights the importance of creating spaces where asymmetry is not just accepted but celebrated, allowing each motif to contribute to a larger whole without losing its uniqueness.

When there is a high similarity in asymmetrical motifs between partners, they may fear losing their unique asymmetry. In contrast, significant disparity in asymmetry may undermine intimacy, potentially leading to concerns regarding abandonment. This oscillation between extremes can create chaotic wobble effects that destabilize the relationship. When these extremes become unbalanced (which can happen easily), feelings of being trapped, overly dependent, or fearful of abandonment may develop. This can set the stage for a potentially life-changing experience.

The asymmetrical traits in all formative entities strengthen and enable their survival and growth. Asymmetrical characteristics of life form motifs assert, affirm, and deepen their uniqueness by empowering groups of similar (but distinctly different) life forms. Birds of a feather may flock together, as "families" of species form with each their unique position within the configuration of the "flock."

While the uniqueness of asymmetry can boost a species' survival and evolution when it functions adaptively in its environment, it can also cause that species to become part of a "family" of similar life forms or grouped events in space and time. Being pulled into a synchronization of merging events could become a life-changing experience. Consider the extinction of dinosaurs 65 million years ago caused by a meteor. While it ended the unique adaptation of enormous dinosaurs, it spurred the evolution of small mammals, eventually leading to the rise of humans. One person's meat (or meteor) is another's poison—especially if you are a dinosaur.

An adolescent's unique rebelliousness can help them stand out from their family. However, it can also become self-destructive if it does not evolve into a higher form of growth—such as rebellion to do what one wants, even if others also want it! These asymmetrical traits in our life patterns drive the ongoing search, quest, and striving toward higher forms of emerging consciousness.

Finally, I want to end with a reflection on spirituality and religion as strong influences that shape our lives. How we see cause and effect in our lives relates to our ideas of God, Higher Power, and/or Universal Causal Agency. Believing that events are somehow meant, divined, or destined (God's will, Divine Providence, etc.) significantly affects how we interpret life-changing moments. To what extent can losses, whether financial, personal, career-related, marital, or physical, be attributed to predetermined factors rather than coincidence? Was it all preordained by God, or was it co-created through some form of interactive interdependence?

Finding purpose and meaning through life-changing experiences shapes our understanding of what God (if we believe in such a Being) truly is. How we interpret—and are interpreted—by these profound moments at a higher level of consciousness influences the core themes that can create powerful alignments. These themes seem to possess a self-organizing life energy of their own. When we access higher levels of consciousness filled with pure formative potential, we open gateways to endless possibilities. Multidimensional resources become accessible to us, and we become receptive to them as we expand our consciousness to such levels of inspiration.

Holy books like the Bible describe creation beginning with the Word, seen as inspiration that 'breathes life" (respiration) into all living beings. However, there is not just one "Word of God." The Word of God is the idea and capacity for words. The "Word" is what is formative, not necessarily a fixed, literal form. Just as many languages have their own unique structural designs, there is a language of languages — a meta-language — with its own "family" of coded meanings and constructs. Syntax, subtle nuances, word combinations, and wordplay all shape the layered meanings of ideas and constructs. Concepts such as love, freedom, and surrender are connected to groups of similar processes, each with its own nuanced meanings and purposes. These are features of distinct design structures within motifs. For example, the construct of 'coldness' has over 80 nuanced meanings in the language of the Inuit.

The idea of "Word" serves as inspiration—a vital breath of life—expressing the endless creative force of life energy, which "breathes itself" through the unique design of each organism. It is the individual design of every living being that we define and label when we name it, "word it," "call it," or give it a logo.

This intricate balance of personal choice and shared resonance recurs not only in human psychology but also in ecological systems and larger social structures. Just as Viktor Frankl's individual responsibility helped him survive and grow under tough conditions, the interaction of asymmetric motifs also influences outcomes in families, communities, and ecosystems. These dynamics show that individuality and interconnectedness are not naturally opposed but are instead complementary forces that, when coordinated, can drive meaningful change.

For instance, the principle of "entrainment" extends into the natural world, where species come together to form ecosystems shaped by patterns of mutual adaptation and survival. Birds of a feather flock together not only by choice but out of necessity, creating groups that thrive through their collective yet unique contributions to their shared environment. The distinctiveness of each bird's flight pattern enhances the flock's unity, reflecting the balance between individuality and harmony seen in human relationships.

This interplay of attraction and divergence occurs not only in personal relationships but also within larger ecological and societal systems. The balance of harmony and discord in uneven patterns influences the paths of individual and collective growth, often leading to important insights or shifts in awareness. These shifts are frequently shaped by our ability—or inability—to reconcile the natural tension between individuality and interconnectedness.

That is why consciousness, as "the Word" or idea/construct (epigenesis), creates and "breathes" the manifestation of abstract ideas— which are "things" in themselves— into concrete, behavioral experience. What we conceive and believe, we tend to "achieve" through entraining motifs— whether we realize it or not. It concerns not only beliefs and thoughts but also the way they are structured, which leads to entrainment.

Living creatures are unique structures with their symmetry. To "word" them into existence stems from formativeness, which represents the infinite design possibilities beyond literal, rigid, set forms. We create our lives through "wording"—both verbal and non-verbal—from prebirth experiences to our most mature years, even up to the moment of physical death and beyond. How we, through consciousness, engage with the attractor patterns of our distinctive motifs produces the operant (or observable variables) that manifest as cause and effect in our lives (Hawkins, 2002).

This dynamic interplay of attraction and divergence underpins much of human relational patterns, as well as broader ecological and societal structures. Whether at an individual level or within communities, these asymmetrical motifs act as catalysts for both harmonious integration and destabilizing friction. The intricate resonance between similarities and differences governs the alignment—or misalignment—of relationships, influencing the collective evolution of shared consciousness. In such contexts, the challenge is balancing mutual entrainments while maintaining individual boundaries and identities. This task requires not only awareness but also deliberate efforts to cultivate personal and collective growth.

For example, if we are taught to set the attractor patterns of our motifs around victimization—rather than victorious journeys of freedom and conquest over personal "demons"—then these operant variables contribute to repeated outcomes of suffering or joy. The balance we establish in our attractor patterns increases the likelihood of skewed, dysfunctional synchronizations.

Consciousness can reveal and shape countless variations of attractor patterns hidden within our unique motifs. The patterns that emerge from significant life experiences demonstrate the relationship between cause and effect, suggesting that unconscious involvement can shape perceptions into a perceived absolute reality. The challenge isn't to play God but to harness our natural "gifts" of formative consciousness—rephrasing and expressing new attractor patterns that can act as new causes and effects in our lives.

Learning to establish new synchronizations or motifs creates fresh attractor patterns for altered states of entrainment. The first step is to become aware of our consciousness and its capabilities. Consequently, taking responsibility for our personal growth is essential for improving and transforming our life experiences, especially when working to overcome challenges related to developing our strengths and characteristics.

We are each responsible for, and have control over, the identity structure from which the attractor patterns of our motifs are drawn and generated.

Each person's identity structure—and therefore boundary design—is complex and multi-layered, reflecting subtleties that must be respected in various interactions. Establishing and maintaining boundaries fosters individual diversity. The process of asserting, empowering, and affirming selfhood for growth involves the emergence of differences throughout life.

Consider that Illinois has a boundary shape that is different and unique from California. Crossing each state's border is more than just crossing a line; it's a shift into a different mindset based on that state's theme. The collective mindset in California may differ from what is in Illinois. Still, both are beautiful in their own way.

Boundary configuration involves a state of consciousness that develops through protective, empowering, and asymmetrical motifs that assert and confirm each entity's identity within formative entrainments. The development and establishment of these motifs influence which selective entrainments will occur, as well as those that may lead to significant experiences.

While we don't have full control, we do have significant influence and input over the outcome of even our most unpredictable events—like how long we live. The way we think, feel, and care for ourselves greatly impacts both the quality and length of our lives and deaths.

Recently, I read that Sen. John Kerry's first wife died of cancer at age 61. She had struggled with depression for much of her life. Research suggests that agitated states, like anger and depression, negatively impact health and can lead to diseases such as cancer, diabetes, and alcoholism. Stress is a killer when it gets out of control and unbalanced in our lives.

When we adopt a transformed lifestyle that is uniquely purposeful and aligned with the multi-dimensional boundaries of our own identity, we increase the likelihood that our life-changing experiences will be more profound and more beneficial.

I want to share some summary thoughts as I finish this work. This interdependence of internal and external forces emphasizes the deep responsibility we hold in shaping our realities. By actively engaging with the multi-dimensional aspects of life, we allow ourselves to embrace the fluidity of existence instead of succumbing to its apparent rigidity. Every boundary we cross becomes a threshold of opportunity—a space to redefine old patterns and envision new paradigms.

At the heart of this transformative process is a delicate balance: maintaining one's boundaries while fostering immersive connections that go beyond them. This dynamic balance between preservation and integration captures the essence of growth, allowing us to explore our motives more deeply. Through this exploration, we recognize our ability to create change, not only in our own lives but also within the collective fabric of human experience.

I believe our experiences of space, time, energy, and matter emerge as complete acausal wholes rather than being caused individually. For example: critical mass effects of nuclear chain reactions (including the metaphorical "nuclear family"), graduating from college, a child "graduating" from living at home, "intimacy" online through technology (e.g., 120 million text messages on Valentine's Day in 2006), Planck's constants of "energy," "space," and "length" determining "chunk size" at the quantum level, and all-or-nothing events like pregnancy, birth, psychosocial stage developments, and death—all are experiences that emerge through discrete steps of completion.

Each step is a separate unit or whole, building on itself into larger entities. The "gestalts" or wholes of our formative life experiences are "digitalization" (discrete units or wholes) that may seem like analog processes (gradations). However, they are design motifs—unique, discrete, quantum units of form.

Life-altering experiences occur when the core elements of our lives collide or reach a "critical mass' of instability, like when the tech bubble bursts in the stock market.

These motifs are not fixed; they are dynamic forces pulsing with the potential for change. Whether through personal reflection or collective upheavals, the connections we build in our lives are like weaving threads into a tapestry—each thread representing a decision, interaction, or realization. The fabric of these connections not only fosters personal growth but also sends ripples across larger contexts, reshaping societal norms and global paradigms.

For example, a moment of clarity, such as recognizing previously overlooked possibilities, can lead to changes that shape a person's life path. When amplified, these moments spread through collective awareness, inspiring movements, innovations, or revolutions. This interaction between small-scale and large-scale levels of synchronization demonstrates the fractal nature of reality, where repeating patterns emerge at different levels.

Think about how these events might connect and lead to a significant, life-changing shift: the subprime housing crisis, job loss, the Iraq war and its costs, fears of nuclear conflict in Iran and Pakistan, the 9/11 terrorist attacks, cancer, heart disease, and others. What role do oil and energy play in this picture?

I will leave the synchronization of these uncommon denominators to your motifs so they can align in your way. Seemingly unrelated events can unintentionally converge as a wave of transformation. Keeping deviations within unstable levels of organization can only last so long before chaotic, volcanic "bubbling over" effects happen. However, the sources of such deviations often originate from multi-dimensional aspects of reality.

Stephen Leeb, Ph.D. (2006), illustrates this point in his discussion of the accelerating oil crisis. He describes the impending, global, life-altering event when oil prices reach $200 per barrel. His emphasis on prevention highlights the actions governments need to take in pursuing alternative energy sources before this "gestalt" event entirely unfolds. Leeb also mentions that stock market analysts have "predicted" seven out of the last two recessions. He refers to French mathematician René Thom, who developed Catastrophe Theory, explaining how distinctly discontinuous (quantum "chunked") events often happen in nature.

Formativeness is a core attribute of existence. The tangible physical world of our personal, psycho-social, cultural, and global experiences depends on sensory materializations that are fundamentally formative. The physical structure of chains and individuals, much like a symphony's arrangement, is made up of atoms, molecules, and other basic components. What distinguishes one configuration from another is formativeness at every level of organization.

Energy and mass are interchangeable (Einstein's $E = mc^2$), representing different levels of concentrated density in a multi-dimensional form. Einstein's formula describes reality as manifesting through patterns of proportionality—an alteration of energy, mass, and light in relative proportions of unity.

For example, what we call force, energy, or mass are lower-level materializations of fundamental design patterns. The "force of gravity" (which famously pulled Sir Isaac Newton's apple to the ground) is, in fact, an illusion. Einstein showed that gravity results from the curvature caused by masses in spacetime.

Quantum mechanics shows that what we call solid matter (subatomic particles, atoms, and molecules) is a probability density of quantum wave clouds that tend to form specific patterns—imperfect, asymmetrical motifs.

The concept of energy and electron movement (electricity) can be understood not as isolated particles in motion but as neighboring electrons passing energy to each other. This illustrates the pattern of the energy wave function. Just as a series of lights outside a theater (synchronized on/off lights in serial patterns) creates the perception of motion through coordinated illumination, energy is transmitted via a sequence of deliberate design patterns of synchronized on/off signals. The illusion of motion is produced by the stroboscopic lighting of wave peaks and troughs reflecting design motifs.

These principles of formativeness are not just theoretical concepts; they are applied across various fields and practices, from ecological design to computational systems. The interconnectedness of patterns in nature challenges our linear way of thinking, fostering a holistic view of interactions and innovations. For example, in the emerging field of biomimicry, nature's complex patterns inspire sustainable solutions to human problems. By studying the fractal geometry of leaves or the efficiency of honeybee hives, innovators find ways to enhance energy efficiency, construction methods, and even social systems.

These connections reveal the hidden potential of rethinking the fabric of existence—not as separate phenomena but as active, interconnected possibilities. For example, advances in quantum computing, where manipulating subatomic particles and their probabilities redefine how we understand processing power. In these systems, the patterns of quantum states are used to achieve computational feats once thought impossible. Such breakthroughs demonstrate the latent power of multi-dimensional patterns in shaping the tangible realities of our world.

Similarly, in the realm of social change, efforts that align individual and collective goals can produce powerful results. Social movements, often triggered by a single catalytic event, show how synchronization can inspire widespread change. Through shared visions, collective meditations, or grassroots activities, the interaction between individual and systemic factors shapes societal changes and future developments.

The piezoelectric effect—deforming crystal lattices, shifting polarities, and rearranging patterned electron structures—is another example of how multi-dimensionality creates the illusion of motion, mass, and energy.

Speaking of illusions: Freud once said that time itself is an illusion—with a purpose.

The power of multi-dimensional motifs in creating tangible, life-changing experiences becomes clear when we understand what "physical reality" truly is. Even space itself has been envisioned (Smolin, 2001) in quantum gravity as composed of loops, weaves, and quantum "foam." If it were possible to travel at the speed of light, time and spatial location would not be experienced in the usual way; one would occupy all positions in space and time simultaneously.

What would happen if faster-than-light travel caused asymmetry in the concept of unity? Disrupting the symmetry of this resonant point means moving beyond "forward to the past." Such infinity might define the essence of multidimensional oneness.

In 2005, a study in New York City aimed to cut crime by 25%. Over 4,000 people meditated for six weeks to achieve this goal. The results were impressive: crime rates decreased. This demonstrates that awareness of multi-dimensionality both influences and is influenced by what we call animate and inanimate beings—and physical reality itself.

Whether through prayer, meditation, intuition, spiritual focus, core sensing of self, or a Higher Power, empowerment in our lives is rooted in our access to the essential abilities of multidimensional consciousness. Our life-changing experiences are inherently formative—and reflect empowered outcomes of acausal possibilities that have come into being because they have completed themselves.

It is our choice to pre-empt these experiences in the "future-now" and empower new, emerging formative futures—enriching the present with renewed potential.

Consciousness is our core. Our choice.

By connecting—in our own unique ways—to the multi-dimensionality of reality (at least eleven dimensions, where membranes touch all points in space-time), we can "put our ear to the ground" and listen (or "see" or "feel") what storms—or resources—may be approaching into our lives and the lives of those we love, cherish, and value.

Being receptive and intuitively open to the vibrations and ripples of entraining motifs allows us to access the core attributes and uncommon factors of our complex life challenges. These motifs can become empowering and resourceful solutions, helping us prevent or intervene in life-altering experiences.

Mindfulness, as a key practice, may involve living in the "eye of the hurricane." The paradox is that we do not need more objectivity in life — but more subjectivity — to define the unique, evolving boundaries of our core self-motif.

Expanded consciousness entails the development of a person's distinct sense of self.

"To thine own self be true..."

Well, you know the rest of this motif.

EPILOGUE

MINDFUL MOTIFS OF LIFE ALTERING EXPERIENCES

We are each a unique, self-organizing pattern with asymmetrical configurations, similar to hanging mobile chimes. These are idiosyncratic to our own "golden ratio." Our core motifs are inherent, epigenetic ways of organizing how we design responses to lifestyle events: inner thoughts, feelings, behaviors, and interpersonal experiences.

Motifs orchestrate asymmetrical themes—never complete, never static—unfolding infinitely like the calculation of pi. They guide how and when to organize what needs organizing to fulfill life functions. Motifs emerge as self-orchestrated entities, resembling an orchestra that synchronizes without a single conductor. In their case, there is no single conductor but an emergent property, motif-ness, inherent within each part, like in a holograph, where every piece contains the wholeness.

In this state of expansive awareness, we uncover how multi-dimensionality resonates not only within individuals but also across collective and systemic paradigms. Each person's unique motif interacts with unseen forces of the universe, forming a web of interconnected vibrations. This interaction suggests that our lives are influenced by more than just luck or circumstance — they are shaped by a deeper design, one that aligns with the unseen geometries of existence.

These motifs are not random; they reflect patterns seen in nature, like the spirals of galaxies or water flowing down a mountain. These natural patterns remind us that individuality is linked to universality. They inspire us to explore our ways of existence, observing how our rhythms blend with the larger symphony of life.

With this understanding, we can begin to tune into the symphony of our surroundings intentionally, perceiving subtle cues that guide us toward growth and alignment. When we align with our inherent geometry, we bridge the gap between the visible and the invisible, the conscious and the unconscious, empowering ourselves to create meaningful transformations in our realities.

Each cell contains the entire epigenetic motif of an individual. The motif is the emerging, asymmetrical identity pattern present in all living beings—what enables starling birds to move in sync and fertilized zygotes to coordinate complex, multi-level differentiation into humans.

These self-organizing motifs rearrange themselves and influence our lifestyle experiences. They entrain and resonate in how we shape and structure our behavioral, emotional, and cognitive experiences. As motifs emerge amid the apparent chaos of life's randomness, they often hide in plain sight—camouflaged among the countless people, places, and events we encounter. Like a jungle puzzle, we might ask: how many monkeys are hiding in the trees?

As a result, we may unknowingly align with both healthy and unhealthy interactions—or internal interactions within ourselves. For example, resonating with fast-paced music while driving can shift our focus toward the "rush,' increasing the risk of a life-changing accident. Often, the consequences of tangled, unconscious actions are only recognized in hindsight.

The purpose of this work is to clarify the hidden empowerment—and danger—of entraining motifs. Recognizing our recurring patterns in daily life reveals familiar yet distinct themes, much like interconnected schemas forming a unified whole. How we organize work, play, and love is guided by these interacting motifs, which both shape and define the experience itself. When we act irrationally, altruistically, or darkly without understanding why, our motif may have been unconsciously influenced.

Through careful exploration, we begin to understand the dynamic relationship between our internal patterns and the external stimuli that influence them. This awareness allows us to see how small shifts in our thoughts, feelings, and actions can alter the connection between ourselves and our environment. For example, the gentle pace of a breeze or the rhythm of meaningful conversation often mirror the complex dance of our inner tendencies, offering opportunities for reflection and growth.

Motifs demonstrate how subtle moments—such as an unspoken word or missed gesture—can shape our lives. They motivate us to stay open to possibilities, where mindfulness turns fleeting moments into meaningful insights, influencing who we are and who we may become.

In this complex interplay of subjectivity and resonance, motifs function not as fixed blueprints but as evolving symphonies. They challenge us to find a balance between accepting and intentionally changing, helping us move beyond reactive patterns and build a meaningful connection with our core configurations. It is within this balance that the essence of mindfulness lies, fostering a harmonious relationship with both our inner and outer worlds.

Something nuanced within us—or between us and our environment—may have synchronized in a way that "switched on" a genome, much like how epigenetics turns genes on or off. This could include subtle combinations of mood, associative thought, biochemistry, and sensation, creating a unique synchronization (a motif) that activates a specific lifestyle expression. This resonance is not just about mirroring external stimuli—it emanates from one's inner "DNA frequency," a person's unique motif.

Motifs are influenced by factors such as beliefs, genetics, culture, and social imprinting; however, their significance extends beyond these elements. They are innate organizing templates embedded in the proportional geometry of our being, formed at conception. This geometry exists before our name is given. In practices of mindfulness and meditation, individuals achieve pure awareness, a state that corresponds to these essential motif patterns. These patterns can also be reached through mindful attention to one's movements—emerging as geometric proportions of formative being. Stillness reveals these motifs.

Imagine a kaleidoscope: each turn reveals new swirling patterns of color and shape. Every moment is unique but originates from the same basic geometry. Similarly, each person is a kaleidoscope of potential growth, capable of mindful self-creation. When left unconscious, these patterns are vulnerable to resonating with whatever aligns—even dysfunctionally—with our innate tendencies.

Each person has unique proportions of mood, energy, ambition, social interaction, and introspection. An imbalance in how we allocate time and energy to work, relationships, and spirituality can impact our health. These ratios resemble kaleidoscope patterns, but each person's motifs arise from within as a self-propagating form of individuality.

These thematic motifs serve as guiding frameworks—shaping our reinvention of self in both familiar and unexpected ways. When we respect their unique rhythmic styles, we find harmony, peace, and achievement. However, if we fixate on imposed social roles—such as striving to become a business owner to meet family expectations—we may become angry, anxious, and conflicted.

Pushing ourselves to achieve goals we should not desire, at the cost of what we truly want, causes inner conflict. We become conditioned to distorted parts of our motivation that break our connection with our authentic, unique self. Embracing our uneven motivation frees us from unhealthy patterns and heals suffering through empowered authenticity.

Motifs have a self-reflective structure that interacts with both internal and external contexts. Their interactions reshape our ecological reality and tell new stories. These stories reinterpret our conversations—giving growth and presence new meaning.

Motifs transfer, moving from mental to physical forms within and between people. This pattern of formation is shown through verbal and nonverbal communication, physical sensations, and more. Transduction allows motifs to affect the mind, body, spirit, and also our social and ecological environments.

This has important implications in the digital age. Motifs are basic wave patterns, each with uneven cognitive, emotional, and behavioral signatures. They reflect our self-views, temperament, and tendencies.

We are also energetic beings composed of electromagnetic fields. These bioelectric fields exist at every level: cellular, tissue, organ, neuroimmune, mental, emotional, and behavioral. Our patterns both influence and are influenced by these energy fields. For example, low-level electromagnetic waves can impact mood, thinking, and actions. The effect depends on how well these external frequencies match our pattern's internal frequency. Just as hydrogen atoms have unique energy levels, so do we.

There is no static "you." Instead, there is a wholeness of formativity—manifested through your unique proportional geometry. Just as a symphony embodies the conductor, and the conductor in turn embodies the music, a larger geometric musical motif guides both. This composition displays a structured approach, though it does not adhere to a predetermined form. Its formative variations are infinite—emerging, diverging, and converging with creative influence.

Motifs are not just about reframing; they are a current and evolving key element of what defines us. They shape other frameworks. Each one displays a unique proportional geometry, resonating in its own way. Every motif allows for different forms of expression, but no single form can fully capture its unique qualities. Motifs are like families — no one member embodies the whole, but their shared traits reveal a collective pattern.

Take the Kennedy family: high achievement, charisma, tragedy, and public visibility—no single Kennedy embodies all of these, but collectively they reflect a common theme. Likewise, each person has a "family" of trait levels that shape their overall motif.

Examples include introversion/extraversion, thinking/feeling, sensing/intuition, verbal/sensory abilities, and emotional/conceptual intelligence. These ratios shape personality profiles—mainly stable but capable of changing based on age, health, environment, and lifestyle. These variations display a system of motifs within motifs—emerging, evolving, or regressing over time.

Motifs are geometric ratios, but they are not "things." They are proportional properties that generate things; for example, pi is not a number but a ratio that creates circular forms. Motifs are variable, with each person having their own distinctive set of ratios. One could say, each of us have our "piece" or share of the pie. What about you?

Just as pi is infinite, so is the motif. It is not a fixed quantity but a formative state, always in flux. In metaphorical terms, the motif may be the "Planck unit" of our psychic quantum reality, the irreducible piece of our being.

It is vital to understand that life continues regardless of my conscious awareness. My entrainments, whether fully or partially active, persist until I choose to re-synchronize and realign with my main asymmetrical motif. When I do, I improve my outcomes, whether responding to my child's specific needs or noticing the fine print of a scam. I engage my motif with full awareness, participating in holistic entrainments that shape the best possible, most likely future.

I'm not leaving it up to chance.

I am proactive in my approach to my motif.

Motifs originate from each person's unique core of geometric potential. Body shape proportionality, individual biochemistry, emotional temperament, brain structure, and cognitive conceptualization style all exhibit core proportional geometric patterns that are characteristic and reflect individual core motifs. These distinctive proportional differences arise through resonant, interacting geometric patterns that develop as motifs combine and evolve within each person.

Incorporating motifs into everyday life fosters mindfulness and self-awareness, functioning as a subtle way to express oneself through fashion.

When a proportional part or element of one's motif merges with the same part of another, they can blend harmoniously. However, it can also, often to varying degrees, be harmful because the combined resonance becomes dystonic and grating—like striking a dissonant note on a piano. For example, everything might seem fine in a friendship, but if one partner uses a tonal gesture that signals a dissonant emotional tone—such as a husband telling his wife she only makes $10.00 an hour and does not have a "real job"—this can trigger a life-changing "War of the Roses" experience. The husband's motif of achieving success through his law firm is how he measures his self-worth. This creates a disparaging clash with his wife's motif of enjoying the process of earning her money, regardless of the amount.

This mixture of "resonating" dissonant parts within each other's motifs creates small fissures that can develop into major earthquakes and life-changing experiences of divorce, or worse. When there is respect and space for each person's motifs, healthy resonance of mutuality is established. However, a lack of awareness of each person's unique motif reflects a kind of mindlessness that runs counter to formative motifs.

If the husband recognizes that his wife also earns her own income and is successful in her own way, then the subtle proportions of each partner's motives align. The proportionality of motives is the key aspect of their developing awareness. The ratio of each person's various motives has its own subtle level. These different levels—measured as ratios between traits—include qualities like moving quickly or slowly through time, being passive or active, intuitive or factual, analytical or artistic, and cognitively or emotionally expressive. The proportional contribution of these elements shapes a unique artistic motif called the self.

What greater proof of inherent motifs exists than the astonishing orchestration of the fertilized egg—zygote—differentiating into its distinct, proportional, specialized areas: the central nervous system, skeletal system, alimentary canal, endocrine system, and more? Guiding, unique motifs are widespread throughout the life cycle.

This zygote exhibits self-organizing properties. There might be a synchronicity between The Zygote and the origin of the universe 13.7 billion years ago, when the supersymmetry (sameness) of the entire universe—infinitely small, with no space and no time—exploded with acceleration and formed asymmetrical (more matter than antimatter) patterns.

This interaction between individuality and interconnectedness vividly expresses life itself. Each motif, whether at the cellular, personal, or cosmic level, can lead to both harmony and disruption. The challenge lies in recognizing these patterns and aligning with resonances that foster growth, while being cautious of those that could cause discord. While some "discord" is a natural part of living, an excessive degree of dissonance beyond an asymmetrical "balance" appears to be destabilizing and could severely disrupt one's well-being in the long run.

In the human experience, this is especially important in relationships, where the unique patterns of individuals can either complement or conflict with one another. The art of living lies in cultivating attunement—not only to one's internal patterns but also to the larger harmony of existence. It is through this awareness of engaging with the flow of patterns that one finds both purpose and growth, serving as a living testament to the emerging, evolving nature of reality. Self-organizing motifs embody this kind of "balance".

This idea of self-organization was explored by Alan M. Turing, FRS (1952), in his publication The Chemical Basis of Morphogenesis, University of Manchester, England. He considered morphogenesis as a process where chemical substances—called morphogens—spread through organic tissues and, by interacting with them, produce distinctive pattern designs like those seen in cows, zebras, and similar animals.

He stated that relatively simple mathematical formulas could describe such patterning by using straightforward rules that reflect themselves. That is, the result of a calculation with these rules would be fed back into the same formula, producing the following output, and so on. This process could continue iteratively, leading to living patterns that are similar but have different origins (asymmetrical), so that patterns within organic tissues result in self-organization.

Notice the fascinating patterns formed by wind blowing over grains of sand in dunes: the properties of the sand and attractive forces between particles interact with wind variations and angular wind velocities, creating self-organizing, artistic flow patterns.

In the human zygote, we work with stem cells. Flow effects on powerful, formative stem cells in specific areas develop interactively into specialized structures for creating tissues, organs, and body systems. Embryonic stem cells' potential is activated by the movement of specific proteins and enzymes generated from DNA/RNA coding. The movement of these formative chemicals through the stem cells is affected by their position within the growing zygote and by the additional flow of epigenetic factors. Location plays an important role in this process.

The organization of embryonic ecology "appropriately" disrupts balance, resulting in asymmetrical outcomes. This asymmetry in the fundamental nature of formative motifs results from the interactive flow of the previously noted formative variables. The entire formative embryonic system reflects an inherent instability in maintaining a consistent equilibrium. There's an innate tendency for the system to move, develop, and evolve. It is a systemic motif characterized by progression rather than stasis, constantly iterating upon itself. Emerging patterns serve to develop increasingly distinctive, self-similar yet differentiated themes. In this way, they are more than fractals—they are organic, life-giving evolutionary properties that go beyond mere self-similarity. Instead, they evolve toward quantum leaps in transformative motifs.

The flow of biochemical coding and epigenetic context both influences and is influenced by the potency of stem cell formation during the embryonic stage and beyond. Asymmetry arises from stem cell interactions with biochemical and epigenetic factors. This causes stem cells to differentiate into specialized cells, leading to the formation of tissues, organs, and entire organisms.

Notice also the flow of the solar wind interacting with Earth's electromagnetic field, created by the rotation of Earth's iron core. The solar wind's stream of electron particles interacts with Earth's magnetic field, forming shapes that resemble almost human figures. Just as an ocean breeze fills the sails of a boat, the solar wind boosts Earth's magnetic field, shaping it into a human-like pattern. This interactive pattern occurs on a cosmic scale.

However, the hierarchy of levels—from the very small to the very large—does not follow a simple one-to-one pattern (i.e., "as above, identical to below"). The density ratio at the smallest levels is unevenly distributed at higher levels of organization (from quarks to galaxies). Therefore, there is a proportional imbalance—an asymmetry—when moving from one level of organization to higher levels: from quantum levels of subatomic particles that are part of the atom to planets orbiting the sun. Similar, but quite different. For example, electrons are energy-dense wave probabilities, whereas planets are more matter-dense.

The asymmetry in logical levels may impact our interpretation of what it means to understand statements literally versus metaphorically when analyzing our universe.

I encouraged my daughter to observe how her traits and needs for space, time, and energy interact with people, environments, and activities, helping her recognize and develop her sense of self and her lifestyle expectations. Her focus is uniquely on how her flow states of being herself connect with her own reflexivity and that of others.

Since differentiation of motifs truly reflects the motif itself, the fundamental origins of motifs are never fully reached—only approached. No one's motif exists in just one place or moment. The paradox is that mindful awareness of motifs arises from the inside out, as the center or "I" of a storm is where stillness and expansiveness reside. The subjective core sense of the motif is the basic objective awareness. The inherent paradox of being the mindful observer of one's motif is that we must observe from within—participating in what we "observe"—our core outward to our expanding and differentiating self. This subjective/objective participation provides a vantage point—looking outward at the ripple effects of our expanding, complex motifs and potential future lifestyles. It is from the "eye of the storm" that we see the boundary horizon of our future possibilities. Just as there is no "core" of the universe, there is, paradoxically, no "core" self. Instead, consciousness is how we experience awareness in the "core" of each experience! The asymmetrical, self-organizing arrangement of these "core" experiences is what we feel as our "core"—our felt sense of selfhood.

Recognize that subtle facets, connections, and unintended entrainments with unexpected combinations of events can become life-changing experiences. Life unfolds in this way—through surprising, interconnected encounters. (Meeting that special person while intriguingly sipping their coffee at the coffee shop; being a victim of assault because of being short.) These moments awaken our awareness of realities beyond our limited world. Enlightened by the interconnectedness of people, places, and events with specific proportional qualities, we begin to see how motifs function. We cannot change our innate traits; however, we can become aware of those aspects that unduly attract unwanted attention.

Motifs can influence each other in surprising and unexpected ways. The tone of a salesperson's voice and the gestures of drivers in rush hour traffic—such as cutting each other off—are small sound bites that can easily trigger large, out-of-balance motif entrainments.

When motifs lack harmony and subtle expression, they may operate subconsciously and seem like a fragmented creation rather than a unified masterpiece like Beethoven's 5th Symphony. Motifs guide our mind, body, and spirit, but trauma becomes victorious when we "mis-align" our consciousness with those who resonate with what we are NOT meant to be.

Much of the anxiety and depression people experience may "stem" from an intuitive grasp of motifs and the complexities of interconnectedness. There might be a vague sense of something bigger than what we focus on directly. However, our fixations and preoccupations with our private worlds keep us from seeing the larger implications of our radiating motifs.

In social and personal relationships, our mood, attitude, words, and phrases attract others through our energy. This "shapes" our interpersonal space with people who have similar patterns, and we blend with them. Our unique, proportional expressions of motifs draw others into a web of motifs, creating waves of gravitational-like ripples that affect everyone involved.

The classic psychologist joke: one psychologist walking down a clinic hallway says "Good morning" to another psychologist coming the other way. The other psychologist remains silent and keeps walking. They both reflect on their thoughts: "I wonder what is meant by that?"

A lack of awareness of our motives and empathy for others causes anxiety and uncertainty about how our actions will impact outcomes. Consequently, our ability to regulate emotions and control expressions and feelings becomes limited. Many people seek therapy not necessarily due to mental illness but because of mental blind spots regarding their motives and those of others.

Motifs are real, subtle, and nuanced organizing forces that influence how and why we perceive the world around us. They establish the principles of perception and serve as the foundation for forming beliefs and values.

We can change many limiting beliefs or distorted conclusions. However, if we ignore learning how beliefs and values are formed, we become vulnerable to constant stress caused by misperceptions. The result is rigidity and fundamentalist views of the world as fixed and absolute.

For example, when police pull over a car for a traffic stop, if both sides show resistance and defiance, a confrontation is likely. Imagine the police ask for a driver's license and registration, and the driver resents being stopped because they believe there's no reason for it and can't see the officer's justification.

This can lead to mutual mistrust and tense behavior. Tragic consequences may follow.

When each party understands itself and is honest about its rigid preconceptions, they both have a better chance of removing false distortions. Self-awareness takes courage, helping us keep our beliefs and actions genuine and transparent when engaging with others.

Motifs are key elements in creating distinctive, proportional geometric patterns. The process of making these unique proportional features is also called a "motif." For example, the enthusiasm and refined skills shown by a highly motivated tennis player can also be seen as positive traits in their demeanor and various aspects of their life beyond the court.

However, if agility, skillful movements, and intricate strategies displayed on the tennis court are suppressed elsewhere—at work, in love, or in friendship—the creative potential found in motifs becomes stagnant and limited. This leads to repression and constraints in one's lifestyle, to the point where being an athlete becomes the only outlet for creative expression, risking the loss of fulfillment in other areas of life.

Limited life motifs can create pressure, leading to distorted thinking and harsh self-criticism. Their talent becomes their prison. Playing tennis is the only way the athlete expresses their wide range of skilled, creative movements and subtle artistry—until it takes over their identity, becoming dehumanizing.

Reifying fluid patterns into fixed forms, which decreases their adaptability, leads to abnormal, dysfunctional behavior, and possibly even evil. Formativeness—the innate ability of each unique motif to creatively develop into multiple kaleidoscopic, interconnected variations of itself in similar but distinct ways—is at the heart of the subjective experience that anchors a person to objectively embrace the mindful, moment-by-moment flow of their present-focused experience—their "here and now" phenomena.

The form of the motif's formativeness is similar in shape to water. When someone loves another unconditionally, the presence of love is felt all around them. It is as if they are floating in an ocean of water—their medium when together. The motif of love is that "felt presence," which is one of "being all around," as it has the mosaic formativeness, or the "shape of water" (as in the movie).

The shapes and forms of each person's unique, proportional motifs emit a distinctive, thematic signature across the endless variations and derivations of that person's core themes. The phrase "the shape of water" alludes to the truth of this medium of unique quantum fluctuations generated by motifs.

What is the shape and form of what is being shaped and formed? It is the motif's formative fluidity, which presents itself as fluctuating, configurative variations of that individual's unique proportional geometric designs.

The versatility of motifs enables adaptation and change beyond rigid structures. Like water flowing around obstacles, motifs allow individuals to navigate life's constantly shifting currents, freeing them from fixed patterns of behavior, thought, and emotion. This fluid movement supports the development of a person's creative core, where balanced geometries interact as a living expression of harmony and growth. Recognizing this fluidity broadens perspectives that go beyond binary distinctions and encourages a deeper understanding. In this way, motifs serve as a mirror to the limitless potential within each person, reflecting a journey of ongoing growth rather than being stuck in static states.

Much like how the derivation of pi (the ratio of a circle's circumference to its diameter) does not produce an exact value, an individual's unique proportional geometric design asymmetry can be approximated but can never be precisely fixed at a constant. This reflects the nature of each person's ongoing uniqueness. Despite constant change, its distinctive progression remains coherent. The "shape of water" continually evolves in a way that is reliably surprising yet familiar.

The transformative power of motifs relies on their interaction with both internal and external worlds. Internally, motifs serve as guides, shaping our thoughts, feelings, and goals. Externally, they influence how we connect with the environment and others, forming pathways that are uniquely tailored to our individualities and resonances. When the inner and outer worlds align, motifs reveal their deepest transformative potential, enabling individuals to embody a harmonious existence that transcends rigid structures.

Furthermore, the idea of a "felt presence" becomes central to this process. The process involves more than just recognizing or categorizing oneself; it includes experiencing how fundamental patterns consistently connect with the varied complexities of the external world. This presence becomes most meaningful when we accept the mysterious nature of existence, finding joy in the process of becoming rather than in reaching fixed goals. Motifs, with their kaleidoscopic range, remind us that life's richness is found in its asymmetry and unpredictability, opening the door to deep self-discovery and growth.

Like in pi, the range of derivations within an individual's motif shows an asymmetrical, distinctly familiar ratio pattern, the calculation of which remains only partially precise. The pattern ratio of geometric proportionality defies both exact measurement and broad generalization into a single thematic pattern. There is no common denominator, as the denominator is actually uncommon.

That is to say: one can approximate and gain a felt sense of an individual's unique motif. However, its complex, embedded, evolutionary nature resists precise description.

Each person's unique motif is an uncommon denominator—an asymmetrical ratio patterning that is ultimately undefinable. This uncommon denominator aspect, embedded within an individual's motif, defies common sense and is therefore beyond linear thinking. It is similar to trying to calculate the square root of -1. Science had to introduce the use of imaginary numbers to suggest an answer. Scientists express this by placing i under the square root symbol. Although this is not an actual number, it serves as a placeholder—formatively—to solve real-world problems.

Imaginary numbers are crucial in calculations used by control towers to help safely land jet airliners.

We rely on approximations to understand each other. However, it's important to realize that we don't truly understand each other completely. We have to use imaginary patterned models just to approximate and identify each other's motives.

Recognizing that we can never fully understand each other is valuable. It's humbling but healthy to see that everyone has "unknowns," which helps us let go of assumptions and labels — categorizing people and creating perceptual boxes.

Under trauma conditions, the critical prefrontal cortex becomes less active, and the fight-flight-freeze-faint amygdala survival response is triggered. While these neurobiological and emotional circuits are evolutionary in origin, they can hinder long-term creative resolution and the integration of isolation and shock experiences into the broader framework of developing cognitive and emotional relationships.

Accessing flow states of one's unique, sensory-based patterns helps integrate "walled-off" traumatic events and "frozen" cognitive-affective-behavioral episodes of shock reactivity. Many mind-body interventions use this principle, such as thought field therapy, eye movement desensitization and reprocessing, exposure therapy, somatic healing, hypnotic procedures, timeline therapy, and more.

Such exuberance of motifs, congruent in their "familiar surprise," elevates one's lifestyle to a sensory level of self-actualization. This sense of actualization can be accessed through mindfulness, which offers a means for experiencing motifs as they naturally occur. To understand the constructs of motifs and their formative, asymmetrical nature, one needs a stillness of the mind-body connection, as if in the eye of a hurricane or the vortex of a violent storm. This is where one perceives—without a fixed sense—the presence of innate knowing regarding configurations unfolding and permeating life-altering events.

If one tries to understand this phenomenon without embracing the genuine uncertainty of its unfolding—holding on too tightly and attempting to control life events—it leads to a compression of what's happening and missed opportunities slipping away. It's more about a felt sense of wholeness that allows the "empty center," the void, to become the fullness of spatial configurations of opportunity and resolution.

The spacetime of motifs is a synchronization of unfolding configurations of interconnected life events, meaningful in unique ways for each person caught in the web of motif connections. These appear as life task fields in work, love, and friendship—nurtured and spread as beautiful labors of love. Motifs are paths of emerging, interconnected configurations capable of guiding the individual to align with their uniqueness, striving in familiar, surprising ways to be reborn.

It's essential to recognize that any event or series of events that resonate, whether partially or fully, with our inherent motifs will influence—and be influenced by them. Resonance with individuals who share perceptual or personality traits (such as charisma, dominance, introversion, gregariousness, etc.) draws both parties into an emerging connection. This may or may not lead to life-changing outcomes. Some connections can result in all-consuming passions in romantic entanglements, driven by glowing smiles, youthful figures, and/or rebellious "bad boy" behavior. Encounters can lead to beautiful outcomes or tragic long-term consequences like divorce, financial ruin, and emotional upheaval.

There was a bridge built over a ravine in one of the southern states of America. The day it opened, people walked across it, admiring its beauty and splendor. However, as they walked, they developed a certain rhythm and pace, and surprisingly, the bridge began to sway and twist in sync with the crowd's footsteps. Eventually, people had to run for their lives as the resonance between the crowd's pace and the vibrating, undulating bridge reached such a peak that the bridge shattered into thousands of pieces.

Well, people aren't exactly bridges, but resonance between partners can cause relationships to fall apart as the connection starts to weaken due to discordant vibrations that spread through it.

The remarkable quality of unique motifs is that there is only one specific motif of its kind in any given individual. Other people can come close to duplicating the asymmetrical beauty of perfectly imperfect balance (think of hanging lopsided mobiles). The inherent resilience of each person is exhilarating when it resonates with their unique, idiosyncratic motif! It reveals one's capacity to manifest liveliness in that moment!

Skilled couples' dancers move gracefully with intricate dance steps of unity. Still, subtle differences appear. The mirroring of one partner with the other complements each other's motifs. In this scenario, the movements on one partner's left side align with the right-side movements of the other partner. Opposites both attract and complete each other.

When we attune and attend to moving in our unique ways. Especially in close relationships and life in general, we're more likely to free ourselves from entangling, unhealthy, life-changing experiences. Expressive assertiveness of our unique motifs helps to organize and reflect our own distinctive ways of solving and resolving core issues of meaning, purpose, and living well.

It is well worth the time, patience, and careful, artistic-like attention to center ourselves in alignment with our fundamental uniqueness of being and becoming, ever diverse and different in our own unique patterns of self-emergence.

This dynamic resonance reaches beyond personal relationships into the areas of communities, cultures, and even civilizations.

This resonance is not just a poetic idea; it is a real force that influences our interactions and choices. Think about the delicate balance of harmony and discord when motifs weave together. The interaction forms a dynamic mosaic, often unpredictable, but full of potential for growth and change.

Shared motifs within a group can create a collective dynamic, representing interconnected individuals working toward coordination and growth. However, when these motifs clash or fall out of sync, the resulting discord can cause fragmentation, misunderstandings, and conflict. Recognizing and respecting the unique rhythm of each person within the group can serve as a foundation for developing resilient and adaptable social structures.

When we resonate with another person, we may discover that synchronization of motifs creates an exhilarating dance of being fully alive together! Our resilience is strengthened through such synchronizing motifs!

To your own self be true, and you can't be false to anyone.

Bibliography

Ader, R., & Cohen, H. (1975). Behaviorally conditioned immunosuppression. Psychosomatic Medicine, 37, 333–340.

Ansbacher, H. L., & Ansbacher, R. R. (1956). The individual psychology of Alfred Adler. New York: Harper Torch Books.

Atwater, P. M. H. (1996). Future memory. New York: Carol Publishing Group.

Barbour, J. (2001). The end of time. New York: Oxford University Press.

Bateson, G. (1972). Steps to an ecology of mind. New York: Ballantine.

Bateson, G. (1979). Mind and nature. New York: Dutton.

Becker, R. O., & Selden, G. (1985). The body electric. New York: Quill/William Morrow.

Begley, S. (1999). Shaped by life in the womb. Newsweek.

Benson, D. F. (1996). Consciousness, personal identity and the divided brain by Roger Sperry. In The dual brain. New York: The Guilford Press.

Benson, H. (1996). Timeless healing. New York: Fireside.

Benson, H., & Klipper, M. (1976). The relaxation response. New York:

Avon Books.

Berne, E. (1961). Transactional analysis in psychotherapy. New York: Grove Press.

Bleu, H. (2005). Perturbations of cells. Discovery Channel, Stanford University.

Bohm, D. (1980). Wholeness and the implicate order. London: Routledge & Kegan Paul.

Bouchard, T., et al. (1990). Sources of human psychological differences: The Minnesota study of twins reared apart. Science, 250, 223–228.

Bowen, M. (1978). Family therapy in clinical practice. New York: Jason Aronson.

Briggs, J. (1992). Fractals: The patterns of chaos. New York: Simon & Schuster.

Briggs, J. (1988). Fire in the crucible. Los Angeles: Tarcher.

Brown, D., & Fromm, E. (1986). Hypnotherapy and hypnoanalysis. Hillsdale, NJ: Lawrence Erlbaum Associates.

Carrere, S., & Gottman, J. (1999). Predicting divorce among newlyweds from the first three minutes of a marital conflict discussion. Family Process, 38(3), 293–301.

Chomsky, N. (1967). Recent contributions to the theory of innate ideas. Synthese, 17.

Chomsky, N. (2001). 9-11. New York: Seven Stories Press.

Cousins, N. (1983). Anatomy of an illness. New York: W.W. Norton.

Csikszentmihalyi, M. (1975). Play and intrinsic rewards. Journal of Humanistic Psychology, 15(3), 39–54.

———. (1990). Flow. New York: Harper & Row.

———. (1997). Creativity. New York: Harper Perennial.

Dabrowski, K. (1967). Personality shaping through positive disintegration. Boston: Little Brown.

Dabrowski, K., & Piechowski, M. (1977). Theory of levels of emotional development: Vol. 1. Multilevelness and positive disintegration. Oceanside, NY: Dabor Science Publications.

Darwin, C. (1871). The descent of man and selection in relation to sex. London: John Murray.

Dawkins, R. (1976). The selfish gene. Oxford: Oxford University Press.

Dilts, R., et al. (1990). Beliefs: Pathways to health and well-being. Portland, OR: Metamorphous Press.

Dodson, C., et al. (1997). The verbal overshadowing effect: Why descriptions impair face recognition. Memory & Cognition, 25(2), 129- 139.

Edelman, G. (1987). Neural Darwinism: The theory of neuronal group selection. New York: Basic Books.

Ekman, P., & Friesen, W. (1978). Facial action coding system (Parts 1 & 2). San Francisco: Dept. of Psychiatry, University of California.

Erickson, M. (1980). Hypnotic investigation of psychosomatic phenomena: A controlled experimental use of hypnotic regression. In E.

Rossi (Ed.), The collected papers of Milton H. Erickson on hypnosis: II.

Hypnotic alteration of sensory, perceptual and psychophysical processes (pp. 169–174). New York: Irvington.

Erikson, E. H. (1950). Childhood and society. New York: Norton.

———. (1968). The life cycle: Epigenesis of identity. In Identity and youth and crisis (pp. 8–26). New York: Norton.

Feeney, D. (1984). A model framework for alcoholism counseling. American Journal of Drug & Alcohol Abuse, 10(3), 403–415.

———. (1996). Purposeful self: Accessing sensory motifs. Journal of Humanistic Psychology, 36(4), 94–115.

———. (1999). Entrancing relationships. Westport, CT: Praeger Press.

———. (2001). Motifs: The transformative creation of self. Westport, CT: Praeger Press.

———. (2003). Creating cultural motifs against terrorism. Westport, CT: Praeger Press.

Feeney, K. (2001). Reiki healing session personal consultation. In D. J. Feeney, Motifs.

Frankl, V. (1963). Man's search for meaning. New York: Washington Square Press.

Gardner, H. (1993). Frames of mind. New York: Basic Books.

Gladwell, M. (2005). Blink: The power of thinking without thinking. New York: Little, Brown & Co.

Glatzmaier, G., & Olson, P. (2005). Geodynamic magnetism. Scientific American, 4.

Gleick, J. (1987). Chaos: Making a new science. New York: Penguin Books.

Goodwin, B. (1994). How the leopard changed its spots. London: Weidenfeld & Nicolson.

Goldberg, E. (2005). The wisdom paradox. New York: Gotham Books. Grof, S. (1993). The holotropic mind. New York: HarperCollins.

Haley, J. (1963). Strategies of psychotherapy. New York: Grune & Stratton.

———. (1973). Uncommon therapy: The psychiatric techniques of Milton Erickson, M.D. New York: W.W. Norton.

———. (1977). Problem-solving therapy. San Francisco: Jossey-Bass.

Hawking, S., & Penrose, R. (1996). The nature of space and time. Princeton, NJ: Princeton University Press.

Hawking, S. (1988). A brief history of time. New York: Bantam Books.

Houston, J. (1982). The possible human. Los Angeles: J.P. Tarcher.

James, T., & Woodsmall, W. (1988). Timeline therapy. Cupertino, CA: Meta Publishing.

Jung, C. G. (1960). The structure and dynamics of the psyche (Vol. 3). Princeton, NJ: Princeton University Press.

———. (1964). Man and his symbols. New York: Bantam Doubleday.

———. (1971). Psychological types. Princeton, NJ: Princeton

University Press.

Kabat-Zinn, J. (1990). Full catastrophe living. New York: Dell.

Kane, G. (2005). Mysteries of mass. Scientific American, 293(3).

Koestler, A. (1964). The act of creation. New York: Hutchinson.

Lamarck, J. (1914). Zoological philosophy. London: Macmillan.

Lienhart, J. (1983). Multiple personality and state dependent learning (Doctoral dissertation). US International University, San Diego.

Klein, G. (1998). The power of intuition. In Sources of power (Ch. 4). Cambridge, MA: MIT Press.

Klin, A., et al. (2002). Quantifying the social phenotype in autism. American Journal of Psychiatry, 159, 895–908.

Mallett, R. (2003). The gravitational field of a circulating light beam. Foundations of Physics, 33(9), 1307–1314.

Maslow, A. (1968). Toward a psychology of being. New York: Harper.

Mehrabian, A. (1972). Non-verbal communication. Chicago: AldineAtherton.

Mehrabian, A., & Ferris, S. (1976). Influence of attitudes from nonverbal communication in two channels. Journal of Consulting Psychology, 31, 248–252.

Neimark, J. (2004). Pattern circumstance: The power of coincidence. Psychology Today, July/Aug., 47–87.

Ornstein, R. (1986). Multi-mind. Boston: Houghton Mifflin.

———. (1986). The psychology of consciousness. New York: Viking Penguin.

Perls, F. (1971). Gestalt therapy verbatim (8th ed.). Lafayette, CA: Real People Press.

Piaget, J., & Inhelder, B. (1964). The early growth of logic in the child. Atlantic Highlands, NJ: Humanities Press.

Piaget, J. (1979). Behavior and evolution. London: Routledge & Kegan Paul.

Progoff, I. (1973). Jung's psychology and its social meaning. Garden City, NY: Anchor Press.

Ramachandran, V. S., & Blakeslee, S. (1988). Phantoms in the brain. New York: Quill/William Morrow.

Restak, R. (1995). Brainscapes. New York: Bantam Books.

Rogers, C. (1951). Client-centered therapy. Boston: Houghton Mifflin.

———. (1980). Psychological shocks and creative moments. In E. Rossi (Ed.), The collected papers of Milton Erickson on hypnosis: IV. Innovative hypnotherapy (pp. 447–463). New York: Irvington.

Rossi, E. (1986). The psychobiology of mind-body healing. New York: W.W. Norton.

———. (2002). A conceptual review of the psychosocial genomics of expectancy and surprise. American Journal of Clinical Hypnosis, 45(2), 103–117.

Schooler, J., et al. (1993). Thoughts beyond words: When language overshadows insight. Journal of Experimental Psychology, 122(2), 166– 183.

Searle, J. (1997). The mystery of consciousness. New York: New York Review Books.

Seligman, M. (1975). Learned helplessness. San Francisco: W.H. Freeman.

Sheldrake, R. (1981). A new science of life. London: Blond & Briggs.

———. (1988). The presence of the past. Rochester, VT: Park Street Press.

Siegel, B. (1986). Love, medicine, and miracles. New York: Harper & Row.

Smolin, L. (2001). Three roads to quantum gravity. New York: Basic Books.

Stone, K. (1979). Impro: Improvisation and the theatre. New York: Theatre Arts Books.

Strachey, J. (1960). Jokes and their relation to the unconscious. New York: W.W. Norton.

Strogatz, S. (2003). Sync. New York: Hyperion.

Szegedy-Maszak, M. (2005). Mysteries of the mind. U.S. News & World Report, Feb. 28, 53–61.

Tart, C. (1969). Altered states of consciousness. New York: John Wiley & Sons.

Thorne, K. (1994). Black holes and time warps. New York: W.W. Norton.

Thoreau, H. D. (1985). Walden. New York: The Library of America.

Watzlawick, P., et al. (1967). Pragmatics of human communication. New York: Norton.

———. (1974). Change: Principles of problem formation and problem resolution. New York: Norton.

Yogananda, P. (1974). Autobiography of a yogi. Los Angeles: SelfRealization Fellowship.

Zimbardo, P. (2007). The heart of the matter. Psychotherapy Networker, Mar/Apr, 13–14.

www.ingramcontent.com/pod-product-compliance
Lightning Source LLC
LaVergne TN
LVHW052213200926
848481LV00001B/95